This study breaks new ground in setting the Oxford Movement in its historical and theological context. Peter Nockles conducts a rigorous examination of the nineteenth-century Catholic revival in the Church of England associated with the *Tracts for the Times* in 1833, and shows that in many respects this revival had been anticipated by a renewal of the Anglican High Church tradition in the preceding seventy years. Having established this element of continuity, Dr Nockles is able to identify the distinctive features of Tractarianism in a manner which challenges many long-established views of the movement. He demonstrates the extent of the divergence of Tractarianism from the older High Churchmanship and reveals the human drama and trauma between erstwhile allies which this ideological breach engendered. The book draws on a wide range of little-known printed and manuscript sources, and provides an indispensable basis for a radical reassessment of the Anglo-Catholic tradition.

THE OXFORD MOVEMENT IN CONTEXT

THE OXFORD
MOVEMENT IN CONTEXT

Anglican High Churchmanship, 1760–1857

PETER BENEDICT NOCKLES

Assistant Librarian, The John Rylands University Library of Manchester

CAMBRIDGE
UNIVERSITY PRESS

PUBLISHED BY THE PRESS SYNDICATE OF THE UNIVERSITY OF CAMBRIDGE
The Pitt Building, Trumpington Street, Cambridge CB2 1RP, United Kingdom

CAMBRIDGE UNIVERSITY PRESS
The Edinburgh Building, Cambridge CB2 2RU, United Kingdom
40 West 20th Street, New York, NY 10011-4211, USA
10 Stamford Road, Oakleigh, Melbourne 3166, Australia

First published 1994
Reprinted 1995, 1996
First paperback edition 1997

Printed in the United Kingdom at the University Press, Cambridge

Typeset in 11/13 Monotype Baskerville

A catalogue record for this book is available from the British Library

Library of Congress cataloguing in publication data

Nockles, Peter Benedict
The Oxford Movement in context: Anglican high churchmanship,
1760–1857/Peter B. Nockles.
p.   cm.
Includes bibliographical references and index.
ISBN 0 521 38162 2 (hardback)
1. High Church movement – England – History – 18th century.
2. High Church movement – England – History – 19th century.
3. Oxford movement – England – History. 4. Anglo-Catholicism –
England – History – 19th century. 5. England – Church history – 18th century.
6. England – Church history – 19th century. I. Title.
BX5121.N63 1994
283´.42´09033 – dc20   93-4799   CIP

ISBN 0 521 38162 2 hardback
ISBN 0 521 58719 0 paperback

In constructing his *Catenae Patrum* he [the Tractarian] closes his list with Waterland and Brett, and leaps at once to 1833 ... The history of a party may be written on the theory of periodical occultation; but he who wishes to trace the descent of religious thought, and the practical working of religious ideas, must follow these through all the phases they have actually assumed.

Mark Pattison, 1860

It is easy to talk of the persecutions of ultra-protestants, but those who shall examine the history of this [Tractarian] movement when the present heats have subsided will find, that ... [a] spirit of puritanical mar-prelacy has had more to do with drawing Mr Newman and his party into formal schism than has been suspected; – and will find reason to doubt, whether any violence or extravagance of ultra-protestants has been, or could have been, more detrimental to the church.

John Crosthwaite, 1846

To my parents

Contents

Contents

Preface

The research for this study commenced in the autumn of 1976 when I was a postgraduate student at Worcester College, and subsequently St Cross College, Oxford. The present work derives from part of a thesis entitled 'Continuity and Change in Anglican High Churchmanship in Britain, 1792–1850' for which the Theology Faculty of the University of Oxford awarded me the degree of Doctor of Philosophy in 1982.

The extensive use made of the thesis by scholars, particularly students of the Oxford Modern History School Special Subject 'Church, State and Society, 1829–54', along with the repeated encouragement of one of my examiners Dr John Walsh, led me to undertake a thorough revision and recasting of the work for publication. My contribution to volume VI of the *History of the University of Oxford*, focusing on the Oxford Movement in its academic context, delayed the process of revision, but proved an invaluable prelude to that task, deepening and broadening my ideas and arguments. Much fresh research has also been conducted on the more theological aspects of the subject, with greater attention accorded to the later Hanoverian period. There is also an additional chapter on the sacraments incorporating discussion on the baptismal and eucharistic controversies of the 1850s and a radically revised and largely new chapter on spirituality.

In writing this book I have incurred innumerable debts of gratitude to various individuals. Thanks must go to my long-suffering editor, Alex Wright of Cambridge University Press. It was his initiative, foresight and enthusiasm back in 1988 that set in progress plans for the publication of a revised version of my dissertation. Without his wise counsel, this work would be longer and less focused than it now is. Particular thanks must also go to my undergraduate tutor at Worcester College in the mid-1970s, Harry Pitt. In suggesting that I write an essay on the Oxford Movement, he helped prepare the ground of which this work is the fruit. Moreover, it was David Newsome's incomparable and moving *Parting of Friends*, to which Harry Pitt introduced me, that first fired my historical imagination and set me on the course of Oxford Movement studies. In recent years, it has become my great privilege to meet and get to know Dr Newsome. His kindly interest in my research and helpful advice regarding the progress of this work is much appreciated.

Although always personally a committed Roman Catholic who could identify wholeheartedly with the positions outlined in John Henry Newman's *Lectures on Anglican Difficulties* as well as in his *Apologia pro vita sua*, I was drawn by a combination of factors into studying a religious tradition different from my own. The *genius loci* of Oxford exerted its magic spell so that 'the very stones did speak'. It took no great leap of the historical imagination to be carried back to the stirring days when the Tractarian Newman held sway from St Mary's pulpit. But it was not so much the intellectual reasons for Newman's conversion that engaged my interest but the interplay of rival personalities as well as religious ideas among the Movement's followers and their opponents. I began to feel that, while the Tractarian triumvirate of Newman, Keble and Pusey loomed large in historical consciousness, the lesser-known figures, sometimes disparaged by those leaders, had become forgotten. It was my own Worcester College connection that helped foster my initial interest in the grossly neglected and shadowy figure of William Palmer who had attached himself to Worcester College on the eve of the rise of the Oxford Movement. Palmer had become obscured in Newman's shadow. College pride and the encouragement of my other main undergraduate tutor James Campbell, along with that of the then Provost of Worcester Asa Briggs, led me to attempt to rehabilitate Palmer. As a consequence, my historical attention turned back towards a broader exploration of the whole, multi-faceted High Church tradition within Anglicanism, from the Irish branch of which Palmer sprang. It took me on to the central theme of this study – the relationship between that older historical tradition and the Oxford Movement itself. The evidence gleaned revealed deep discontinuities as well as obvious continuities, and caused that questioning of some of the assumptions of the received Anglo-Catholic historiography which characterises the following pages. Moreover, the events of 1845–51 may find an echo in the minds of those troubled by the modern crisis in Anglicanism created by the recent decisions of the General Synod of the Church of England. Considering that some commentators interpret this current crisis as signalling the final end of the Oxford Movement, the present study perhaps has a contemporary resonance and timely quality. Church history can be put to the service of offering insights in the current debate, as Fr Aidan Nicholls has admirably demonstrated in his book *The Panther and the Hind*. The following work, however, does not attempt such an ambitious approach. It is necessarily historical and not polemical. It is for the reader to judge, but I hope that my own personal religious distance from the High Anglican tradition does not detract from the strict historical objectivity of the following pages.

Particular thanks must also be accorded to The Rev Dr Geoffrey Rowell of Keble College, Oxford, who supervised my doctoral thesis and from whose profound and sympathetic knowledge of the subject I much profited. As for Dr John Walsh of Jesus College, Oxford, mentioned above, no words can do justice to the degree of my debt to his academic inspiration, unstinting kindness and moral support over many years. Without his unflagging interest, guidance and advice, this book would never have appeared. In this respect, I am but one of a whole generation of scholars who could say the same.

One of the great delights of protracted academic study in a specialised field is the opportunity for friendship and contacts with other scholars. In this I have been especially fortunate. Pride of place here must go to Dr Sheridan Gilley whom I have had the privilege of knowing since 1989. In a short period he has become a real academic mentor and friend, whose tireless encouragement and helpful advice have been a source of inspiration. Another great scholar whom I got to know and who helped me in so many ways was the late Emeritus Professor F. C. Mather. In several discussions with him at Southampton University in the mid-1980s, he kindly shared with me that profound knowledge of Georgian Anglicanism of which his posthumous biography of Samuel Horsley is fitting testimony. Professor Mather is greatly missed. Dr Walsh's series of church history seminars in the Trinity Term at Oxford over which he and Dr Rowell together presided from 1981–92, has also proved an invaluable boon to my scholarly progress. The friendly atmosphere of the seminars, thanks to the tone set by the organisers, was

almost unique in its relaxed informality. Eschewing the worst forms
of academic competitiveness, the contributors came together to
exchange ideas, and numerous friendships were forged. The conference at Winchester in July 1990 on the eighteenth-century Church
of England was an offshoot of the Oxford seminars and proved an
invaluable forum for the airing and refining of my ideas on the
increasingly important pre-Tractarian period of my study.

In the process of converting my thesis to a book, it has been the
help and insights of some of the many contributors to the Oxford
church history seminars that I wish, above all, to acknowledge. I
want to single out Dr David Maskell of Oriel College, Oxford, for
his tireless efforts in reading, commenting on, and discussing the
text with me. I have been saved from more than one slip by his
friendly and constructive advice, and have particularly benefited
from his profound knowledge of his forebear, William Maskell. I
am also particularly indebted for the exchange of ideas and arguments, and for the reading of portions of various drafts of my
manuscript, to the following: Dr Arthur Burns of King's College,
London, Christopher Zealley of Wolfson College, Oxford, Dr
Grayson Carter of Brasenose College, Oxford, Michael Millard
and Richard Sharp. My ideas on historiography have been sharpened by discussion with Arthur Burns, and on spirituality I have
been helped by Christopher Zealley. On the subject of baptism, the
eucharist and Justification I profited especially from discussion
with Michael Millard and Grayson Carter. Others who have
helped me in various ways, sometimes generously providing me
with useful comments or references, include The Rev Dr Perry
Butler, Dr George Herring, The Rev Peter Cobb, Dr John Findon,
Dr David Bebbington, Dr Mark Curthoys, Richard Sharp, Dr
Stephen Taylor, Dr Brian Young, Dr James Garrard, Dr Mark
Smith, Dr Jeremy Morris, Dr Frances Knight, Dr Clive Dewey, Dr
Richard Brent, Dr James Bradley, Dr Jeremy Gregory, Kenneth
Hylson-Smith, Fr Ian Ker, The Rev Professor Donal Ker, The Rev
Professor John McManners (who supervised me for a term), Canon
Peter Hinchliff, Jerry Jones, Laurence Crumb, Mrs E. Thomas,
Dr Nigel Aston, The Rev Henry Rack, Dr Stephen Conway,
Michael Perrott, Stephen Hancock, Dom Alberic Stacpoole, Simon
Skinner, Dr Peter Erb, Fr James Pereiro, Roger Turner and James
Docherty. The latter two have shared with me a common interest in
William Palmer involving considerable historical detective work.

Alan Rose also deserves special thanks for kindly compiling the index.

Mention should also be made of Dr Jonathan Clark whose ground-breaking book *English Society* when it appeared in 1985 was a source of intellectual inspiration and stimulation to me. I much appreciate Dr Clark's subsequent advice and moral support. I would also like to thank some professional colleagues at the John Rylands University Library of Manchester. In particular, I wish to record my thanks to Dr Peter McNiven and Dr Dorothy Clayton for their support and friendship. Thanks are also owing to Dr David Brady for discussion on one or two finer points of the history of the prophetical interpretation of scripture. I also acknowledge the generous financial assistance of the British Academy which has helped me to conduct further research in recent years.

I am grateful to my friends in Walton Well Road whose house has been a favoured Oxford 'bolt-hole' in recent years. Their genial good-humour in putting up with me on my frequent visits is appreciated. Moral support and a sympathetic ear in Oxford were also provided by Mrs Margaret Wheeler. Mention should also be made of 'The Royal Oak Society' genially presided over by Richard Sharp, for helping to keep alive my historical enthusiasm for a particular side of the tradition examined in this study. Above all, thanks must go to my parents for their constant encouragement and for providing me with the physical and mental space for working retreats in their large Surrey family home over innumerable weekends and vacations for many years. The bulk of the writing and real mental graft of this study was conducted here and it is fitting that this work should be dedicated to them.

This study also owes a great deal to the patience and understanding of the staff of the Bodleian Library, Pusey House Library, the libraries of Oriel College, Keble College, Pembroke College, Wadham College, Lincoln College and Christ Church, Oxford; the Cambridge University Library and Trinity College, Cambridge; the British Library, Lambeth Palace Library and Sion College Library in London; the library of Trinity College, Dublin; and the Record Offices in Gloucester, Chichester, Lewes and Lincoln; the cathedral libraries at Durham, Exeter and Canterbury. My debt is also due to the following custodians of private or family papers: (Churton) Victor Churton of Sutton Coldfield, Warwickshire; (Hook) Mrs E. Coatalen of Bucklebury, Oxfordshire; (Watson) Canon Reade of

Marychurch, Torquay. The weekend spent at the home of Mr Victor Churton in November 1981 when I was given full access to his outstanding collection of family papers of which great use has been made in this study, remains a memorable experience.

While acknowledging all those who have read and commented on various drafts of this work, I accept its blemishes as entirely my own responsibility. A text, once complete, is launched into the stream and inevitably will be tested and modified by subsequent research and fresh insights. The natural process of historical scholarship will ensure that this work is no exception. It is in this spirit that it is offered to the reader.

Manchester, April 1993

Abbreviations

BL	British Library
Bodl. Lib	Bodleian Library
CUL	Cambridge University Library
DCL	Durham Cathedral Library
DNB	*Dictionary of National Biography*
ECA	Exeter Cathedral Archives
ECS	*Eighteenth-Century Studies*
EHR	*English Historical Review*
ESCRO	East Sussex County Record Office
GCRO	Gloucestershire County Record Office
HJ	*Historical Journal*
HLQ	*Huntington Library Quarterly*
JEH	*Journal of Ecclesiastical History*
KCA	Keble College Archives
LBV	Liddon Bound Volumes
LCRO	Lincolnshire County Record Office
LPL	Lambeth Palace Library
NLS	National Library of Scotland
OCA	Oriel College Archives
ODCC	*Oxford Dictionary of the Christian Church*
PCA	Pembroke College Archives
PH	Pusey House
SC	Sutton Coldfield
SCH	*Studies in Church History*
TCD	Trinity College Dublin
TRHS	*Transactions of the Royal Historical Society*
WCA	Wadham College Archives
WSCRO	West Sussex County Record Office

Historiographical introduction

HISTORICAL AND FAMILY CONTEXT

This study will involve a historical re-evaluation of the Oxford Movement from the 1830s to 1850s in the context of a rich and varied 'High Church' tradition within the Church of England. As an episode in the cultural, intellectual and ecclesiastical history of the nineteenth century, the Oxford Movement has never lacked historians. However, much of the historiography of the Movement until recently has been shaped by either Anglo-Catholic partisans or Protestant detractors.

Apart from the contemporaneous accounts by A. P. Perceval and William Palmer of Worcester College,[1] the first accounts of Tractarian Oxford were given not by its heirs but by critics or renegades such as J. A. Froude and Mark Pattison.[2] Thomas Mozley's *Reminiscences* (1882) was the work of a sympathetic one-time disciple but it was whimsical and eccentric as well as indiscreet enough to be regarded as a degradation by the surviving leaders of the

---

[1] A. P. Perceval, *A Collection of Papers Connected with the Theological Movement of 1833* (London, 1842); W. Palmer [of Worcester], *A Narrative of Events Connected with the Publication of the Tracts for the Times; with Reflections on Existing Tendencies to Romanism, and on the Present Duties and Prospects of the Church* (Oxford, 1843).

William John Copeland (1804–85), scholar of Trinity College, Oxford, Fellow from 1832 to 1849, and curate of Farnham, Essex, 1849–85, collected materials over many years for what would have been a highly sympathetic insider's history of the Oxford Movement. Although always retaining connections with the old High Church party, Copeland became a close ally of the Anglican Newman and remained a lifelong friend, editing Newman's eight-volume *Parochial and Plain Sermons* (1868). Partly owing to ill-health, Copeland's history of the Oxford Movement remained uncompleted and was never published. The manuscript of Copeland's sketch account, dated 1881 and edited by his nephew W. C. Borlase, remains in the archives of Pusey House Library, Oxford. A scholarly edition would enhance Oxford Movement studies enormously. For Copeland, see *DNB*; H. Broxap, *The Later Nonjurors* (Cambridge, 1924), pp. 303–5.

[2] J. A. Froude, 'The Oxford Counter-Reformation', *Short Studies on Great Subjects*, 4 vols. (new edn London, 1893), vol. IV, pp. 231–360; M. Pattison, *Memoirs* (London, 1885).

Movement.[3] Yet though notably hostile sketches of John Henry
Newman's leadership of the Movement by his brother Francis and
by Edwin Abbott and Walter Walsh[4] followed in the 1890s, much of
the subsequent historiography bordered on Anglo-Catholic hagio-
graphy.

The primary focus of Tractarian historiography has been on the
Movement's leaders: Newman, Froude, Keble and Pusey. This
historiography presupposed that the 'Tractarians' represented the
dominant group within Anglicanism after the rise of the Movement
from 1833 onwards. Although historical attention has also been
given to the Evangelicals and 'Broad Churchmen',[5] 'the old High
Church party', as distinct from the Tractarians, has been com-
paratively neglected. There has been no serious historical evaluation
of a distinctively High Church response to the Oxford Movement,
partly because traditional High Churchmanship and Tractarianism
have often been treated as synonymous. These lines of continuity
between Georgian and Victorian High Churchmanship will be fully
explored. The often-overlooked discontinuities will also be given
attention.

To a great, if often unconscious extent our historical understanding of the Oxford Movement has been coloured by the personal
drama of the peculiar religious odyssey of Newman as so movingly
unfolded in his masterpiece of spiritual autobiography, the *Apologia
pro vita sua*. Yet, as Newman himself admitted, he had a much better
memory for what he called 'anxieties and deliverances' than outer
facts and circumstances.[6] Thus, while it is certainly a dramatic
account of spiritual heroism and imbued with moral truths,
Newman's *Apologia* is not accurate or balanced history. On the
contrary, it is best regarded as an example of that 'rhetoricisation of
history' of which Newman's Protestant critics have complained.

[3] O. Chadwick, 'The Oxford Movement and Its Reminiscencers', *The Spirit of the Oxford
Movement: Tractarian Essays* (Cambridge, 1990), ch. 7.
[4] F. W. Newman, *Contributions Chiefly to the Early History of the Late Cardinal Newman* (London,
1891); E. A. Abbott, *The Anglican Career of Cardinal Newman*, 2 vols. (London, 1892);
W. Walsh, *The Secret History of the Oxford Movement* (London, 1897).
[5] Examples of notable recent studies of Anglican Evangelicalism in the period include:
P. Toon, *Evangelical Theology, 1833–1856: a Response to Tractarianism* (London, 1979); D. W.
Bebbington, *Evangelicalism in Modern Britain* (London, 1989); K. Hylson-Smith, *Evangelicals
in the Church of England, 1734–1984* (London, 1988).
    The most notable recent study of Broad Churchmanship is: I. Ellis, *Seven against Christ: a
Study of 'Essays and Reviews'* (Leiden, 1980).
[6] W. E. Houghton, *The Art of Newman's 'Apologia'* (London, 1945), p. 22.

Nevertheless, with a few notable recent exceptions, most historians have tended to accept uncritically Newman's personal interpretation of events. Of course, there are dangers in interpreting Newman's religious writings in terms of devious strategies or as a mere 'rhetorical device'.[7] Yet while Newman should be judged on his own religious terms, and loaded terminology avoided, the Anglican Newman was not above party tactics and special pleading. A degree of reappraisal of his role as leader of the Oxford Movement is called for. Such a reappraisal cannot detract from his overall religious greatness. He himself could be candid about his own limitations as Tractarian leader. He never pretended that the *Apologia* was intended to be the objective account which some later partisan writers assumed. He told his friend William Copeland that the *Apologia* was not 'a history of the movement but of me – it is an egotistical matter from beginning to end'.[8]

A serious misconception implicit in Tractarian historiography is the assumption that the followers of the Oxford Movement alone were the true heirs of the High Church tradition in the Church of England, and that it was only because the episcopal and academic authorities in opposing the Movement repudiated that tradition, that the secessions to the Roman Catholic Church ensued.

Tractarian historiography has been characterised by selectivity. For the Tractarians found the history of the Church of England to be something of a Noah's Ark, full of beasts clean and unclean. They tended to associate the High Church tradition almost exclusively with a portion of the seventeenth century and in their doctrine of Justification were forced to limit their appeal to a mere thirty-year period following the Restoration in 1660.[9] Thereafter, the Tractarians maintained, there was a 'tunnel period' in the history of the tradition from about 1689 until the apparent dawn of the Oxford Movement in 1833. Hurrell Froude dated the rise and fall of what he called the Church of England's 'genus of Apostolical divines' from the beginning of the reign of King James I till the Revolution of 1688–9 and the separation of the first

---

[7] See review of Stephen Thomas's *Newman and Heresy: the Anglican Years* (Cambridge, 1992) by E. Griffiths, 'Doing Service in the Church', *TLS*, No. 4639 (28 February 1992), 12.

[8] J. H. Newman to W. J. Copeland, 19 April 1864, in C. S. Dessain and E. Kelly, eds., *Letters and Diaries of John Henry Newman*, vol. XXI (London, 1971), p. 97.

[9] A. McGrath, 'The Emergence of the Anglican Tradition on Justification, 1600–1700', *Churchman*, 98 (1984), 40.

Nonjurors.[10] Froude's notorious repudiation of the English Reformers obviously removed them as potential Apostolical witnesses, though others pushed an Anglo-Catholic line back as far as the Elizabethan divine, Bishop Cheney.[11]

Tractarian historiography assumed that the Revolution of 1688–9 marked the collapse of what Newman called 'the experiment' of operating the High Church theory in the Church of England. With the decline of the Nonjurors, the theory was all but deemed to have 'sunk once and for all'.[12] By 1841, Newman's never-very-generous estimate of the eighteenth-century Church of England had so far hardened that he could complain of 'the last miserable century which has given us to start from a much lower level and with much less to spare than a churchman in the 17th century'.[13] Pusey took a similarly severe view of the negative impact of the Revolution, likening it to 'some dreadful taint taken into one's system, poisoning all our strength, and working decay and all but death'.[14] Henry Manning likewise shared the Tractarian assumption of a century and a half of decay following a Caroline 'golden age'; a decay which only the Oxford Movement helped to reverse.[15] It was because the eighteenth century was deemed such a sterile period that, apart from the Nonjurors and a few figures within the establishment such as Daniel Waterland, Jones of Nayland and George Horne, the laboriously constructed Tractarian *catenae patrum* overwhelmingly relied on a narrow span of the seventeenth century. As the, by then, liberal critic of the Movement, Mark Pattison complained of the Tractarian polemicist in 1860, 'in constructing his "Catenae Patrum" he closes his list with Waterland and Brett, and leaps at once to 1833'.[16]

10 [J. H. Newman and J. Keble, eds.] *Remains of the Late Richard Hurrell Froude, M.A. Fellow of Oriel College Oxford*, 4 vols. (vols. I–II, London, 1838; vols. III–IV, Derby, 1839), vol. II, p. 381. See also Froude's comment (vol. I, p. 327): 'It seems to me that Saravia and Bancroft [late Elizabethan divines] are the revivers of orthodoxy in England.' Many modern historians likewise date the true beginning of Anglicanism to Richard Hooker and the first five books of his *Ecclesiastical Polity* (1594–7). Peter Lake even claims that Hooker 'invented' Anglicanism. P. Lake, *Anglicans and Puritans? Presbyterianism and English Nonconformist Thought from Whitgift to Hooker* (London, 1988), pp. 227, 230.
11 *Puseyism; or the New Apostolicals* (London, 1838), pp. 4–5, 142–4.
12 [J. H. Newman], 'Home Thoughts from Abroad', *British Magazine*, 9 (March, 1836), 247.
13 PH, Ollard Papers, J. H. Newman to R. W. Church, 25 December 1841 (copy).
14 PH, Pusey Papers, LBV [Transcripts], E. B. Pusey to H. E. Manning, 9 August 1844.
15 WSCRO, Wilberforce Papers, Ms 98 No. 66, H. E. Manning to S. Wilberforce, 24 April 1849.
16 M. Pattison, 'Tendencies of Religious Thought in England, 1688–1750', *Essays and Reviews* (London, 1860), p. 255.
     Daniel Waterland (1683–1740), Archdeacon of Middlesex, was a leading theologian

Why were the Tractarians so selective in their historiography? Why were they so dismissive of the eighteenth-century Church of England and its High Church tradition? J. A. Froude felt that it was partly because they underestimated the strength which existing institutions and customs possess as long as they are left undisturbed.[17] It can also be maintained, however, that the Tractarians deliberately exaggerated the supposed evils of the Hanoverian church in order to add lustre to their own religious endeavours. Moreover, Tractarian historiography was shaped by the extent to which the Movement's leaders identified with the later Nonjurors. The latter had castigated the post-1689 Church of England for compromises and creeping secularity, and the Tractarians readily imbibed this critique.[18]

Another factor suggested by J. Wickham Legg was an ubiquitous feature of nineteenth-century Whig historiography with which in all other circumstances the Tractarians had no sympathy. Wickham Legg argued that 'there was a leaning on the part of the writers of the nineteenth century and of the Victorian epoch to plume themselves on the supposed excellency of their own age, as an age of "progress", "enlightenment", etc. The lustre of the age in which they wrote would be heightened by darkening the age which went immediately before.'[19] When usually applied by Whig theorists to support the inevitability of the 'progress' of principles of civil and constitutional liberty or material advancement, the Tractarians disdainfully repudiated such apparent historical determinism. However, as a rationale for the 'progress' of 'catholic' opinions and moral and spiritual values, such an historicism was at least in tune with Tractarian assumptions.

The assumption of a moral and spiritual superiority of the present over the immediately preceding age was no less a feature of Evangelical writings. The difference was that for the Tractarians both ages were decadent in comparison with the age of Christian antiquity. The Tractarians also put a different gloss from that of the

---

within the moderate High Church tradition in the earlier Hanoverian era. *DNB*; T. Holtby, *Daniel Waterland, 1683–1740: a Study in Eighteenth-Century Orthodoxy* (Carlisle, 1966). See ch. 2, n. 54.

17 Froude, 'Oxford Counter-Reformation', pp. 245–6.

18 On the link between the Tractarians and Nonjurors, see chapters 1 and 2, and Broxap, *Later Nonjurors*, ch. 9.

19 J. Wickham Legg, *English Church Life from the Restoration to the Tractarian Movement* (London, 1914), p. viii.

6 *The Oxford Movement in context*

Evangelicals on their denigration of the previous century. For
Evangelicals, the eighteenth century was to be faulted for not
sufficiently 'preaching the Gospel'; for Tractarians, for losing sight
of 'catholic' principle and practice.

The Tractarians were fascinated by and made much use of
history. Yet theirs was an essentially romantic reading of church
history. For all Newman's debt to Gibbon for style, it was the
writings of Walter Scott which fired his historical imagination. The
imaginative influence of the Evangelical, Joseph Milner, on
Newman's patristic historiography was also crucial. Ultimately, the
discernment of *ethos*[20] mattered more than the probing of evidence in
the modern, technical sense.

The myth of the collapse of High Churchmanship in the
eighteenth-century Church of England gained ground in later Tractarian polemic. According to William Bennett, 'a deep ignorance of
catholicity' developed among both clergy and laity. Bennett insisted
that it was only the Oxford Movement that restored the heritage of
the Caroline Divines which had been previously lost.[21] However, it
was in R. W. Church's *Oxford Movement: Twelve Years* (1891) and
H. P. Liddon's four-volume biography of Pusey (1893–4) that the
Tractarian historiography became enshrined in its most appealing
as well as most comprehensive form. These works, while outstanding
monuments of historical biography and scholarship, had limitations.
The close relations that Dean Church and Liddon had with
Newman and Pusey respectively, ensured that they wrote as partisans. Both magnified the Tractarians at the expense of the older
tradition.[22] They looked back on the 1830s and 1840s in a spirit of
hagiographic devotion, in which their respective heroes were cast as
innocent victims of intolerance and misunderstanding on the part of
the ecclesiastical authorities. Facts which did not fit the picture were
subtly downplayed or omitted. Liddon chose not to dwell on or
explain the extent of Pusey's early theological liberalism, while

20 'What Froude and others discovered continually was *ethos*, the predominant moral habit or
proclivity.' T. Mozley, *Reminiscences Chiefly of Oriel College and the Oxford Movement*, 2 vols.
(London, 1882), vol. I, pp. 211–12.
21 W. J. E. Bennett, 'Some Results of the Tractarian Movement of 1833', in O. Shipley, ed.,
The Church and the World: Essays and Questions of the Day in 1867 (London, 1867), pp. 3–6;
R. I. Wilberforce, *The Evangelical and Tractarian Movements: a Charge to the Clergy of the
Archdeaconry of the East Riding* (London, 1851), p. 4.
22 For example, see R. W. Church, *The Oxford Movement. Twelve Years, 1833–1845* (London,
1891), pp. 8–9; H. P. Liddon, *The Life of Edward Bouverie Pusey*, 4 vols. (London, 1893–4),
vol. I, pp. 256–60.

Church did not highlight the many provocations which Newman presented to the episcopal and academic authorities in the early 1840s. Subtle and appealing as Church's pleading of Newman's case was, he was much less candid than in his masterly dissection of Hurrell Froude's character.

In less able and eloquent hands the essentially one-sided perspective of Church and Liddon was restated in cruder form by subsequent generations of Anglo-Catholic writers. Of these, the works of S. L. Ollard and especially F. L. Cross are the most impressive.[23] The period around the centenary of the Oxford Movement in 1933 witnessed a burgeoning of Anglo-Catholic historiography, some of it of inferior quality.[24] On the other hand, Yngve Brilioth's *Anglican Revival* (1925), injected an original note into Tractarian studies, with much fresh and perceptive insight. Yet in all these works, Brilioth's included, the old High Church party remained a background or foil for the fuller treatment accorded to the Oxford Movement.[25]

The magisterial scholarship of Norman Sykes corrected the grosser charges against the Augustan Church of England made by Victorian historiography. Sykes, however, chose to highlight the more latitudinarian characteristics of the Anglicanism of the age somewhat to the neglect of its residual High Church features.[26] More recent scholarship has been less inclined to regard such figures as Hoadly and Richard Watson, on whom Sykes focused, as representative figures of that age.

Two recent studies by John Spurr and Paul Avis have shed much light on links between the seventeenth-century divines and the Tractarians. Some of the historiographical conclusions of John Spurr's challenging study of Restoration Anglicanism support the present author's contention that the Tractarians distorted the Caro-

[23] S. L. Ollard, *The Anglo-Catholic Revival* (London, 1925); F. L. Cross, *The Oxford Movement and the Seventeenth Century* (London, 1933).

[24] Examples include: H. L. Stewart, *A Century of Anglo-Catholicism* (London, 1929); C. B. Moss, *The Orthodox Revival. 1833–1933* (London, 1933); D. Morse-Boycott, *The Secret Story of the Oxford Movement* (London, 1933); T. H. Whitton, *The Necessity of Catholic Reunion* (London, 1933); N. P. Williams and C. Harris, eds., *Northern Catholicism: Centenary Studies in the Oxford and Parallel Movements* (London, 1933).

[25] Y. Brilioth, *The Anglican Revival. Studies in the Oxford Movement* (London, 1925), ch. 2; F. W. Cornish, *The English Church in the Nineteenth Century* (London, 1910), pp. 62–76; G. Wakeling, *The Oxford Church Movement. Sketches and Recollections* (London, 1895); J. R. H. Moorman, 'Forerunners of the Oxford Movement', *Theology*, 25 (June, 1933), 6–11.

[26] N. Sykes, *Church and State in England in the XVIIIth Century* (Cambridge, 1924).

line heritage of the Church of England.[27] Spurr rightly insists that
Anglicanism would be subject to what he calls 'recreations' and be
defined in different ways; it was never the monolithic theological
system which the Tractarian 'recreation', with its careful selectivity,
sought to make out. Nevertheless, we shall point to the continued
vitality of a religious tradition which not only survived 1689 but
flourished in the Georgian era, being less dependent on political or
historical circumstances than is sometimes assumed.

Along with Stephen Sykes and others, Paul Avis recently has
explored the historical roots of the identity of Anglicanism in its
various manifestations.[28] Avis's conclusions support some of those
advanced in this study.[29] Unfortunately, albeit for reasons which he
explains, he passes straight from Waterland to the Tractarians.
Other historians, however, have demonstrated that Hanoverian
Anglicanism represented more than an ideal of comprehensiveness,
and that 'latitude' and 'moderation' were not its only defining
characteristics.

Historians of Georgian Anglicanism are particularly indebted to
J. C. D. Clark's ground-breaking, revisionist study, *English Society*.
Clark has clothed the political debate of the period in a theological
context which for too long had been denied it. His penetrating, if
sometimes provocative, elucidation of the long neglected tradition of
what he aptly describes as 'orthodox political theology' in
eighteenth-century Anglicanism,[30] forms a point of reference in our
own study. Nonetheless, a feature of Clark's revisionism – a reassertion of the centrality of Anglicanism in eighteenth-century English
religious history – had already been reasserted by the American

---

[27] J. Spurr, *The Restoration Church of England, 1646–1689* (London, 1991), especially ch. 8.

[28] P. Avis, *Anglicanism and the Christian Church: Theological Resources in Historical Perspective*
(Edinburgh, 1989), especially pp. 1–18; P. Avis, 'What Is Anglicanism?', in S. Sykes and
J. Booty, eds., *The Study of Anglicanism* (London, 1988), especially pp. 413–16. See also,
P. E. More and F. L. Cross, eds., *Anglicanism: the Thought and Practice of the Church of
England, Illustrated from the Popular Literature of the Seventeenth Century* (Milwaukee, 1935);
H. R. McAdoo, *The Spirit of Anglicanism* (London, 1965); S. Sykes, *The Integrity of Angli-
canism* (London, 1978). For a penetrating Roman Catholic appraisal of the self-contradic-
tions of historic Anglicanism in the context of the current crisis of Anglican identity, see
A. Nicholls, *The Panther and the Hind: A Theological History of Anglicanism* (Edinburgh, 1993),
especially pp. xiv–xx.

[29] P. Avis, 'The Tractarian Challenge to Consensus and the Identity of Anglicanism', *King's
Theological Review*, 9.1 (1986), 14–17.

[30] J. C. D. Clark, *English Society, 1688–1832: Ideology, Social Structure and Political Practice during
the Ancien Régime* (Cambridge, 1985), especially pp. 216–34. See also J. C. D. Clark, *The
Language of Liberty: Political discourse and social dynamics in the Anglo-American world* (Cambridge, 1994).

literary historian Donald Greene in a series of articles in the late 1960s and early 1970s.[31]

Other current scholars such as Stephen Taylor, Paul Monod, Robert Hole, John Gascoigne, James Bradley and James Sack have all recently extended our understanding of eighteenth-century Anglican religion and politics.[32] Some take issue with Clark on particular points but give additional credence to his view of the paramountcy of religious concerns in political life and of the continued importance in contemporary debate of the 'Orthodox' tradition in Anglicanism. To other aspects of this tradition, notably ecclesiology, sacraments and worship, Clark gives less emphasis. However, much of this gap has recently been filled by the late F. C. Mather who has revealed the depth of the sacramental and spiritual dimension of the pre-Tractarian High Church tradition.[33]

The early nineteenth-century component of the pre-Tractarian era has also been the subject of some recent reappraisal along the lines pursued by Clark for the eighteenth century. One of the most original studies of the High Churchmanship of this period has been by the Italian scholar, Pietro Corsi. Corsi's fresh insights into the pre-Tractarian High Churchmen of the 1820s and early 1830s has been matched by a complementary study by Richard Brent of the

---

[31] For example, see D. Greene, 'The Via Media in an Age of Revolution: Anglicanism in the 18th Century', in P. Hughes and D. Williams, eds., *The Varied Pattern: Studies in the 18th Century* (Toronto, 1971) pp. 297–320. See also J. A. W. Gunn, *Beyond Liberty and Property* (Kingston, 1983).

[32] S. Taylor, 'Church and State in England in the Mid-Eighteenth Century: the Newcastle Years, 1742–1763', unpublished Ph.D thesis, University of Cambridge, 1987; P. Monod, *Jacobitism and the English People, 1688–1788* (Cambridge, 1989); R. Hole, *Pulpits, Politics and Public Order in England, 1760–1832* (Cambridge, 1989); J. Gascoigne, *Cambridge and the Enlightenment* (Cambridge, 1989); J. Bradley, *Religion, Revolution and English Radicalism: Nonconformity in English Politics and Society* (Cambridge, 1990); J. J. Sack, *From Jacobite to Conservative: Reaction and Orthodoxy in Britain, c. 1760–1832* (Cambridge, 1993).

See also J. Walsh, C. Haydon and S. Taylor, *The Church of England, c. 1689–c. 1833: From Toleration to Tractarianism* (Cambridge, 1993), esp. 'Introduction: The Church and Anglicanism in the 'long' eighteenth century'. See also, F. Knight, 'The Hanoverian Church in transition: some recent perspectives', *HJ*, 36, 3 (September, 1993), 745–52; N. Aston, 'Horne and Heterodoxy: The Defence of Anglican Beliefs in the Late Enlightenment', *EHR*, 108 (October, 1993), 895–919.

[33] F. C. Mather, *High Church Prophet: Bishop Samuel Horsley (1733–1806) and the Caroline Tradition in the Later Georgian Church* (Oxford, 1992); F. C. Mather, 'Georgian Churchmanship Reconsidered: Some Variations in Anglican Public Worship, 1714–1830', *JEH*, 36, (1985), 255–83; R. Sharp, 'New perspectives on the High Church tradition: historical background 1730–1780', in G. Rowell, ed., *Tradition Renewed: the Oxford Movement Conference Papers* (London, 1986), pp. 4–23. For the philosophical dimension of later Georgian High Churchmanship, see N. Aston, 'Horne and Heterodoxy: The Defence of Anglican Beliefs in the Late Enlightenment', *EHR*, 108 (October, 1993), 895–919.

religious concerns of Whig churchmen or 'liberal Anglicans' of the same period.[34] Both works reveal the primacy of religious concerns in contemporary political, social and educational debate. A. M. C. Waterman's study of Christian political economy for the first third of the nineteenth century has extended the evidence for such a primacy, even in matters of economic debate.[35] Further noteworthy recent scholarship elucidating aspects of the role and principles of the 'Orthodox' party in the Church of England includes the work of Clive Dewey, Elizabeth Varley, Nancy Murray, Mark Evershed, R. Braine, Arthur Burns, Brian Young and Frances Knight.[36]

Yet while scholars are indebted to the work of Mather and the broad survey by Hylson-Smith, the need for a comprehensive, integrated account drawing together the many strands of pre-Tractarian High Churchmanship has not been superseded. The High Church tradition still awaits fuller consideration in relation to the Oxford Movement that followed.

Our own study aims to set the Oxford Movement more firmly than hitherto within the historical context of a long and continuous as well as rich and varied High Church tradition in the Church of England. Our *terminus a quo* has been fixed at approximately the year 1760 as this marked the dawn of something of a High Church revival in the wake of the accession of King George III and the ending of the long era of so-called 'Whig ascendancy' when High Churchmen were out of political favour. Our *terminus ad quem* has been set at approximately 1857 so as to encompass not only the strictly Oxford

[34] See P. Corsi, *Science and Religion: Baden Powell and the Anglican Debate, 1800–1860* (Cambridge, 1988); R. Brent, *Liberal Anglican Politics: Whiggery, Religion and Reform, 1830–1841* (Oxford, 1987).

[35] A. M. C. Waterman, *Revolution, Economics and Religion: Christian Political Economy, 1798–1833* (Cambridge, 1991).

[36] C. Dewey, *The Passing of Barchester: a Real Life Version of Trollope* (London, 1991); E. A. Varley, *The Last of the Prince Bishops: William Van Mildert and the High Church Movement of the Early Nineteenth Century* (Cambridge, 1992); N. Murray, 'The Influence of the French Revolution on the Church of England and Its Rivals', unpublished D.Phil thesis, University of Oxford, 1975; M. Evershed, 'Party and Patronage in the Church of England, 1800–1945', unpublished D.Phil thesis, University of Oxford, 1985; R. Braine, 'The Life and Writings of Herbert Marsh (1757–1839)', unpublished Ph.D thesis, University of Cambridge, 1989; A. Burns, 'The Diocesan Revival in the Church of England, c. 1825–1865', unpublished D.Phil thesis, University of Oxford, 1990; B. W. Young, '"Orthodoxy Assailed": an historical examination of some metaphysical and theological debates in England from Locke to Burke', unpublished D.Phil thesis, University of Oxford, 1990; F. Knight, 'John Kaye, and the Diocese of Lincoln, 1827–53', unpublished Ph.D thesis, University of Cambridge, 1991. For a general historical survey of the High Church tradition, see K. Hylson-Smith, *High Churchmanship in the Church of England: from the Sixteenth Century to the late Twentieth Century* (Edinburgh, 1993).

phase of the Tractarian era but the subsequent Gorham and Denison theological controversies which engaged old High Church-men and Tractarians in constructive debate, prior to the rise of Ritualism in the Church of England.

The presuppositions of Tractarian historiography were challenged by some contemporaries. This rival viewpoint has attracted little attention from recent historians. Yet the view that it was traditional High Churchmen who were dominant in the pre-Tractarian Church of England had found eloquent expression in a scholarly four-volume *Summary History of the English Church*, by the little-known Vicar of Kentish Town, one Johnson Grant, and published between 1811 and 1825. Johnson Grant's study, full of illuminating insights by a contemporary 'Orthodox' churchman, has been neglected by historians as a source. Johnson Grant's testimony to the influence of the 'Orthodox' prior to the rise of Tractarianism, was to be echoed by J. B. Marsden in another little-known ecclesiastical history published in 1856.[37] Moreover, this perspective came to colour numerous biographical studies and works of personal reminiscences in the later part of the century, though few have enjoyed the attention that they deserve. Some of the better-known of these works include Edward Churton's two-volume *Memoir of Joshua Watson* (1861), William Palmer of Worcester College's extended and revised edition of his *Narrative of Events connected with the Publication of the 'Tracts for the Times'* (1883), John William Burgon's *Lives of Twelve Good Men* (1888), Charles Wordsworth's *Annals of My Early Life* (1891) and G. W. E. Russell's 'Catholic Continuity in the Church of England' in his *Household of Faith* (1902).

Burgon insisted that High Church feeling was not created by the Oxford Movement. According to Burgon, 'the smouldering materials for the cheerful blaze which followed the efforts made in 1832-3-4 had been accumulating unobserved for many years: had been the residuum of the altar-fires of a long succession of holy and earnest men'. Burgon records a lengthy list of old High Churchmen active in the later decades of the eighteenth and early decades of the nineteenth centuries, insisting that 'time would fail me, were anything like a complete enumeration to be attempted'.[38]

---

[37] J. B. Marsden, *A History of Christian Churches and Sects from the Earliest Ages of Christianity*, 2 vols. (London, 1856), vol. I, pp. 322-3. On Grant, see n. 109, 121.

[38] J. W. Burgon, *Lives of Twelve Good Men*, 2 vols. (4th edn, London, 1889), vol. I, pp. 154-5. Burgon's list included the following.

The later private correspondence of a leading pre-Tractarian High Churchman, Joshua Watson, repeatedly echoes the refrain that he felt disquiet at 'the inclination to make a great era of the year 1833'. Watson's niece, Mary, recorded that he often maintained in his last years, 'I am only solicitous to get rid of all the history of the agitation.'[39] Likewise, even a one-time contributor to the series of *Tracts for the Times*, Benjamin Harrison, complained in 1843 of the widespread 'notion, which it is most desirable to get rid of, of church principles being altogether a creation of the last ten years'.[40]

The continued importance of the influence of the separatist Non-jurors on the inner life of the Church of England in the eighteenth

Samuel Horsley (1733–1806). Trinity Hall, Cambridge, 1751–8; living, 1759; FRS, 1767; Prebendary of St Paul's, 1777; Archdeacon of St Albans, 1781; Prebendary of Gloucester, 1787; Bishop of St David's, 1788; Bishop of Rochester, 1796; Bishop of St Asaph, 1802-d. *DNB*.

John Randolph (1749–1813). Son of Thomas Randolph, President of Corpus Christi College, Oxford; Westminster and Christ Church. BA 1771; Tutor 1779–83; Professor of Poetry; Regius Professor of Greek; Professor of Moral Philosophy; Regius Professor of Divinity, 1783; Canon of Christ Church, 1789; Bishop of Oxford, 1799; Bishop of Bangor, 1807; Bishop of London, 1809-d.

William Cleaver (1742–1815). Brasenose College, Oxford; Principal, 1785; Bishop of Chester, 1787; Bishop of Bangor, 1880; Bishop of St Asaph, 1806-d. *DNB*.

Alexander Knox (1757–1831). A somewhat eclectic Anglo-Irish High Churchman who admired the Methodists and maintained close links with various Evangelicals. *DNB*. On Knox's role as a precursor of the Oxford Movement, see G. T. Stokes, 'Alexander Knox and the Oxford Movement', *Contemporary Review*, 3 (1887), 184–205; J. T. Gunstone, 'Alexander Knox, 1757–1831', *Church Quarterly Review*, 157 (1956), 466–72; Brilioth, *Anglican Revival*, pp. 331–3.

Charles Daubeny (1745–1827). Winchester and New College, Oxford. Fellow. Prebendary of Salisbury, 1784; Archdeacon of Salisbury, 1804. *DNB*.

John Jebb (1775–1833). Rector of Abington, co. Limerick, 1809; Bishop of Limerick, 1823-d. Lifelong friend and correspondent of Alexander Knox. *DNB*.

Martin Joseph Routh (1755–1854). Magdalen College, Oxford, 1770–1854; BD 1785; President, 1791-d. See J. W. Burgon, 'Martin Joseph Routh: the Learned Divine', *Lives of Twelve Good Men*, vol. I, pp. 1–115.

William Van Mildert (1765–1836). Merchant Taylor's; Queen's College, Oxford, 1784; BA 1787; curacies; Rector of St Mary-le-Bow, London, 1796–1820; Boyle Lecturer 1804; Preacher, Lincoln's Inn, 1813–19; Regius Professor of Divinity, Oxford, and Rector of Ewelme, 1813–26; Bampton Lecturer, 1814; Bishop of Llandaff, 1820–6; Dean of St Paul's, 1826-d; Bishop of Durham, 1826-d. Owed early preferment to Archbishop Manners-Sutton, later to Lord Liverpool. *DNB*.

Charles James Blomfield (1786–1857); Archdeacon of Colchester; Bishop of Chester, 1824–8; Bishop of London, 1828-d.

[39] Quoted in A. Webster, *Joshua Watson: the Story of a Layman* (London, 1954), p. 29. In complete contrast to the Tractarians, the pre-Tractarian High Church leader Joshua Watson eulogised the age of Waterland. E. Churton, *Memoir of Joshua Watson*, 2 vols. (London, 1861), vol. II, p. 169. Similarly, William Van Mildert viewed the era of Waterland as 'a brilliant period in our Church annals'. Varley, *Van Mildert*, p. 105.

[40] BL, Gladstone Papers, Ms. Add. 44204, fols. 114–15, B. Harrison to W. E. Gladstone, 16 November 1843.

century has been well attested.[41] However, High Church groupings within the establishment in the same period have been accorded less attention. The two groups that stand more prominently in the so-called 'tunnel period' between the Hanoverian Succession and 1833 include the 'Hutchinsonians' and the 'Hackney Phalanx'. Of the two, the Hutchinsonians remain the less well known. They comprised the followers of the somewhat eccentric anti-Newtonian scientific theories of the Hebraist author of *Moses principia*, John Hutchinson, who died in 1737.[42] Yet, the Hutchinsonians do not deserve to be defined exclusively in such terms. For most of the group, philosophical 'Hutchinsonianism' was somewhat peripheral to the High Church ecclesiastical, political and sacramental principles which they upheld. Closely connected with the University of Oxford, the Hutchinsonians comprised such figures as Nathaniel Wetherell, Master of University College, Thomas Patten of Corpus Christi,[43] George Horne (1730–92) of University College and later President of Magdalen College,[44] and Samuel Glasse (1735–1812) of Christ Church.[45] Other notable followers included William Jones of Nayland (1726–1800),[46] William

---

[41] For example see T. T. Carter, *Undercurrents of Church Life in the Eighteenth Century* (London, 1899); Wickham Legg, *English Church Life*; Broxap, *Later Nonjurors*.

[42] On Hutchinsonianism, see Churton, *Memoir of Joshua Watson*, vol. 1, pp. 39–42; R. Spearman, *Life of John Hutchinson Prefixed to a Supplement to the Works of John Hutchinson Esq.* (London, 1765), pp. i–xiv; G. Horne, *An Apology for Certain Gentlemen in the University of Oxford, Aspersed in a Late Anonymous Pamphlet* (Oxford, 1756); [J. A. Park], *Memoirs of William Stevens Esq.* (London, 1812), pp. 22–7. See also, L. Stephen, *History of English Thought in the Eighteenth Century*, 2 vols (London, 1876), vol. 1, pp. 389–91; C. B. Wilde, 'Hutchinsonianism, Natural Philosophy and Religious Controversy in Eighteenth-Century Britain', *History of Science*, 18 (1980), 1–24.

[43] Nathaniel Wetherell (1727–1807). Fellow of University College, Oxford; Master, 1764–1807.

Thomas Patten (1714–90), Fellow of Corpus, had been a one-time member of John Wesley's 'Holy Club' at Oxford, thereby providing one of several links between early Methodism and Hutchinsonianism.

[44] George Horne (1730–92). University College, Oxford, 1746; Fellow, 1750; President, 1768; Vice-Chancellor of Oxford University, 1776; Chaplain-in-Ordinary to King George III, 1771–81; Dean of Canterbury, 1781; Bishop of Norwich, 1790–d. *DNB*. Comparisons were later drawn between the Hutchinsonian and Tractarian movements at Oxford. Edward Churton maintained: 'Bishop Horne, long before he was bishop, had as much influence on the minds of the young men at Oxford, as ever Newman or Pusey have lately had.' PH, Gresley Papers, GRES 3/7/68, E. Churton to W. Gresley, 25 May 1846.

[45] Samuel Glasse (1735–1812). MA Christ Church, Oxford 1759; Vicar of Epsom, 1782; Rector of Wanstead, Essex, 1786; an 'intimate friend' of George Horne. *DNB*.

[46] William Jones (1726–1800). Charterhouse and University College, Oxford; BA 1749; curacies; FRS; perpetual curate of Nayland, his subsequent residence, 1777. Biographer of his friend George Horne. *DNB*. See also G. M. Ditchfield and B. Keith-Lucas, 'Reverend William Jones of Nayland (1726–1800): some new light on his years in Kent', *Notes and Queries*, 238 (New Series, 40), No. 3 (September, 1993), 337–42.

Stevens (1732–1807),[47] George Berkeley junior, George Gaskin (1751–1824),[48] John Prince (1754–1833) and Jonathan Boucher (1738–1804).[49]

Directly connected to the Hutchinsonians by personal ties, the 'Hackney Phalanx' represented a succeeding generation of High Churchmen.[50] The group was large and rather amorphous, loose membership determined by residence in, or links with, the metropolis of London. The Phalanx, which was most active for the three decades from the early 1800s to the mid-1830s, took its name from the then village, north-east of London, where one of its leading figures, Archdeacon John James Watson, was the Vicar (afterwards Rector).[51] Archdeacon Watson was the elder brother of Joshua Watson,[52] the real father figure of the Hackney circle. The other

47 William Stevens (1732–1807). Hosier in the City of London. Treasurer of Queen Anne's Bounty, 1782-d. A cousin of George Horne and biographer of his lifelong friend William Jones of Nayland, Stevens belonged to that tradition of High Anglican lay piety represented by such figures as Isaak Walton, John Evelyn and Robert Nelson.
   Another contemporary layman in this tradition was Thomas Calverley, a chemist, and an intimate of Stevens 'since their earliest youth'. *DNB*. See also [Park], *Memoirs of William Stevens*. The lawyer James Allan Park was another lay member of Stevens's circle. *DNB*.
48 George Gaskin (1751–1824). Secretary to the SPCK; Rector of Stoke Newington, London, 1797. Like Horne and Stevens, a vigorous supporter of the Scottish episcopal church. *DNB*.
49 Jonathan Boucher (1738–1804). Ordained 1762; emigrated to North America, living in Virginia, then Maryland; MA of King's College, New York, 1774; defended Anglican Church in the North American colonies and, as a Loyalist, forced to return to England in 1775; Vicar of Epsom, 1785. Became a close friend of Horne, Jones and Stevens. See J. Bouchier, ed., *Reminiscences of an American Loyalist* (Boston, 1925); *DNB*.
50 The best account of the 'Hackney Phalanx' is in Churton's *Memoir of Joshua Watson*. See also Webster, *Joshua Watson*; Corsi, *Baden Powell*, pp. 9–20; Varley, *Van Mildert*, especially ch. 3. On the composition of the Phalanx, see Dewey, *Passing of Barchester*, 'Appendix', pp. 149–68. Dr William Hales, Rector of Killesandra, Ireland, first coined the term 'Hackney Phalanx' to describe the motley group of London High Churchmen who entertained him on visits to the capital. Churton, *Memoir of Joshua Watson*, vol. 1, p. 97.
51 John James Watson (1767–1839). Charterhouse; University College, Oxford (contemporary of Lord Liverpool, Prime Minister, 1812–27); curate to J. Boucher at Epsom; Rector of Hackney, 1799–1839; Archdeacon of St Albans, 1816; Prebend of St Paul's, 1825–39. Owed his later preferment to William Howley, Bishop of London, 1813–28 and Archbishop of Canterbury, 1828–48. *DNB*. Howley was patron of numerous High Church clergy and counted several notable High Churchmen among his chaplains at Lambeth. See Dewey, *Passing of Barchester*, p. 155; J. Garrard, 'William Howley (1766–1848): Bishop of London, 1813–28: Archbishop of Canterbury, 1828–48', unpublished D.Phil thesis, University of Oxford, 1992.
52 Joshua Watson (1771–1855). In early years, a friend of Horne, Jones of Nayland and Stevens. London wine merchant and contractor (1792–1814), retiring to devote his life to service of the Church of England; Treasurer of the SPCK and active in the SPG; co-founder of the National Society 1811, and first Treasurer, 1817; co-founder of the Church Building Society, 1817, and the Additional Curates Society, 1837. In 1811, Watson bought up and reconstituted the then ailing High Church review, the *British Critic* (first

leading dignitary in the Phalanx was Watson's close friend, the
Rector of South Hackney, Henry Handley Norris.[54] Joshua
Watson's London residence in Park Street for many years proved
to be the focal point for gatherings of the Phalanx. After Watson
came increasingly to reside in Daventry in later years, it was
Norris's residence at Grove Street, South Hackney, that assumed
this role.

Both groups accounted for only a small but significant proportion
of those who might be identifiable as 'the Orthodox' in the pre-
Tractarian Church of England. There were numerous figures, such
as John Oxlee[54] mentioned in Burgon's list, who are best regarded as
witnesses to a tradition, but not always as possessing a developed
sense of theological group identity. Yet if ideological cohesion was
often lacking, a sense of cultural and social cohesion in pre-Tractarian High Churchmanship was fostered by patronage and family
networks. Continuity extended to parochial livings. For instance,
Jonathan Boucher succeeded Samuel Glasse as Vicar of Epsom, and
John James Watson became Boucher's curate there before moving
on to Hackney. It was such ties of patronage, family and kinship as
well as of friendship that forged a sense of union among High
Churchmen, and bestowed the character of a succession or school.
Within the Hackney circle, family interrelationships and inter-
marriages created a myriad of clerical dynasties, as Clive Dewey has
demonstrated in the case of the family of the Phalanx member,
W. R. Lyall, Archdeacon of Colchester, then Maidstone, and later
Dean of Canterbury.[55] For example, Joshua Watson, himself the
nephew of the most prominent High Churchman of his day, Archdeacon Daubeny, married Mary Sikes, the daughter of another
prominent Phalanx High Churchman, Thomas Sikes, Rector of

established by Horne and Jones in 1792); one of the founders of King's College, London,
1828. *DNB*.

[53] Henry Handley Norris (1771–1850). Perpetual Curate (1809–31) and Rector (1831–50) of
South Hackney; Prebend of Llandaff, 1816; Prebend of St Paul's, 1825 (owed preferment
to William Howley). Norris 'largely ruled' the SPCK from 1793–1834. *DNB*.

[54] John Oxlee (1779–1854). Rector of Scrawton, Yorkshire. An extreme High Churchman
and an important precursor of the Oxford Movement. See Wakeling, *Oxford Church
Movement*, pp. 16–17; *DNB*.

[55] William Rowe Lyall (1788–1857). Rector of Fairstead, Essex, 1827–33; Rector of Had-
leigh, Suffolk, 1833–42; Archdeacon of Maidstone, 1841–5; Dean of Canterbury, 1845–57.
An accomplished editor of the *British Critic*, *Encyclopaedia Metropolitana* and of the *Theological
Library*, Lyall owed his preferment, prior to becoming Dean of Canterbury, to William
Howley. See Dewey, *Passing of Barchester*, especially chapters 1–3, 8.

Guilsborough.[56] Henry Handley Norris married the sister of Archdeacon Watson. Sikes himself had married another sister of Archdeacon Watson. Moreover, intermarriage further cemented the
succeeding generation in the Hackney circle. Thus, Christopher
Wordsworth junior (1807–85),[57] son of Joshua Watson's close friend
Christopher Wordsworth senior, Master of Trinity College, Cambridge,[58] married Elizabeth Frere, daughter of George Frere (1774–
1854) who in turn was the son of John Frere (1740–1807),[59] the
Hutchinsonian ally of Horne and Stevens. Edward Churton
(1800–74), Joshua Watson's biographer, was the son of the Phalanx
member, Ralph Churton (1754–1831).[60] Edward Churton married
Mary Watson, daughter of Archdeacon Watson, thus making him
the nephew of Joshua Watson. Moreover, John David Watson, who
became Rector of Guilsborough on the death of Thomas Sikes and
who was the son of Archdeacon Watson and nephew of Joshua
Watson, proceeded to marry Edward Churton's sister. In short, the
dynasties of Sikes, Watson, Frere, Wordsworth and Churton, along
with Crawley and Bowdler (to name two more), represent but a few
examples of the essentially hereditary nature of old High Church-

56 Thomas Sikes (1766–1834). St Edmund Hall and Pembroke College, Oxford; Rector of
    Guilsborough, Northants., 1792-d. A nephew of Archdeacon Daubeny. *DNB.*
57 Christopher Wordsworth, the Younger (1807–85). Fellow and Tutor, Trinity College,
    Cambridge; Headmaster of Harrow, 1836–44; Canon of Westminster, 1850; Bishop of
    Lincoln, 1869-d. *DNB.*
58 Christopher Wordsworth, the Elder (1774–1846). Chaplain to Archbishop Manners-
    Sutton to whom he owed his subsequent preferment; Dean of Bocking, Surrey, 1808;
    Master of Trinity College, Cambridge, 1820–41; friend and associate of Joshua Watson
    and Norris; acted as liaison between Archbishop Manners-Sutton and the Phalanx;
    co-founder of the National Society, 1811. *DNB.*
    Charles Manners-Sutton (1755–1828). Bishop of Norwich, 1792–1805; Archbishop of
    Canterbury, 1805–28. Manners-Sutton was a 'staunch supporter' and patron of the
    Hackney Phalanx. His chaplains (George Owen Cambridge, George D'Oyly, Charles
    Lloyd, John Lonsdale and Richard Mant as well as the elder Christopher Wordsworth)
    were all High Churchmen. Manners-Sutton 'guided and animated' the SPCK and pre-
    sided over the first meeting of the National Society in 1811. *DNB.*
59 George Frere (1774–1854). A zealous High Church layman. His father, John Frere
    (1740–1807) had married Janet Hookham, a disciple and spiritual confidante of William
    Stevens. At Stevens's home, John Frere became acquainted with Horne and Jones of
    Nayland. He became one of Stevens's 'most intimate friends'. *DNB.*
60 Ralph Churton (1754–1831). Orphaned son of a Cheshire yeoman; taken up by the Rector
    of Malpas, Thomas Townson, a High Church divine. Brasenose College, Oxford, MA
    1772, Fellow; Bampton Lecturer, 1785; Rector of Middleton Cheney, Northants, 1788-d;
    Archdeacon of St David's, 1805. *DNB.*
    Edward Churton (1800–74). Charterhouse; Christ Church, Oxford; curate to Archdea-
    con Watson at South Hackney and Headmaster of Watson's school at Hackney; Rector of
    Crayke, Yorkshire, 1835; Archdeacon of Cleveland, 1846-d. *DNB.*

manship, of 'the faith of the father' being handed down to a succeeding generation.[61]

Personal and family links were not always a guarantee of theological coherence. There was an assumption that the old tradition in all its integrity would be bequeathed in the family line, but there were exceptions. Ideological defections could seem like family betrayals, as in the case of defections to the Church of Rome from Evangelical family dynasties such as the Wilberforces which David Newsome has movingly portrayed.[62] Defections could also occur in an opposite theological direction. An example was provided by one of Edward Churton's brothers, Thomas Townson Churton. Edward and Thomas Townson's father, Ralph, had imbibed Orthodox principles while curate at Malpas, Cheshire, from his ecclesiastical mentor, Thomas Townson. Ralph Churton became an exemplar of Orthodox churchmanship as Rector of Middleton Cheney, Northamptonshire. During the 1830s while he was a young Fellow of Brasenose College, Thomas Churton embraced Evangelicalism, much to the disapproval of the Principal of Brasenose, A. T. Gilbert.[63] As the apologist of Hackney who kept a critical but not unfriendly eye on the Oxford Tract writers, Edward Churton regarded this apparent defection as a family betrayal as well as ideological error. Thus, after T. T. Churton achieved notoriety as one of the four Oxford tutors who called on the Heads of Houses to censure Newman's *Tract 90* in March 1841, Edward expostulated with him in an angry letter, 'I have not foresaken the friends of my youth, nor my father's friends. It is not I, who have learnt to condemn the principles he learnt at Malpas and taught at Middleton, or those still cherished at his friends' houses, at Guilsborough as at Hackney.'[64] For Edward, Thomas had broken with the Orthodox faith no less than if he had gone in an opposite direction and embraced Rome. It was a blow from which Edward Churton never recovered. As he remarked sadly to William Copeland after his

---

[61] See the testimony of James Hicks-Smith in 1868: 'I claim to have inherited Church principles. The idea that any one fifty years ago could have inherited Anglo-Catholic principles, such as I understand them, will be new to many. Yet it is a fact to be asserted that previous to 1833 church principles did exist. The torch of Andrewes and of Ken had been handed down. Catholic tendencies were ... hereditary'. [J. Hicks-Smith], *Reminiscences of Fifty Years. By an Hereditary High Churchman* (London, 1868), pp. 1–2.

[62] D. Newsome, *The Parting of Friends: a Study of the Wilberforces and Henry Manning* (London, 1966), especially ch. 8.

[63] SC, Churton Papers, E. Churton to W. J. Copeland, 1 February 1842.

[64] SC, Churton Papers, E. Churton to T. T. Churton, 17 April 1841.

brother's death in 1865, 'it cannot be a simple cross, for one who has
been educated in the school of loyal Church principles, with all
hereditary ties to bind him to them, – to foresake the instruction of
his fathers, the teaching of Bull and Waterland, Townson and
Winchester, and all my dear father's friends ... truly it may be said
of poor T. T., that he "went astray in the wilderness out of the way,
and found no city to dwell in" ... he fell into strange company, –
became one of the "Four Tutors"'.[65]

Consternation afflicted Hackney households when another of
their sons, Baden Powell (1796–1860) eventually embraced what
was regarded as infidelity. In his early years, Baden Powell had
espoused a moderate High Churchmanship and contributed to
Orthodox journals, only to emerge as 'an acknowledged leader of
the infidel party within the Anglican Church' and a contributor to
Essays and Reviews. As a result of this apostasy, Edward Churton
deliberately ignored Baden Powell in his own *Memoir of Joshua
Watson*. Churton wished to spare his mentor embarrassment and
protect his own family good name[66] – Baden Powell was a cousin of
Edward Churton's wife.

The cohesion of pre-Tractarian High Churchmanship was
fostered by factors of geographical location. The concentration of
High Churchmen in London was striking, if hardly surprising
given the proximity to Hackney influence.[67] Northamptonshire
also had a high concentration of High Churchmen in the pre-
Tractarian era. Ralph Churton was Rector of Middleton Cheney,
while his neighbour as Rector of Guilsborough was Thomas Sikes,
in turn succeeded by John David Watson. Another clerical neighbour was Charles Crawley, Rector of Stowe,[68] a position which he

65 SC, Churton Papers, E. Churton to W. J. Copeland, 18 December 1865.
66 Corsi, *Baden Powell*, p. 10.
67 A selection includes: Thomas Rennell senior (1763–1840), Master of the Temple, 1798
(Dean of Winchester, 1805-d.); George Gaskin, Rector of Stoke Newington; Francis
Randolph (1755–1831), Rector of St Paul's, Covent Garden; William Van Mildert, Rector
of St Mary-le-Bow; John Prince, chaplain to the Magdalen Hospital; Gerard Andrewes
(1750–1825), Rector of St James's, Westminster; Robert Hodgson (1777–1844), Rector of
St George's, Hanover Square; Thomas Rennell, junior (1787–1824), Vicar of Kensington;
Samuel Wix (1771–1861), Vicar of St Bartholomew-the-Less; Thomas Fuller (1790–1861),
Vicar of St Peter's, Pimlico; James Endell Tyler (1789–1851), Rector of St Giles-in-the-
Fields; John Hume Spry (1767–1854), Rector of St Marylebone; Christopher Benson
(1789–1868), Master of the Temple; John Russell (1787–1863), Headmaster of the
Charterhouse; George Chandler (1779–1859), Rector of All Souls, St Marylebone.
68 Charles Crawley (1788–1871). Rector of Stowe, Northants. His younger brother, George
Abraham Crawley (1795–1862), was Treasurer of the Additional Curates Society.

held for sixty-one years. Again nearby there was Henry Bayley, Archdeacon of Stowe,[69] while at neighbouring Daventry, Joshua Watson spent his later years residing at the home of his brother's widow. Significantly, in 1833, the Tractarian Thomas Mozley, then a young curate at Moreton Pinckney in Northamptonshire, found a welcome reception for the *Tracts for the Times* which he distributed on horseback.[70]

The coherence of pre-Tractarian High Churchmanship was promoted by common membership of various church organisations. These included the SPG, the SPCK, the National Society (1811) and the Church Building Society (1818). They served as a medium of Hackney Phalanx influence. The cohesion of the Phalanx was underpinned by similarities in social composition and professional background. Clive Dewey has demonstrated how far the Phalanx represented metropolitan mercantile interests as well as the clerical and landowning element of society.[71] The strength of City of London High Churchmanship has also been shown.[72] High Church identity was further bestowed by common membership of a powerful private society of establishment dignitaries. 'The Club of Nobody's Friends' was founded in 1800 in honour of the Hutchinsonian High Churchman, William Stevens,[73] the epithet 'Nobody' being one which Stevens appropriated for himself. The complete

---

[69] Henry Vincent Bayley (1777–1844). Trinity College, Cambridge; Examining-Chaplain to George Pretyman-Tomline, Bishop of Lincoln, 1804–6 (tutor to one of Pretyman-Tomline's sons); Sub-Dean and Prebend of Lincoln, 1806–14; Archdeacon of Stowe, 1826–44. *DNB*.

Thomas Fanshawe Middleton (1769–1822) was another Northamptonshire clergyman in the Hackney circle. Rector of Tansor, Northants, 1795–1812; Archdeacon of Huntingdon, 1812–14; first Bishop of Calcutta, India, 1814-d; editor of *British Critic*, 1812–14. See C. Le Bas, *The Life of the Rt. Rev. Thomas Fanshawe Middleton, Late Lord Bishop of Calcutta*, 2 vols. (London, 1831); *DNB*.

[70] Mozley, *Reminiscences Chiefly of Oriel College and the Oxford Movement*, vol. I, pp. 329–33. For Thomas Mozley (1800–93), see *DNB*.

[71] Dewey, *Passing of Barchester*, 'Appendix', pp. 149–68.

[72] A. Howe, 'Free Trade and the City of London, *c.*1820–1870', *History*, 77 (October, 1992), 395; Boyd Hilton, *The Age of Atonement: the Influence of Evangelicalism on Social and Economic Thought, 1785–1865* (Cambridge, 1991, paperback edn), p. 386.

[73] ESCRO, Locker-Lampson Papers, 3/3/85, W. Stevens to J. Boucher, 15 August 1800; Park, *Memoirs of William Stevens*, p. 164; S. Egerton, *Censura literaria: Containing Titles, Extracts and Opinions of Old English Books*, 4 vols. (London, 1807), vol. IV, pp. 219–23. The editor of a Victorian edition of Stevens's *Memoirs* claimed that 'the members of this Society may be regarded, in a certain sense as his posterity'. *Memoirs of the Late William Stevens, Esq. Treasurer of Queen Anne's Bounty. By the Late Hon. Sir James Allan Park. A New Edition. Revised and Enlarged* (London, 1859), p. iv.

biographical list of members from 1800 onwards serves as a sort of 'Who Was Who' of High Churchmen.[74]

This study also contends that, in the era of the Oxford Movement, the lineal ideological descendents of pre-Tractarian High Churchmanship were those whom Hurrell Froude idiosyncratically labelled the 'Zs' rather than the Tractarians themselves. The 'Zs' were deemed to be distinct from the Tractarians themselves whom Froude labelled as 'Ys' or 'Apostolicals', while Evangelicals were honoured with the label 'Xs' or 'Peculiars'.[75] The continuity of the 'Zs' with pre-Tractarian High Churchmen, and the divergence of the Tractarians from both of the former will be illustrated by focusing on five main areas of debate: 'orthodox politics' and the question of church, state and establishment; the rule of faith, patristic antiquity and its relation to scripture; ecclesiology and ministry, involving attitudes to the Church of Rome, Protestant Dissent and the foreign reformed bodies; and spirituality, worship, liturgy and sacramental theology. Finally, the differences between old High Churchmen and Tractarians will be explored more fully at the historical and personal level.

The 'Zs' included Hugh James Rose (1795–1838);[76] William Patrick Palmer (1803–85) of Worcester College, Oxford, and Arthur Philip Perceval (1799–1853);[77] Walter Farquhar Hook (1798–1875);[78]

---

74 See *'The Club of Nobody's Friends': a Biographical List of the Members since Its Foundation, 21st June 1800 to 30th September 1885*, printed for private circulation (1938), pp. 1–161.
75 [Newman and Keble, eds.], *Remains of Hurrell Froude*, vol. 1, p. 429.
76 Hugh James Rose (1795–1838). Trinity College, Cambridge (owed preferment to his tutors, Charles Blomfield and J. H. Monk, both on the fringes of the Hackney circle); curate of Buxted, Sussex, 1819 (Rector was George D'Oyly, Chaplain to Archbishop Manners-Sutton and prominent Hackney divine); Vicar of Horsham, 1821–30; Select Preacher and Christian Advocate, Cambridge, 1826; Dean of Bocking and Rector of Hadleigh, Suffolk, 1830–3; Rector of Fairstead, Essex, 1833–4; Regius Professor of Divinity at newly founded University of Durham, 1834 (owed appointment to the University's benefactor, Bishop Van Mildert); Principal of King's College, London, 1836-d. *DNB*; J. W. Burgon, 'Hugh James Rose: the Restorer of the Old Paths', *Lives of Twelve Good Men*, vol. 1, pp. 116–283.
77 William Patrick Palmer (1803–85). Trinity College, Dublin; studied for ordination under John Jebb, Bishop of Limerick, 1823. A notable liturgical scholar. Incorporated at Magdalen Hall, Oxford, 1828; Worcester College, 1831; Rector of Whitchurch Canonicorum, Dorset, 1846–c. 70; Prebend of Salisbury, 1858; Editor of *English Review*, 1844–52. *DNB*.
   Arthur Philip Perceval (1799–1853). Chaplain to King George IV; Rector of East Horsley, Surrey. Although the author of numbers 23, 35 and 36 of *Tracts for the Times*, Perceval later distanced himself from the Oxford Movement. *DNB*.
78 Walter Farquhar Hook (1798–1875). Curate of Whippingham, Isle of Wight, 1822; Vicar of Holy Trinity, Coventry, 1828–37; Vicar of Leeds, 1837–61; Dean of Chichester, 1861-d. *DNB*.

Edward Churton; Benjamin Harrison (1808–87);[79] George Ayliffe Poole (1809–83);[80] William Gresley (1801–76),[81] William Sewell (1804–74)[82] and Richard William Jelf (1798–1871).[83]

It was through the anxious communication between younger 'Zs' like Churton and Rose on the one hand, and the Hackney elders like Wordsworth, Watson and Norris on the other, that the drama of the painful breach that came to separate old High Churchmen and Tractarians was played out. For if Edward Churton lectured his errant Evangelical brother, his stern message to the young Oxford zealots similarly was to stand by 'the good old men, who really have done something for right principles in their day'.[84] In Churton's eyes, this would best be achieved by the Oxford men acting as if they were really but heirs to a long and honourable tradition, instead of chasing after 'new lights'. The message was eloquently pleaded in a letter to Churton's friend, William Gresley, in May 1846. 'The value', wrote Churton, 'of the labours of Bishop Horne, Jones of Nayland and their friends, will not be forgotten by any faithful historian of the church of the eighteenth century.' Churton wanted Gresley in forthcoming writings 'to refer to such good men's names, (you might add William Stevens, and the late Judge Park, if you thought proper) not only as a matter of justice but because I believe nothing will tend more to make what you are now doing more

[79] Benjamin Harrison (1808–87). Christ Church, Oxford; Scholar; Fellow 1828–48; Select Preacher, Oxford 1835–7; co-founder with Joshua Watson of Additional Curates Society, 1837; Domestic Chaplain to Archbishop Howley, 1838–48; Archdeacon of Maidstone and Canon of Canterbury 1845–87. Like Palmer of Worcester, Harrison was an accomplished liturgical scholar. He was also a popular preacher and effective administrator. Although the author of numbers 16, 24 and 49 of the *Tracts for the Times*, like Perceval, Harrison increasingly distanced himself from the Movement. *D.N.B.*

[80] George Ayliffe Poole (1809–83). Perpetual Curate, St James's, Leeds, 1839, where he was a close ally of W. F. Hook; Vicar of Welford, Northants, 1843. *D.N.B.*

[81] William Gresley (1801–76). Prebend of Lichfield. A prolific populariser of High Church teaching and author of several religious novels. A close friend and confidante of Edward Churton. He was described as 'a thorough going High Churchman, of what may be called the sensible school'. S. C. Austen, *The Scepticism of the Nineteenth Century. Selections from the Latest Works of William Gresley. With a Short Account of the Author* (London, 1879), p. xii; *D.N.B.*

[82] William Sewell (1800–74). Exeter College, Oxford; Fellow; Vice-Rector; Professor of Moral Philosophy, Oxford, 1835; founder of St Columba's College in Ireland, 1841; founder of Radley College, 1847. After 1841 Sewell distanced himself from the Movement. *D.N.B.*

[83] Richard William Jelf (1798–1871). Oriel College, Oxford; Fellow and Tutor; Bampton Lecturer, 1844; Principal of King's College, London, 1843–68. Lifelong friend and correspondent of Pusey in spite of growing theological differences. A regular contributor to the *English Review* under Palmer of Worcester's editorship.

[84] PH, '*British Critic* Papers', E. Churton to J. H. Newman, 17 November 1837.

acceptable to my good old friends'. For Churton, nothing was more important 'than to show that Anglicanism, as it is now called, is not a new party, but has come down to us in regular descent from the Reformation, from Hooker to Andrewes, Andrewes to Laud, Bramhall, and Hammond, thence to Pearson and Jeremy Taylor, thence to Bishop Bull, thence to Hickes and Robert Nelson, Leslie and other names'. Thereafter, there was no breach, as some Tractarians would have it. On the contrary, 'after the succession of George III these principles were again enquired for, and Horne and Jones answered to the call. Horne and Jones have their disciples still living. Tell the world this.'[85] Gresley was to transcribe this passage from a private letter virtually word for word into a subsequent pamphlet.[86] Moreover, the names in this roll-call, including those of Horne and Jones of Nayland, were cited in various *catenae* in the *Tracts for the Times*. Yet if the letter was sometimes observed, the spirit of Churton's advice was imperfectly heeded by Tractarian partisans.

The role of the younger 'Zs' rather than of Tractarians alone in the Church Revival, deserves fuller recognition. At the diocesan level, Arthur Burns and Frances Knight have highlighted the impact of the Orthodox contribution. Knight demonstrates the strength of the 'Z' contribution to the ecclesiastical revival at parochial level in the diocese of Lincoln in the 1840s.[87] Moreover, I have elsewhere delineated the extent of 'Z' involvement in a High Church revival in the Church of Ireland.[88]

The Orthodox role in the Church Revival and the reality of the divergence between the two schools was recognised and illustrated in such works as Burgon's *Lives*, Charles Wordsworth's *Annals* and the biography of George Moberly, *Dulce Domum* (1911). The perspective of these writers had been shaped by links with the Hackney Phalanx and earlier Hutchinsonian divines. Charles Wordsworth had impeccable Hackney credentials. Burgon had been a curate to William Palmer, Rector of Mixbury, Oxfordshire. Palmer was related to the High Church but anti-Hutchinsonian bishop, Samuel

85 PH, Gresley Papers, GRES 3/7/68, E. Churton to W. Gresley, 25 May 1846. See also chapter 6 n. 11.
86 W. Gresley, *A Second Statement on the Real Danger of the Church of England* (3rd edn, London, 1847), p. 14.
87 F. Knight, 'John Kaye and the Diocese of Lincoln', pp. 249, 254–60, 377–8.
88 See P. B. Nockles, 'Continuity and Change in Anglican High-Churchmanship in Britain, 1792–1850', unpublished D.Phil thesis, 2 vols., University of Oxford, 1982, ch. 5.

Horsley, and had been tutored by Jones of Nayland whose memory he revered.[89] Similarly, the loyalty of George Moberly to the older tradition owed much to his family background and connections. Moberly married Mary Ann Crokat, the god-daughter of that Hackney stalwart, Judge Allan Park, at whose London house she often stayed. Another member of 'Nobody's', Sir John Richardson, lived opposite the house.[90] Significantly, both Judge Park and Sir John Richardson had been Hutchinsonian friends of William Stevens and Jones of Nayland.

The need remains for a structured evaluation of the old High Church response to Tractarianism, to complement Peter Toon's delineation of the Evangelical response. For while the Evangelical response was important, it was predictable. The old High Church strand of response was distinguished by its discriminating nature. Recent studies, notably by Perry Butler of Gladstone's religion, recently supplemented by P. J. Jagger, have begun to fill the gap.[91] Nevertheless, many of the 'Zs' remain shadowy figures. William Palmer of Worcester's liturgical and theological treatises have been recently analysed by an American scholar, William Seth Adams.[92] Yet there remains a need for further work on Palmer's personal relation to Newman and the Oxford Movement from an historical perspective to build on the unpublished study by another American scholar, R. H. Greenfield.[93] Given that such different contemporaries as Döllinger and Gladstone considered Palmer to be the most accomplished contemporary theologian in the Church of England, and Newman remained in awe of his learning,[94] more should be known about Palmer's life as well as thought. Ultimately, for

[89] R. Palmer, *Memorials. Part I: Family and Personal. 1766–1865* (London, 1896), p. 6; G. W. E. Russell, 'John William Burgon', *The Household of Faith: Portraits and Essays* (London, 1902), pp. 95–131; S. Baring-Gould, *The Church Revival. Thoughts Thereon and Reminiscences* (London, 1914), p. 72.

[90] C. A. E. Moberly, *Dulce Domum. George Moberly: His Family and Friends* (London, 1911), pp. 47–8; George Moberly (1803–85). Balliol College, Oxford; Fellow, 1834; Warden of Winchester College, 1835; Bishop of Winchester, 1869-d. *DNB.*

[91] P. Butler, *Gladstone. Church, State and Tractarianism: a Study of his Religious Ideas and Attitudes, 1809–1859* (Oxford, 1982). See also, P. Jagger, Gladstone: the Making of a Christian Politician. The Personal Religious Life and Development of William Ewart Gladstone, 1809–1832 (Alison Park, Pa., 1991), especially chs. 5 and 6.

[92] W. S. Adams, 'William Palmer's *Narrative of Events*: the First History of the *Tracts for the Times*', in J. E. Booty, ed., *The Divine Drama in History and Liturgy: Essays in Honor of Horton Davies* (Alison Park, Pa., 1984), pp. 81–106.

[93] R. H. Greenfield, 'The Attitude of the Tractarians to the Roman Catholic Church', unpublished D.Phil thesis, University of Oxford, 1957.

[94] J. H. Newman, *Apologia pro vita sua* (London, 1864), p. 108.

Newman, Palmer's Irish background told against him in an Oxford context.[95] However, Palmer's eventual estrangement from Newman represented in human terms a real 'parting of friends' provoked by a theological divergence between Tractarianism and old High Churchmanship.

The work of reappraisal and revision of the history of the Oxford Movement has recently been advanced by the scholarship of Owen Chadwick and Rune Imberg. Chadwick has shed light on the inner motivations that underscored Dean Church's classic version of the history of the Movement and Newman's part in it.[96] Imberg's penetrating scholarly analysis with its injection of fresh insights, lies in the tradition of that earlier Swedish scholar, Brilioth. Imberg's conclusions support a major contention of this study that there was a marked theological evolution within the Movement itself from its early to later phases.[97]

Important reassesments of the Movement's leaders have recently been made. Keble's limitations have come under the scrutiny of Georgina Battiscombe and Owen Chadwick.[98] Pusey has been the focus of comprehensive re-evaluation, freed from Liddon's distorting lens,[99] while the Anglican Newman has been the subject of the most searching reappraisals by Sheridan Gilley, David Newsome and Stephen Thomas.[100] The present study aims to be a further contribution to this reappraisal, and to set the Oxford Movement in historical context.

[95] *Ibid.*   [96] Chadwick, 'The Oxford Movement and Its Reminiscencers', pp. 142–3.

[97] R. Imberg, *In Quest of Authority: the 'Tracts for the Times' and the Development of the Tractarian Leaders, 1833–1841* (Lund, 1987). For another recent Swedish study of the Oxford Movement, see M. Selen, *The Oxford Movement and Wesleyan Methodism in England, 1833–1882: a Study in Religious Conflict* (Lund, 1992).

[98] G. Battiscombe, *John Keble: a Study in Limitations* (London, 1963); O. Chadwick, 'The Limitations of Keble', *The Spirit of the Oxford Movement*, ch. 2.

[99] P. Butler, ed., *Pusey Rediscovered* (London, 1983); D. Forrester, *The Young Doctor Pusey* (London, 1989). Liddon played down Pusey's early liberalism. See G. Best, 'A Letter from Pusey to Bishop Maltby', *Theology*, 61 (January, 1958), 19.

[100] S. Gilley, *Newman and His Age* (London, 1990); Thomas, *Newman and Heresy*. See also I. Ker, *Newman and the Fullness of Christianity* (Edinburgh, 1993), especially chs. 4, 6. For a masterly reappraisal of both Newman and Henry Manning, see D. Newsome, *The Convert Cardinals: Newman and Manning* (London, 1993), especially chs. 2–3.

THE NOMENCLATURE OF CHURCH PARTIES: PROBLEMS OF
DEFINITION AND IDENTITY

'High Church' or 'Orthodox' in the pre-Tractarian Church of England,
1760–1833

The emergence of more self-conscious church party divisions after
1833 caused followers and historians of the rival traditions of Tractarian and Evangelical to project back the intensity of their own
later disputes to a seemingly more harmonious period. Therefore the
dismissal in later Tractarian historiography of many who had once
passed for 'High Churchmen' in an earlier period, as merely 'High
and Dry', 'Church and King men' or as 'Two Bottle Orthodox',
should be viewed in context. For these were essentially slang epithets
initially applied only in a facetious spirit, but which came to be
solemnly paraded by later Tractarians as indicators of the moral or
spiritual bankruptcy of much pre-Tractarian High Churchmanship.

No party label has been more subject to misapplication than that
of 'High Church'. As J. C. D. Clark has observed, 'the Victorian
conception of High Church was one largely drawn from the Oxford
Movement'.[101] Yet there was an earlier, different conception too
often lost sight of. The term 'High Church' has a long and early
historical lineage.[102] But it needs to be rescued from misappropri-
ation in later historiography. In short, the challenge which John
Walsh issued more than twenty-five years ago deserves to be taken
up. For, as Walsh puts it, 'in the century between the death of Anne
and the rise of the Oxford Movement, "High Churchman" could be
a Protean label, with variations doctrinal, ecclesiastical and political
that have yet to be disentangled by the historian'.[103]

In order to disentangle the layers encrusting the term, the following broad definition might serve as applicable to the pre-Tractarian
era. A High Churchman in the Church of England tended to uphold
in some form the doctrine of apostolical succession as a manifestation

[101] J. C. D. Clark, *Revolution and Rebellion: State and Society in England in the Seventeenth and
Eighteenth Centuries* (Cambridge, 1986), p. 109.
[102] P. B. Nockles, 'Church Parties in the pre-Tractarian Church of England, 1750–1833: the
Orthodox – Some Problems of Definition and Identity', in J. D. Walsh, S. Taylor and
C. Haydon, eds., *Church of England, c. 1689 to c. 1833*, pp. 334–59.
[103] J. D. Walsh, 'The Origins of the Evangelical Revival', in G. V. Bennett and J. D. Walsh,
eds., *Essays in Modern English Church History in Memory of Norman Sykes* (London, 1966),
p. 138.

of his strong attachment to the Church's catholicity and apostolicity as a branch of the universal church catholic, within which he did not include those reformed bodies which had abandoned episcopacy without any plea of necessity. He believed in the supremacy of Holy Scripture and set varying degrees of value on the testimony of authorised standards such as the Creeds, the Prayer Book and the Catechism. He valued the writings of the early Fathers, but more especially as witnesses and expositors of scriptural truth when a 'catholic consent' of them could be established. He upheld in a qualified way the primacy of dogma and laid emphasis on the doctrine of sacramental grace, both in the eucharist and in baptism, while normally eschewing the Roman Catholic principle of *ex opere operato*. He tended to cultivate a practical spirituality based on good works nourished by sacramental grace and exemplified in acts of self-denial and charity rather than on any subjective conversion experience or unruly pretended manifestations of the Holy Spirit. He stressed the divine rather than popular basis of political allegiance and obligation. His political principles might be classed as invariably Tory though by no means always in a narrowly political party sense, and were characterised by a high view of kingship and monarchical authority. He upheld the importance of a religious establishment but insisted also on the duty of the state as a divinely-ordained rather than merely secular entity, to protect and promote the interests of the church. Of course, some of these features of our definition would be held more prominently and unequivocally by some than by others to whom the term 'High Church' has been applied. Many might prove to be beyond categorisation or be claimed by more than one party in the Church. As Gladstone in later years reminded contemporaries, not 'all which was not under the Evangelical "mot d'ordre" was in sharp antagonism with it. For example, Bishops Barrington of Durham, Porteus of London, and Burgess of Salisbury were, like Bishop Horne and Jones of Nayland at an earlier date, men who had in them many elements kindred to it.'[104]

[104] W. E. Gladstone, *Gleanings of Past Years, 1843–79*, 7 vols. (London, 1879), vol. VII, p. 216; B. Hilton, *Age of Atonement* (Cambridge, 1988, hardback edn), pp. 26–31.
   Thomas Burgess (1756–1837). Bishop of St David's, 1803–25; Bishop of Salisbury, 1825-d. Partly on account of his patronage of the British and Foreign Bible Society, Burgess has been mistakenly labelled an Evangelical. See Braine, 'Life and Writings of Herbert Marsh', p. 3n; *DNB*. Burgess has also been considered a 'staunch High Churchman'. See Corsi, *Baden Powell*, p. 27.

The term 'High Church' appears to have been first coined by Richard Baxter in the 1650s[105] but only gained common currency in political and theological discourse in the 1690s and 1700s. It had clear political connotations even in John Evelyn's definition in 1705, 'a strong Church of England man in public life'.[106] For Whig pamphleteers, the label was a pejorative synonym for 'Tory'. In consequence, few willingly identified themselves with the label. But the insistence of pre-Tractarian High Churchmen that they belonged to no party but were simply part of the Anglican mainstream was a rhetorical defence against an opprobrious label bestowed by the Church's external critics.[107] Therefore the common repudiation of the term by those invested with it need not be taken at face value. After Bishop Horsley had urged churchmen not to fear 'the idle terror of a nickname' but rather to accept and even glory in the name once properly understood,[108] there was a greater readiness to acknowledge the theological significance of the term.[109] Nevertheless, the relentless propagation by Dissenters and political radi-

---

105 M. Sylvester, ed., *Reliquiae Baxterianae*, 2 vols. (London, 1696), vol. II, p. 387; H. Sacheverell, *The Character of a Low-Churchman: Drawn in Answer to the True Character of a Churchman* (London, 1702), p. 27.

106 G. Every, *The High Church Party. 1688–1718* (London, 1956), p. 1. See also, J. Spurr, 'Anglican Apologetic and the Restoration Church', unpublished D.Phil thesis, University of Oxford, 1985, pp. 314–17. On the distinction between High Churchmen and Low Churchmen in the 1700s, see G. V. Bennett, 'Conflict in the Church', in G. Holmes, ed., *After the Glorious Revolution, 1689–1714* (London, 1969), p. 166.

107 See [S. Heywood], *High Church Politics, Being a Seasonable Appeal to the Friends of the British Constitution, Against the Practices and Principles of High Churchmen* (London, 1792), especially ch. 3; *High Church Claims Exposed, and the Protestant Dissenters Vindicated ... By a Layman* (London, 1808), pp. 71–2. For evidence of clerical 'apprehension of being stigmatised as High Churchmen', see *British Critic*, 12 (October, 1819), 401. See also Jones of Nayland's comment on party: 'I would willingly have avoided a party name [Hutchinsonian], being conscious that I am not a party man.' W. Jones, *New Preface to the Second Edition of the Memoirs of the Rt Rev George Horne* (London, 1799), p. xi.

108 *The Charge of Samuel, Lord Bishop of St Davids to the Clergy of His Diocese, Delivered at His Primary Visitation in the Year 1790* (London, 1801), p. 28. See ch. 1, n. 65.

109 For examples of revived theological usage of the term, see C. Daubeny, *A Guide to the Church in Several Discourses* [1798], 2 vols. (2nd edn, London, 1804), pp. 431–2; T. Le Mesurier, *The Nature and Guilt of Schism ... in a Course of [Bampton] Lectures Delivered before the University of Oxford in the Year 1807* (Oxford, 1808), p. 431; J. Brewster, *A Secular Essay. Containing a Retrospective View of Events Connected with the Ecclesiastical History of England* (London, 1802). Another contemporary insisted that the title 'High Churchman' should not be accorded to the Nonjurors alone in the eighteenth century, since many had held 'High Church' views 'who never disputed the measures adopted by Parliament at the Revolution'. J. Grant, *A Summary History of the English Church*, 4 vols. (1811–25) (London, 1820), vol. III, pp. 79–80. I am grateful to Christopher Zealley of Wolfson College, Oxford, for drawing my attention to this neglected source. On Grant, see n. 121.

cals of a label designed to insult, ensured that a term apparently less capable of misconstruction, 'Orthodox', came to be preferred. For even George Horne regarded 'High Church' as 'a name invented, according to Mr Leslie, under which the Church might be abused with greater security'.[110] Moreover, as F. C. Mather suggests, as a synonym for intolerant Toryism fighting Whig oligarchy, the term lost much of its earlier political significance with the collapse of the two-party system in the early years of George III's reign.[111]

Contemporary churchmen, then, came to see the label 'Orthodox' as less indicative of a particular sub-division or 'party' within the Church than was 'High Church'. Many historians have taken up this usage, the phrase 'Orthodox party' being most widely employed to denote adherents of a particular religious tradition in the pre-Tractarian Church of England.[112] Some rightly use the two terms interchangeably, but others have given it their own, often partial and misleading, gloss, sometimes too rigidly separating the two.[113] The best model would be one that recognised a relatively broad Orthodox spectrum on the lines suggested by Newsome, within which it can be acknowledged that some were more High Church than others.[114] This allows for the differences of theological emphasis within the spectrum that clearly separated some such as Daubeny

---

110 W. Jones, *Memoirs of the Life, Studies and Writings of the Rt Rev George Horne* D. D. Late Lord Bishop of Norwich (London, 1795), pp. 324–5.

111 Mather, *Horsley*, p. 22. But Sack (*From Jacobite to Conservative*, p. 50) argues that High Churchmanship formed the key element of post-Jacobite Toryism.

112 Francis Blackburne (1705–87), was one of the first to equate the term 'Orthodox' with that of 'High Church'. See F. Blackburne, ed., *The Works, Theological and Miscellaneous . . . of Francis Blackburne, M.A. Late Rector of Richmond, and Archdeacon of Cleveland*, 7 vols. (Cambridge, 1805), vol. I, p. xxxiii. The Unitarian and lapsed Anglican Gilbert Wakefield, referred to Oxford as a seat of 'Orthodox theology, high church politics, and passive obedience to the powers that be'. *Memoirs of the Life of Gilbert Wakefield* (London, 1792), p. 60.

The title of the *Orthodox Churchman's Magazine*, established in 1801, represented a conscious appropriation of the label by High Churchmen. For the review's own definition of the term, see *Orthodox Churchman's Magazine*, 5 (November, 1803), p. 301; [Park], *Memoirs of Stevens* (1812), pp. 20–1.

113 For example, see Murray, 'Influence of the French Revolution on the Church of England', p. 75; Braine, 'Life and Writings of Herbert Marsh', pp. 1–4.

114 Newsome, *Parting of Friends*, p. 318; G. Parsons, 'Introduction', in G. Parsons, ed., *Religion in Victorian Britain*, 4 vols. (Manchester, 1988), vol. I, p. 32.

and Van Mildert on the one hand, and Herbert Marsh[115] and George Pretyman-Tomline[116] on the other.

Prior to the rise of Tractarianism, such differences mattered less than they would later. Moreover, a greater degree of consensus pertained prior to 1833 than afterwards. As A. M. C. Waterman has recently shown, the cause of orthodoxy at Cambridge in the later decades of the eighteenth and early decades of the nineteenth century was represented by a so-called 'intellectual party'[117] which encompassed some erstwhile latitudinarians such as William Paley[118] and Richard Watson on the one hand, as well as more rigidly Orthodox divines such as Marsh and Pretyman-Tomline. Similarly, Corsi has demonstrated links even between the High Church Hackney Phalanx and liberal Oriel *Noetics* – links which would dismay the Tractarians. Convergence between different church parties in the 1810s and 1820s is revealed by the evidence which Corsi presents of the contacts of even such a rigid High Churchman as Van Mildert with *Noetic* divines such as John Davison and Baden Powell.[119] Clearly, the less dogmatically precise character of pre-Tractarian High Churchmanship compared to a later period ensured that such churchmen could feel that differences of emphasis upon collateral points did not impair the substance of Orthodox apologetic against the Church's Dissenting and Unitarian opponents. The Orthodox position was bounded by certain para-

---

115 Herbert Marsh (1757–1839). Lady Margaret Professor of Divinity, Cambridge, 1807; Bishop of Llandaff, 1816; Bishop of Peterborough, 1819-d. *DNB.* Has been described as 'probably the most learned Anglican divine of the early nineteenth century'. Corsi, *Baden Powell,* p. 16. Braine, ('Life and Writings of Herbert Marsh'), p. 10, argues that Marsh was 'Orthodox' but in no sense a High Churchman. Marsh's correspondence with Norris and Joshua Watson, however, points to his links and alliance of interest with the Hackney circle. See chapter 2 and Varley, *Van Mildert,* pp. 57–8.

116 George Pretyman-Tomline (1750–1827). Bishop of Lincoln and Dean of St Paul's, 1787–1820; Bishop of Winchester 1820–7. *DNB.* Owed his earlier preferment to being tutor, then private secretary and ecclesiastical adviser to William Pitt the Younger. Although emanating from the Cambridge Whig school of moderate latitudinarian churchmanship, Pretyman-Tomline increasingly assumed a rigidly 'Orthodox' position. Mather describes him as 'a High Churchman of a drier kind'. Mather, *Horsley,* p. 20. Pretyman-Tomline became the patron of several members of the Hackney Phalanx.

117 A. M. C. Waterman, 'A Cambridge *Via Media* in Late-Georgian Anglicanism', JEH, 42 (1991), 419–36.

118 William Paley (1743–1805). Fellow and Tutor of Christ's College, Cambridge 1766–76; Archdeacon of Carlisle, 1782-d. See D. S. Wayland, ed., *The Works of William Paley with a Biographical Sketch of the Author,* 2 vols. (Derby, 1825), vol. I, pp. iii–xxxvii; *DNB.*

119 Corsi, *Baden Powell,* especially pp. 22, 34–5.

meters and there was unity on certain essentials of the faith, but
otherwise there was no single, monolithic viewpoint.

The High Church theological overtones of the label 'Orthodox'
go back at least as far as the 1620s when Laud coined the term to
describe those clergy who were not 'Puritan'.[120] Similar overtones
are evident in the usage of the term by Johnson Grant in his *Summary
History*. Grant preferred the term 'Orthodox' to that of 'High
Church' but he implied the same principles by another name.[121]
Grant's *Summary History*, like James Brewster's similarly neglected
Secular Essay (1802), is evidence that the concept of 'church party'
was countenanced in the pre-Tractarian Church of England. Grant
divided the contemporary Church of England into four distinct,
though not always mutually exclusive, parties – the 'Orthodox', the
'Latitudinarian', the 'Evangelical' and the 'Secular'. In fact, Grant
merely accepted these labels as drawn up by a contemporary author
of another recent history of the Church of England. This history,
entitled *An Ecclesiastical Memoir of the First Four Decades of the Reign of
George the Third*, was by an Evangelical, J. W. Middelton, and first
published in 1822.[122] Although both authors belonged to different
poles of the current ecclesiastical spectrum, the third and fourth
volumes of Grant's work agreed with Middelton's categorisation of
contemporary church parties. Middelton's use of party labels in turn
drew upon a similar earlier categorisation made by the Evangelical
opponent of Daubeny, John Overton, as early as 1801, in his *True
Churchman Ascertained*. Significantly, when Overton was criticised for
using the labels 'Orthodox' and 'Evangelical' as the major terms of
theological division in the Church, he insisted that they were then
widely used as 'terms of distinction' and had 'use to a theologian'.[123]
This view was shared by the anonymous author of a revealing
pamphlet entitled *Call to Unanimity in the Established Church*. The
author maintained that it was, 'well known that independently of
smaller differences of opinion, there are at present two grand divisions or parties in the Church of England, both professing to have

[120] P. Collinson, *The Religion of Protestants. The Church in English Society, 1559–1625* (Oxford, 1982), p. 81.
[121] Grant, *Summary History*, vol. III, pp. 79–80. Johnson Grant (1773–1844). Vicar of Kentish Town, London, 1820-d. *DNB.*
[122] J. W. Middelton, *An Ecclesiastical Memoir of the First Four Decades of the Reign of George III* (London, 1822), p. 20; Grant, *Summary History*, vol. IV (1825), p. 29.
[123] J. Overton, *Four Letters to the Editor of the 'Christian Observer': Being a Reply to That Author's 'Occasional Strictures' on 'The True Churchman Ascertained'* (York, 1805), p. 24.

the same end in view, but aiming to accomplish that end by somewhat different means, and both zealous in inculcating their respective sentiments'. He designated these differences by the terms 'Evangelical and Orthodox', though adding the qualification that these terms had 'been assumed or applied as marks of distinction on both sides, though they do not of themselves sufficiently discriminate the parties'.[124]

This terminology continued to be used in the Tractarian era. In an historical survey of the Church of England for the *Encyclopaedia Metropolitana* first published in 1845, Hugh James Rose's brother, Henry, explained that in employing the labels 'Orthodox' and 'Evangelical', it was 'not intended ... to use any such terms as implying approbation, but these have been known for so long a time as distinctive terms, that to disdain their use would be idle affectation'.[125] Similarly, an Evangelical writer in 1835 could observe that, while contemporaries might 'lament that such terms of distinction' as 'Orthodox' and 'Evangelical' 'should be used', yet 'as long as men can convey their meaning in a word, which otherwise would require much explanation, they will always do it'.[126]

The theological divide between Orthodox and Evangelical was not synonymous with differences separating 'Arminians' and 'Calvinists'.[127] Contemporaries sometimes used 'Arminian' as shorthand for 'High Church' or 'Orthodox', and 'Calvinist' as interchangeable with 'Evangelical'[128] or even 'Puritan'. Yet historically there was no such correlation between them.[129] A pre-Laudian combination of

---

124 *A Call to Unanimity in the Established Church, by a Clerical Member* (London, 1816), p. 7; *Considerations on the Probable Effects of the Opposition of the Orthodox Clergy to Their Evangelical Brethren* (London, 1818).

125 *Encyclopaedia Metropolitana*, 13, ch. 205 [H. J. Rose], 'Ecclesiastical History from A.D. 1700 to A.D. 1815' (1845), p. 1141. For another example of late usage of 'Orthodox' and 'Evangelicals' as descriptions of the two main party divisions, see J. King, *A Letter Addressed to the Churchmen of Hull on the Present Crisis of Affairs in the Church* (Hull, 1846), p. 14.

126 *An Address to the Most Rev. and Rt. Rev. Fathers in God, the Archbishops and Bishops on the Internal Discipline of the Church of England by a Low Churchman* (London, 1835), p. 18; R. Vaughan, *Religious Parties in England: Their Principles, History and Present Duty* (London, 1839), p. 106.

127 Nockles, 'Church Parties', pp. 342–3.

128 *Orthodox Churchman's Magazine*, 5 (1803), 183; 12 (1807), 72; A. H. Kenney, *The Principles and Practices of Pretended Reformers in Church and State* (London, 1819), p. 412. For a contrary view, see E. Pearson, *Remarks on the Controversy Subsisting, or Supposed to Subsist between the Arminian and Calvinist Ministers of the Church of England* (London, 1802), pp. 6–8.

129 Anglican Evangelicals complained that the confounding of Calvinist with Puritan was an historical fallacy deriving from partisan High Church writers such as Peter Heylin and Jeremy Collier. *Christian Observer*, 3 (July, 1804), 429; G. S. Faber, *Thoughts on the Calvinistic and Arminian Controversy* (London, 1804), p. 42. Peter Heylin, a prominent Laudian exile under the Commonwealth, was the author of *Cyprianus Anglicanus* (1668).

High Church episcopal claims with a highly Protestant emphasis on Justification by faith that had moderate Calvinist overtones continued to characterise the churchmanship of some individual divines such as G. S. Faber and Charles Smith Bird and their strand of opposition to Tractarianism in the 1840s.[130]

An Evangelical in the pre-Tractarian era was not a Low Churchman. As Gascoigne has shown, the epithet 'Low Church' was not levelled at Evangelicals prior to 1833.[131] The term was confined to the Latitudinarian school associated with Benjamin Hoadly and Francis Blackburne.[132] Evangelicals criticised this school as sternly as any of the Orthodox. The anti-Low Church credentials of many Evangelicals were pronounced enough in the 1820s to attract the attention of a visiting American High Churchman. The American observer actually described the Evangelical Bishop Ryder as a 'High Churchman'.[133] It was only from the 1840s onwards that Evangelicals in the Church of England came to acquire the label 'Low Church' from Tractarian polemicists, though it would appear that by that date Evangelicals did not appear to resent the label; one of its earliest uses in this sense dates from 1835, when an Evangelical pamphleteer appeared proud to adopt the title 'Low Churchman'.[134]

130 George Stanley Faber (1773–1842). Oxford BA, 1789; Fellow of Lincoln College, 1793–1803; Master of Sherburn Hospital, 1830-d. Faber's churchmanship has been variously described as Evangelical and High Church. For evidence on this, see ch. 2, ns. 87, 137–9, ch. 6, n. 67.
    Charles Smith Bird (1795–1862). Trinity College, Cambridge 1815, Fellow, 1820; Rector of Gainsborough, Lincs, 1843-d. A moderate Evangelical, Bird boasted: 'he [Bishop Kaye] says, that my views of Doctrine and discipline are moderate, removed on the one hand from Tractarianism, and on the other from Low Church laxity'. LPL, Golightly Papers, Ms 1804, fols. 41–2, C. S. Bird to C. P. Golightly, 25 May 1843. *DNB*.
    John Kaye (1783–1853). Christ's College, Cambridge; Fellow; Margaret Professor of Divinity, Cambridge, 1812; Bishop of Bristol, 1820–7; Bishop of Lincoln, 1827-d; a moderate High Churchman with Hackney connections, and accomplished theologian. On relationship with Tractarians, see chapter 2; Knight, 'John Kaye and the Diocese of Lincoln', especially ch. 1; *DNB*.
131 J. Gascoigne, 'Anglican Latitudinarianism and Political Radicalism in the Late Eighteenth Century', *History*, 71 (1986), 24.
132 See Le Mesurier, *Nature and Guilt of Schism*, p. 431.
133 *Address to Protestant Episcopalians on the Subject of a Tract called 'Origin of the Terms High and Low Churchman'. By a High Churchman* (New York, 1827), pp. 1, 3–4.
134 *Address to the Archbishops ... By a Low Churchman.* An early example of an Evangelical being labelled a 'Low Churchman' was W. F. Hook's designation of Charles Sumner as such in 1826. W. R. Stephens, *The Life and Letters of Walter Farquhar Hook*, 2 vols. (London, 1878), vol. 1, p. 109. For discussion of the historical distinction between 'Evangelical' and 'Low Church' and later fusion of the terms, see G. R. Balleine, *A History of the Evangelical Party in the Church of England* (London, 1908), p. 209; Toon, *Evangelical Theology*, pp. 207–9; M. A. Crowther, 'Church Problems and Church Parties', in G. Parsons, ed., *Religion in Victorian Britain*, vol. IV, 'Interpretations', p. 11.

THE TRACTARIAN REDEFINITION OF CHURCH PARTY LABELS

The Tractarians altered the nomenclature of Anglican church parties, as a result of their distortion of the pre-existing theological spectrum. As William Gresley observed in 1846, 'the Church is not what she was. Parties within her have shifted their ground. New combinations have taken place.'[135]

As early as 1828, while Newman could describe the two main parties in the Church as 'Orthodox' and 'Evangelical', he proceeded to distance himself from both. Already vaunting the future Tractarian claim that the Movement's followers were the real heirs of Laudianism, Newman insisted that the 'old divines' of the Church of England, whose example he avowed to follow, fitted neither of the modern church party labels; that they were 'neither orthodox nor evangelicals, but untractable persons'.[136] In Tractarian eyes, a residue of apparent compromise and equivocation attached itself to those who had been labelled 'the Orthodox'. Certainly, the term 'orthodoxy' in the sense of opposition to heresy retained a perennial hold on Tractarian regard. However, when Tractarians referred to 'the Orthodox party' there was the same note of disdain as when the epithet 'Z' was employed. Thus John Keble would refer to 'the old Orthodox Two Bottles',[137] while even Benjamin Harrison used the term 'orthodoxistical' and 'orthodoxism' in an unflattering sense akin to Pusey's use of the same term to describe the 'dead orthodoxy' of a party within the eighteenth-century German Lutheran church.[138] Moreover, the use of the term 'High and Dry' in a less than flattering sense was not confined to Tractarians.[139]

The hitherto accepted High Church credentials of various con-

---

[135] W. Gresley, *The Real Danger of the Church of England* (London, 1846), p. 3.
[136] *Letters and Diaries of John Henry Newman*, I. Ker and T. Gornall, eds. vol. I, (Oxford, 1978), pp. 309–10.
[137] See Bodl. Lib, Ms Eng Lett d. 134, fol. 283, J. Keble to J. T. Coleridge, 1 May 1839. Thomas Mozley asserted: 'in my time, and I suspect long before my time, the expression "three-bottle orthodox", was often used to denote some class supposed to exist in the last century and reaching down into this'. Mozley, *Reminiscences Chiefly of Oriel College and the Oxford Movement*, vol. I, p. 324.
[138] BL., Gladstone Papers, Ms Add 44204, fol. 73, B. Harrison to W. E. Gladstone, 6 January 1837.
[139] Samuel Wilberforce employed the term, defining it as being 'meant to express the school of High Churchmen who adhere rather to the arid stiffness of the "Establishment" than to the spiritual powers of the Church ... He is stiffer as to forms, rubrics etc. than the High Churchman. Dr Spry of St Mary-le-Bow is considered the typical specimen.' Bodl. Lib, Ms Eng Lett d. 367, fols. 277–8, S. Wilberforce to J. W. Croker, 5 May 1851.

temporary churchmen were questioned by the Tractarians. Another Tractarian controversial gambit was to invest many, sometimes moderate, opponents with such epithets as 'Ultra-Protestant' or 'Puritan'.[140] Admittedly, some of the pre-Tractarian Orthodox employed the term 'Puritan' interchangeably with 'Evangelical',[141] but the Tractarians were freer in the application of pejorative epithets. For example, while that notorious opponent of the Tractarians, Charles Portales Golightly, was claimed as 'fundamentally High Church' by his friend, Edward Goulburn,[142] the Tractarians invoked the bugbear of 'Puritanism' to explain away Golightly's inveterate anti-Tractarianism. For Thomas Mozley, Golightly was 'a decided, not to say extreme, Evangelical, showing more sympathy for Puritans than for High Churchmen'.[143] But High Church Evangelicals such as G. S. Faber and C. S. Bird resented being labelled 'Genevan' or 'Puritan' merely on account of their opposition to the *Tracts for the Times*.[144]

An early consequence of the rise of the Oxford Movement was to divest High Churchmanship of its hitherto accepted meaning. Even Hugh James Rose was led to concede in 1836, 'I was asked by a very eminent person about a month ago, to define High Churchmanship. I was obliged to say that I could only state my own view, not speak with any confidence of any general or fixed standard.'[145] Another younger 'Z', Edward Churton, conceded in 1839, 'I was not aware till lately that there were so many who in the last generation fancied themselves High Churchmen, and who were not ... One or two of them are writing against us, such as Godfrey Faussett and Mr

---

[140] Pusey especially was prone to this. For examples, see *Tract 81*, p. 4, 28; E. B. Pusey, *A Letter to His Grace the Archbishop of Canterbury, on Some Circumstances, Connected with the Present Crisis in the English Church*, (2nd edn, Oxford, 1842), p. 84.

[141] For example, see Bodl. Lib, Norris Papers, Ms Eng Lett c. 789, fol. 106, W. Johnson to H. H. Norris, 27 November 1822.

[142] E. M. Goulburn, *Reminiscences of Charles Portales Golightly* (Oxford, 1886), p. 13; R. W. Greaves, 'Golightly and Newman, 1824–1845', *JEH*, 9 (October, 1958), 216. See Golightly's avowal in 1840: 'I am not, I repeat it, one of them [Evangelicals]; they would not own me, and I have not always received kind usage from them.' LPL, Golightly Papers, Ms 1809, fol. 50, C. P. Golightly to P. Shuttleworth, 29 December 1840. See *DNB*.

[143] T. Mozley, *Reminiscences Chiefly of Towns, Villages and Schools*, 2 vols. (2nd edn, London, 1885), vol. 1, p. 12.

[144] See Bird's indignant assertion: 'This alternative [i.e. Latitudinarian or Puritan] is modestly offered us ... We are not reduced, thank God! to the necessity of accepting the alternative. We are too dogmatic to be latitudinarians. And we are too sincerely attached to Episcopacy and the whole framework of our Church, to be Puritans. Yet never will we be Tractarians. Nor need we. We desire to be true Church-of-England men.' C. S. Bird, *A Defence of the Principles of the English Reformation from the Attacks of the Tractarians; or a Second Plea for a Reformed Church* (London, 1843), p. 290.

[145] PH, Pusey Papers, LBV [Transcripts], H. J. Rose to A. P. Perceval, 2 April 1836.

Holden.'[146] Suddenly, High Churchmanship became 'a very indefinite characteristic'. Not surprisingly since Tractarianism itself was but a variant new form of High Churchmanship, the latter's 'ample folds' came to embrace proponents and opponents of the Movement alike.[147]

A controversy between W. F. Hook and F. D. Maurice over the correct meaning of the term 'High Church' in 1841, exemplified the new degree of ambiguity and complexity in current usage. On the one hand, Hook, who was a 'Z' but still somewhat identified with the Tractarians, made an unqualified distinction between supporters of the Movement whom he classed as 'High Church' and opponents of the Movement whom he labelled 'Low Church'.[148] On the other hand, Maurice criticised the basis of this division as facile, arguing that 'the phrase "High Churchman" is most equivocal; it would be claimed by persons with whom Dr Hook has no sympathy, and who have no sympathy with him; I do not say which has the older or better title to the name'.[149]

Newman and Froude's appropriation of the term 'Apostolicals' for themselves entailed a surrendering of an exclusive claim to the 'High Church' label. Pusey conceded the distinction between the two terms when in 1836 he described the Evangelical party as having 'no ground to stand upon against Catholic principles, although they may against mere High Churchism'.[150] Newman was even more candid. In an article in the *British Magazine*, he allowed one of the parties in a dialogue to assert that the

element of High Churchmanship (as that word has commonly been understood) seems about to retreat again into the depths of the Christian temper, and Apostolicity is to be elicited instead, in greater measure ... High-churchmanship – looking at the matter historically – will be regarded as a temporary stage of a course ... I give up High-churchmanship.[151]

This distinction between High Churchmen and the 'Oxford divines' came to be widely employed in the 1840s. In 1841 Richard

---

146 PH, Pusey Papers, LBV [Transcripts], E. Churton to A. P. Perceval, 23 February 1839. Godfrey Faussett (1771-1853). Canon of Christ Church; Margaret Professor of Divinity, 1811-d.
147 *Christian Remembrancer*, 7 (June, 1844), 702.
148 W. F. Hook, *A Letter to the Rt. Rev. the Lord Bishop of Ripon, on the State of Parties in the Church of England* (London, 1841), pp. 5-6.
149 F. D. Maurice, *Reasons for Not Joining a Party in the Church. A Letter to the Ven. Samuel Wilberforce* (London, 1841), p. 12.
150 PH, Pusey Papers, LBV [Transcripts], E. B. Pusey to J. Keble, 7 November 1836; E. B. Pusey to W. F. Hook, 12 August 1838.
151 [Newman], 'Home Thoughts from Abroad', *British Magazine*, 9 (April, 1836), 358.

Monkton-Milnes differentiated 'the church and state or High Church party' from the 'catholic, or, as it is now accidentally denominated, the "Puseyite" party'.[152] Similarly, in 1842 W. F. Hook, abandoning his earlier dichotomy between 'High Church' and 'Low Church' as determined by one's attitude to the Tractarians, now clearly distinguished 'the High Churchmen of the old school, the Church of England men', from 'those who are usually called the Oxford Divines'.[153] A contemporary German observer surveying in 1844 the existing parties in the Church of England, likewise separated 'the Puseyites' from 'the Orthodox'.[154]

The term 'Tractarian' which soon became the most widely employed as a description of followers of the Oxford Movement, was first coined by the then Master of the Temple, Christopher Benson, in a sermon at the Temple church in 1839.[155] The term was more acceptable to friends of the Movement than the no less commonly used nickname 'Puseyite'[156] which had more of the quality of offensive slang. 'Tractarian' was also preferred by the Movement's supporters to other nicknames, some invented by Richard Whately, such as 'Tractites', 'Tractators' or 'Tractists',[157] 'Newmanites' or 'Neomaniacs'.[158]

As first defined by Benson, the term 'Tractarian' appeared to be quite specific and narrow in its application, referring to 'the authors, editors and approvers of the "Tracts for the Times"'.[159] Of

---

152 [R. Monckton-Milnes], *One Tract More, or the System Illustrated by the 'Tracts for the Times' Externally Regarded by a Layman* (London, 1841), p. 3.
153 W. F. Hook, *Reasons for Contributing towards the Support of an English Bishopric at Jerusalem* (London, 1842), p. 38.
154 H. Uhden, *The Anglican Church in the Nineteenth Century: Indicating Her Relative Position to Dissent in Any Form*, W. C. Humphreys, tr. and ed. (London, 1844), pp. 89–90.
155 *British Critic*, 26 (October, 1839), 508. Years later, Newman confirmed that Benson had been the first to use the term. On noticing that Benson's authorship had been acknowledged by Sir John Coleridge in his biography of John Keble, Newman commented: 'Yes – Mr Benson gave the name "Tractarian" to us in his sermon. I thought no one recollected this but myself.' C. S. Dessain and T. Gornall, eds., *Letters and Diaries of John Henry Newman*, vol. XXXI (London, 1972), p. 82, J. H. Newman to Sir J. T. Coleridge, 7 February 1869.
156 'Puseyism' as a term gained currency after Pusey had added his initial to his Tract (No. 18) on Fasting in 1834. Brilioth, *Anglican Revival*, p. 18.
157 E. J. Whately, *The Life and Correspondence of Archbishop Whately*, 2 vols. (London, 1866), vol. I, p. 418; OCA, Hawkins Papers, Letterbook III No. 290, R. Whately to E. Hawkins, 17 December 1849.
158 Chadwick, 'The Oxford Movement and Its Reminiscencers', p. 135. For an early example of the punning phrase, 'New Mania', see LPL, Golightly Papers, Ms 1805, fol. 165, J. Evans to C. P. Golightly, 11 December 1841. It was a favourite quip of Bishop Blomfield that the Oxford Movement 'was nothing but a Newmania'. *Church Quarterly Review*, 116 (October, 1864), 539.
159 C. Benson, *Discourses upon Tradition and Episcopacy* (London, 1840), p. 101. See definition of 'Tractarian' in *ODCC* (p. 1388): 'a name for the earlier stages of the Oxford Movement,

course, 'approvers' widened the application considerably, but it was maintained that Benson only really meant the term to cover 'the writers of a certain well-known series of Tracts – neither less nor more'.[160] Yet, even if thus narrowly circumscribed, 'Tractarianism' as the sum of the doctrine contained in those Tracts was itself no more of a monolith than had been the old High Churchmanship. The Tracts were the work of individuals beholden to no committee of revision, and thus did not exemplify uniformity in doctrine, aspiring as they did to a particular catholic standard. It became as easy for a supporter of the Movement to cover his tracks by denying formal allegiance to the 'Tractarian party' as it was for an unscrupulous opponent to brand even traditional High Churchmen with the stigma of an equivocal nickname.[161] Richard Whately mocked such disavowals of Tractarianism by even noted supporters of the Movement. 'Tractism', he noted in a letter in 1846, 'is very like the Fens where no one can ever reach. "Oh no, this village is not in the Fens, only near; you must go to such and such village, and then you will be in the Fens"; you go there and are told, "oh no, this is not in the Fens, you must go to the next village" etc. etc.'[162]

The term acquired an ever looser meaning once the series of Tracts ceased in 1841. Rune Imberg's informed scholarly analysis of Tractarianism suffers from his confining of evidence of 'Tractarian' attitudes and allegiance to a literal involvement in the series of *Tracts for the Times*.[163] As an index of 'Tractarian' credentials, this is both unreliable and too narrow. Both Benjamin Harrison and William Palmer of Worcester College were authors or part-authors of one or two of the *Tracts for the Times*. Yet neither was in full sympathy with the tenor and direction of the Movement and expressed private disagreement at an early date. On the other hand, there were numerous individuals who became enthusiastic followers of the Movement but who had had no hand in the composition of the Tracts and in some cases had scarcely even read them. Moreover, the

derived from the *Tracts for the Times* issued under its aegis'; Imberg, *In Quest of Authority*, p. 15.

[160] *Christian Remembran.er*, 3 (October, 1842), 254.

[161] See the comment of Henry Newland in 1852: 'There are also certain publications called *Tracts for the Times*, but many of us have never seen them, few of us have read them at all, none of us I suppose would like to be bound by them, or to make them our Confession of Faith. In truth we were called Tractarians, not because the name was appropriate, but because people could find no better for us'. H. Newland, *South Church Union. Three Lectures on Tractarianism Delivered in the Town Hall, Brighton* (London, 1852), pp. ix, 5.

[162] OCA, Hawkins Papers, Letterbook III, R. Whately to E. Hawkins, 11 February 1846.

[163] Imberg, *In Quest of Authority*, p. 18.

Tractarian leaders themselves came to define the term as encompassing a whole range of doctrines and practices that went beyond standard Orthodox teaching. Some of these doctrines and practices might have been advocated in the *Tracts for the Times*, but others might only have been hinted at in the later numbers of the series. A few would only come to be developed after the termination of the series in 1841. In 1845, Samuel Wilberforce defined the term thus:

> I used the words 'Tractarian' ... to imply a leaning to those doctrines and practices advocated by the writers of the Tracts or any of them which are at variance with the received interpretation of the formularies of the English church. I might refer to many, but I will only mention No. 90 as falling in my judgment eminently under this category.[164]

Of course, Wilberforce's definition of the term is slippery and begs the question, since old High Churchmen and Tractarians would each claim that theirs was the most faithful interpretation of Church of England formularies. Yet, there was a consensus that the key to the difference lay in the fact that one purported to adhere to the letter of those formularies in a way which the latter did not; in short, that Tractarianism implied more than what Newman, echoing Jeremy Bentham's disparaging phrase, called 'Church-of-Englandism'.[165]

During the 1840s, the term 'Oxfordism' came to be used interchangeably with 'Tractarianism' as well as the more obnoxious 'Puseyism', to distinguish the system cultivated by the Tractarians from that of old High Churchmanship. The term only became commonplace after Newman's secession and in some cases applied primarily to followers of the Movement who had not embraced 'Romanism' or were not 'Romanisers'.[166] Yet though the phrase 'Oxford Tracts' was commonplace in the 1830s, until the 1880s the term 'Oxford Movement' was rarely employed without inverted commas.[167]

There were many prominent individuals involved in the theological controversies of the 1840s and early 1850s, such as William

---

[164] Bodl. Lib, Ms Wilberforce c.8, fol. 73, S. Wilberforce to Lord Lyttleton, 30 December 1845.
[165] For an example of Newman's derogatory usage, see PH, Copeland Papers, J. H. Newman to F. Rogers, 19 June 1837.
[166] LPL, Wordsworth Papers, Ms 2149, fol. 329, C. Wordsworth (Sen.) to C. Wordsworth (Jun.), 17 May 1845.
[167] Chadwick, 'The Oxford Movement and Its Reminiscencers', p. 136.

Maskell,[168] William Scott of Hoxton[169] and George Anthony Denison,[170] who cannot neatly be categorised as either unreservedly 'old High Church' or 'Tractarian', and whose mature churchmanship contained elements or a mixture of both. They might best be described as advanced old High Churchmen. As before 1833, lines of party division remained blurred. Within the umbrella of the 'Tractarian' label, different shades of opinion manifested themselves. At the one extreme, there was the advanced 'Romanising' strand represented by W. G. Ward and Frederick Oakeley. At the other end of the spectrum, a moderate Tractarian strand, comprising the so-called 'Bisley school' of Isaac Williams, Sir George Prevost and Thomas Keble, remained much closer in spirit to the older High Churchmen. After the secessions to Rome in 1845, when the residue of the advanced Tractarian party – though less extreme than the Wardites – regrouped under Pusey's leadership, the more conservative 'Bisley school' virtually merged with the younger generation of old High Churchmen.[171] Nevertheless, for all its variations, 'Tractarianism' had specific points of ideological reference which bestowed a certain cohesion on the principles of its adherents. A common identity was provided by both the philosophical and ethical, and moral and spiritual dimensions of the Movement. These dimensions extended support for the Tractarians among those who had reservations on particular doctrinal points. For example, while the old High Churchman William Sewell took issue with the Tractarians from 1841 onwards, in the intellectual and philosophical debates at Oxford between Tractarians and Liberals in the 1830s he was closely identified with the former camp.[172]

The labels 'Anglican' and 'Anglo-Catholic', so familiar in current theological discourse, also underwent a modification of their original meaning in the Tractarian era. The term 'Anglican' is of relatively modern origin. In the seventeenth century, it was mainly used in its Latin forms of 'Anglicanus' or 'Anglicanae' as a description of the reformed and established church in England. Early examples of its

---

[168] William Maskell (1814–90). University College, Oxford; MA 1838; Rector of Corscombe, Dorset, 1842; Perpetual Curate of St Marychurch, Torquay, and Domestic Chaplain to Bishop Phillpotts, 1847–50; Joined Church of Rome, 1850. *DNB*.

[169] William Scott (1813–72). Perpetual Curate of Hoxton, London, 1839–60; joint editor of the High Church *Christian Remembrancer* in the 1840s. Friend of William Maskell. *DNB*.

[170] George Anthony Denison (1805–96); Christ Church, Oxford, 1823–6; Oriel College, 1828; Tutor, 1830–6; Vicar of East Brent; Archdeacon of Taunton. *DNB*; G. A. Denison, *Notes of My Life, 1805–1878* (Oxford, 1878).

[171] On the Bisley school, see O. W. Jones, *Isaac Williams and His Circle* (London, 1971).

[172] See P. B. Nockles, 'An Academic Counter-Revolution: Newman and Tractarian Oxford's Idea of a University', *History of Universities*, 10 (1991), 137–97.

usage to denote individual membership of that church, i.e. an 'Anglican', can be dated to Edmund Burke in 1797,[173] and to George Stanley Faber in 1804.[174] It was not descriptive of a theological system in the way that 'Calvinism' or 'Romanism' was. 'Anglican' took a long time to acquire an '-ism'. Its earliest modern use as denoting a particular theological tradition was by Newman in his formulation of the *via media* in 1837.[175] Yet even as late as 1846, its use in this sense was of sufficiently recent date for Edward Churton to refer to 'what is now called Anglicanism'[176] when describing the Orthodox tradition bequeathed by Hooker and the Caroline Divines. In the Tractarian controversies, 'Anglican' acquired party connotations. The term now denoted a particular understanding of the Church of England rather than simple membership of that Church itself. Thus William Gresley applied the title as a substitute for a 'High Churchman' and in direct contradiction to 'Evangelical' which he used interchangeably with 'Puritan'.[177] Certainly, the term 'Anglican' acquired sufficiently unacceptable 'High Church' resonances in Evangelical eyes for it to become suspect and almost synonymous with 'Puseyite'.[178]

On the other hand for the Tractarians, the term 'Anglican' came to denote a 'High and Dry' form of attachment to the Church of England. Thus, Palmer, Hook and Edward Churton were dubbed 'mere Anglicans',[179] to distinguish them from those whom the

---

[173] *OED.*   [174] Faber, *Thoughts on the Calvinistic and Arminian Controversy*, p. 43.

[175] J. H. Newman, *Lectures on the Prophetical Office of the Church Viewed Relatively to Romanism and Popular Protestantism* (London, 1837), p. 21.

On the historical origins of the terms 'Anglican' and 'Anglicanism', see Sykes and Booty, eds., *Study of Anglicanism*, pp. 405–41, especially J. R. Wright's essay on terminology, pp. 424–8. Sykes concludes that the term 'Anglicanism' was 'a neologism of the 1830s'. S. Sykes, 'The Genius of Anglicanism', in D. G. Rowell, ed., *The English Religious Tradition and the Genius of Anglicanism* (London, 1992), p. 227.

[176] PH, Gresley Papers, GRES 3/7/68, E. Churton to W. Gresley, 25 May 1846.

[177] Gresley, *Real Danger of the Church of England*, pp. 5–6, 46; *A Second Statement on the Real Danger of the Church of England* (London, 1846), p. 15.

[178] F. Close, *An Apology for the Evangelical Party* (London, 1846), p. 11. By 1863, Mark Pattison was complaining that the Church of England had become 'Anglicanised'. *Quarterly Review*, 157 (April, 1898), 302. For Pattison, 'Anglican' had become shorthand for 'High Church'. By 'Anglicanised', he suggested that the Church of England had become 'a party Church' on the High Church side. Ellis, *Seven against Christ*, p. 248.

[179] See Pusey's comment in 1844: 'I have no fears whatever about the fall of what is called Anglicanism.' PH, Pusey Papers, LBV [Transcripts], E. B. Pusey to J. H. Newman, 25 August 1844. Even Edward Churton in 1847 maintained: 'there is a sort of exclusive Anglicanism, too near to High and Dry, which I do not wish to see prevalent'. PH, Churton Papers, E. Churton to W. Gresley, 16 September 1847. In contrast, in 1851 the Tractarian convert to Rome William Dodsworth labelled residual followers of the

Tractarian leaders regarded as unequivocal followers of 'apostolical' principles. Only old High Churchmen took pride in the 'Anglican' label and increasingly criticised the Tractarians for being 'essentially un-Anglican'.[180] Significantly, in his famous article on church parties in the *Edinburgh Review* in 1853, W. J. Conybeare distinguished an 'Anglican' or 'normal type' of High Churchman from the 'High and Dry' as well as from a 'Tractarian' or 'exaggerated type' of High Churchman.[181]

The label 'Anglo-Catholic' also underwent transmutation. The original meaning of 'Anglo-Catholic', like that of 'Anglican', had been a descriptive term for mere membership of the Church of England, and was of seventeenth-century lineage. The term could be used interchangeably with 'Anglican'. The non-party meaning of the term endured well into the nineteenth century as was witnessed by Newman's use of the phrase 'Anglo-Catholic Church' in his *Lectures on the Prophetical Office of the Church*.[182] The same usage was employed in the very title *Library of Anglo-Catholic Theology* by its Tractarian editors. Similarly, William Palmer of Worcester used the term interchangeably with the 'orthodox Church of England position' in his *Treatise on the Church of Christ* (1838),[183] and William Gresley adopted the same meaning in his theological manual, *Anglo-Catholicism* (1844).[184]

The addition of the '-ism' symbolised a new degree of theological precision in the title. For Gresley, 'Anglo-Catholicism', like 'Anglicanism', represented a distinctive theological tradition; a

Movement as of 'the Anglican school', as distinct from 'the old high church school'. W. Dodsworth, *Anglicanism Considered in Its Results* (London, 1851), p. 3.

180 Samuel Wilberforce complained of the Tractarians, that 'from the very first they have been essentially un-Anglican ... This has become more and more clear, but it was always so.' Bodl. Lib, Ms Eng Lett d. 367, fol. 13, S. Wilberforce to J. W. Croker, 31 January 1842. Similarly, Edward Churton related that the elder Christopher Wordsworth condemned the Tractarians for a 'spirit of Anti-Anglican Novelty'. PH, Churton Papers, CHUR 2/3/2, E. Churton to Joshua Watson, 7 September 1842.

181 [W. J. Conybeare], 'Church Parties', *Edinburgh Review*, 98 (October, 1853), 301–30. A writer in the Tractarian *English Churchman* in 1858 distinguished between 'Romanists', 'Romanizers', 'semi-Romanizers', 'consistent Anglicans', 'wavering Anglicans', 'old fashioned High Churchmen', 'neutrals', 'Broad Churchman' and various shades of 'Evangelical'. *English Churchman*, 15, No. 817 (August, 1858), 801–2.

182 Newman, *Lectures on the Prophetical Office*, p. 21.

183 W. Palmer [of Worcester], *A Treatise on the Church of Christ*, 2 vols. (London, 1838), vol. 1, p. 527.

184 W. Gresley, *Anglo-Catholicism. A Short Treatise on the Theory of the English Church* (London, 1844), p. 1.

reinvigorated version of traditional High Churchmanship. Yet the label increasingly was appropriated by the Tractarian party. In short, 'Anglo-Catholic' ceased to be a merely descriptive term for the Church of England as a whole and instead became a particular sub-division of the Church of England itself.

Later generations of the Movement's followers, including the 'Ritualists', would claim the term 'Anglo-Catholic' exclusively for themselves. Old High Churchmen objected to this hijacking of a once neutral, unequivocal terminology. They strove to reclaim the term for supporters of what they deemed Orthodox Church of England principles. As a writer in the *Church of England Quarterly Review* put it in 1843, 'because the writers of the Tracts choose to call themselves Anglo-Catholics, surely we are not to give up our own claim to the title, nor yet to concede to those individuals, a designation which they have assumed, but which belongs to all sound members of the Anglican Church'.[185] G. S. Faber, who had proclaimed himself an 'Anglican' as early as 1804, maintained in 1842 that his opposition to 'Tractarian principles' was based 'on the real principles of our Reformed Anglo-Catholic Church'.[186] Some old High Churchmen even appropriated the term exclusively for themselves. George Ayliffe Poole, a 'Z', and friend and ally of W. F. Hook in Leeds, in 1842 distinguished three separate parties in the Church of England; the 'Evangelical or Low Church', the 'moderate churchmen or Anglo-Catholics', and the 'ultra-churchmen or Oxford school'.[187] Likewise, the elder Christopher Wordsworth in 1845 asked his son, Christopher junior, whether he might induce the editor of the *English Churchman*, an avowedly Tractarian publication, to make it 'a really Anglo-Catholic paper'.[188] It was a conscious throw-back to an older meaning, when Charles Wordsworth in his *Annals* (1891) made his indictment of the Oxford Movement that it had so soon ceased to be '"bona fides" Anglo-Catholic'.[189] As late as

---

[185] *Church of England Quarterly Review*, 14 (July, 1843), 248.

[186] G. S. Faber, *Provincial Letters from the County-Palatine of Durham Exhibiting the Nature and Tendency of the Principles Put Forth by the Writers of the 'Tracts for the Times'* (London, 1842), p. iv.

[187] G. A. Poole, *The Present State of Parties in the Church of England* (London, 1842), pp. 4–6. In 1846, Edward Churton referred to himself and his friend William Gresley as 'us Anglo-Catholics'. PH, Pusey Papers, LBV [Transcripts], E. Churton to W. Gresley, 6 February 1846.

[188] LPL, Wordsworth Papers, Ms 2149, fol. 326, C. Wordsworth (Sen.) to C. Wordsworth (Jun.), 14 May 1845. Reference was also made to 'the Pseudo-Anglo-Catholicism of the Tractarians'. *Church of England Quarterly Review*, 25 (April, 1849), 431.

[189] Cha. Wordsworth, *Annals of My Early Life* (London, 1891), p. 351.

1877, 'Anglo-Catholic principles' were defended as synonymous with the 'old historic High Church school'.[190]

The history of changing nomenclature points to that divergence of Tractarianism from old High Churchmanship which will be a theme of this study. It illustrates a common perception among contemporaries of the divergence of a Tractarian minority from a High Church majority, in contrast to later historical assumptions that many distinctive features of the High Church tradition were attributable to the Oxford Movement alone. For instance, the estimates of the respective clerical adherents of the various church parties made by W. J. Conybeare in his 1853 article in the *Edinburgh Review* revealed a total of 3,500 for what he called the 'Anglican' or 'normal type' of High Church, compared to 2,500 for the 'High and Dry' or 'stagnant type' and a mere 1,000 for the 'Tractarian' or 'exaggerated type'.[191] The reliability of Conybeare's figures were questioned at the time, more particularly those relating to Evangelicals, but they at least represent a useful pointer by a seasoned contemporary observer. Moreover, for the diocese of Lincoln up until the 1850s, Frances Knight has found little evidence of Tractarian support in comparison with that for old High Churchmanship.[192] Evidence from another source for the diocese of London in 1844 puts the numbers of clergy classed as 'Tractarian or more' in a much higher ratio to other church parties including the category of 'moderate or High and Dry Churchmen'.[193]

---

[190] *Anglo-Catholic Principles Vindicated.* Edited by C. J. S. (Oxford, 1877). As late as 1877, a High Church writer insisted that the Tractarian school was 'certainly not the High Church of other days, and never ought to have been called by its name'. N. Dimock, *Confession and Absolution in the Church of England* (London, 1877), p. 34.

[191] [Conybeare], 'Church Parties', 338.

[192] Knight, 'John Kaye and the Diocese of Lincoln', p. 254. In a sample of clergy for one part of Lincolnshire, however, James Obelkevitch found the percentage identifiable as 'moderate High Church' falling from thirty-seven in 1851 to only fourteen in 1875. At the same time, the percentage identifiable as 'advanced High Church' or 'Tractarian' rose from thirteen to twenty-three in the same period. J. Obelkevitch, *Religion and Rural Society: South Lindsey, 1825–75* (Oxford, 1976), p. 122. According to Conybeare in 1853, the main strength of the Tractarian Party was concentrated in the two south-western dioceses of Exeter and Bath and Wells. Conybeare, 'Church Parties', 322.

[193] See Bodl. Lib, Ms Add c. 290, 'The Principal Clergy of London Classified According to Their Opinions on the Great Church Questions of the Day' [1844]. The statistics for a sample of 89 clergy were as follows: 23 – 'Tractarian or more'; 8 – 'leaning or supposed leaning towards Tractarianism'; 14 – 'Moderate or High and Dry'; 3 – 'Moderate, inclined to High'; 22 – 'Evangelical or more'; 13 – 'Moderate Evangelical'; 3 – 'Moderate or Low'. In total, 31 were placed in the 'Tractarian' camp, 37 in the 'Evangelical' camp, and only 17 in the 'Moderate' category. Nonetheless, the value of this evidence is weakened by the vagueness and indeterminate character of the party labels used.

CHAPTER I

Church and state: the politics of High Churchmanship

ORTHODOX 'POLITICAL THEOLOGY', 1760–1833

One consequence of the constitutional revolution between 1828 and 1833 for the Church of England was that religion and politics could no longer be presented as but 'two aspects of the same thing'. The gradual divorce of the two in subsequent decades made it increasingly difficult for later generations of High Churchmen to appreciate the mental framework within which the pre-Tractarian High Church operated. For the Orthodox prior to 1828, political concerns were a necessary ingredient of churchmanship and were perceived as a legitimate sphere for the application of principles which were essentially theological. In the much-altered political climate of the second half of the century when the Church of England's constitutional status had suffered erosion, the Church's theology necessarily carried less of a political load. As a result, the centrality of the political interests of pre-Tractarian High Churchmen came to appear anomalous. A later Nonconformist observer, Guinness Rogers, in contrasting High Churchmen at the beginning of the century with those in his own day, maintained, 'the political idea which was supreme with the former is of very slight importance to the latter'.[1] A reviewer of Churton's *Memoir of Joshua Watson* in the High Church *Christian Remembrancer* in 1861 felt called to explain away Watson's political links at the end of the preceding century with such contributors to the *Anti-Jacobin Review* as William Gifford, John Bowles, John Reeves, 'and others opposed to the Horne Tooke school'. The reviewer insisted that 'these Tory interests were,

---

[1] J. Guinness Rogers, *The Church of England in the Nineteenth Century* (London, 1881), p. 115.

however, only digressions from the main object of his life'.[2] Yet as
Churton made clear in his biography, at the time, such political
priorities, precisely because they had a religious dimension, were
regarded as central to the Orthodox cause. Churton took pride in
the efforts of his Hackney mentors in stemming the 'tide of anarchy
and sedition' in the era of the French Revolution and Napoleonic
wars.[3] The success of the anti-Jacobin crusade was the fruit of the
ascendancy of a tradition of 'Orthodox political theology' which was
as vital an ingredient of old High Churchmanship as was ecclesiology and sacramental or liturgical concerns.

The political dimension of the High Church tradition, too often
overlooked or misunderstood by later historians, has been explored
in recent works by J. C. D. Clark, Robert Hole, James Bradley,
James Sack and Andrew Waterman. Clark's account of pre-Reform
England as an *ancien régime* underpinned by a theological ideology
which gave divine legitimation to the Church of England's political
hegemony, has convincingly overturned the secularist assumptions
of earlier social historians with little interest in theology. Clark has
shown that at the root of Orthodox political theology lay a concern
'to emphasise the patriarchal, not contractual origin of the state, to
deny a right of resistance, and to insist that obedience for con-
science-sake in a Christian commonwealth extended only as far as
the doctrine of passive obedience'.[4] James Sack has also demonstrated that 'High Church' ecclesiastical values infused the 'Tory'
mentalité of the British 'Right' in the pre-Reform era.

The Hutchinsonians were leading exponents in the eighteenth-
century Church of England of a revival of the Orthodox political
theology associated with the Caroline Divines. Hutchinson's own
pyscho-theological theories had philosophical and political implications; the emphasis was on man's dependence on God, with
political and social subordination one aspect of that dependence.
However, as Jones of Nayland explained, the Hutchinsonians were
'loyalist and true churchmen' but they learnt their loyalty and

[2] 'Joshua Watson', *Christian Remembrancer*, 42 (July 1861), 35. The editor of the *Anti-Jacobin Review* declared in 1800: 'We profess ourselves to be *Tories* and *High Churchmen*.' *Anti-Jacobin Review* v (March, 1800), 290.
[3] PH, Gresley Papers, GRES 3/7/68, E. Churton to W. Gresley, 25 May 1846. See n. 6 for attribution of the source of the revival of Orthodox political principles in the 1790s.
[4] See Clark, *English Society*, ch. 2. The key seventeenth-century source of the High Church doctrine of Passive Obedience and theories of political obligation was Sir Robert Filmer's *Patriarcha*. See P. Laslett, ed., *Patriarcha; and Other Political Works of Sir Robert Filmer* (Oxford, 1949).

churchmanship 'not from Hutchinson's writings *per se*, though it was found in them, but from what he taught them to find, by taking their principles from Scripture'.[5]

Orthodox political theology embodied a critique of the apparently secular theories of government and of the origin of civil society associated with John Locke. For the Hutchinsonians, Locke's political theories had inescapable theological implications. George Horne and Jones of Nayland found an antidote to Locke in their rediscovery of the political writings of the Nonjurors, Charles Leslie and George Hickes, in the early1750s.[6] The consequent Hutchinsonian restatement of the latter's political theology found its fullest expression in Horne's Oxford assize sermon, *The Origin of Civil Government* (1769), and in Jones of Nayland's *Discourse on the English Constitution* (1776). It was precisely because the Hutchinsonians insisted that the English constitution had a divine sanction and theological rationale that the appeal was made to the testimony of even the early Fathers such as Clement, Ignatius and Cyprian.[7]

The revolt of the American colonies in the 1770s prompted an outpouring of Orthodox politico-theological apologetic, much of it directed against the Lockean principles espoused by American proto-revolutionaries such as Jonathan Mayhew. In fact, Clark and others have demonstrated that Locke's political ideas were less influential in eighteenth-century England than had been supposed.[8]

[5] Jones, *Memoirs of Horne. Second Edition, with a New Preface, on Certain Interesting Points in Theology and Philosophy* (1799), p. xxv. For other examples of High Anglican statements on the principles of civil government, see LPL, Horsley Papers, Ms 1767, fols. 198–203, S. Horsley, 'Thoughts upon Civil Government and Its Relation to Religion'; J. Whitaker, *The Real Origin of Government* (London, 1795), especially pp. 1–23.

[6] As Jones of Nayland puts it: 'The sight of Mr Leslie's two theological folios prepared Mr Horne for the reading of such of his political works as should afterwards fall in his way: and it was not long before he met with a periodical paper, under the title of The Rehearsals, which the author [Charles Leslie] had published in the time of Queen Anne ... This paper ... dissected Sidney and Locke, confuted the republican principles ... According to his own account, he [i.e. Horne] had profited greatly by the reading of it; and the work which gave to one man genius and discernment so much satisfaction, must have had its effect on many others; insomuch that it is highly probable that the loyalty found amongst us at this day [1795], and by which the nation has of late been so happily preserved, may have grown up from some of the seeds then sown by Mr Leslie'. Jones, *Memoirs of George Horne* pp. 70–1. Horne proudly styled himself a Tory. BL, Berkeley Papers, Ms Add 39312, fol. 100, G. Horne to G. Berkeley, 17 July 1789.

[7] G. Horne, 'A Charge Intended to Have Been Delivered to the Clergy of the Diocese of Norwich, at the Primary Visitation' [1791], Jones, ed., *Works of George Horne*, vol. IV, pp. 528–9.

[8] Clark, *English Society*, pp. 57–8, 120n; H. T. Dickinson, 'The Eighteenth-Century Debate on the "Glorious Revolution"', *History*, 61 (1976), 28–45.

The American Loyalist and Hutchinsonian, Jonathan Boucher, noted that the American conflict helped further discredit Lockean ideas in England.[9]

High Church theorising on the origin of government reached an apogee in response to the French Revolution. Historians have tended to present the conservative reaction to events in France in primarily secular political or military terms. Yet as Professor Christie, H. T. Dickinson and Philip Schofield have demonstrated, the challenge to the existing social order from Jacobinism was countered not only by the physical force of the state but by the enunciation of a coherent conservative ideology.[10] In short, there was more to English anti-Jacobinism than the Loyalist Associations founded by John Reeves. A national martial campaign was only one aspect of Loyalism[11] which also had a theological dimension. Reeves was an Orthodox churchman allied to the emergent Hackney Phalanx as well as a political pamphleteer.[12] The conservative political ideology, most famously represented by Burke's *Reflections on the Revolution in France*, took a variety of forms. An important ingredient was a so-called 'theological utilitarianism' associated particularly with William Paley.[13] Nevertheless, among some of the later Hutchinsonians, Paley's political principles were as suspect as his theological ideas.[14] In comparison, as we shall see in other contexts, the Hackney Phalanx tended to be less dismissive of Paley.

[9] See J. Boucher, 'Discourse XII: On Civil Liberty, Passive Obedience, and Non-Resistance', *A View of the Causes and Consequences of the American Revolution in Thirteen Discourses, Preached in North America between 1763 and 1775* (London, 1797). p. 495–560; [W. Stevens], *The Revolution Vindicated and Constitutional Liberty Asserted in Answer to the Rev. Dr Watson's Accession Day Sermon, Preached before the University of Cambridge, on October 25th 1776* (Cambridge, 1777), p. 67. See also, Sack, *From Jacobite to Conservative*, p. 126. G. M. Ditchfield, however, questions the extent of a resurgence of Tory High Churchmanship in the 1770s. G. M. Ditchfield, 'Ecclesiastical policy under Lord North', in Walsh, Taylor and Haydon, eds., *Church of England, c. 1689–c. 1833*, pp. 228–46.

[10] I. Christie, *Stress and Stability in Late Eighteenth-Century Britain: Reflections on the British Avoidance of Revolution* (Oxford, 1984); H. T. Dickinson, *Liberty and Property: Political Ideology in Eighteenth-Century Britain* (London, 1977); J. P. Schofield, 'Conservative Political Thought in Response to the French Revolution', *HJ*, 29 (1986), 605–16.

[11] On the military aspect of the Loyalist movement, see A. Mitchell, 'The Association Movement of 1792–93', *HJ*, 4 (1961), 56–77; D. E. Ginter, 'The Loyalist Association Movement of 1792–3 and British Public Opinion', *HJ*, 9 (1966), 179–80.

[12] John Reeves (?1752–1829). Eton; Merton College, Oxford 1771; Fellow of Queen's College, 1778; various government appointments; an accomplished liturgical scholar as well as lawyer. *DNB*.

[13] Waterman argues that Paley's intellectual sway among the Orthodox remained marked for more than a generation. Waterman, *Revolution, Economics and Religion*, p. 126.

[14] Clark, *English Society*, pp. 270–4.

In their reaction to the French Revolution, High Churchmen sought to refute natural right theories by a rigorous reassertion of the patriarchal theory of the origin of government which they derived from Scripture. It was Jones of Nayland who gave publicity to the High Church political counter-attack with the foundation in 1792 of a *Society for the Reformation of Principles* and with the publication in 1795 of a new, expanded edition of the *Scholar Armed*, a compendium of tracts first published in 1780.[15] This publication included tracts by Charles Leslie against disloyalty as well as infidelity, and in defence of 'scriptural' principles of government as well as of ecclesiastical polity.

A conviction of the inseparable connection between political insubordination or disloyalty and theological heterodoxy was commonplace among pre-Tractarian High Churchmen. It was partly because episcopacy was deemed to be conducive to sound principles of obedience to political authority that High Churchmen in the 1770s lamented the failure of various attempts to establish bishops among the American colonies. According to Jones of Nayland, had the colonists been given resident bishops, 'the country would not have begun that extraordinary republican dance, which like the long minuette, may extend itself to all that are on the stage of the world'.[16]

The equation between loyalism and orthodoxy extended well beyond those who were strictly High Church in theological terms.[17] Even Anglican Evangelicals, whom many of the Orthodox regarded as the heirs of seventeenth-century Puritanism, identified themselves no less closely with political loyalism and anti-Jacobinism in the era of the French Revolution. The identification of Calvinist Evangelicals with 'political republicanism' by High Church zea-

15 *The Scholar Armed Against the Errors of the Time; or a Collection of Tracts on the Principles and Evidences of Christianity, the Constitution of the Church, and the Authority of Civil Government*, 2 vols. (London, 1795).
16 Quoted in J. Freeman, *The Life of the Rev. William Kirby, MA* (London, 1852), p. 38. See J. Bradley, 'The Anglican Pulpit, the Social Order, and the Resurgence of Toryism during the American Revolution', *Albion*, 21 (1989), 361–88.
17 Moderate churchmen such as Beilby Porteus and Latitudinarians like Richard Watson became zealous defenders of the existing political order. See H. T. Dickinson, 'Popular Loyalism in Britain in the 1790s', in E. Hellmuth, ed., *The Transformation of Political Culture: England and Germany in the Late Eighteenth Century* (London, 1990), p. 514. On the growing political conservatism of many Whig Latitudinarians in the 1790s, see also, J. Gascoigne, *Cambridge in the Age of Enlightenment* (Cambridge, 1989), p. 35; Waterman, 'A Cambridge Via Media'.

lots,[18] while in accord with a strong polemical tradition, rarely matched political reality. The Evangelical theological critique of the writings of Orthodox contemporaries such as Daubeny did not contain any note of political disagreement. As Johnson Grant later recalled, Evangelicals such as John Overton might repudiate the 'orthodox construction of the Articles' enshrined in such writings, but they 'were well enough pleased with its loyalty'.[19] It was the Evangelical Hannah More who popularised anti-Jacobin political ideology in her *Village Politics*, known as 'Burke for beginners'.[20] Moreover, many Evangelicals would join High Churchmen in rebutting the 'theological utilitarianism' associated with Paley. Thus, for the Evangelical Joseph Milner, Paley was as 'loose in his politics as in his religion'.[21] In fact, as Hole shows, Evangelicals such as Thomas Gisborne in his *Principles of Moral Philosophy* (1789) were among Paley's sternest philosophical critics.[22]

In political terms, J. C. D. Clark's argument that 'Anglican Evangelicalism' and even Methodism represented just another 'new branch' of 'Orthodox' churchmanship[23] is valid. Yet orthodoxy had other defining principles, ecclesiastical, liturgical and sacramental, beyond mere political conservatism. Moreover, even at the political level, the common bond that tended to unite Evangelical and Orthodox in the face of the Jacobin threat in the 1790s, remained fragile. The High Church backlash in 1790 against the campaign to repeal the Test and Corporation Acts, which revived old stereotypes of Dissenters as king-killing, Oliverian rogues, became exacerbated by a growing anti-Jacobin phobia. Many, Bishop Horsley included, were provoked into condemning as politically subversive various independent manifestations of religious zeal among not only Dissenters but also Methodists and Evangelicals within the Church of

---

[18] For examples, see H. H. Norris, *A Practical Exposition of the Tendency and Proceedings of the British and Foreign Bible Society* (London, 1814), p. 359; W. H. Whithead, *A Letter to the Rev. Daniel Wilson* (London, 1818), pp. 31–2; Kenney, *Pretended Reformers in Church and State*, pp. 412–14.

[19] Grant, *Summary History*, vol. IV, p. 148; J. Overton, *True Churchman Ascertained*, (London, 1801), p. 16.

[20] Clark, *English Society*, p. 246.

[21] Quoted in R. I. and S. Wilberforce, *The Life of William Wilberforce*, 2 vols. (London, 1838), vol. II, p. 3.

[22] Hole, *Pulpits, Politics and Public Order*, p. 81.

[23] Clark, *English Society*, p. 235. Hole questions whether Anglican political and social attitudes were as distinctive as he thinks Clark assumes and argues for a broader multi-denominational spectrum of shared political ideals in the Revolutionary era. Hole, *Pulpits, Politics and Public Order*, pp. 266–7. See also Sack, *From Jacobite to Conservative*, pp. 194–8.

England.[24] It was a mentality well exemplified by John Randolph, Bishop of Oxford, when in 1802 he complained of Evangelicals, 'that while they bring everything within private suggestion, they encourage in Religion the very principle, which in Politics has proved so fatal to the peace and good government of states; being no other than giving the reins to private opinion, in opposition to public authority'.[25] Similarly, Daubeny referred to the Evangelical *Gospel Magazine* in 1799 as 'one of the most dangerous publications to the constitution of this country at this day in circulation'.[26]

At the philosophical level, some Evangelicals as well as most Protestant Dissenters regarded High Churchmanship as much in terms of a hated political authoritarianism and Filmerite patriarchialism, as of episcopal tyranny and 'popish' doctrine. The twin-headed bugbear of political and ecclesiastical despotism was sometimes invoked by Evangelicals within the church as well as more commonly by Protestant Dissenters. For instance, in 1807, a reviewer in the Evangelical *Christian Observer* revealed the extent to which contemporary High Churchmen were still perceived in such quarters as upholding a certain set of philosophical notions which applied not only to individual morality but which also underpinned a distinctive view of the nature of society and political obligation. High Churchmen, according to the reviewer, 'in the relation subsisting between the creature and his Creator ... contemplate nothing but precept and duty: the system is made up altogether of injunction and submission'.[27]

The element in Orthodox political theology which perhaps most distinguished pre-Tractarian High Churchmen from other church parties was an almost mystical, sacral theory of monarchy.

HIGH CHURCHMANSHIP AND MONARCHY: THE THEORY OF SACRAL KINGSHIP

The theory of kingship enshrined in the High Church tradition had found full expression in the writings of the Caroline Divines and

24 S. Horsley, *A Charge Delivered to the Clergy of the Diocese of Rochester* (London, 1880), pp. 3–10, 12–14, 16, 18–27, 32–4. Nevertheless some High Anglican critics of Dissent conceded that 'Methodists, as far as we can learn, are real friends to the King and Constitution'. G. Croft, *Thoughts Concerning the Methodists and the Established Clergy* (London, 1795), p. 49.
25 J. Randolph, *A Charge Delivered to the Clergy of the Diocese of Oxford,* (Oxford, 1802), p. 11.
26 ESCRO, Locker-Lampson Papers, B/5/76, C. Daubeny to J. Boucher, 10 April 1799.
27 *Christian Observer*, 6 (May, 1807), 319.

Nonjurors, notably in Charles Leslie's *Case of the Regale and Pontificate* (1700). However, an emphasis on monarchy as a sacred office transcended and endured long after any formal dynastic preference for the House of Stuart had ceased to be politically tenable. For the assumption that the Hanoverian Succession destroyed an older, seventeenth-century sacral royalism cannot be sustained. At one level, High Church royalist instincts were translated into a residual but merely sentimental Stuartite feeling among the Hutchinsonians and Hackney Phalanx. Thus, William Stevens always remained critical of the writings of the pro-Whig, French Huguenot historian, Rapin, as 'undertaken after the Revolution in order to justify the proceedings of that time, and, as a necessary step to blacken the character of the excluded family from the beginning'.[28] On the other hand, Stevens commended the Jacobite Thomas Carte's *General History of England* (1747–52). Moreover, Stevens never felt at ease with the 5 November state thanksgiving service enshrined in the Prayer Book. This did not denote dissatisfaction with the state service commemorating deliverance from the Gunpowder Plot in 1605 on that day; rather, it reflected Stevens's sense that the arrival of William of Orange on English soil in 1688, also commemorated, had amounted to no such further 'deliverance'.[29]

In contrast to the commemoration of the 'Glorious Revolution' of 1688, those other major state services, commemorating the martyrdom of King Charles I in 1649 on 30 January, and the Restoration of the monarchy in 1660 on 29 May, took on the aura of 'red-letter' days among Hutchinsonian High Churchmen. From 1649 onwards, a cult of the 'Royal Martyr' had developed into an integral part and potent symbol of the High Church tradition. Throughout the eighteenth century, the annual commemoration of the martyrdom and the 30 January sermon helped keep alive a distinctively High Church political identity nourished on a perennial sense of grievance against what were regarded as the twin evils

[28] Park, *Memoirs of William Stevens* (new edn, 1859), pp. 162–3.
[29] The young Henry Phillpotts also questioned the epithet 'Glorious Revolution' to describe the events of 5 November, 1688. Phillpotts protested against the 'speaking of a Revolution, even if it were real, and justified by being necessary, without some palliative caution; much more from eagerly representing it as a subject of glory and emulation'. H. Phillpotts, *A Sermon Preached before the University of Oxford, at St Mary's, on Monday November 5, 1804* (Oxford, 1804), p. 16. For biographical details on Phillpotts, see n. 56. For criticism of 1688, see also J. Reeves, *Thoughts on the English Government* (London, 1795).

of political Whiggery and theological heterodoxy.[30] In the era of the French Revolution, the analogy drawn in Anglican apologetic between political republicanism and religious error was reinforced.[31] Even as late as the 1820s, High Churchmen could invoke the cult of the Royal Martyr as a political weapon in defence of Orthodoxy and to discredit Protestant Dissenters who were branded as heirs of the regicides.[32]

By the end of the eighteenth century, altered political circumstances ensured that the Royal Martyr cult had become less of a source of political or theological division within the Church of England. Once the heat of the earlier dynastic conflict subsided after 1760, there was a certain political realignment, but the underlying principles of High Church monarchical allegiance endured as a distinctive political emphasis. Monarchy was eulogised, but the chief concern of High Churchmen was no longer with the precise form of government *per se* but with the divine sanction underpinning it. As Clark puts it, 'the uniting of old Whig and old Tory allowed the monarchy to be progressively hedged with a certain divinity, but as a diffused sense of reverence which also embraced the whole social order, not as the sharply-focused spotlight which early eighteenth-century dynastic conflict had made it'.[33] Earlier Jacobite proclivities faded. Ironically, many Orthodox churchmen in the half-century preceding the rise of the Oxford Movement built their constitutional

---

30 H. W. Randall, 'The Rise and Fall of a Martyrology: Sermons on Charles I', *HLQ*, 10 (1946–7), 164–5. Sack, however, on the evidence of Charles I Remembrance sermons, points to a decline in the divine-right kingship tradition during George III's reign. *From Jacobite to Conservative*, ch. 5. He notes (p. 86) that in 1789, Bishop Pretyman-Tomline preached 'one of the most anti-Charles I sermons of the eighteenth century'. See also, B. S. Stewart, 'The Cult of the Royal Martyr', *Church History*, 38 (1969), 186.

31 For an example of the genre, see W. Jones, *A Letter from Thomas Bull to His Brother John* (London, 1792).

32 Christopher Wordsworth senior invoked the cult in establishing Charles I's authorship of the martyrology, *Eikon Bazilikeh*. See LPL, Wordsworth Papers, Ms 1822, fol. 240, W. Van Mildert to C. Wordsworth, 17 December 1824; fol. 81, J. Jebb to C. Wordsworth, 20 January 1825; fols. 39–40, C. Forster to C. Wordsworth, 7 February 1825; Churton, *Memoir of Joshua Watson*, vol. 1, pp. 248–9. As late as 1824, a Whig writer assailed High Churchmen for seeking 'to make the Crown despotic' and aiming at 'the joint domination of priestcraft and kingcraft'. *Edinburgh Review*, 41 (October 1824), 2. There were also complaints about an apparent revival of 'a strange sort of speculative Jacobitism ... The praises of the Cavaliers are lavishly chanted; the devotion of the Stuart partisans is consecrated as something more than human'. 'Jacobite Relics', *Edinburgh Review*, 34 (August, 1820), 149. Sack, (*From Jacobite to Conservative*, p. 58), argues that the political collapse of Jacobitism after 1760 coincided with a heightened retrospective emotional enthusiasm for the movement.

33 Clark, *English Society*, p. 194.

principles on the basis of the same 1688 settlement which their predecessors had questioned, if not rejected. It was the 'Ultra Tories' such as Lord Eldon, who, in the 1810s and 1820s, appeared to take on the mantle of the 'old Whigs' in their adulation of 1688, even arguing that they were better Whigs than the radical exponents of constitutional reform. The 'Ultras', according to Clark, were 'defending a doctrine essentially similar to that which ministerial Whigs had held since the days of Burnet, Wake, Gibson and Potter'.[34] Yet the vastly altered political context ensured that like was not thereby being compared with like. In both cases, 1688 might have been the idol, but the spirit in which it was invoked and the principles guiding the invocation were very different. For behind the apparent outward *volte-face* by the Orthodox, a deeper current of ideological continuity remained. The sacral royalism inherent in the Orthodox political tradition was not abandoned or even diluted, but was transmuted, manifesting itself under a new form and external colouring.

HIGH CHURCHMANSHIP AND CHURCH–STATE THEORY, 1688–1790

The Oxford Movement represented an anti-Erastian, moral protest against the apparently popular notion that the Church of England was but a human establishment, subservient to the material and secular interests of the state. The term 'Erastianism' derived from the teaching of the sixteenth-century writer, Thomas Erastus, sometimes known as Thomas Luber. Erastianism implied that all religious truth was at the mercy of the civil power, and that political convenience was the sole test of belief. In the eighteenth century, there were advocates of such a viewpoint, such as Benjamin Hoadly, who maintained that the church had no inherent spiritual rights or independence from the civil power. Other more moderate Whig latitudinarian divines such as William Warburton, Thomas Balguy and William Paley, while less extreme in their Erastianism, also based their rationale of the church–state union not on religious truth but on the utilitarian interests of the civil power and mere political

---

[34] Clark, *English Society*, p. 408; P. Langford, 'English Clergy and the American Revolution', in Hellmuth, ed., *Transformation of Political Culture*, p. 284, 287; Bradley, *Religion, Revolution and English Radicalism*, pp. 24–5. By the 1820s, modern Toryism was being proclaimed as the equivalent of 1688–1714 Whiggism. Sack, *From Jacobite to Conservative*, p. 73.

convenience.[35] Pre-Tractarian High Churchmen based their rationale for the union of church and state on quite different principles.

The Orthodox theory had found its classic expression in Richard Hooker's *Laws of Ecclesiastical Polity*, and was restated by the Caroline Divines such as Taylor, Hammond, Bramhall and Sheldon. The underlying assumption was that the church in a sense was the state, and vice versa. As yet, reality went some way to matching theory. Elizabethan legislation assumed an absolute identity of church and commonwealth. For instance, an Act of 1592 which empowered magistrates to drive out Dissenters, sought to enforce such an identity.

Unscrupulous politicians might exploit ecclesiastical patronage for overtly secular ends, but the Orthodox rationale for the union stressed the inherent spiritual independence of the church. On the one hand, it was deemed to be the awesome responsibility of the state to protect and succour the church; on the other, it was the mission of the church to consecrate or sanctify the state in a spirit of service. Moreover, this ideal was not jettisoned but continued to inspire the early Nonjurors.[36] There was always the implication in the Hookerian theory that, when the old balance of church and state broke down under pressure from an unsympathetic civil power, then passive obedience might dictate putting the interests of the church above civil allegiance.

The events of 1688–9 marked the first dents in the integrity and tenability of the Hookerian ideal. Moreover, the establishment of the Presbyterian church in Scotland in 1707, the Hanoverian succession in 1714 and the suspension of Convocation in 1717, each in turn marked the divergence of constitutional reality from Hooker's theory. In consequence, later Nonjurors such as Thomas Deacon and William Cartwright reacted against the notion of a church–state union on any terms as an unacceptable 'political

---

35 [W. Warburton], *The Alliance between Church and State, or the Necessity and Equity of an Established Religion and a Test-Law Demonstrated, from the Essence and End of Civil Society, upon the Fundamental Principles of the Law of Nature and Nations* (London, 1736). See also, T. Balguy, 'On Church Authority', Discourse VII, *Nine Discourses on Various Subjects; and Seven Charges, Delivered to the Clergy of the Archdeaconry of Winchester* (London, 1817), p. 114. For the impact of the *Alliance*, see n. 44.

36 See L. M. Hawkins, *Allegiance in Church and State. The Problem of the Nonjurors in the English Revolution* (London, 1928); J. Findon, 'The Nonjurors and the Church of England, 1689–1716', unpublished D. Phil dissertation, University of Oxford, 1977; J. P. Kenyon, *Revolution Principles: the Politics of Party, 1689–1720* (Cambridge, 1977), p. 86.

entanglement' inimical to the church's spiritual integrity.[37] Cartwright's position was challenged by Hutchinsonian High Church friends in the establishment such as Jonathan Boucher and John Douglas, Bishop of Salisbury. Furthermore, it should not be forgotten that the original Nonjurors had taken their stand in 1689 on what John Findon aptly calls the 'state point' rather than the 'church point' which concerned the later Nonjurors; and that Sancroft and Ken had actually accepted the canonical legitimacy of the lay deprivations of Nonjuring bishops in 1689–91.[38] Thus, Nonjurors such as Charles Leslie retained their devotion to the old church–state ideal of an organic union as postulated by Hooker. It was Leslie's restatement of the Hookerian theory, just as it was Leslie's disquisition on the nature of political obligation, which Hutchinsonian and later eighteenth-century High Churchmen imbibed and passed on to their successors in the Orthodox tradition.

In their identification with the later Nonjurors, some of the Tractarians, especially Froude and Newman, did much to perpetuate a historical misrepresentation of Orthodox teaching on church and state. Increasingly, in Tractarian polemic, 'Erastianism', like 'Puritanism' or 'ultra-Protestantism', became a 'catch all' rhetorical device. Eventually, it was argued that the Church of England even in its Laudian glory was infused by what John Mason Neale termed a 'fearful Erastianism'.[39]

This aspect of Tractarian historiography still finds an echo in some recent writings. For instance, one noted American scholar delineates what he calls a 'conservative tradition' in theorising on

37 Bodl. Lib, Cartwright Papers, Ms Bodl. Add D. 30, fol. 45, W. Cartwright to J. Boucher, 26 March 1787, fol. 51, W. Cartwright to J. Boucher, 26 March 1787. William Cartwright (1730–99), an apothecary in Shrewsbury, consecrated Nonjuring Bishop of Shrewsbury, 1780. See J. H. Overton, *The Nonjurors: their Lives, Principles, and Writings* (London, 1902), pp. 364–71.

38 Findon, 'Nonjurors and the Church of England', p. 156. The acceptance by Sancroft and Ken of the legitimacy of the deprivations dismayed Tractarian advocates of the Nonjuring case. See [W. J. Copeland], 'Account of the Non-Jurors', *British Critic*, 21 (January, 1837), 51. The Tractarians lamented that most High Churchmen had conceded the legitimacy of the Nonjuring deprivations. See Froude's comment: 'The High Church party had cut the ground from under their feet by acknowledging Tillotson. Would that the Nonjurors had kept up a succession'. [Newman and Keble, eds.] *Remains of Hurrell Froude*, 1 (1838), p. 395. In fact, Archbishop Sancroft initially opposed consecrations issued under a new royal mandate by William of Orange, but eventually consented to grant a commission for the purpose, for fear of incurring the penalties of *praemunire*. G. D'Oyly, *The Life of William Sancroft Archbishop of Canterbury*, 2 vols. (London, 1821), vol. 1, pp. 438–9. But for examples of High Church defence of the deprivations, see n. 50 and ch. 3, n. 5.

39 J. M. Neale, 'The Laudian Reformation Compared with That of the Nineteenth Century', *Lectures Principally on the Church Difficulties of the Present Time* (London, 1852), p. 172.

church and state, but includes in its ample folds three very different treatises, Hooker's *Ecclesiastical Polity*, Leslie's *Regale and Pontificate*, and Warburton's *Alliance of Church and State* (1736). With some lack of discrimination, it is maintained that all of these works, when reduced to first principles, merely regarded 'the church as a department of government and the clergy as agents of the state'.[40] In similar vein, Ursula Henriques has argued that the Orthodox regarded the challenge of Protestant Dissent mainly as a threat to the state, and only incidentally as a violation of church order.[41] Likewise, R. G. Cowherd contrasts a supposed preoccupation of the Orthodox with the material trappings of establishment, with an Evangelical primary devotion to the church's 'inherent zeal and excellence'.[42]

Edward Norman has argued that such historical misconceptions, including those spawned by Tractarian historiography, 'derived from a later uncritical acceptance of the polemical views put out by Dissenters in their early nineteenth-century attacks upon the church'.[43] Moreover, such viewpoints rest upon the mistaken assumption that all Orthodox churchmen adhered to what many regarded as the cynical Warburtonian theory of an 'alliance' of two powers that became incorporated merely out of mutual self-interest. As Stephen Taylor has argued, Warburton's theory was not as representative of even mid-eighteenth-century Anglican apologetic as some historians have assumed.[44] On the contrary, the eighteenth-century Orthodox were more likely to appeal to the older Hookerian theory of an integral, organic union, from which Warburton's theory notoriously had departed. For as Norman has maintained, Orthodox apologetic assumed 'the interdependence of

[40] J. R. Griffin, 'The Anglican Politics of Cardinal Newman', *Anglican Theological Review*, 55 (October, 1973), 435.

[41] U. Henriques, *Religious Toleration in England, 1787–1833* (London, 1961), p. 69.

[42] R. G. Cowherd, *The Politics of English Dissent* (London, 1959), p. 33.

[43] E. Norman, *Church and Society in England, 1770–1970: an Historical Study* (Oxford, 1976), p. 19.

[44] S. Taylor, 'William Warburton and the *Alliance of Church and State*', *JEH* 43 (April, 1992), 271–86. Cf. R. W. Greaves, 'The Working of the Alliance: a Comment on Warburton', in Bennett and Walsh, eds., *Essays in Memory of Norman Sykes*, pp. 163–80.

The Dissenter Samuel Heywood described Warburton's *Alliance* as 'the sheet-anchor of modern High Churchmen'. In contrast, Francis Blackburne asserted: 'when Dr Warburton's book of Alliance between church and state first appeared, the old orthodox phalanx was highly scandalised, that the author should desert the old posture of defence, and subject the church to such a humiliating dependence on the state'. *Works of Francis Blackburne*, vol. I, p. xxxv.

church and state, and not the dependence of the church upon the state'.[45]

HIGH CHURCHMANSHIP AND THE ROYAL SUPREMACY: IN
DEFENCE OF THE PROTESTANT CONSTITUTION, 1760–1829

The pre-Tractarian High Church identification with monarchy always had both an important theological basis and practical religious application. It drew as its scriptural source of inspiration the text of Isaiah 49, v. 23: 'And Kings shall be thy nursing fathers, and their queens thy nursing mothers'. The text was interpreted to justify an understanding of the Royal Supremacy that was consciously anti-Erastian. Thus, for traditional High Churchmen, the Supremacy was but a reflection of the sacral, quasi-religious character of the office of monarch. The duties of that office as enshrined in the coronation oath were primarily to watch over and protect the church as a 'nursing father' or 'mother'. The binding religious nature of that oath and of the whole coronation service served as a symbolic theological guarantee of the church's right to be thus protected. For as the liturgical scholar, E. C. Ratcliff has explained, 'from the time of Edgar, the English King was recognised as in some sense an ecclesiastical person'. Up until the coronation of Charles II, the monarch was even described as 'mediator betwixt the clergy and the laity'. The obligation of the monarch was 'to defend and advance the Church and to "pursue heretics no less than infidels"'. It was 'his function "to nourish and instruct, defend and teach" Church as well as people'.[46]

As exponents of this tradition of sacral royalism, the Hutchinsonian High Churchmen regarded the *jure divino* basis of monarchy and the constitutional order as inextricably linked to the *jure divino* basis of episcopacy and the ecclesiastical order. They imbibed the anti-Erastian understanding of the Royal Supremacy as formulated by the Nonjuror, Charles Leslie. The direct nature of the link is clear from the avowal of William Green, Fellow of Magdalen College, Oxford, made in 1792 in a letter to the wife of his Hutchinsonian friend, George Berkeley junior:

pray tell Dr Berkeley that I am got into the marrow of Leslie's "Rehearsals" which have convinced me that the jure divino principles may be

[45] Norman, *Church and Society*, p. 19.
[46] E. C. Ratcliff, *The English Coronation Service* (London, 1937), pp. 23–4.

supported on constitutional grounds (which I knew not before) as well as on religious grounds (which I was well assured of). I mean as to the monarchy; for the divine right of episcopacy needs not the aid of erastianism.[47]

Queen Anne had kept up, albeit selectively, the symbolic trappings of royal ceremonial,[48] but the disputed legitimacy of the first two Hanoverian monarchs had not been favourable to this aspect of royalist tradition. The accession in 1760 of George III, the first Hanoverian monarch to be an unqualified adherent of the Church of England, had enabled High Churchmen for the first time since 1714 to focus their theoretical royalist sentiments once more on the person of a living monarch.[49] Horne's rapturously royalist sermon *The Christian King*, preached at Oxford in 1761, celebrated this apparent return to a non-Erastian Caroline order of church and monarchy working in harmony.

Apart from the small knot of later Nonjurors, few pre-Tractarian High Churchmen regarded the Revolution settlement as inimical to the power or independence of the church. The primacy of the 'state point' in the motivation of original Nonjurors such as Sancroft acted as a precedent for subsequent generations of High Churchmen in defending the principle of the lay deprivations as a legitimate application of the monarch's role as a 'nursing father' of the church. On this point, most later pre-Tractarian High Churchmen parted company with Leslie, who had regarded the deprivations as an act of Erastian tyranny. For instance, some members of the 'Hackney Phalanx' were more critical of Leslie than their Hutchinsonian predecessors had been, for limiting the Royal Supremacy purely to civil matters. These Hackney critics were uncompromising in their avowals of anti-Erastianism and on that basis attacked the theories of Warburton and Paley. However, they tended to draw a distinction between the theory postulated by Hooker, Bramhall and the Caroline Divines, and that expounded by Leslie and other Nonjurors, the logic of which they regarded as the 'desire for a perpetual empire in the Church, independent even in Christian countries, on

[47] BL, Berkeley Papers, Ms Add 39312, fol. 131, R. Green to Mrs Berkeley, 26 Feb. 1792.
[48] R. O. Bucholz, '"Nothing but Ceremony": Queen Anne and the Limitations of Royal Ritual', *Journal of British Studies*, 30 (July, 1991), 288–323.
[49] The Loyalist spirit inspired by the American war encouraged Stevens's circle to take up the 'Church and King' cry and to make 'sundry other constitutional toasts after the manner of the Tories of old time'. ESCRO, Locker-Lampson Papers, B/3/3, W. Stevens to J. Boucher, 12 November 1777.

the sovereign power'. As Archdeacon Pott explained, 'the dread of Erastian principles, and the peculiar sentiments of some in a season of much difficulty, led them to forsake the just and uniform agreement of our best authorities in times preceding, until new principles advancing, produced a partial schism of no small duration'.[50] A few extreme High Churchmen, notably John Oxlee, took up the later Nonjuring line and prefigured the absolutist stance of the Tractarians. Oxlee uncompromisingly denounced the deprivations of 1689 in the mode later popularised by Keble, Bowden and Copeland: 'to me these deprivations have always seemed an act of civil tyranny and persecution; and I feel no hesitation in declaring that as long as Archbishop Sancroft continued to survive, Dr Tillotson was an intruder in the chair of Canterbury'.[51]

Such differences within the High Church spectrum became less significant, once the dynastic issue faded and the Nonjurors had dwindled into a tiny rump. By the late eighteenth century, a broad consensus among High Churchmen had emerged as to the high ecclesiastical status with which the Revolution settlement had actually invested the Church and monarch. In short, 1688 could be defended on Tory principles.[52] Some of the Orthodox, notably Pretyman-Tomline, still used Whiggish argument in defence of the Revolution settlement, arguing that in 1688 church–state relations had been placed on a new and much surer foundation than had

[50] J. Pott, *The Rights of Sovereignty in Christian States Defended in Some Chief Particulars: a Charge Delivered to the Clergy of the Archdeaconry of London ... 1821* (London, 1821), p. 142.

Joseph Holden Pott (1759–1847). Eton; St John's College, Cambridge; Chaplain to Lord Chancellor Thurlow, 1784; various London livings, 1787–1824; Archdeacon of St Albans, 1789–1813; Archdeacon of London, 1813–42. *DNB*. For Pott's links with the Hutchinsonians and Hackney Phalanx, see Churton, *Memoir of Joshua Watson*, vol. I, p. 237.

George D'Oyly, in his biography of the Nonjuror, Archbishop Sancroft, conceded the ecclesiastical legitimacy of Sancroft's deprivation for refusal to take the oaths to William and Mary, while commending his conscientious adherence to principle. D'Oyly, *Life of William Sancroft*, vol. I, pp. 448–9.

George D'Oyly (1778–1846). Corpus Christi College, Cambridge, 1796; BA, 1800; Hulsean Christian Advocate, 1811; Domestic chaplain to Archbishop Manners-Sutton, 1813; Rector of Lambeth, 1820-d. A frequent contributor to the *Quarterly Review*. *DNB*.

[51] J. Oxlee, *A Sermon with Notes in Which All Due and Lawful Claim of the Protestant Dissenters to Any Part of the Christian Ministry Is Further Disproved and Rejected* (York, 1821), p. 66. For the Tractarian attitude to the deprivation of Nonjuring bishops, see n. 174.

[52] For example, see S. Horsley, *A Sermon Preached before the Lords Spiritual and Temporal, January 30th 1793 on the Anniversary of King Charles' Martyrdom* (London, 1793), p. 3. On the political dimension of Horsley's High Churchmanship, see Mather, *Horsley*, ch. 11.

been the case in the Caroline era.[53] Yet the new idol of the Protestant constitution was less a denial of the spirit of Sacheverell than
the apparent ideological volte-face might suggest.

The realignment was symbolised by George III's scrupulous
exercise of his royal prerogative as enshrined in the coronation oath,
when in 1801 he refused to countenance Catholic Emancipation
and thereby overruled the wishes of his Prime Minister, William
Pitt the Younger. Thereafter, Catholic Emancipation was
portrayed as a move against the monarch in his twin capacity as
head of the church and the state. As John Reeves's *Considerations on
the Coronation Oath* (1801) exemplified, Protestant constitutionalism
thus became identified with the royalist and political dimensions of
High Churchmanship.

In his *Considerations*, Reeves emphasised the scriptural image of
the monarch as 'nursing father' in a way intended to rebut claims
by Dissenters that the Church of England was a mere 'parliamentary church'; claims which the standard Warburtonian defence
of the church–state union had helped promote. According to
Reeves, the sacral nature of the royal office rendered the monarch a
more fitting symbol or representative of the church than the collective popular will as embodied in even an exclusively Anglican
parliament. Like other mainstream High Churchmen, Reeves
argued that the greater powers undoubtedly bequeathed to parliament in relation to the crown by the 1688 settlement had extended
much more to matters of state politics than to the church. Following
Hooker, Reeves conceded that parliament could assume the guise of
a lay synod of the church. Moreover, with Convocation in abey-
ance, parliament had the right of legislating solely for the church.
This right was subject to the watchful approval of the church's true
guardian, the crown. For the monarch's duty as determined by
oath, was 'to watch over any laws, that may be proposed to him by
his Parliament, for alteration in church matters, with more conscientious solicitude, than he exercises on other occasions of legislation'. The monarch, Reeves concluded, 'is thus made more peculiarly the guardian of the church, than he is of the state; and
happily, he can completely execute this office by himself, without

---

[53] Pretyman-Tomline asserted: 'the principles of a Church Establishment, and of Toleration
of those who dissent from the National Religion, can scarcely be said to have been
thoroughly understood, till the time of the Revolution'. G. Pretyman-Tomline, *A Charge
Delivered to the Clergy of the Diocese of Lincoln* (London, 1812), p. 11.

the aid of the many advisers who are necessary towards the conduct of civil affairs'.[54]

Even in the 1810s and 1820s most of the Anglican apologetic in defence of establishment retained a dominantly religious rather than secular basis, and was infused by a spirit of sacral royalism.[55] Henry Phillpotts, one of the most vocal ideologues on behalf of the Protestant constitution in this era, developed Reeves's argument. For Phillpotts, not only did the coronation oath bind the monarch to 'the Protestant reformed religion established by law', but to argue otherwise, was to 'attack the Church by law'. The monarch was answerable to God alone in his interpretation of the oath, and not dependent on the advice of any ministers.[56]

Robert Hole exaggerates the degree to which the ideological *raison d'être* of the confessional state was undermined prior to the final removal of the legislative props that supported it between 1828 and 1833.[57] Hole is right to stress the greater emphasis which concerns of social order came to assume in establishment apologetic.[58] In the case of latitudinarian divines such as Paley and Balguy, this emphasis entailed a utilitarian and secular rationale. But for the more High Church element among the Orthodox, the increased emphasis on social order was not made at the expense of more theological considerations. On the contrary, *jure divino* principles were merely adapted and given a wider applicability.

In the half-century prior to the rise of Tractarianism, allegiance to the principle of the Protestant constitution ensured a degree of common ground encompassing different parties in the pre-Tractarian Church of England. The Orthodox in the University of Oxford may have been at the forefront of the anti-Emancipationist cause, but Evangelicals in the Church tended to invest establishment with similar overtones of Protestant exclusiveness. It was the *Noetic* party

---

54 J. Reeves, *Considerations on the Coronation Oath to Maintain the Protestant Reformed Religion, and the Settlement of the Church of England* (London, 1801), pp. 22, 36.

55 Clark, *English Society*, pp. 387–93; G. Best, 'The Protestant Constitution and Its Supporters, 1800–1829', *TRHS*, 5th Series, 8 (1958), 107–27.

56 H. Phillpotts, *A Letter to an English Layman on the Coronation Oath* (London, 1828), pp. 7–8, 52, 83.
  Henry Phillpotts (1778–1869). Corpus Christi College, Oxford, 1791–; Fellow of Magdalen College, Oxford, 1795–1804. Ordained, 1804. Married Lord Eldon's niece. Chaplain to Bishop of Durham, 1806; Prebend of Durham, 1809; Dean of Chichester, 1828; Bishop of Exeter, 1830-d. *DNB*.

57 Hole, *Pulpits, Politics and Public Order*, p. 267 especially ch. 8.

58 For examples of the genre, see S. H. Cassan, *Obedience to Government. A Religious Duty* (London, 1819); J. H. Spry, *The Duty of Obedience to Established Governments* (London, 1819).

at Oxford, while no less devoted upholders of establishment, who
were the least inclined to idolise 1688. Ironically, in view of later
connotations, in the context of 1828–9, to be 'Orange' and 'High
Church' were almost synonymous terms.[59] In fact, the extent to
which apparent consistency and soundness in constitutional principles could be made the ultimate test of orthodoxy is revealed by
the episode of the Peel election at Oxford in 1829.[60] Thus, when
the University of Oxford rejected Sir Robert Peel as its MP for his
volte-face over Emancipation, it was to Sir Robert Inglis, a
staunch Tory but reputedly a doctrinal Evangelical, that the
Orthodox majority turned. When Sir Philip Bliss, the University
Registrar, complained that Inglis 'would not "go down" with a
large majority of our members of Convocation, on account of his
principles in religion being supposed to be Evangelical', the editor
of the Orthodox newspaper, *The Standard*, spoke for many when he
insisted that what mattered was 'Inglis's attachment to the Church
of England' and the fact that he 'was more high church than most
of the bishops ... in the matter of the Test and Corporation
Acts'.[61]

This exaltation of the outward framework of establishment into
the kernel of orthodoxy could entail a neglect of the deeper High
Church principle of the church being a divine society which ultimately did not depend on its connection with the state. An element
among the Orthodox undoubtedly considered themselves primarily
as servants of the establishment and were concerned above all with
the church as an established institution.[62] Typical of such a brand of
Orthodox churchmanship was the 'Ultra Tory' statesman and Lord
Chancellor, Lord Eldon, who, as his biographer admitted, 'opposed
the Dissenters and the Roman Catholics, not because he looked at
them through any jaundice of theological dislike, but simply because
he believed the the Church Establishment would be undermined by

[59] J. S. Boone, *Men and Things in 1823: a Poem in Three Epistles with Notes* (London, 1823),
    p. 33. On the growing identification of Tory High Churchmanship with anti-Catholicism,
    see Sack, *From Jacobite to Conservative*, ch. 9.
[60] J. C. D. Clark, 'England's Ancien Régime as a Confessional State', *Albion*, 21 (fall, 1989),
    461n.
[61] BL, Bliss Papers, Ms Add 34750, fol. 148, P. Bliss to unnamed correspondent, 19 February
    1829.
[62] For example, for George Nott, the notion 'that True Religion and all Ecclesiastical
    Establishments are point in themselves totally distinct' was the error of 'Enthusiasts'.
    G. Nott, *Religious Enthusiasm Considered; in Eight Sermons Preached before the University of Oxford
    in the Year MDCCCII. At the Lecture Founded by John Bampton* (Oxford, 1803), p. 372.

their admission to the functions of the state'.[63] The Tractarians would later react against such 'high establishmentism' or 'Eldonism', as much as against Whig Latitudinarianism. Nevertheless, Protestant constitutionalism could coexist as happily with very high notions of the spiritual independence of the Church as with very high views of monarchy.

HIGH CHURCHMANSHIP AND CHURCH–STATE THEORY, 1790–1833

The conservative reaction in the Church of England to the French Revolution bolstered the case for establishment. This was sometimes expressed in Erastian terms. Nonetheless, anti-Jacobinism was by no means inimical to high claims in favour of ecclesiastical independence. On the contrary, the reaction to events in France helped engender a renewed awareness of the *jure divino* grounds of ecclesiastical power, as of the grounds of monarchical authority, the origin of government and political obligation. Significantly, the most celebrated mouthpiece of the anti-Jacobin reaction, Edmund Burke in his *Reflections*, upheld the Hookerian rather than Warburtonian or Paleyite theories of the church–state union. In Burke's apologetic, Erastianism was eschewed; the church was not swallowed up in the state. On the contrary, Burke insisted that the church manifestly was not 'a mere representative of individuals. Rather, the church was an oblation of the state itself'.[64]

It was this Hookerian understanding of church–state theory in terms of an organic union of two interrelated divinely-ordained powers rather than of the pragmatic Warburtonian theory of an alliance, which infused the churchmanship of Bishop Horsley. Thus while Horsley remained a staunch defender of the Test and Corporation Acts, his line of defence differed widely from that employed earlier by Warburton as well as by Hoadly. Horsley was careful to point out that the Test and Corporation Acts 'neither establish the Church nor create its rights'. The Church would be injured by their repeal; otherwise, 'with equal truth it might be said, that a building is not served by a buttress, and would not be injured by its removal; because the buttress is no part of the foundation'. Pursuing the

---

[63] H. Twiss, *The Public and Private Life of Lord Chancellor Eldon, with Selections from His Correspondence*, 3 vols. (2nd edn, London, 1844), vol. III, pp. 488–90.
[64] A. Cobban, *Edmund Burke and the Reaction against the Eighteenth Century* (London, 1960), p. 5.

64   *The Oxford Movement in context*

analogy to its logical end, Horsley could conclude that 'buildings have been known to fall, while the foundations have been unimpaired'.[65]

Members of the Hackney Phalanx were also committed to the Hookerian rather than Warburtonian church–state theory. Moreover, they strove to put the theory more effectively into practice. Certainly, in the years immediately prior to 1828, with the Phalanx in the political ascendancy and in effective control of ecclesiastical patronage, the union of church and state appeared to be working more in the church's interests and in accordance with Hooker's ideal, than at any time since the reign of Charles II.

Pre-Tractarian High Churchmen were not unaware of the compromises inherent in the status quo in church–state relations. There was an awareness that in practice the benefits of the union could appear to be one-sided, always weighted in favour of the state. John Bowles, a High Church layman, conceded that the church 'considered as a spiritual institution' was apt to receive from its connection with the state 'somewhat of a secular alloy'.[66] Similarly, in his Bampton Lectures at Oxford in 1820, that later *bête noire* of the Tractarians, Godfrey Faussett, admitted that 'unsound' views of the union had, 'in greater or lesser degree impaired the beneficial effects of ecclesiastical establishments'.[67] Faussett regretted that many contemporaries thought that the Church derived her authority from the civil magistrate. Citing the Nonjuror George Hickes as well as Thomas Sherlock, Horsley and Daubeny, Faussett assailed the error 'of those who wholly confound their idea of the Church of Christ

[65] [S. Horsley], *A Review of the Case of Protestant Dissenters: with Reference to the Corporation and Test Acts* (London, 1790), pp. 52–3. I cannot concur with Paul Langford's surprising assertion that 'Warburton's tolerant Erastianism fitted the 1790s as thoroughly as it had fitted the 1730s, in some ways more so, for there was no one in the 1790s who took seriously the high view of the church and its jurisdiction over laymen to which men of Gibson's generation had remained loyal.' The evidence of Mather's *Horsley* and of this study does not support this view. Dr Langford also misinterprets a famous passage in Horsley's Charge of 1790 cited above (p. 27 and n). See P. Langford, *Public Life and Propertied Englishmen, 1689–1798* (Oxford, 1991), p. 88.

[66] [J. Bowles], *The Claims of the Established Church Considered as an Apostolical Institution* (London, 1815), pp. 1–5.

    John Bowles was a younger member of Stevens's circle. He was a campaigning barrister active in High Church causes such as relief for the Scottish episcopal church in the 1790s, the SPCK and church education. *DNB*; Churton, *Memoir of Joshua Watson*, vol. I, pp. 85–92.

[67] G. D. Faussett, *The Claims of the Established Church to Exclusive Attachment and Support, and the Dangers Which Menace Her from Schism and Indifference, Considered in Eight Sermons Preached before the University of Oxford in the Year MDCCCXX. At the Lecture Founded by the Late Rev. John Bampton* (Oxford, 1820), p. 318.

with that of a political establishment', and explicitly linked Warburton's *Alliance* with 'the Erastian notion of ecclesiastical subordination and civil supremacy'.[68] Moreover, Faussett lamented the practical deviations from the original Elizabethan ideal of a federal union of independent powers, such as in the silencing of Convocation. Such abuses, Faussett insisted, echoing Daubeny's view, did not invalidate the constitutional theory of the union and might be remedied in time.[69] Of course, in practice the church was no longer strictly conterminous with the Commonwealth. As James Bradley has shown, the theoretical barriers of the confessional state were increasingly breached by Nonconformists at a local level in the later decades of the eighteenth century.[70] Yet parliament still represented the church as a lay synod, as Hooker envisaged. Furthermore, royal appointments only could be made to communicants, though legislation under the first two Georges had opened elections to corporate offices to non-communicants.

Hutchinsonian and Hackney divines were particularly sensitive to the anomalies that had accrued both in the theory and in the practical working of church–state relations. The elder Christopher Wordsworth in a letter to his friend, Joshua Watson, in 1815, explicitly warned of the danger 'of laying too much stress upon the Church as an "Establishment", and so of losing sight of its spiritual character and claims'.[71] Such High Churchmen were insistent that, while establishment was a useful appendage, it was by no means essential to the church's existence.[72] As Daubeny put it, 'when the state came into being the church, these two separate kingdoms became united in the same civil society. But in this case the union, being an accidental circumstance, did not affect the original independent rights of either party'. Citing the examples of the non-established episcopal churches in Scotland and the United States of America, Daubeny emphasised that, should a separation 'again take place between these two kingdoms, the state will leave the church, so far as respects its government, just in the same

---

[68] Faussett, *Claims of the Established Church*, pp. 330–1.   [69] *Ibid.*, p. 328.

[70] Bradley, *Religion, Revolution and English Radicalism*, ch. 2.

[71] In Cha. Wordsworth, *Annals of My Early Life*, p. 330; Churton, *Memoir of Joshua Watson*, vol. I, pp. 130–1. See Watson's comment: 'Call me, if you will, an Establishmentarian. It is a soubriquet, which, as a hearty lover of my country, I cannot conscientiously repudiate'. Churton, *Memoir of Joshua Watson* (2nd edn, London, 1863), p. 279.

[72] W. Stevens to Bishop John Skinner, 1 May 1797, [Park], *Memoirs of William Stevens* (1812), p. 138; W. Stevens, *Cursory Observations on a Pamphlet Entitled 'An Address to the Clergy of the Church of England in Particular and to All Christians in General'* (London, 1773), pp. 10–11.

condition in which it was, previous to their original connexion'.[73] Even Bishop Marsh, whose High Church credentials have been disputed, distinguished between 'true Religion' and 'established Religion', and cited the example of the era of the Great Rebellion for the view that 'true Religion' could endure without the aid of establishment.[74]

The strenuous efforts of High Churchmen such as Horne, Horsley, Boucher and Stevens on behalf of the disestablished and once persecuted episcopal church in Scotland in the 1790s, was a practical application of their concern for the inherent spiritual rights and independence of the church. Moreover, this concern motivated a large number of the English episcopate in the parliamentary campaign on behalf of Scottish episcopacy in 1791. Significantly, Jones of Nayland devoted much space to this episode in his biography of Bishop Horne, precisely in order to show

not only that the bishops of Scotland are true Christian bishops, but that the bishops of England, from the part they kindly took in the affair, do little deserve the clamour which some have raised against them, as if they were so dazzled by their temporalities, as to lose sight of their spiritual character, and bury the Christian bishop in the peer of Parliament.[75]

The characteristic Orthodox rhetoric of pre-Tractarian establishment apologetic has been the subject of historical misunderstanding by later Anglo-Catholic writers. It was not always easy for post-Tractarian churchmen who had experienced the decline of the confessional state, to appreciate that earlier in the century the state was commonly viewed much more in its then ecclesiastical aspect than was possible later. Thus, rhetoric which might have seemed equivocal or Erastian in the context of the 1850s, could have had a very different connotation in the 1800s. In such phrases as 'our happy establishment' which would lend themselves to Tractarian caricature, the word establishment could mean not merely a con-

---

[73] C. Daubeny, *An Appendix to the 'Guide to the Church'*, 2 vols, (London, 1799), vol. I, pp. 114–15.

[74] H. Marsh, *A Charge Delivered to the Clergy of the Diocese of Peterborough in July 1827* (London, 1827), p. 16. Like his Hackney allies, Marsh was a friend and correspondent of the staunchly Republican and anti-Erastian American High Churchman, John Henry Hobart. See Bodl. Lib, Norris Papers, Ms Eng Lett c. 789, fol. 126, H. Marsh to H. H. Norris, 31 July 1824.

[75] Jones, *Memoirs of Horne*, p. 152. On High Church involvement in the campaign for relief of the Scottish episcopal church in 1789–92, see F. C. Mather, 'Church, Parliament and Penal Laws', *JEH*, 28 (1977), 540–72.

dition of the church, but rather, the church itself.[76] For the Tractarians, 'establishment' simply meant 'the establishment of the church by the state'. However, in unequivocally High Church apologetic prior to 1833, such as Stevens's *Constitution of the Catholic Church* (1776) and Daubeny's *Guide to the Church* (1798), the term 'national establishment' was employed in a sense synonymous with that of 'the church' or 'the catholic church'.[77] Establishment implied the spiritual constitution as well as temporal framework of the church. In this sense, it was argued, 'the church itself has ever been an establishment, and the very fact of its being an establishment with inherent powers of government proves its independence'.[78]

THE POLITICAL DIMENSION OF EARLY TRACTARIANISM

The essentially political origins of the rise of the Oxford Movement are too often overlooked. In many ways, Tractarianism represented a revolt of Oxford Toryism at the reforming measures which the Grey ministry brought into parliament in the early 1830s. Yet, historians taking their cue from Tractarian historiography have tended to regard the Movement as always unconcerned with constitutional and political questions. Pusey himself had encouraged this misunderstanding. For example, when, in 1864, the clerical historian William Nassau Molesworth asked Pusey for information on the political background of the Oxford Movement, Pusey was dismayed that such a question should even be posed. For by this date, Pusey shared the view expressed by his Tractarian friend, William Copeland, 'that the political element, the Reform Bill, had not any effect in producing the "Tracts for the Times"'.[79] Copeland maintained that Tractarianism had not been a response to the political crisis of the early 1830s. Moreover, he could not even 'imagine how the two subjects could be brought into any intelligible relation to each other'.[80] Later writers, especially those writing from an Anglo-

---

[76] *Church and Reform: Being Essays Relating to Reform in the Government of the Church of England* (London, 1902), p. 75.

[77] For example, see C. Daubeny, *An Appendix to the Guide to the Church* (2nd edn, London, 1804), p. 337.

[78] *British Critic*, 22 (July, 1837), 223.

[79] PH, Pusey Papers, LBV [Transcripts], W. J. Copeland to E. B. Pusey, 30 October 1864. According to Liddon, in later life Pusey had 'little heart for themes which did not more directly concern the well-being of souls'. Liddon, *Life of Pusey*, vol. II, p. 27.

[80] PH, Pusey Papers, LBV [Transcripts], W. J. Copeland to W. N. Molesworth, 2 November 1864.

Catholic perspective, have taken for granted this assumption of a
dichotomy between politics and theology in the Oxford Movement.
In his study of Tractarian social thought, Peck concluded that the
Tractarians consciously retreated from the political sphere to the
'innermost sanctuary of religion'.[81] More recently, J. H. L. Rowlands has questioned this view. Rowlands rightly points out the
extent to which early Tractarian political thought is to be found
enshrined in the sermons and meditations of the Movement's leaders,[82] and was thus far more integral to Tractarian theology than is
usually recognised.

At the root of Tractarian attitude to politics was an apparent
'otherworldliness' which seemed to contrast with the mentality of at
least the 'High and Dry' element among the Orthodox of the
preceding generation. Ultimately, Newman and Keble would
foresee and brand as 'apostasy' our modern preoccupation with
politics.[83] Party politics was eschewed. Tractarian theological views
would increasingly cut across the political spectrum, with the liberal
Conservative Roundell Palmer and even the radical Whig politician
Sir W. Page Wood coming under the Movement's influence.[84]
Nonetheless, the early Tractarians remained devoted to the underlying principles of Orthodox political theology which had animated
preceding generations of High Churchmen. The early Tractarians
were unashamedly Tories, but theirs was primarily a moral Toryism
that was distinct from the more political Toryism associated with
Lord Eldon or from what Copeland called 'the semi-infidel Conservatism of many of the maintainers of our so-called happy establishment'.[85]

[81] W. G. Peck, *The Social Implications of the Oxford Movement* (London, 1933), pp. 48–98;
V. Pitt, 'The Oxford Movement: a Case of Cultural Distortion?', in K. Leech and
R. Williams, eds., *Essays Catholic and Radical* (London, 1983), pp. 205–24.
[82] J. H. L. Rowlands, *Church, State and Society: the Attitudes of John Keble, Richard Hurrell Froude
and John Henry Newman, 1827–1845* (Worthing, 1989), pp. ix–x.
[83] Rowlands, *Church, State and Society*, pp. 220–2. See Newman's comment to his friend Mary
Giberne, 'the Queen of Tractaria', in 1837: 'We have nothing to hope or fear from Whig or
Conservative governments. We must trust to our own ethos'. A. Mozley, ed., *The Letters and
Correspondence of John Henry Newman*, 2 vols. (London, 1891), vol. II, p. 241.
[84] *The Advance of Tractarianism. Four Letters Reprinted by Request from Avis's Birmingham Gazette*
(Birmingham, 1853), p. 6.
[85] PH, Copeland Papers, W. J. Copeland to M. A. Copeland, 3 May 1836. For a Tractarian
critique of the political character of Eldon's churchmanship, see 'Life of Lord Eldon',
Christian Remembrancer, 8 (September, 1844), 274–86. The Tractarian Henry Woodgate
commented: 'Mr Norris of Hackney ... I find is a Churchman in a better sense of the word,
and not like Lord Eldon, whom he disapproves of entirely, considered as a friend of the

Political concerns, albeit infused by deeper religious principles, underlay the very genesis of the Movement. In many ways, it was a political episode, Oxford University's repudiation of Peel in 1829, that deserves to be regarded as an even more appropriate date for the rise of the Movement than was Keble's Assize sermon on July 14, 1833. For it was the campaign against Peel which first brought together the future Tractarian constellation on the basis of political discontent infused by moral principle.[86] Significantly, Newman dramatised a political contest, which to some contemporaries seemed trivial, into an almost apocalyptic struggle against the forces of darkness. These forces summed up for Newman in the dreaded phrase 'liberalism' might have seemed merely political, but for him they were no less symptomatic of spiritual and moral evil.

The early Tractarians repeatedly applied a moral, religious and philosophical colouring to apparently political differences dividing them from Whig and latitudinarian opponents, and even from Peelite Conservatism. Newman may not have written any treatise on political obligation, in the manner of High Churchmen of the previous century, but he imbibed the philosophical presuppositions of earlier Orthodox political theology. Martin Svaglic has maintained that 'Newman's early political thought is a blend of the conservatism of Burke, which dominated Oxford, with the Nonjuring principle taught in the Anglican Homily on Wilful Disobedience (1569).'[87] In the note on 'Liberalism' in the appendix to his *Apologia*, Newman included among the eighteen propositions which he listed as having 'denounced and abjured', the tenets that 'the people were the legitimate source of power', and that 'it is lawful to rise in arms against legitimate princes. Therefore, e.g. the Puritans in the 17th century, and the French in the 18th, were justified in their Rebellion and Revolution respectively'.[88]

Newman's response to contemporary manifestations of the Whig, radical, or what he ironically called 'march of mind' ideology, was partly shaped by his Burkean presumption in favour of an inherited

Church'. H. A. Woodgate to J. H. Newman, 22 February 1830, Mozley, ed., *Letters and Correspondence of Newman*, vol. I, p. 224.

86 See P. B. Nockles, 'The Great Disruption: the University and the Oxford Movement', in M. Brock and M. C. Curthoys, eds., *The History of the University of Oxford*, vol. VI (forthcoming).

87 Newman, *Apologia pro vita sua*, J. Svaglic, ed. (Oxford, 1967), p. 506.

88 *Ibid.*, pp. 260–2. For an example of Newman's Toryism, see [J. H. Newman], 'Affairs of Rome', *British Critic*, 22 (October, 1837), especially 261–83.

system of institutions as well as by Tory scepticism about abstract
political panaceas that made too little allowance for original sin. As
Rowlands shows, the basis of Newman's critique of Peel was that
'Peel's legislation, in its attitude to man's place in society, its views
on knowledge and benevolence, religion and the church, reflected
much of the prevailing Benthamite spirit'. In contrast, Newman
assailed what he regarded as the false, unspiritual philosophy of
Benthamite Utilitarianism, with its liberal theory of education and
glorification of natural and physical science as unqualified 'norms of
truth'.[89] For Newman, the root of what he perceived as the false
idols of Benthamism lay in 'the cheerful, hopeful view of human
nature, which prevails at all times (especially since the "Glorious"
1688!) Such was Paley's, Addison's, Blair's, and now Maltby's and
the Liberals.'[90]

Yet the nightmare vision of a church engulfed in political crisis
which Newman invoked in the early 1830s, was to be met, as
Stephen Thomas shows, by an essentially eschatological rather than
political response.[91] Nevertheless, here also there was continuity
with the recent High Church past. In the 1790s, Bishop Horsley,
Jones of Nayland and other High Churchmen had indulged in
prophetical interpretation of Scripture in order to brand Jacobinism
as partaking of Antichrist.[92] It was in similar vein in the 1830s that
Newman identified prevailing forces of rebellion, sedition and insubordination with that same spirit of Antichrist 'which scared the
world some forty or fifty years ago'.[93]

With Keble, the link with the High Church political heritage was
explicitly acknowledged. As late as 1841, Keble devoted a review in
the *British Critic* to castigating not only what he regarded as the lax
theology but also the lax politics of the school of Warburton in the
preceding century. For Keble, the Whig Warburton's 'proud spi-
rited' abstract notions of liberty were deemed to emanate from the
same tainted source as his claims for unbridled religious enquiry and
doctrinal latitude. It was a spirit which he detected and lamented

[89] Rowlands, *Church, State and Society*, pp. 168–9.
[90] *Letters and Diaries of John Henry Newman*, I. Ker and T. Gornall, eds., vol. III (Oxford, 1979),
p. 35.
[91] Thomas, *Newman and Heresy*, pp. 55–7.
[92] W. H. Olliver, *Prophets and Millennialists: the Use of Biblical Prophecy in England from the 1790s
to the 1840s* (Auckland, 1978), pp. 50–1; Hole, *Pulpits, Politics and Public Order*, pp. 170–2;
J. A. Oddy, 'Eschatological Prophecy in the English theological tradition, c. 1700–c.
1840', Ph.D. thesis, University of London, 1982, ch. 3.
[93] J. H. Newman, *Discussions and Arguments on Various Subjects* (London, 1885), p. 69.

even in some of the Tory, Protestant High Church eulogisers of the old constitution. As Keble put it, 'in this overweening talk of human dignity and civil liberty, Warburton was but following the fashionable quasi-idolatry of that era, perhaps we might say, of our country, for a century and a half: a superstition not confined to any one school in theology'.[94] Significantly, Keble excepted not only the Nonjurors but the Hutchinsonians from this verdict. The Nonjurors had invoked the true spirit of the primitive Christians first in passively obeying King James II and then at the Revolution heroically refusing to compromise their principles and suffering for conscience's sake. For Keble as for Newman, an insistence on the duty of obedience and on the horror of rebellion as a form of blasphemy, stemmed from theological principle; it was but 'one inseparable branch of the universal doctrine of resignation and contentment'.[95] Rebellion was akin to heresy; both were breaches of the natural moral order and forms of sacrilege. As Liddon justly observed, it was Keble's 'moral temper' which 'led him to view reform and change with distrust: his faith in God's presence and guidance made all high-handed self-willed action on man's part appear more or less irreverent'.[96] It was a comfort for Keble to find this message rooted in the Homilies and in the classic treatises of the Caroline Divines. Yet it would be wrong to suggest that this was a political theology deterministically controlled by the dynamics of the *ancien régime*. For like other Tractarians, Keble's political principles transcended the particular constitutional order under which they had been nurtured.

With Pusey, under the formative influence of Keble, an abandonment of a youthful political liberalism in favour of a 'moral Toryism' precisely coincided with a jettisoning of an early moderate latitudinarianism and his emergence as one of the Tractarian leaders. Given the popular historical assumption that Tractarianism bade a 'farewell to Toryism', there was a paradox here, though one more apparent than real. A striking passage in a letter of Pusey's to Edward Churton in 1865 has been cited to demonstrate Pusey's own 'farewell to Toryism'. Pusey told Churton, 'I could have been a

[94] [J. Keble], 'Unpublished Papers of Bishop Warburton', *British Critic*, 29 (April, 1841), p. 427.

[95] J. Keble, 'The Danger of Sympathising with Rebellion. Preached before the University of Oxford on 30th January 1831, Being the Day of King Charles' Martyrdom', Sermon V, *Sermons Academical and Occasional* (London, 1848), p. 124.

[96] Liddon, *Life of Pusey*, vol. II, p. 29.

Tory; but 1830 ended Toryism. I could not be a mere Conservative, i.e. I could not bind myself, or risk the future of the Church on the fidelity or wisdom of persons whose principle it is to keep what they think they can, and part with the rest.'[97] Yet the real implication of this passage was that Pusey actually regarded his theological volte-face into the vanguard of the Movement in the 1830s as a kind of substitute for that deeper philosophical Toryism which the triumph of Reform appeared to have denied any other form of political expression. Pusey rightly sensed that it was almost impossible, in the wake of the events of 1828–33, to translate such Tory principles into political reality again. It was partly because, for the Tractarians, party politics were no longer deemed an appropriate forum for the pursuit of the High Church cause, that the tradition of Orthodox political theology gained in Pusey a wholehearted convert.

THE TRACTARIANS, MONARCHY AND THE ROYAL SUPREMACY

The early Tractarians also were heirs of the Orthodox political tradition in their espousal of sacral theory of monarchy. Keble's Toryism was infused by a romantic, almost mystical reverence for the House of Stuart and that potent symbol, the Royal Martyr, Charles I. For Keble, the office of monarch represented the 'anointed of the Lord, a living, type of the supreme dominion of Jesus Christ'.[98] Like pre-Tractarian High Churchmen, Keble's sacral royalism was reflected in a theological understanding of the Royal Supremacy. Thus, in the face of Whig ministerial interference in matters ecclesiastical in 1833–4, Keble sought part refuge in an advocacy of the Royal Supremacy which echoed that espoused by Reeves and others in an earlier generation. In the spirit of Hooker, Keble clung to the ideal of the godly prince. In an Accession Day sermon in 1855 on the text from Isaiah, 49, v. 23, 'And Kings shall be thy nursing fathers', etc., Keble expounded the ideal. Like his High Church predecessors, he denied that to put one's trust in princes amounted to Erastian temporising.[99] As the crown failed in the 1830s to protect the church from secular encroachment, Keble's sense of the dangers of such reliance increased. This did not diminish

[97] Quoted in Liddon, *Life of Pusey*, vol. IV, p. 199.
[98] J. Keble, 'Kings to be Honoured for Their Office's Sake' [Accession Day Sermon, 1835], *Plain Sermons*, vol. 1 (London, 1839), p. 243; J. Keble, 'On the Death of a King' [July 9, 1837], *Plain Sermons*, vol. IV (London, 1842), pp. 76–7.
[99] Keble, *Sermons Academical and Occasional*, p. 149.

his faith in the old theory rightly interpreted. As he explained in 1839, for some, the phrase 'nursing father' had 'acquired a trite and almost proverbial use ... in a very different sense: as though the church were a helpless infant in the arms of some defender of the faith'. Keble insisted that the true imagery of the text from Isaiah was of the church as a mother with her children lodged in her arms; 'monarchs were essentially foster fathers and mothers'.[100]

Significantly, Pusey acknowledged his conversion to Keble's brand of Toryism by reference to his own changed attitude to symbols of the royalist tradition in High Churchmanship. As he wrote movingly to Keble in November 1837,

It was at Fairford, many years ago, when I was thoughtlessly or rather I must say confidently taking for granted that the Stuarts were rightly dethroned, that I heard for the first time a hint to the contrary from you; your seriousness was an intended reproof to my petulant expression about it, and so it stuck by me, although it was some time before it took root, and burst through all the clouds placed upon it.[101]

Pusey's 5 November sermon in 1837, *Patience and Confidence the Strength of the Church*, dedicated to Keble, was a fitting fruit of the latter's influence.

Pusey's repudiation of the 'Glorious Revolution' of 1688 led many contemporaries to treat the sermon as an anachronistic piece of neo-Jacobite polemic, comparable to Sacheverell's notorious sermon in 1709, *In Peril among False Brethren*.[102] In another historical parallel, just as Warburton and Samuel Parr had denounced the

100 *British Critic*, 26 (October, 1839), 373–5.
101 PH, Pusey Papers, E. B. Pusey to J. Keble, 15 November 1837. Pusey's dedication of the sermon to Keble made explicit the influence: 'To the Rev. John Keble, M.A. Professor of Poetry, and late Fellow of Oriel, who in years past unconsciously implanted a truth which was afterwards to take root, himself and dutiful disciple of its ancient guardian and faithful witness in word and action, the University of Oxford'.
102 Liddon, *Life of Pusey*, vol. II, p. 27. Pusey was accused in the Evangelical press of wishing 'to restore the doctrines and practices of Laud and Sacheverell'. *Christian Observer*, 37 (September, 1837), 586; R. Fisher, *Tractarianism Opposed to Truth* (London, 1843), pp. 15–16.
   Even moderate High Churchmen warned against a revival of 'Jacobite' political notions by the Tractarians. See J. Beavan, *Warnings from History, Political and Ecclesiastical: a Discourse Delivered before the University of Oxford on the 30th January 1838, being the Day of King Charles' Martyrdom* (Oxford, 1838). On residual Jacobite sentiment among the Tractarians, see n. 157.
   As late as mid-century, political Toryism remained a bond between the old High Churchman Edward Churton and the Tractarian Robert Wilberforce. See Churton's comment to Wilberforce: 'under a Whig dynasty "sufferance is the badge of all our tribe"'. E. Churton to R. I. Wilberforce, 5 June 1849, PH, Churton Papers, CHUR 2/4/20.

'Jacobite' or 'Tory' politics of the sermons of Horne and Horsley in the 1760s and 1790s respectively, Thomas Arnold in January 1838 was complaining that Pusey had quoted texts 'which appear to advocate pure despotism'.[103] Yet, while it was true that Pusey cited such authorities as Filmer, Overall's *Convocation Book*, Sanderson and Horsley in favour of the 'high doctrine of Non-Resistance',[104] it was moral and religious lessons not party politics that concerned him. Those who accused Pusey of wishing to restore the Stuarts missed the point. As Pusey made clear, 'with regard to the special instance of the English revolution of 1688, the question is now happily of practical importance only, as relates to men's feelings and principles, not to any political mode of acting'.[105] 'Non-resistance or passive obedience, in the sense to which they are generally limited' were 'but two sides of the same doctrine' – faith and humility in religion, obedience and submission in political allegiance.[106]

Keble's influence on Pusey was revealed also by the latter's adherence to the notion of the monarch as 'nursing father' of the church. In a sermon on behalf of the SPG in 1838, Pusey stressed the role of the crown in the church's missionary endeavour, declaiming that the 'princes of this world shall reverence the Church, and shall find their glory and their joy in ministering to her necessities'.[107] Far from complaining of the monarch's interference, Pusey faulted the crown's occasional neglect of her duties of protection and succour, as in the failure in the previous century to introduce episcopacy to the North American colonies. The old theme of American Loyalists such as Jonathan Boucher that this failure helped contribute to the revolt of the 1770s was reiterated by Pusey.[108] Pusey blamed royal advisers rather than the crown itself. He was critical of ministerial interference in church matters precisely because he felt that it stifled the

---

[103] Quoted in A. P. Stanley, *The Life and Correspondence of Thomas Arnold*, 2 vols. (4th edn, London, 1845), vol. II, p. 93. Even a current historian of Jacobitism maintains, 'The last Oxford Jacobite sermon was preached by Dr Pusey on 5 November 1837', P. K. Monod, *Jacobitism and the English People*, p. 152.

[104] E. B. Pusey, *Patience and Confidence the Strength of the Church: a Sermon Preached on the 5th of November, before the University of Oxford at St. Mary's* (Oxford, 1837), p. xv. Liddon described the sermon as 'imbued with the old moral as well as political temper of Toryism'. Liddon, *Life of Pusey*, vol. II, p. 27.

[105] Pusey, *Patience and Confidence*, p. vi.   [106] *Ibid.*, p. v.

[107] E. B. Pusey, *The Church, the Converter of the Heathen. Two Sermons Preached in Conformity with the Queen's Letter in Behalf of the SPG* (Oxford, 1838), p. 23.

[108] 'Far different might the relations of our great colony the United States have been ... had our state then known her duties to her colonies or to the church'. Pusey, *The Church, the Converter of the Heathen*, p. 56.

true role of the monarch as 'nursing father'. For Pusey, the 'blessed influence of George the Third' was a model worthy of emulation, but as he lamented, 'even he could not undo the evil which had been done by the ministers of the first two sovereigns of his line'.[109] Yet while Pusey could complain that the role of politicians as ecclesiastical advisers prostituted the office of bishop, he took comfort in the fact that 'their interference grew only with the weakness of the House of Hanover, and even Pitt could not carry his own Archbishop of Canterbury (Tomline)'.[110] It was because, as Pusey said, 'this modern plan, wherein ministers are virtually the patrons, and the king a cypher, did not come in until the middle of the last century', that he hoped that 'with a struggle we might again recover the old system'.[111] Even Pusey's desire for a veto by the chapter and consecrating bishop in the case of bad episcopal appointments was not intended to restrict the due exercise of royal authority. He agreed with Keble that 'His Majesty's Prerogative would gain more than it would lose by taking from him the nominal appointment and giving the real one to that party who we know are always surest to stand by him'.[112]

As he advanced theologically, Pusey adhered to the ideal of sacral monarchy as a bulwark of the church. As we shall see, in the Gorham crisis, it was an emphasis which divided him from many other Tractarians and allied him with old High Churchmen with whom on other theological issues he had become estranged. In his treatise, *The Royal Supremacy Not an Arbitrary Authority* (1850), Pusey explicitly appealed to that tradition of Orthodox political theology which 'owed the ancient authority of the Crown' and which provided him with precedents to 'justify the principle which the Church had conceded'.[113]

Newman's royalist instincts were no less marked. He had a notorious horror of 'republicanism' which was represented on the index of eighteen 'Liberal' propositions which he anathematised. After about 1829, Newman adopted the cult of the Royal Martyr and, like High

---

109 E. B. Pusey, *Remarks on the Prospective and Past Benefits of Cathedral Institutions in the Promotion of Sound Religious Knowledge and of Clerical Education* (2nd edn, London, 1833), p. 96.
110 Bodl. Lib, Wilberforce Ms d. 17, fol. 336, E. B. Pusey to S. Wilberforce, 9 September 1836.
111 PH, Pusey Papers, LBV [Transcripts], E. B. Pusey to W. E. Gladstone, March, 1836.
112 Bodl. Lib, Wilberforce Ms. d. 17, fol. 338, J. Keble to S. Wilberforce, 19 September 1836.
113 E. B. Pusey, *The Royal Supremacy Not an Arbitrary Authority but Limited by the Laws of the Church, of Which Kings Are Members* (Oxford, 1850), p. 159.

Churchmen of an earlier generation scrupulously observed 30 January as the day of the Martyrdom.[114]

Newman's royalism was expressed in a passionate appeal to the crown to use her Supremacy to defend the church against ministerial thraldom. When Bishop Phillpotts in a fighting speech in the House of Lords in June 1833 urged the crown to veto Whig legislation by recourse to the coronation oath, thereby clashing with Lord Grey, Newman rallied to the former's side. After Newman's old mentor, Richard Whately, had defended Grey's interpretation of the coronation oath, Newman exploded, 'as to Whately and his evasions about the Coronation oath, it is quite distressing to think about him'.[115] As yet, Newman still regarded the Royal Supremacy as a bulwark of the spiritual rights of the church. When Whig legislation threatened to infringe those rights in 1833, it was natural for him to appeal to William IV as 'Defender of the Faith'. As he explained in a letter to the *British Magazine* in 1834,

If it be said that the Act of Settlement secures to the people certain liberties, I reply that the Coronation Oath has secured to the Church its liberties also to the utter annulment of all former precedents of tyranny – and that we stand by that oath as our law as well as our Sovereign's sanction and acknowledgment of it, and that any power in the state that innovates on the spirit of that oath tyrannises over us.[116]

When it became clear that William IV in 1833–4, unlike George III in 1801, was not prepared to stand by his oath in the way Tractarian leaders urged, Newman's disillusionment was patent. William IV's acquiescence in the creation of the Ecclesiastical Commission in 1835 further deepened Newman's feeling that the Church was being betrayed by the Crown and that she would have to confide her trust elsewhere.[117] Newman's readiness to bow to the totems of Protestant constitutionalism purely as a rhetorical device to disarm contemporary churchmen should not be underestimated. The suspicion

[114] T. Gornall, ed., *Letters and Diaries of John Henry Newman*, vol. v, (Oxford, 1981), p. 216. Newman's diary entry for 30 January 1836 reads: 'Saturday 30th January. The Martyrdom – tried to find a church open in vain'. *Letters and Diaries*, vol. v, pp. 220, 302. Newman also expressed theoretical Jacobite sentiments, holding that 'the rightful heir was lost in the Revolution'. J. H. Newman to R. H. Froude, 7 January 1830, *Letters and Diaries*, vol. ii, p. 186.
[115] J. H. Newman to H. A. Woodgate, 7 July 1833, I. Ker and T. Gornall, eds., *Letters and Diaries of John Henry Newman*, vol. iv (Oxford, 1980), pp. 26–7. See also A. P. Perceval, *A Letter to the Rt. Hon Earl Grey on the Obligation of the Coronation Oath* (London, 1833), pp. 6–7.
[116] *Letters and Diaries*, vol. iv, p. 164.
[117] J. H. Newman to J. W. Bowden, 5 February 1835, *Letters and Diaries*, vol. v, p. 24.

lingers that Newman's letter to the *British Magazine* may have been something of a tactical ploy. At any rate, thereafter, Newman, under the powerful influence of his friend Hurrell Froude, allowed himself to be pulled in another direction.

For all Froude's own personal devotion to the Martyr King and royalist idealism, he never shared Keble's or Newman's apparent faith in the Royal Supremacy. Froude's reactionary Romanticism had even less in common with the spirit of Protestant constitutionalism than had the political outlook of any other Tractarian leader. He despised 1688 to such an extent that the Act of Settlement could never have been a point of reference for him in the way it seemed to be for Newman in 1833. By 1836, Froude had induced Newman altogether to abandon his belief in the Royal Supremacy. Yet, already by the autumn of 1833, Newman's ambivalence towards the Church's traditional political props was evident. As he confided to R.F. Wilson at this time,

It is most natural and right proper that the Monarchy and Aristocracy should be our secular instruments of influence – but if these powers will not, lo! we turn to the people. The King has tied his own hands – he has literally betrayed us ... Our first duty is the defence of the Church. We have stood by Monarchy and Aristocracy till they have refused to stand by themselves.[118]

Ultimately, Newman had to ask which mattered more, monarchy or church? As J. C. D. Clark puts it, 'in 1688–9 the political classes ultimately chose the second; in 1828–9 they reversed that choice'.[119] Newman could not respect that reversal and, in consequence, he sought out new 'secular instruments'. Yet as he insisted to Froude, 'theoretically and historically' he remained 'a Tory'. It was only altered external political circumstances that forced him to 'begin to be a radical practically'. For him, 'the most natural and becoming state of things' was 'for the aristocratical power to be the upholder of the church'.[120] He made clear to Rose in 1836 that, had circumstances not thus altered, he would have gone on clinging to the old order;

Now suppose one had been born 30 years sooner, I think one should have kept quiet. But the times will not allow of this ... outward circumstances are changing ... we have a reason for being bolder ... men like Hooker,

118 J. H. Newman to R. F. Wilson, 8 September 1833, *Letters and Diaries*, vol. IV, p. 33.
119 Clark, *English Society*, p. 419.
120 J. H. Newman to R. H. Froude, 31 August 1833, Mozley, ed., *Letters and Correspondence of Newman*, vol. I, p. 450.

Andrewes, and Laud, acted in the system they found themselves. The single difference between their views and those I seem to follow is this – they had a divine right king – we in matter of fact have not.[121]

In short, Froude may have helped undermine the basis of Newman's Toryism as a practical outlet for his ecclesiastical principles, but Newman's historical and emotional attachment to a Laudian monarchical and hierarchical ideal lingered on into his later Tractarian years. This attachment was well exemplified in Newman's article on the Court of James I in the *British Critic* in 1840.[122] On reading the article, the Tractarian Charles Marriott confided to Newman, 'the very broad avowal of the Anglican notion of Royal Supremacy ... made me open my eyes an eighth of an inch wider than usual. But I think facts bear you out'.[123]

Newman's Tory and royalist sympathies acted as a brake in his drift towards Rome, even as his theological objections were being overcome. For example, it was the apparent identification of the Church of Rome with the cause of Daniel O'Connell in Ireland and of the Whigs in England in the late 1830s that especially troubled him. On the other hand, as he told a friend in 1840, if there were 'a movement in the English Roman Catholics to break the alliance of Exeter Hall, strong temptations will be placed in the way of individuals, already imbued with a tone of thought congenial to Rome, to join her communion'.[124]

As Paul Misner, Gilley and Rowlands have demonstrated, the hard edges of Newman's Toryism would be softened, and his passage towards Rome consequently eased, by his rediscovery and reappropriation after 1840 of the 'Evangelical prophetical tradition' in which he had been educated. As 'the World' and even its secular princes and powers began to assume the guise of Antichrist rather than Whiggery or Popery as at an earlier date in Newman's always

---

[121] J. H. Newman to H. J. Rose, 23 May 1836, *Letters and Diaries*, vol. v, p. 304.

[122] [J. H. Newman], 'The Court of James I', *British Critic*, 27 (January 1840), especially 34–5.

[123] PH, Ollard Papers, C. Marriott to J. H. Newman, 15 January 1840. See also Newman's comment about W. G. Ward on his joining the Movement after 1838: 'I cannot help liking him very much, in spite of his still professing himself a Radical in politics'. J. H. Newman to J. W. Bowden, May 1839, Mozley, ed., *Letters and Correspondence of Newman*, vol. II, p. 282. On Ward's political iconoclasm in High Church eyes, see n. 141.

This evidence contradicts Professor Griffin's assertion that the Anglican Newman lacked religious patriotism and had little or no respect for the 'Church and King' tradition. Griffin, 'The Anglican Politics of Cardinal Newman', 435.

[124] Newman, *Apologia*, p. 237.

active eschatology, so his political Toryism was modified by an 'otherworldliness'. This 'otherworldliness' drew out of Newman that latent 'Calvinist sense of the satanic significance of contemporary events' which was but one of several extreme Evangelical traits which never left him and which were never far below the surface.[125]

THE TRACTARIANS AND ESTABLISHMENT: THE BREACH WITH THE 'ZS'

A divergence of attitude towards establishment between 'Apostolicals' and 'Zs' was implicit from the dawn of the Movement. The very words of Joshua Watson's lay loyal address to the Primate in 1834, with its insistence that the 'consecration of the state by the public maintenance of the Christian religion' was the 'paramount duty of a Christian people' were words, as Palmer later recalled, 'which were anathema to Froude'.[126]

In 1833, 'Zs' stressed the religious, cultural and educational advantages of establishment in terms of clerical provision and endowment, and regarded tithes as symbols of outward blessings.[127] Nonetheless, the portrait of the conservatism and immobility of 'Z' attitudes to establishment presented by Froude, and Newman in his *Apologia*, was exaggerated. At this date, apart from the exception of Froude himself, inner differences between the two sides had scarcely surfaced. Not only were the Tractarians still imbued with elements of the 'Church and King' mentality, but the 'Zs' also were alive to the implications of the constitutional revolution of 1828–33. In 1836, one observer actually traced the first anti-establishment stirrings at Oxford back to 1827 when Godfrey Faussett as Margaret Professor warned in a public sermon, 'that Oxford would (as under James II) cease to preach passive obedience to the temporal power, so soon as that power ceased to rule in conformity with her suggestions'.[128] In his Bampton Lectures in 1834 Faussett returned to the theme of those he had given in 1820. What had then been but 'deviations' from the church–state ideal had now become crippling abuses. Far from instilling complacency, Faussett called for protests

[125] See S. Gilley, 'Newman and Prophecy, Evangelical and Catholic', *Journal of the United Reformed Church History Society*, 3 (March, 1985), 160–83; P. Misner, *Papacy and Development: Newman and the Primacy of the Pope* (Leiden, 1976), pp. 50–7; Rowlands, *Church, State and Society*, pp. 181–96.
[126] Palmer, *Narrative of Events*, p. 15.   [127] *British Magazine*, 4 (July, 1833), 91.
[128] *The State of Parties in Oxford* (Oxford, 1836), p. 16.

against 'the degrading and ruinous anomaly of our present position,
as a church practically, though not constitutionally, deprived of the
privilege of legislating for herself, yet subjected to laws forced on her
by aliens from her communion, and individually calculated to work
her destruction'.[129]

Froude's response was different in kind. His radical message was,
'let us tell the truth and shame the devil; let us give up a national
church, and have a real one'.[130] Establishment was an incubus and
ought to be jettisoned; all 'secular' interferences in the church even
by the crown was a 'usurpation'. But in his famous article, *Remarks on
State Interference in Matters Spiritual* first published in the *British
Magazine* in November 1833 and later reprinted as *Tract 59*, Froude
sought to persuade rather than provoke the old High Churchmen.
For in advocating that the church face constitutional reality and
adopt a new line of policy in relation to the state, Froude insisted
that such a new course could be justified on the very principles of
Hooker's church–state theory. Froude pointed out that,

according to Hooker . . . the representatives of the Commonwealth, i.e. the
Parliament of England, were at the same time representatives of the Church,
and thus a lay *Synod of the Church of England*. And it was because parliament
was such a synod, and only because it was so, that Hooker justified himself
in consenting to its interference in matters spiritual.[131]

The logic of the constitutional revolution of 1828–33 was that 'the
conditions on which our predecessors consented to parliamentary
interference in matters spiritual are *cancelled*'.[132] This argument
enabled Froude apparently to turn the tables on the old High
Churchmen. Against those mistrustful of the radical implications of
his message, he could retort, 'open your eyes to the fearful change
which has been so noiselessly effected; and acknowledge that *by
standing still you become a party to Revolution*'.[133]

For Froude, however, the appeal to Hooker had been an essentially rhetorical, tactical device to disarm the 'Zs'. His instinct was to
'have the "Zs" thrown overboard',[134] and to follow the logic of his own

---

[129] G. Faussett, *The Alliance of Church and State Explained and Vindicated in Eight Sermons Preached
before the University of Oxford, in the Year MDCCCXXXIV. At the Lecture Founded by the Late
Rev. John Bampton* (Oxford, 1834), p. 28.
[130] [Newman and Keble, eds.], *Remains of Richard Hurrell Froude*, vol. III, p. 274.
[131] *Ibid.*, pp. 199–200.
[132] *Ibid.*, p. 197.   [133] *Ibid.*, p. 196.
[134] *Letters and Diaries*, vol. IV, p. 33. For instance, Froude privately confessed himself 'out of
conceit with old Hooker's notion of a lay synod: it is unecclesiastical and Whig. We must

radicalism on the church–state question. In reality, Froude's church–state ideal was not the constitutionalism of Hooker or even the Laudian theocracy of the Caroline Divines. Rather, it found its model exemplified by that unqualified ecclesiastical supremacy over the civil power in all capacities, symbolised by Becket and the twelfth-century church dictating to monarchs.[135] Whereas old High Churchmen condemned the late medieval church's claim to spiritual dominion over the secular power as championed by Hildebrand, Froude's perspective was diametrically opposite. Froude faulted the church for alienating too many of her ecclesiastical powers to the domain of temporal rulers in the fourteenth century, not vice versa. Inspired by the romanticised notion of the *pauperes Christi*, he argued that the 'usurpations' of Roman Pontiffs in the fourteenth century were 'usurpations, not on the rights of Kings and Governors, but on the rights of the Church itself, of the congregations of Christ's little ones, the poor, the halt, the lame and the blind'. In a striking echo of the Tractarian complaint about the eighteenth-century episcopate, Froude lamented that fourteenth-century bishops had 'shrunk from asserting their station as successors of the Apostles, for fear of losing their station in society'.[136]

The context of the Orthodox stand in the 1830s against Protestant Dissent made Froude an unreliable ally. Old High Churchmen had often warned of the analogy between the hostility of the modern Protestant sectarian to the church–state connection, and that of 'those who, in the Middle Ages, were devoted to the Popedom'.[137] Froude's espousal of Becket and Hildebrand seemed to bear out the analogy. Thus, while Froude's radical objection to the payment of tithes was on the ground that, since it was enforced by the civil power, it partook of 'desecration',[138] it was an attitude that

only be popular in the choice of church officers'. [Newman and Keble, eds.], *Remains of Richard Hurrell Froude*, vol. I, p. 333.

[135] See Froude's article on Becket in the *British Magazine*, 2 (September, 1832), especially 334–5. The article was reprinted as volume IV of the *Remains of Richard Hurrell Froude* (Derby, 1839). Even Newman thought the 'Becket papers might frighten people considerably – on Church and State'. J. H. Newman to J. Keble, 13 September 1838, *Letters and Diaries*, vol. VI, p. 317.

[136] Newman and Keble, eds., *Remains of Richard Hurrell Froude*, vol. III, pp. 223, 227.

[137] W. F. Hook, *On the Church and the Establishment. Two Plain Sermons* (London, 1834), p. 44. See Churton's comment: 'What can be more plain, than that all other systems interfere with the just authority of the Christian Governor or Chief Magistrate in the state? The Papists claim both swords [temporal and spiritual] – the Presbyterians do the same ... No Lady Abbess was ever greater than Lady Huntingdon. See the extremes meet'. PH, Gresley Papers, GRES 3/7/31, E. Churton to W. Gresley, May 1841.

[138] [Newman and Keble, eds.], *Remains of Richard Hurrell Froude*, vol. I, p. 434.

appeared to put him in league with Dissenters. To the dismay of old High Churchmen, Froude's brand of anti-Erastianism actually led him to identify with the anti-church and -state views of the early Puritans in their struggle with 'High Church' episcopal opponents such as Whitgift and Bancroft.[139] Froude privately even faulted Laud and the Caroline Divines on this point. As Frederic Rogers later confided to Newman, 'he [Froude] said to me of Laud that all he saw in him was that he was a brave man, with some good views, adding that all our divines since the Reformation had been very dark about Church Independence'.[140]

Froude may have been a Tory and 'Romantic reactionary', but the radical implications of his anti-establishment mentality should not be underestimated. For anti-establishmentism would seep into the bloodstream of later Anglo-Catholicism and, as shaped by W. G. Ward[141] and others, would overshadow the Tory and royalist instincts with which Froude had still been imbued. Ultimately, it would inspire objections even to that once sacred High Church highlight of the liturgical calendar, the Prayer Book's 30 January Thanksgiving rite, on the ground that it was but a 'state service' imposed by the civil power.[142]

Froude's influence on the attitude of other Tractarian leaders to establishment was potent. During the 1820s, Keble's constant refrain was of the 'danger to the Church Establishment'.[143] Far from at this stage looking to the apparently 'independent' American church for inspiration, Keble scornfully referred to 'American

---

139 *Ibid.*, pp. 325–8.

140 F. Rogers to J. H. Newman, 21 January 1839, G. E. Marindin, ed., *Letters to Frederic Lord Blachford* (London, 1896), pp. 45–6.

141 Wilfrid Ward described the consternation which his father W. G. Ward provoked when he asserted 'at a dinner of Puseyites and zealous worshippers of the Martyr-King that the execution of Charles I was the only defensible or possible course under the circumstances'. W. Ward, *William George Ward and the Oxford Movement* (London, 1889), p. 214.
    William Gresley cautioned advanced Tractarians in 1847: 'we must not set down the old cry of "Church and King" as altogether Erastian. Good men used it as well as mere politicians'. Gresley, *Second Statement on the Real Danger of the Church of England*, p. 14.

142 Appropriately, it was left to the octogenarian and one-time Hackney Phalanx associate, Bishop Bethell, to mount the rearguard action in the House of Lords against the abolition of the state service for 30 January in 1858.
    Christopher Bethell (1773–1859). King's College, Cambridge; BA, 1796; Fellow, 1797; Rector of Kirby Wiske, Yorks, 1808–30; Dean of Chichester, 1814–30; Bishop of Gloucester, 1824–30; Bishop of Bangor, 1830–d. Bethell 'was during the whole of his life identified with the high-church party'. *DNB.*

143 PH, Pusey Papers, LBV [Transcripts], J. Keble to A. P. Perceval, 25 March 1829; J. Keble to A. P. Perceval, 29 June 1827; KCA, Keble Papers, J. Keble to J. Davison, 23 June 1827.

notions of church and state' as worthy of obloquy.[144] He was
haunted by the spectre of a separation between church and state.
Ironically in view of their respective later positions, Keble actually
criticised Whately's *Letters of an Episcopalian* (1826) for countenancing such a separation.[145] Even Keble's famous sermon on *National
Apostasy* was arguably more conservative in tone than a sermon by
Rose on a similar theme in 1832. However, in private correspondence Keble began to sound more like Froude, eschewing compromise and even threatening dramatic gestures. As he told Newman in
August 1833,

I cannot take the Oath of Supremacy in the sense which the legislature now
puts upon it. I cannot accept my curacy or office in the Church of England,
but I have not made up my mind that I am bound to resign what I have . . .
I think we ought to be prepared to sacrifice any or all of our endowments,
rather than sanction it. Take every pound, shilling and penny and the
cause of sacrilege along with it, only let us make our own Bishops and be
governed by our own laws.[146]

For all the Froudean bravado and fighting talk, Keble did not put
himself to the ultimate test, though again in 1850 he would contemplate the prospect of lay communion. The pastoral reality of life at
his beloved Hursley dissuaded him from radical courses.

Keble frequently acknowledged his personal debt to Froude in his
later thinking on church and state. Keble's comment on Gladstone's
classic restatement of the Orthodox position, *The State in Its Relations
with the Church* (1838) is revealing. For Keble, Gladstone's book,
which he reviewed in the *British Critic*, was 'exceptionally well-
meant but wants a little reconciling with Froude's view'.[147]

On the other hand, there were limits to Froude's influence on
Keble. For Keble, it was Hooker, albeit with the addition of his own
gloss, rather than Becket or even Ambrose, who remained a sure
guide on church–state matters. Keble would never have classed

---

[144] PH, Pusey Papers, LBV [Transcripts], J. Keble to A. P. Perceval, 15 June 1828.
[145] KCA, Keble Papers, J. Keble to W. R. Churton, 24 June 1827; GCRO, Prevost Papers,
Ms D 2692, no. 8, J. Keble to G. Provost, 3 July 1827.
[146] J. Keble to J. H. Newman, 8 August 1833, Mozley, ed., *Letters and Correspondence of
Newman*, vol. 1, p. 441. For an interpretation of Keble's utterances in 1833 as 'radical' in a
political sense, see J. R. Griffin, 'John Keble, Radical', *Anglican Theological Review*, 59
(1971); J. R. Griffin, 'The Radical Phase of the Oxford Movement', *JEH*, 27 (1976). For
another evaluation, explaining the real nature of Froude's 'radical' influence on Keble in
non-political terms, see P. Brendon, *Hurrell Froude and the Oxford Movement* (London, 1974),
pp. 41–84.
[147] KCA, Keble Papers, J. Keble to J. H. Newman, 31 March 1839.

Hooker's theory as 'conservative-Erastian', even if it required bolstering by Leslie's *Regale*.[148] As late as 1839, when Keble's disaffection with existing church–state relations was total, he could assert that '[Hooker's] theory of Church and State is a development ... of the Holy Catholic Church, i.e. of the continued presence and manifestation of Jesus Christ in the world, through the medium of that society which is called His mystical body'.[149] Yet Keble's Nonjuring source of inspiration for his later attitude to establishment was only marginally less acceptable to 'Zs' such as Palmer and Hook than were the Hildebrandine idols of Hurrell Froude.

If Newman's Tory royalism long outlasted the progress in his theological opinions, his initially conservative attitude to establishment did not. Newman may not have shared Froude's idolisation of Becket, but he was at one with his friend in throwing himself imaginatively into the historical past for the purpose of extracting polemical fodder for contemporary controversy. As Thomas points out, Newman's articles in the *British Magazine* between 1833 and 1836 were designed to draw from the ecclesiastical history of the age of Ambrose, Gregory and Basil, a message for current churchmen grappling with the church–state crisis of the early 1830s.[150] This was not antiquarianism for its own sake. For the Tractarians, history had to be brought alive; it was not an 'old almanac' providing 'curious' records of the past for a detached or cynical 'modern'.

The message which Newman sought to impress upon contemporary churchmen was that, following the example of the age of Ambrose and the Church of Milan, the Church of England might have to take a 'popular', course, and 'flee to the mountains' in order to prove its anti-Erastianism.[151] In the manner of Froude's flattery of Hooker in *Tract 59*, and possibly of his own defence of the Royal Supremacy in 1834, Newman's references to 'good King George' can be read as designed to soothe his country clerical readership which might otherwise baulk at the innovative and disturbing message he was delivering.[152] As Thomas shows, Newman's acute

[148] J. Keble, ed., *The Works of the Learned and Judicious Divine, Mr Richard Hooker: With an Account of His Life and Death by Isaak Walton* [1836] (3rd edn, Oxford, 1845), pp. lxxvii–lxxviii.

[149] [J. Keble], 'Gladstone – the State in its Relations with the Church', *British Critic*, 26 (October, 1839), 373–4.

[150] Thomas, *Newman and Heresy*, ch. 3.

[151] Rowlands, *Church, State and Society*, pp. 147–50, 162–66.

[152] Thomas, *Newman and Heresy*, p. 52.

ambivalence in relation to establishment can be explained in terms of a tension between nostalgia for the *ancien régime*, with its old focus of monarchical loyalty, and the pull of a patristic ideal. Certainly, the contrast between Newman's theoretical defence of establishment in 1833–4 and the tone of his articles on 'The Convocation of the Province of Canterbury' in the *British Magazine*, 1834–5, is marked.[153] In the latter, Newman reproduced, albeit toned down, Froude's earlier polemic against the constitutional basis of the Henrician settlement itself. Having only a year previously been prepared to make the Act of Settlement the basis of his stand, for the first time, Newman now actually questioned in print the legitimacy of the Church's apparent surrender of juridical power to the state in 1534 as well as in 1689.[154] By 1836, Newman's disenchantment not merely with what the state had done to the church since 1828 but with what she had done ever since the Reformation, especially after the Revolution of 1688–9, was made clear to Rose:

The Anglican Church ... discriminated by imposition of hands, not a tyrant's jurisdiction, I love indeed ... But I do not like the adventitious encrusted system in which they [Andrewes, Laud, etc.] found themselves ... I mourn over ... a 'Law Church' ... the creature of Henries and Williams's. I cannot love the 'Church of England' commonly so designated – its very title is an offence ... for it implies that it holds of the state.[155]

Far from being a temporary abuse to which the Church of England had been occasionally subject in her history, Newman already now regarded 'Erastianism' as her essential, natural condition. As he told Pusey in 1836, 'the English Church subsists in the state, and has no internal consistency to keep it together'.[156] This was doctrine subversive not merely of Hoadlyite principles but those of old High Churchmanship itself.

---

[153] See Rowlands, *Church, State and Society*, pp. 108–10.
[154] [J. H. Newman], 'The Convocation of the Province of Canterbury', *British Magazine*, 6 (October, 1834), 517–24, 637–47; 7, (January–March, 1835), 33–41, 145–54, 259–68.
[155] J. H. Newman to H. J. Rose, 23 May 1836, *Letters and Diaries*, vol. v, pp. 301–2. Even in the *Lectures on the Prophetical Office*, p. 11, Newman questioned whether the Church had not forfeited her juridical rights by the deprivations of 1689, the establishment of Presbyterianism in Scotland in 1707 and the silencing of Convocation in 1717. In an echo of earlier Nonconformist rhetoric, he even conceded the possibility 'that King William and his party did but complete what King Henry began'. See n. 174.
[156] J. H. Newman to E. B. Pusey, 24 January 1836, *ibid.*, p. 214.

THE OLD HIGH CHURCHMEN AND ESTABLISHMENT, 1833–45: THE REACTION TO TRACTARIANISM

Rose considered Newman's censures of establishment to be alarmingly indiscriminate. If William III as a Presbyterian might have merited criticism, Rose objected to Newman's railing at Archbishop Wake's 'Revolution-Protestantism'. Newman was reminded that Wake had been a High Churchman as well as a Whig and no mere Erastian.[157]

Against the emergence of Tractarian anti-establishmentism, old High Churchmen restated the Caroline ideal. To refute Froude's Hildebrandine notions of the 'ecclesiastic power' as 'an absolute independent commonwealth, able to make laws by itself', William Sewell offered the contrary testimony of the Church's seventeenth-century divines who did not 'hold up Becket to reverence, or allow him to be a martyr'.[158] Old High Churchmen, while not denying the gravity of the changes of 1828–33, questioned whether these justified Tractarian theorists in foregoing 'the vantage-ground of the Establishment, and, in common with the Dissenters, to adopt the cry of religious freedom'.[159] Sewell insisted the the Church of England by 1842 was 'in no worse position with respect to the state, than she had been in either the Elizabethan or Hanoverian eras'.[160] The Hookerian theory was more than a rationalisation of a common identity between church and commonwealth which no longer pertained. For the younger Christopher Wordsworth, there was no 'greater historical mistake than to entertain such an idea. Do we suggest that there were no Romanists in Parliament in Hooker's days?'[161] The

---

[157] H. J. Rose to J. H. Newman, 13 May 1836, *ibid.*, p. 302. The Revolution of 1688 remained a source of contention among High Churchmen in the 1840s. Edward Churton cautioned William Gresley on the subject: 'those who submitted to the change of Government [in 1688], having no share in the guilt of the Revolution, acted on the old principles. I wish you therefore to speak with more moderation on this doubtful question'. PH, Gresley Papers, GRES 3/7/57, E. Churton to W. Gresley, 17 November 1845.

[158] [W. Sewell], 'Divines of the Seventeenth Century', *Quarterly Review*, 69 (March, 1842), 500–1. Churton likewise objected to Tractarian writers who claimed Becket as 'a Holy Martyr'. For Churton, Becket was 'a man who died in defence of a false principle, excommunicating a man for what cannot be pretended to have been an offence against the church'. PH, Gresley Papers, GRES 4/1/1, E. Churton to F. E. Paget, 24 January 1846.

[159] *Scottish Ecclesiastical Journal*, 1, 21 (September 16, 1851), 195.

[160] [Sewell], 'Divines of the Seventeenth Century', 499. Similarly, Churton considered the Church of England to have been in greater Erastian thraldom 'in the times of Clarke, Hoadly and Queen Caroline'. BL, Gladstone Papers, Ms Add 44370, fol. 309, E. Churton to W. E. Gladstone, 19 September 1851.

[161] *Scottish Ecclesiastical Journal*, 1, 21 (September 16, 1851), 195.

changes of 1828–33 offered no more of an excuse for the radical reshaping of the constitutional theory of church and state envisaged by the Tractarians, than had any of the no less profound political changes of the seventeenth century. Moreover, the Tractarians were criticised for misrepresenting Hooker's true principles. Wordsworth appealed to both Hooker and Burke against the Tractarian notion drawn from the later Nonjurors that church and state were two distinct societies only accidentally brought into a condition of union, and in favour of the contrary notion that they represented an organically unified single entity.[162]

Old High Churchmen also faulted Tractarian views of establishment on practical grounds. For instance, while Gladstone's book was without any conscious anti-Tractarian intent, its priorities presented a contrast to the Tractarian approach. It might be said of Froude, Newman and even the later Keble, that they were almost prepared to alienate the nation, so long as they could induce the church of their day to become the church of their Hildebrandine or Ambrosian dream. Their viewpoint was entirely intrinsic to the church. They evinced a reluctance to consider the church's role and mission in relation to the nation at large. In contrast, Gladstone viewed church–state relations from the wider national perspective and on grounds of moral necessity and religious obligation. In consequence, Gladstone was arguably better able to meet the dual challenge of the anti-establishmentism of political Dissent and of the schemes of religious comprehension advocated by Thomas Arnold, on their own terms. Thus, in response to the first stirrings of Tractarian anti-establishmentism, Gladstone rhetorically asked his friend Manning in 1835, 'what however are the interests of the church, which are supposed to be thus injured and corrupted by union with the state? An institution can scarcely be said to be capable of an interest, distinct from that attaching to its members'. On the other hand, once individual members were made the prime object of consideration, Gladstone argued that the real interests of the church were best fulfilled by the state connection. It was lamented that many members of the established church were only nominal adherents, but this did not invalidate the church's wider duty to minister

[162] LPL, Wordsworth Papers, Ms 2149, fol. 342, C. Wordsworth (Sen.) to C. Wordsworth (Jun.), 30 August 1845. Low Churchmen also echoed this point. As early as 1836 one critic argued that the Oxford leaders had 'secretly discovered Hooker's doctrines [on church and state] to be dangerous, though it is willing to shelter under his name still'. *State of Parties in Oxford*, p. 16.

to the whole nation – the grand principle of Hooker's theory. As Gladstone put it,

The truth is we do injustice to our arguments in permitting the Establishment to be judged on the same ground as a sect. That it contains more persons not inwardly religious is nothing to her discredit, if they are persons who but for her would be divested of any feeling of regard to a God, and prospectively of every appointed ... and hopeful means, of being brought within the true fold.[163]

To advocate disestablishment would be to cut off many from possible means of salvation. This would be the real 'national apostasy'.

Even from a perspective intrinsic to the Church, disestablishment could be presented as a desecration of the state which High Churchmen had always invested with a quasi-sanctity. As one establishment apologist reminded Tractarian critics, in accord with Hooker's classic theory, 'the state was the representative not only of the grand body of the nation, but of the laity of the church: because the nation had a faith, and of their faith the church was the visible exhibition, the witness and the guardian'.[164] This was the vital principle which Burke had upheld in the 1790s, and was but restated by the young Gladstone, when he insisted that 'the state is a person, having a conscience, cognisant of matters of religion, and bound by all constitutional and actual means to advance it'.[165]

The younger 'Zs' urged on their Tractarian friends the continued value of establishment. Rose admitted 'the mischiefs' that resulted from the union, but was insistent that these were outweighed by the advantages.[166] Establishment rendered the church better able to fulfil her spiritual duties. Significantly, the examples of the non-established American and Scottish episcopal churches, so frequently appealed to by Tractarians as a model to strive for, were invoked to prove the old High Church case. In the 1820s, the Hackney divines

---

163 BL, Gladstone Papers, Ms Add 44683, fol. 5, W. E. Gladstone to H. E. Manning, 5 April 1835.

164 G. E. Biber, *The Royal Supremacy over the Church, Considered as to Its Origin, and Its Constitutional Limits* (London, 1848), p. 144. George Edward Biber (1801–74). From Ludwigsburg, Germany, and educated at Tübingen University. Settled in England and naturalised, 1826; renounced the Lutheran Church for the Church of England, 1839; curate of Ham, 1842; Vicar of Roehampton, 1842. The author of many articles in Palmer of Worcester's *English Review* between 1844 and 1852. *DNB*.

165 M. E. Maltby, 'Living with Establishment and Disestablishment in Nineteenth-Century Anglo-America', *Journal of Church and State*, 18, 1 (Winter, 1976), 66–7.

166 PH, Pusey Papers, LBV [Transcripts], H. J. Rose to A. P. Perceval, 9 April 1836; Palmer, *Treatise on the Church of Christ*, vol. II, p. 361.

had almost fallen out with their friend, the American bishop John Henry Hobart, after the latter's strictures on the church–state system in England.[167] Hugh James Rose in the *Christian Remembrancer* defended Hobart from the criticisms of the *Quarterly Theological Review*,[168] but even Rose disagreed with Hobart's anti-establishmentism.[169] At a much later date, Joshua Watson could refer disparagingly to 'the pseudo anti-Erastianism of America'.[170] Hook, Samuel Wilberforce and even the younger Keble shared this perspective, in spite of their sympathies with the American and Scottish churches.[171] For the practical weaknesses they detected in those non-established churches proved in their eyes the value of establishment. As Hook explained,

The American churchman is apt, in his nationality, to exaggerate these evils [of establishment], overlooking the various advantages of such a union, both to the country and to the church, by the creation of a kind of religious atmosphere, and entirely blinding his eyes to the still greater disadvantages of his own system. The very circumstance that the churchmen of America are obliged to seek for subscriptions in England for the establishment of a library to be attached to their Theological Seminary at New York, is quite sufficient to show the inadequacy of the voluntary system.[172]

The theological rationale for separation of church and state was also suspect in the view of old High Churchmen. They questioned whether orthodoxy or discipline was thereby better preserved. On the contrary, the American and Scottish churches had 'scarcely any better discipline than our own'.[173] As Edward Churton observed to

167 J. H. Hobart, *The United States of America Compared with Some European Countries, Particularly England; in a Discourse Delivered in the City of New York, October 1825* (London, 1826), pp. 19–35. On Hackney support for the American church, see G. Best, 'Church Parties and Charities: the Experiences of Three American Visitors to England 1823–1824', *EHR*, 78 (April, 1963), 243–67.

168 *Quarterly Theological Review*, 7 (June, 1826), 14–21.

169 *Christian Remembrancer*, 8 (July, 1826), 543–50; Bodl. Lib, Norris Papers, Ms Eng Lett c. 789, fol. 151, H. J. Rose to H. H. Norris, 4 November 1826; Burgon, *Lives of Twelve Good Men*, vol. I, p. 333; Churton, *Memoir of Joshua Watson*, vol. I, pp. 245–60.

170 Mary Watson, Ms 'Reminiscences' (in private possession, Torquay) fol. 348, J. Watson to C. Wordsworth (Jun.), 7 September 1852.

171 For Hook's support of the Scottish episcopal church, see W. F. Hook, *The Peculiar Character of the Church of England Independently of Its Connection with the State. A Sermon Preached at the Primary Visitation of the Bishop of Winchester in the Church of Newport, Isle of Wight ... 1822* (London, 1822), p. 10.

172 [W. F. Hook], 'Preface', in J. McVickar, ed., *The Early and Professional Years of Bishop Hobart* (London, 1838), p. iii; Faussett, *Alliance of Church and State*, p. 11; [S. Wilberforce], 'Ecclesiastical History of the United States', *British Critic*, 20 (October, 1836), 272.

173 PH, Pusey Papers, LBV [Transcripts], E. Churton to E. B. Pusey, 26 May 1843.

William Copeland in 1840 in response to the latter's equation of establishment and heresy,

With regard to your remarks of the bad practices in the Church 'in consequence of its establishment', you must know, my dear Non-Juror, that ... the most dangerous errors of the day do not proceed from our being too much under state-laws. What have the state-laws to do with the principles advocated in the 'Record' and the 'Christian Observer'? The religion of Ultra-Protestantism is essentially a religion against all ordinances, whether of Pope, Prelate or Caesar, and the man who adopts it calls history an old almanac, and writes the year of his own conversion or first formation of a system as the year one of Christianity. It is not the result of an Establishment, but pride of reason and spiritual wickedness and rebellion.[174]

For the Hackney leaders, the example of the later Nonjuring attitudes to establishment with which Keble came to identify, far from validating the Tractarian brand of anti-establishmentism, presented a dangerous precedent of schism and marginalisation. Norris's foreboding was that, as in the case of the last Nonjurors, anti-establishmentism merely as a habit of mind would induce a sectarian spirit.[175] By the middle of the century, many old High Churchmen, viewing the later history of the Oxford Movement, felt that Norris had been proved right.[176]

HIGH CHURCHMANSHIP AND THE CRISIS OF CHURCH AND STATE, 1845–51

The Maynooth Affair, 1845–6

By 1845, the question dividing High Churchmen was whether to oppose the government's secularising policy by, on the one hand reasserting the Church of England's constitutional claims as they

---

174 SC, Churton Papers, E. Churton to W. J. Copeland, 30 May 1843. Churton's greeting 'dear Non-Juror', was a playful reference to Copeland's sympathies. Although it was Copeland's Hackney mentors, Thomas Sikes and Joshua Watson as well as Dr Hamilton of University College, Oxford, who first introduced him to the works of the Nonjuror, George Hickes, Copeland drew different conclusions from the history of the Nonjurors from that drawn by the Phalanx leaders. Copeland compared the position taken by Sancroft and Ken with 'the protest of Athanasius and a handful of Catholics against the Arianising Emperor Constantius' in the fourth century. [Copeland], 'Account of the Non-Jurors', *British Critic* (January, 1837), 51. See also ch. 2, n. 73–5, and Broxap, *Later Nonjurors*, ch. 9.

175 PH, Copeland Papers, H. H. Norris to W. J. Copeland, 7 February 1839. On the history of the Nonjuring papers temporarily in Norris's possession at this date, see ch. 2, n. 75.

176 SC, Churton Papers, E. Churton to W. J. Copeland, 27 September 1859.

were prior to 1828, or, on the other hand, by arguing that the state's duties to the church were individual and that a restriction of those duties might be a price worth paying for the church's freedom. The former view was upheld by the Hackney remnant, including the Wordsworths; the latter represented the position of the Tractarian rump and of detached allies such as Manning.[177] Gladstone emerged as a spectacular convert to the latter's camp during the Maynooth affair. This crisis surfaced in February 1845 when Peel announced 'a liberal increase of the vote for the College of Maynooth', a Roman Catholic seminary near Dublin, which had first received a government grant in 1795. The increase in the grant was effected without making 'any regulations in respect of the doctrines and discipline of the Church and Rome'.

As John Wolffe has shown, Peel's measure was the occasion for an explosion of anti-Catholic protest spearheaded by Anglican Evangelicals and Protestant Dissenters.[178] There was also a parallel, but distinct, conservative High Church reaction, mentioned by Wolffe but not always given as much emphasis in standard accounts which focused on constitutional implications.

The conservative High Church backlash was directed more at the rationale of support adopted by Gladstone and other High Churchmen, not all Tractarian, than against the grant itself. Gladstone fully recognised that his support contradicted the principle of Anglican confessionalism which he had espoused in his book in 1838, and accordingly resigned from Peel's government. Like many of the Tractarians, Gladstone now conceded the principle of a confessional state in the hope of securing 'church liberties'. For Gladstone in 1845, as for Newman ten years earlier, the shift was aided by a conviction that 'the state has ... cut the ground from under its own feet'.[179] But for Gladstone there was also a new ingredient, the liberal principle of 'social justice' which squared even less easily with the Protestant constitutionalist tradition in High Churchmanship.

Many old High Churchmen regarded Gladstone and supporters of the grant as betraying the principles of the anti-Peelites of 1829 around which the future Tractarians had first rallied. For Palmer of

---

[177] BL, Wordsworth Papers, Ms 1822, fols. 147–8, H. E. Manning to C. Wordsworth (Sen.), 7 August 1845.

[178] J. Wolffe, *The Protestant Crusade in Great Britain, 1829–1860* (Oxford, 1991), ch. 6.

[179] BL, Gladstone Papers, Ms Add 44375, fol. 41, 'Autobiographica', 19 June 1843; W. E. Gladstone to J. H. Newman, 19 April 1845, D. C. Lathbury, ed., *Correspondence on Church and Religion of William Ewart Gladstone* (London, 1910), p. 72.

Worcester, the Maynooth question was 'almost precisely parallel in its features to that of 1829; and the conduct of the Ministry and its conservative supporters deserves precisely the same praise or blame as that of Sir Robert Peel in 1829'.[180] It was not denied that the Church had since been the victim of many 'acts of ill-informed and unscrupulous or erastianising politicians', but Gladstone, like the Tractarians, had drawn the wrong conclusion when insisting 'that our constitution in church and state is radically at fault'.[181]

According to its old High Church critics, supporters of Maynooth overlooked the crucial difference between mere civil toleration conceded as early as 1688 and active recognition or even encouragement of what, from a Church of England perspective, must be deemed theological error. It was because the text or basis of establishment for such old High Churchmen was doctrinal truth and not political convenience, that support for the measure appeared tantamount not only to religious 'indifferentism', but also an 'endowment of schism'.[182] Moveover, there were potential political and social dangers inherent in such a constitutional acceptance of the principle of religious pluralism. As the younger Christopher Wordsworth put it,

unity in true religion being the great conservative principle of a Commonwealth, and civil discord and disquiet being the natural consequences of religious dissension, it is certain that when a nation is passing from the Toleration or various forms of religious belief to the Encouragement of them, its civil rulers have great cause for alarm.[183]

Old High Churchmen even drew a parallel between their opposition to the Maynooth grant in 1845, and the principle of opposition by High Churchmen and Tractarians to the Whig suppression of Irish bishoprics in 1833. For the younger Wordsworth, both measures were equally Erastian and acts of political expediency, so that logic determined that the later measure be opposed on precisely

---

180 LPL, Wordsworth Papers, Ms 2143, fol. 141, W. Palmer to C. Wordsworth (Jun.), 22 April 1845.
181 *Scottish Ecclesiastical Journal*, 1, 3 (20 March 1851), 47.
182 C. Wordsworth (Jun.), *Church Principles and Church Measures: a Letter to Lord John Manners, M.P. with Remarks on a Work Entitled, 'Past and Present Policy towards Ireland'* (London, 1845), pp. 21-2; C. Wordsworth (Jun.), *A Review of the Maynooth Bill, Showing Its Fatal Tendencies and of the Debates on the First and Second Reading; with a Proposal for the Conciliation of Contending Parties in Ireland* (London, 1845), p. 131.
183 [C. Wordsworth (Jun.)], *Maynooth, the Crown and the Country* (London, 1845), p. 3; J. H. Overton and E. Wordsworth, *Christopher Wordsworth, Bishop of Lincoln, 1807-1885* (London, 1888), p. 113.

the same grounds as the former.[184] It was the Tractarian and High Church supporters of Maynooth who had forfeited consistency.

The tragedy for old High Churchmen was that for the first time a division opened up within their own ranks on the church–state question. To the dismay of the Wordsworths, Palmer, Sewell and other High Church opponents of Maynooth, some of their ideological allies such as Hook, Churton and John Miller ranged themselves in Gladstone's camp.[185] For instance, Churton was critical of Palmer for leaning 'too much to that very weak principle of making the Church an appendage of the Conservative party'. Churton could respect the old constitutional principle of opposition to the Maynooth grant,

but, seeing that such a view does not enter into the heads of a tenth part of those who are opposing this grant, I am obliged to ask what is likely to be the result if their petitioning is successful. And I really see nothing but a strong levelling Dissenting interest at work, which may as easily be directed against the Establishment, as they call it, at some future time, as it is now against Maynooth.[186]

In provoking such tensions within High Churchmanship, the Maynooth crisis opened a new chapter in the history of the debate over establishment in the Church of England.

The Gorham Crisis, 1847–51: the final denouement

The new note of disillusionment with establishment among a section of the old High Churchmen, which the Maynooth crisis revealed, was further exacerbated by subsequent concern over government educational policy and notably by the elevation of R. D. Hampden to the episcopate in 1847.[187] The vigorous episcopal protest against the appointment was spearheaded by bishops of a conservative High Church disposition. Moreover, the issue of the church's right to

---

184 C. Wordsworth (Jun.), *Church Principles and Church Measures*, p. 29; LPL, Wordsworth Papers, Ms 2143, fols. 139–41, W. Palmer to C. Wordsworth (Sen.), 22 April 1845.
185 LPL, Wordsworth Papers, Ms 2143, fol. 157, W. Palmer to C. Wordsworth (Jun.), 16 May 1845; BL, Gladstone Papers, Ms Add 44213, fols. 71–2, W. F. Hook to W. E. Gladstone, 15 April 1845; PH, Gresley Papers, GRES 3/7/51, E. Churton to W. Gresley, 22 April 1845.
186 PH, Gresley Papers, GRES 3/7/51, E. Churton to W. Gresley, 22 April 1845.
187 See Manning's comment: 'This Hampden affair is a grave one, involving the highest relations of the Church and the Civil Power and the most vital principles of the Church. Of all the questions I can remember it is the most decisive'. Bodl. Lib, Ms Wilberforce, D. 62, H. E. Manning to S. Wilberforce, 27 December 1847.

choose her own bishops was canvassed in this quarter in a way that would have been unthinkable a few years earlier. The subsequent controversy over Lord John Russell's Jewish Disabilities bill in 1847 tended to restore divisions on to the old fault-lines of 'liberal Catholic' versus 'Protestant constitutionalist'.[188] However, the constitutional implications of the notorious Gorham Judgment in 1850 produced an even greater blurring of old ideological demarcation lines than that thrown up by Maynooth.

As is well known, the Gorham crisis was provoked by Bishop Phillpotts's refusal in 1847 to institute the Evangelical George Cornelius Gorham to the living of Brampford Speke in his Exeter diocese, on account of what Phillpotts regarded as Gorham's denial of the doctrine of baptismal regeneration. The case went to the Court of Arches which decided against Gorham's claim that denial of the doctrine was not inconsistent with holding a living in the Church of England. On appeal, the Judicial Committee of the Privy Council reversed this decision.

It was the constitutional as well as theological implications of the Judgment which troubled High Churchmen of all shades. It was not simply the anomaly of the church being invested with the 'latitude' to countenance what for High Churchmen was theological error that provoked concern. The preamble to the Judgment made clear that the Committee regarded themselves as making only legal and not theological pronouncements. However, it was the contrary perception of High Churchmen that theological pronouncements were indeed being made by a court whose legal validity to do so they disputed, that turned the affair into a crisis.

Old High Churchmen and Tractarians in 1850 were at one in their alarm at the idea of a point of doctrine having been apparently settled by a court which represented the civil power. Both agreed that this was an Erastian affront to the Church of England. Where division arose was in the very divergent theories offered as to the extent to which the Church was thus compromised; a division that

---

[188] James Hope made a classic assertion of the 'liberal catholic' position: 'On the Jewish question, my bigotry makes me liberal. To symbolise the Christianity of the House of Commons in its present form is to substitute a new Church and Creed for the old Catholic one, and as this is a delusion, I would do nothing to countenance it'. BL, Gladstone Papers, Ms. Add 44214, fols. 322–3, J. R. Hope to W. E. Gladstone, 9 December 1847. For Charles Wordsworth, this was 'the sort of argument which was used to justify the publication of Mr. Froude's *Remains* - men were to be startled into orthodoxy'. *Scottish Ecclesiastical Journal*, 1, 21 (16 September, 1851), 193.

was to be exacerbated by the clash of rival historical interpretations of the Church's relations with the civil power in an ultimate attempt to settle the validity of the hated Judgment.

After the abolition of the Roman jurisdiction in 1530–4, doctrinal cases had originally been tried by the Court of Delegates, which contained a preponderance of bishops and ecclesiastical lawyers. During the course of the eighteenth century this episcopal element was gradually lost. In 1832, jurisdiction was transferred to the Privy Council. An Act of 1840 then allowed bishops who were privy councillors to sit, if cases were of an ecclesiastical nature. No distinction was drawn between doctrinal and other ecclesiastical matters. As Chadwick has observed, the consequence of this subtle but crucial legal change was that,

it removed the final appeal from a court where the judges, even when junior and inexperienced, were trained in the canon and civil law; and transferred it to a court where some of the judges, though vastly more eminent, were less accustomed to the system of ecclesiastical courts.[189]

In 1832, the significance of the measure was lost on all parties. It was only the Gorham Judgment that forced churchmen to focus on the consequences of what had been then settled, and to take sides accordingly.

For most old High Churchmen and many moderate Tractarians, the Gorham Judgment represented an unacceptable constitutional innovation amounting to a usurpation of the church's inherent spiritual office, but it did not touch or compromise the church's spiritual essence. As Benjamin Harrison put it, 'the present Court of Appeal ... was at variance with the ancient exercise of the Royal Supremacy in the Church of England'.[190] Alarming as was the situation in which the Church of England suddenly found itself placed, it was insisted that there were legitimate constitutional remedies at hand to correct what was but a dangerous 'anomaly'. Thus, George Biber argued,

Nothing more is required than an Act of Parliament, empowering the Crown to nominate, independently of the political administration, a privy council for ecclesiastical purposes, whose business it shall be to advise the

---

189 O. Chadwick, *The Victorian Church*, 2 vols. (London, 1966), vol. 1, p. 258.
190 BL, Gladstone Papers, Ms Add 44248, fol. 39, B. Harrison to W. E. Gladstone, 12 July 1850.

Crown in the exercise of the royal supremacy in convoking church synods, in directing their action, and sanctioning their decrees.[191]

It was maintained that such a council must consist only of communicant members of the Church of England, and should include clergy and bishops.

Old High Church apologetic in the crisis defended the integrity of English Reformation statute law on which the traditional constitutional edifice supporting Hooker's and the pre-1828 church–state theory was based.[192] Pusey and Keble, for all their sense of the practical abuses of establishment, now ranged themselves with old High Churchmen in insisting that the Reformation statutes had never intended the state to act as a judge in matters of Christian doctrine, and that the Church's doctrine remained exactly as it was before. It was only the Act of 1832 that had introduced an entirely new constitutional arrangement by, albeit unintentionally, placing the settlement of doctrinal questions in the hands of a final Court of Appeal which had in fact been constituted for quite other purposes, and to which the church had never assented.[193] Like the old High Churchmen, Pusey maintained that the Reformation had introduced no novelty in the model of church–state relations which he found in antiquity. He insisted that 'what Henry VIII and Queen Elizabeth claimed, and what eminent lawyers have affirmed to be conceded, and what the Church meant to concede, was no other than the ancient prerogative of the Crown, which had been invaded, it was alleged, by the authority claimed by the Pope'.[194] There could be no clearer evidence that for Pusey, the Hildebrandine ideal of Hurrell Froude had no appeal.

To complete the realignment, Gladstone also took his stand with the conservative churchmen on this issue. For Gladstone, it was merely the latter-day illegitimate extension of state interference after 1832 that needed to be checked. Far from being unsettled as to

---

[191] Biber, *The Royal Supremacy*, pp. 277–8.

[192] For example, see F. Vincent, *On the Jurisdiction of the Crown in Matters Spiritual. A Letter to the Rev. H. E. Manning ... in Reply to His Letter to the Lord Bishop of Chichester on the Above Subject* (London, 1851).

[193] F. C. Massingberd, *The Policy of the Church of Rome Promoted by the Abuse of the Royal Supremacy, and the Remedy in Convocation: a Letter to the Rev. Dr. Jeremie* (London, 1852), p. 21.
  Francis Massingberd (1800–72). Rector of South Ormsby, Lincs, 1825-d; Chancellor of Lincoln diocese, 1868-d. Moderate High Church divine and friend of Edward Churton. *DNB*; W. J. Baker, 'F. C. Massingberd: Historian in a Lincolnshire Parish', *Lincolnshire History and Archaeology*, 1 (1968), 3–10.

[194] Pusey, *Royal Supremacy*, p. 162.

the original constitutional basis of the Church, Gladstone's respect
for the pre-1832 constitutional system was more evident than it had
been in 1845 when he made his stand on Maynooth. As he told
Manning in April 1850, 'after the ordeal of this particular time ... I
feel better pleased with the Reformation in regard to the Supremacy
than I did at former times: but also more sensible of the drifting of
the Church since, away from the range of constitutional securities'.[195]

In 1850–1, however, there was another body of High Churchmen
for whom the Gorham Judgment finally revealed the *ab initio* Erastian nature of the church-settlement as bequeathed by the Reformation statutes. For them, regardless of the degree of actual lay composition, the lay status of the Court of Appeal meant that it derived
'its power from the civil authority and from her alone'.[196] In short,
the Judgment destroyed the whole basis of their allegiance, theological and historical, to the Church of England, and would prove a
direct cause of their ultimate secession to the Church of Rome.

It would be misleading to class this group of High Churchmen as
Romanisers or even Tractarian. Some, such as Allies, Dodsworth,
James Hope and Robert Wilberforce, were very advanced High
Churchmen deserving the Tractarian label, but the position of
others such as Manning remained rather more ambivalent. Some of
the group, notably William Maskell, while difficult to categorise,
had had more theological affinity hitherto with old High Churchmen than Tractarians such as Newman and Pusey, and were resolutely anti-Romanist. Maskell perhaps was closest to his mentor
Bishop Phillpotts, whose domestic chaplain he had been, and on
whose assistance Phillpotts had relied in his examination of Gorham.[197] To Phillpotts's dismay, however, his friend and supporter
parted company as the Gorham crisis unfolded.

The collapse of Maskell's faith in the Church of England in 1850
was to be very sudden. It was almost entirely a consequence of a
dawning conviction that the Gorham Judgment, regardless of the
doctrinal issue at stake, far from representing some unprecedented
usurpation of the Church of England's guaranteed spiritual rights,

[195] BL, Gladstone Papers, Ms Add 44248, fol. 39, W. E. Gladstone to H. E. Manning, 29
April 1850; W. E. Gladstone, *Remarks on the Royal Supremacy as It Is Defined by Reason, History
and the Constitution. A Letter to the Lord Bishop of London* (London, 1850), pp. 14, 22.
[196] W. Dodsworth, *The Gorham Case Briefly Considered. In Reference to the Judgment Which Has
Been Given, and to the Jurisdiction of the Court* (London, 1850), pp. 26–7.
[197] See G. C. B. Davies, *Henry Phillpotts, 1778–1869* (London, 1954), p. 232.

actually pointed to the fact that ultimate jurisdiction in spiritual matters had always lain with the crown ever since the Reformation. Thus, the Gorham appeal had been no different in principle from all other previous appeals in matters ecclesiastical. For Maskell, the Judicial Committee was 'nothing more than the necessary organ of the Royal Supremacy as established by the statutes of Henry VIII and Elizabeth'.[198] In contrast to the assumption of High Churchmen on the other side, Maskell actually came to agree with Evangelical supporters of Gorham's cause, such as William Goode, that the Privy Council, as the legitimate representative of the Queen, had been the appropriate arbiter of the Gorham case.[199] In short, the Erastianism of 1850 was no different in kind from the Erastianism of 1530 as well as 1688.

The allegiance of Maskell, Hope and Manning to the Church of England had been grounded on the assumption that the Royal Supremacy was purely civil in its bearing.[200] As a result of the Gorham crisis they concluded that in practice the Royal Supremacy extended to theological matters. This struck at the root of their Anglican allegiance. A mere return to the pre-1832 'constitutional securities' offered no solution. Maskell argued that, even on the old constitutional principles, the state had had no obligation even to consult the Church when it abolished the Court of Delegates and set up the Judicial Committee in 1832. Maskell cited the ready compliance of the then predominantly High Church bishops appointed to sit in the Court, as evidence that old High Churchmen had fully concurred in the measure and had not envisaged that the Judicial Committee would ever become a forum for the settlement of

---

198 See W. Maskell, *A First Letter on the Present Position of the High Church Party in the Church of England* (London, 1850), pp. 9–24; W. Maskell, *The Present Position of the High-Church Party in the Church of England Considered in a Review of the 'Civil Power in Its Relations with the Church' and in Two Letters on the Royal Supremacy and the Want of Dogmatic Teaching in the Reformed Church* (London, 1869), pp. 27–56. James Hope took the same view. See R. Ornsby, *Memoirs of James Robert Hope-Scott*, 2 vols. (London, 1884), vol. II, p. 83; Bodl. Lib, Manning Papers, MS Eng Lett c. 657, fols. 56–64, J. R. Hope to H. E. Manning, 19 January 1850.

199 Maskell, *First Letter*, p. 9; W. Maskell, *Protestant Ritualists* (London, 1872), pp. 14–15.

200 WSCRO, Wilberforce Papers, H. E. Manning to S. Wilberforce, 24 January 1850. Manning's Anglican allegiance had been gradually undermined from the end of 1845. This was partly the result of his reading of the sixteenth-century Spanish theologian Melchior Cano's *De Locis Theologicis*. Thus, for Manning, the Gorham Judgment helped put the seal on a process of disenchantment with Anglican church–state theory which had been germinating for some time. See J. Pereiro, 'Truth before peace: Manning and infallibility', *Recusant History*, 22 (October, 1992), 218–53.

potential doctrinal disputes.[201] For Maskell and Manning, the only solution in 1850 was a return to the pre-1530 Common Law relating to the church.[202] Yet this in itself would invalidate, as Maskell intended it should, the whole constitutional basis of the post-Reformation Church of England.

Robert Wilberforce and Manning were prepared to sign a declaration attempting to distinguish between 'the Royal Supremacy intended by the Articles and Canons of the Church' which they could still accept, and a 'Royal Supremacy as defined and established by statute law'.[203] The logic of Maskell's argument that the civil power had always been envisaged as supreme in all matters spiritual, soon overcame Manning's residual belief in a limited Royal Supremacy. Wilberforce took much longer to reach this position. For a time, he took refuge in the view that under the Tudors and Stuarts even the submission of the spiritual to civil power could be justified because then 'the Church seemed to come before the world as a living body'. It was only in modern times when the 'sovereign is a parliamentary sovereign, and Parliament represents a divided nation', that such a submission had become untenable.[204] Moreover, Wilberforce still maintained that the undoubted civil supremacy in 'spiritual causes' had not extended to doctrinal matters. Wilberforce argued that it was precisely because, prior to the rise of Tractarianism, doctrinal division in the Church had been so limited, that so little scrutiny had been made in 1832 as to the appropriateness of a lay court for presiding over ecclesiastical cases.[205] Robert Wilberforce's brother Henry moved more quickly to the position taken up by Maskell and Manning. For Henry Wilberforce, as for Maskell, the Gorham case was as damaging in its constitutional as in its doctrinal consequences. He was convinced

---

[201] Maskell, *Present Position of the High-Church Party* (1869), p. 22.

[202] BL, Gladstone Papers, Ms Add 44248, fol. 59, H. E. Manning to W. E. Gladstone, 19 June 1850.

[203] Newsome, *Parting of Friends*, pp. 352–3.

[204] R. I. Wilberforce, *An Inquiry into the Principles of Church Authority or, Reasons for Recalling My Subscription to the Royal Supremacy* (London, 1854), p. 279; R. I. Wilberforce, *A Sketch of the History of Erastianism* (London, 1851), pp. 59–61. As late as 1848, Robert Wilberforce had characterised the Caroline theory as 'the highest and holiest view of human society'. R. I. Wilberforce, *Reflections on Church and State: a Charge to the Clergy of the Archdeaconry of the East Riding, Delivered at the Ordinary Visitation, A.D. 1848* (London, 1848), p. 21.

[205] Gladstone also took this view: 'Not bringing heresy into question, nor dealing with morals, it is no wonder that for the scarcely spiritual, scarcely ecclesiastical causes which were the common business of the Court of Appeal, they [churchman] thought less and less of the spiritual element in its composition'. Gladstone, *Royal Supremacy*, p. 80.

that even if the Judgment had gone in favour of High Churchmen, grave implications would still have occurred. As Henry Wilberforce explained, 'if the Church allows such a question to be decided either way by such a Court she will be taking to herself another instead of her only true Spouse'.[206]

The extent of the ideological disarray among High Churchmen on constitutional questions which the Gorham controversy provoked, is illustrated by the way in which some such as Palmer of Worcester who had taken a conservative stand over Maynooth, were driven into taking up almost an anti-establishment position. On the basic issue dividing the two sides, Palmer was with Pusey and Gladstone, not Maskell or Manning. He had never doubted that the Royal Supremacy had had an ecclesiastical bearing and remained insistent that whatever false gloss might be put on the bearings of that Supremacy this could not forfeit the Church of England's claim to apostolical ministry.[207] On the other hand, for Palmer and for Hook, the Gorham crisis meant that relations between church and state could never be the same again. In private correspondence, Palmer began to use language almost reminiscent of the early Tractarian 'agitators' which he had once deplored. Thus, he complained of 'a fixed resolution to Latitudinarise the Church' on the part of the state, and attacked the bishops for being 'fearfully under the influence of the state'. In a striking echo of Froude's and Newman's private sentiments in 1833, Palmer was indignant at the apparent episcopal reluctance to make a stand over Gorham while, 'we, who even mutter protest do so under the feeling that we are considered as agitators and we know that we are acting in opposition to the wishes of our superiors'. If the bishops were so reluctant to act in such a case, Palmer observed, 'how infinitely more so would they be to take any steps such as are really necessary for the purpose of giving liberty to the Church of England'.[208] Like the Tractarian 'agitators' in 1833, Palmer recommended 'a stand for the liberties of the Church' so as to force the bishops' hands. For Palmer, the logic of the Gorham case was that the Royal Supremacy could no longer be defended on historical grounds. As he complained to Gladstone, 'men are now arguing about the Royal Supremacy as if the crown

[206] LPL, Mill Papers, Ms 1494, fol. 25, H. W. Wilberforce to W. H. Mill, 23 January 1850.
[207] BL, Gladstone Papers, Ms Add 44369, fol. 251, W. Palmer [of Worcester] to W. E. Gladstone, 7 June 1850.
[208] BL, Gladstone Papers, Ms Add 44369, fol. 149, W. Palmer to W. E. Gladstone, 16 April 1850.

were now in the same state, or its powers were influenced by the same religious beliefs, as in the time of Elizabeth or James'.[209] Thus there could be no mere return to the pre-Reform situation as he had previously advocated, but only a restoration of that 'liberty enjoyed by the Church before the Reformation and the liberty enjoyed by the establishment in Scotland'.[210] Similarly, in the wake of the Gorham affair, G. A. Denison, a Tory High Churchman not hitherto identified with the Tractarians, began to urge churchmen in and out of parliament to abandon 'the delusion that the relations of the church to the state and of the state to the church, remain such as they were before'. Denison concluded from the Gorham case that the position of the Church of England could no longer be 'strengthened, or as much as maintained by Act of Parliament'.[211]

The Gorham controversy cast old High Churchmen adrift into conflicting responses and a new era of constitutional uncertainty in a way which even the crisis of 1828–33 had failed to do. While some, such as Maskell and Manning, were provoked into abandoning Anglicanism, it was not Tractarianism that was the trigger for this move; rather, it was a decision based on their own individual assessment of the implications of the Gorham Judgment for themselves.

On the other hand, even Palmer of Worcester's somewhat analogous reaction to the crisis was not in itself evidence of belated Tractarianism. Nor was Phillpotts's own new-found anti-establishmentism an index of Tractarian bias in the way Gorham suggested. Nevertheless, it is an indication of Phillpotts's shift away from his earlier Protestant constitutionalist rhetoric that in 1847 he should condemn Gorham for holding a 'low view' of the Church's spiritual prerogatives purely on the evidence of Gorham's use of the expression, 'national Establishment'. For, as Gorham conclusively showed, such a phrase had in an earlier generation been 'one of common

---

209 BL, Gladstone Papers, Ms Add 44369, fols. 251–2, W. Palmer to W. E. Gladstone, 7 June 1850. Churton also espoused this line. See E. Churton, *The Church's Claim to Self-Government: a Charge Delivered to the Clergy of the Archdeaconry of Cleveland at the Ordinary Visitation, A.D. 1851* (London, 1851), p. 18.

210 BL, Gladstone Papers, Ms Add 44369, fol. 152, W. Palmer to W. E. Gladstone, 16 April 1850; f. 162, W. Palmer to W. E. Gladstone, 19 April 1850. Palmer even was prepared to contemplate the hitherto unthinkable: 'I cannot help fearing that the time may come, when the Church of England may stand distinguished from the Established Church – if there be an Established Church'. LPL, Mill Papers, Ms 1491, fol. 47, W. Palmer to W. H. Mill, 22 April 1850.

211 G. A. Denison, *Why Should the Bishops Continue to Sit in the House of Lords?* (2nd edn, London, 1851), p. 36.

usage by the soundest churchmen' and a favourite expression of 'a
High-Churchman, Archdeacon Daubeny' and of 'even bigotted
churchmen' such as 'Dr Marsh, then Margaret Professor of Divinity'.[212] In fact, in his own apologetic for the Protestant constitution in the early decades of the century, Phillpotts himself had
employed precisely such language. Contemporaries, including
Newman, noted the apparent change in Phillpotts.[213] One Nonconformist writer later even described Phillpotts 'as a renegade from
political Protestantism to the side of the reaction Romewards'.[214] In
reality, the difference between the earlier and later Phillpotts represented only development, modification and a new tone in response
to altered external circumstances rather than any sudden ideological volte-face. For once the *ancien régime* in church and state had
been overturned, it was much easier for churchmen of all shades to
transcend party politics and for certain intrinsic features of High
Churchmanship to reveal themselves more fully. Prior to that time,
the attitude of the High Churchman Alexander Knox, with his
insistence 'I am a churchman in grain – not a Tory churchman, for
that is a disease in the church, not its constitutional turn',[215]
remained untypical.

As the above Nonconformist writer put it, after 1832 royal support
was 'seen to fail' so that Phillpotts 'and others of his school began to
look out for a fresh support for the tottering Church Establishment.
They sought it in church principles, and where they sought for it
they found it'.[216] There is a certain truth in this. But the writer
overlooked the extent to which Phillpotts and others such as Horsley
and Van Mildert had been able to combine *jure divino* church
principles alongside their Protestant constitutionalist rhetoric. They
would have repudiated Alexander Knox's distinction which the
later Tractarians echoed, between a 'Tory churchman' and a
'primitive churchman' as unreal. For, as Mather has concluded, no
one believed more firmly than Horsley in the principle of a Prot-

[212] G. C. Gorham, ed., *An Examination before Admission to a Benefice by the Bishop of Exeter Followed by Refusal to Institute on the Allegation of Unsound Doctrine Respecting the Efficacy of Baptism* (London, 1848), pp. 21–2.
[213] See Newman's reference to the 'sensation' caused by Phillpotts's sermonising additions to his Visitation Charge in the Exeter diocese in 1836. Newman concluded that Phillpotts 'has quite thrown off the political ground'. J. H. Newman to F. Rogers, 7 January 1837, Mozley, ed., *Letters and Correspondence of Newman*, vol. I, p. 222.
[214] J. B. Heard, *National Christianity or Caesarism or Clericalism* (London, 1877), pp. 231–2.
[215] J. J. Hornby, ed., *Remains of Alexander Knox*, 4 vols. (London, 1834–7), vol. IV, p. 26.
[216] Heard, *National Christianity, or Caesarism or Clericalism* pp. 231–2.

estant establishment and church–state union as a single entity under the crown, but there was also no more eloquent advocate of the Church's independent spiritual authority.[217] Likewise, Van Mildert appealed to both sources of authority in his own powerful defence of the church's 'ancient basis' in the 1820s and early 1830s.[218] It was only when the legislative props of establishment had been undermined after 1832 that anything like a contradiction between the two began to be perceived.

Phillpotts, like Palmer of Worcester, had not become a Tractarian,[219] but the church–state crisis and the various episodes of theological controversy in the 1830s and 1840s had left an indelible mark on the character of the churchmanship of both. In short, the Gorham crisis finally brought to a head the fact that after twenty years of constitutional turmoil in church and state the option of 'fleeing to the mountains' had ceased to be an exclusively Tractarian shibboleth.

Moreover, the anti-establishmentism of the Tractarians was essentially a tactical weapon. It became pronounced only at times of particular crisis in church and state, as in 1833, 1847 and 1850–1. Ironically, from the 1850s onwards, it was Pusey who often upheld against Gladstone the advantages of the constitutional *status quo*. Pusey opposed, as resolutely as the old High Churchmen, the transition from what he called 'the Catholic to the infidel idea of the state'. Ultimately, the dynamic concept of church authority in Tractarian thought fostered a concern to preserve a residual spiritual character to the state. The state's claim to sovereignty was a challenge to be overcome, rather than conceded by the church's retreat to the margins of society.[220]

---

[217] Mather, *Horsley*, p. 309.   [218] Varley, *Van Mildert*, pp. 198–9.
[219] J. A. Thurmer, 'Henry of Exeter and the Later Tractarians', *Southern History*, 5 (1983), 210–20.
[220] C. K. Gloyn, *The Church in the Social Order: a Study of Anglican Social Theory from Coleridge to Maurice* (Forest Grove, Oregon), pp. 54–8.

CHAPTER 2

Antiquity and the rule of faith

THE PRE-TRACTARIAN HIGH CHURCH LEGACY, 1760–1833

One facet of the High Church tradition on which the Tractarians drew was an appeal to the teaching of the primitive church exemplified in the writings of the early Fathers. High Churchmen did not deny that Holy Scripture, in the words of Article 6, 'contained all things necessary unto salvation', and that it was entirely sufficient as the rule or basis of faith. High Churchmen tended to argue that Scripture needed to be understood in the light of antiquity, properly understood. The documents of early Councils and the writings of the Fathers were generally regarded reverentially as testimonies to the 'Faith once delivered unto the Saints'. In the classic Caroline divinity which embodied this approach, the rule for interpreting Scripture was deemed to consist in a consent of early Fathers and of those Councils of the early church considered truly ecumenical. This entailed an appeal to the authoritative teaching of the universal church of the first four centuries of Christian history. The principle of this appeal had been first formulated by the fifth-century Vincent of Lerins in his *Commonitorium*. It was enshrined in the Vincentian Canon, 'quod semper, quod ubique, et quod ab omnibus'. Catholic truth could be ascertained not merely by reference to the letter of the Bible alone but by what in the early church had been taught always, everywhere, and by all.

The Tractarian appeal to antiquity gave an appearance of continuity between the Oxford Movement and the seventeenth-century divines.[1] As the *catenae patrum* of exponents of the Vincentian rule

[1] On the role of Tradition in seventeenth-century Anglicanism, see McAdoo, *Spirit of Anglicanism*; H. Chadwick, 'Tradition, Fathers and Councils', in Sykes and Booty, eds., *Study of Anglicanism*, pp. 91–105; S. L. Greenslade, 'The Authority of the Tradition of the Early Church in Early Anglican Thought' and G. V. Bennett, 'Patristic Tradition in Anglican

compiled by Manning in *Tract 78* testified, on this question the Tractarians were following in the footsteps of the Caroline and Nonjuring divines. On the other hand, the paucity of testimony drawn from the Georgian epoch was designed to throw the Tractarians into sharper focus as restorers of 'the study of sound theology in an unlearned age'. The Tractarians felt that, apart from a few exceptions such as Martin Routh and Charles Lloyd,[2] the 'ultra-Protestant' principle of the unqualified right of private judgment had become the standard theological method in Anglican apologetic over the previous century.

There was a decline in deference to antiquity among Hanoverian divines compared with their seventeenth-century predecessors. Within the 'latitude men' themselves, a shift of emphasis can be detected between the respect for the Fathers evinced by Simon Patrick and Edward Stillingfleet on the one hand, and the disparaging tone adopted by Hoadly and Richard Watson on the other.[3] Nevertheless Georgian Anglicanism continued to value the Fathers. The Roman Catholic controversialist, John Milner, at the turn of the century, insisted that what he called 'Hoadlyism' was not representative of the Church of England which 'so far from undervaluing the ancient Fathers, requires her clergy to consult their interpretation of the Scriptures in preaching to the people under pain of excommunication'.[4]

Numerous editions and commentaries on the Fathers poured from the university presses in the three or four decades prior to the rise of Tractarianism. Works by Daubeny, Cleaver, Van Mildert, John Jebb,[5]

Thought' – both in *Traditum in Luthertum und Anglikanismus*, [1972] *Oecumenica* (1971/2), 9–33; 72–87.

[2] Charles Lloyd (1784–1829). Regius Professor of Divinity, Oxford, 1821-d; Bishop of Oxford, 1827-d. *DNB*. On Lloyd's influence on the Tractarians, see F. Oakeley, *Historical Notes on the Tractarian Movement* (London, 1865), pp. 12–14; J. H. Philpot, *The Seceders, 1829–1869* (London, 1930), p. 15; W. J. Baker, *Beyond Port and Prejudice: Charles Lloyd of Oxford* (Maine, 1981), pp. 214–15.

[3] N. Sykes, *From Sheldon to Secker: Aspects of English Church History, 1660–1768* (London, 1959), p. 149.

[4] J. Milner, *Letters to a Prebendary ... With Remarks on the Opposition of Hoadlyism to the Doctrines of the Church of England* (London, 1802), p. 385.

[5] Francis Huyshe republished Jebb's *Peculiar Character* in 1839 under the title, *A Tract for All Times, But Most Eminently for the Present*. On the influence of the *Appendix* of Jebb's sermon on Newman's line in his controversy with the Abbé Jager in 1834–6, see C. Forster, *The Life of John Jebb D.D. F.R.S. Bishop of Limerick* (London, 1837), p. 187; L. Allen, *John Henry Newman and the Abbé Jager: a Controversy on Scripture and Tradition* (London, 1975), p. 5.

Routh,[6] Hawkins, Kaye and Edward Burton in this period, stood squarely within the Caroline tradition of theological method and patristic learning. A witness to this tradition was also provided by the lists of books recommended for ordination candidates by various bishops.[7] It was a tradition kept alive, within the University of Oxford, by the annual Bampton Lectures in which the value of patristic theology was a commonplace theme.[8]

The question of the relative value of the testimony of apostolical Tradition and the writings of the Fathers, did not divide the Orthodox and Evangelicals prior to 1833 in the way, or to the extent, that it would divide Tractarians and Evangelicals thereafter. On the contrary, the basis of the Trinitarian apologetic constructed by the High Church Samuel Horsley in his controversy with Joseph Priestley in the 1780s, with its emphasis on patristic testimony, provided a basis of common ground. For Horsley, it was axiomatic that the 'reasonableness of our faith will be best understood from the writings of the Fathers of the first three centuries'.[9] Moderate Evangelicals such as G. S. Faber infused their own defence of the Trinity and other fundamental doctrines such as the Atonement with an appeal to antiquity. Faber explicitly opposed a 'crude exercise of a naked and unformed private judgment'. Although dismissed as a 'Calvinist' by some of the Hackney divines, he was happy not only to cite Van Mildert's writings but also to dedicate his own defence of Trinitarianism to that staunch pre-Tractarian High Churchman.[10]

Many High Churchmen took issue with Evangelicals for championing private judgment and the principle of *sola scriptura*. But Evangelicals rebutted the charge of doctrinal 'indifferentism' raised by the Orthodox. Significantly, Bishop Jebb, notable for being able to bridge the Orthodox–Evangelical gap, detected the rise of a greater respect for ecclesiastical antiquity among Evangelicals in the

---

[6] Bishop Jebb ascribed to Routh's influence, 'a principal share in raising the love, and the spirit of Christian antiquity'. Bodl. Lib, Ms Eng Lett d. 123, fol. 70, Bishop J. Jebb to C. A. Ogilvie, 1 June 1832.

[7] For example, see W. Cleaver, *A List of Books Intended for the Use of the Younger Clergy and Other Students in Divinity, within the Diocese of Chester* (Oxford, 1791).

[8] Two examples of treatment of this theme included the Bampton Lectures by George Croft in 1786 and John Collinson in 1813.

George Croft (1747–1809). Clerical headmaster and leader of the High Church Party in Birmingham in the 1780s and 1790s. *DNB*.

[9] S. Horsley, *Tracts in Controversy with Dr Priestley* (London, 1789), p. 68.

[10] G. S. Faber, *The Apostolicity of Trinitarianism, or, the Testimony of History, to the Positive Antiquity and to the Apostolical Inculcation of the Doctrine of the Holy Trinity*, 2 vols. (London, 1832), vol. 1, pp. vi–vii.

wake of the earlier phase of the Bible Society controversy. For instance, in 1816 the Evangelical *Christian Observer* expressed qualified agreement with Jebb's *Appendix on Tradition* and conceded that 'the communion of the Church of England with the primitive church may have been too little insisted upon in late times'.[11] Citing other examples of the apparent trend, Jebb welcomed the emergence of what he called 'Catholic Evangelicalism' and by 1826, felt that what he called 'gymno-biblicism' was 'less in fashion than it was'.[12]

Nevertheless, even among the Orthodox there was no unanimity of attitude to Tradition and the rule of faith. On the one hand, the apologetic of High Churchmen such as Daubeny, Cleaver, Sikes and Van Mildert emphasised the Church of England's claim as an apostolic church to act as an authorised interpreter of Holy Scripture. While the Church of Rome was assailed for superseding the authority of Holy Scripture by 'setting up her own authority as an infallible guide', John Bowles argued that other, Protestant Christian bodies had erred no less in an opposite extreme with 'still more baneful consequences'.[13] In a direct allusion to the Unitarian movement of the 1770s and 1780s, Bowles insisted that the result of the advocacy of private judgment and *sola scriptura* had been 'more injurious to the interests of Christianity, than even the arrogant pretensions and daring usurpation of the Church of Rome'.[14] Yet, on the other hand, there were leading Orthodox apologists, notably George Pretyman-Tomline in his *Elements of Christian Theology* (1798) and Herbert Marsh in his *Comparative View* (1814), whose apparent repudiation of Tradition, Councils and Fathers even as a polemical weapon in controversy against the Church of Rome,[15] seemed more akin to the theological method of eighteenth-century latitudinarian divines. Behind the facade of Orthodox unanimity in the campaign against Evangelical patronage of the Bible Society, differences on the subject of the rule of faith surfaced. For example, Daubeny was privately critical of the soundness of both Pretyman-Tomline's and Marsh's approaches.[16] Marsh attacked Evangelical supporters of

---

[11] *Christian Observer*, 15, No. 175 (July, 1816), 420.
[12] Bp J. Jebb to A. Knox, 30 May 1826. C. Forster, ed., *Thirty Years' Correspondence between John Jebb D.D. and Alexander Knox Esq.*, 2 vols. (London, 1834), vol. II, pp. 539–40.
[13] [Bowles], *Claims of the Established Church*, p. 21.   [14] *Ibid.*, p. 24.
[15] H. Marsh, *A Comparative View of the Churches of England and Rome* (London, 1814), pp. 1–41, 60–75.
[16] Daubeny said of Bishop Pretyman-Tomline, after publication of his *Elements of Christian Theology*: 'the Bishop of Lincoln's orthodox and apostolical opinions have not long been

the Bible Society for allowing the Scriptures to be distributed without the Prayer Book and hence an authorised interpreter.[17] This seemed to put him at one with Daubeny, Norris and Sikes. But Daubeny was publicly critical of Marsh for deserting the high ground of apostolical authority in his critique of the Bible Society.[18] Moreover, other High Churchmen such as George Glover, who claimed Bishop Cleaver as his theological mentor, disputed with Marsh over his rejection of Tradition.[19] Citing an array of Caroline and later divines, Glover, like Edward Hawkins, in a striking anticipation of Tractarian teaching, even upheld the importance of oral tradition[20] as well as the Vincentian principle of Catholic consent.[21]

Nevertheless, the gulf between the two elements within the Orthodox camp should not be overestimated.[22] Marsh maintained that the Prayer Book was the Church's practical guide to Holy Scripture. His reason for advocating the distribution of the Prayer Book with the Bible was specifically to check false scriptural interpretations by the ignorant. 'Take away the Prayer Book' he insisted, 'and, though we remain Protestants, we become Dissenters'.[23]

---

formed ... if they are at present'. ESCRO, Locker-Lampson Papers, B/5/16, C. Daubeny to J. Boucher, 7 November 1800. Nonetheless, even Bishop Pretyman-Tomline made controversial use of patristic evidence. Almost half of his 600-page *Refutation of Calvinism* (1811) comprised 'quotations from the Fathers opposed to the tenets of Calvinism'.

[17] H. Marsh, *An Inquiry into the Consequences of Neglecting to Give the Prayer Book with the Bible* (2nd edn, London, 1812), p. 5.

[18] C. Daubeny, *Reasons for Supporting the S.P.C.K. in Preference to the New Bible Society. Partly Given in a Charge Delivered to the Clergy of the Archdeaconry of Sarum* (London, 1812), pp. 90–1.

[19] G. Glover, *Remarks on the Bishop of Peterborough's 'Comparative View of the Churches of England and Rome'* (London, 1821), especially p. 60 where ironically, given Marsh's frequent raising of the spectre of revived 'Puritanism', Glover accused Marsh of employing 'the language of Calvin, and of the Puritans in the worst ages of our civil anarchy'. Glover, a Fellow of Brasenose College, Oxford, was Chaplain to the Duke of Sussex. Glover's High Church standpoint owed much to the influence of the theological writings of the Principal of Brasenose, William Cleaver. Glover's criticisms of Marsh for a defective view of Tradition were shared by Alexander Knox. See Forster, ed., *Thirty Years' Correspondence*, vol. II, p. 125.

[20] Glover, *Remarks*, pp. 36–7, 53–4, 60; E. Hawkins, *A Dissertation upon the Use and Importance of Unauthoritative Tradition as an Introduction to the Christian Doctrines* (Oxford, 1819), p. 32. For Marsh's explicit rejection of oral Tradition, see *Comparative View*, p. 68.

[21] Glover, *Remarks*, p. 49; Forster, ed., *Thirty Years' Correspondence*, vol. II, p. 125; J. H. Pott, *Grounds and Principles of the Church of England Considered in a Charge Delivered to the Clergy of the Archdeaconry of London* (London, 1824), pp. 17–18. For Marsh's rejection of the principle of Catholic Consent, see *An Inquiry into the Consequences of Neglecting to Give the Prayer Book with the Bible*, p. 20.

[22] R. Braine, 'Life and Writings of Herbert Marsh', pp. 204–5, 232, 236, 241. Braine overlooks qualifications to his apparently bald rejection of Tradition which Marsh introduced into an appendix to the second edition of his *Comparative View*, and also, in contrast to Pretyman-Tomline, Marsh's eulogies of Laud.

[23] Marsh, *Comparative View* (2nd edn, London, 1816), pp. 286–7.

Moreover, the strictly polemical context of Marsh's apparent repudiation of Tradition should be noticed.[24] In his polemic against the
Bible Society, Marsh had been charged with supporting a popish
principle, not only by a Roman Catholic controversialist, Peter
Gandolphy, but by an Orthodox Anglican divine, Thomas Burgess,
Bishop of St David's.[25] In reaction, Marsh may have been provoked
into appearing more antagonistic to Tradition than he really was. In
fact, Marsh did accept at least a subordinate role for an ecclesiastical
tradita of rites and ceremonies.[26] Moreover, he criticised Burgess for
supporting the Bible Society. Marsh made clear that the very title of
Burgess's *The Bible, and Nothing But the Bible, the Religion of the Church
of England*, was 'a very injudicious one. For it contains a proposition,
which is not only false in one sense, though true in another, but is
false in that sense, in which it is more likely to be understood and
applied.'[27] Furthermore even Van Mildert, who took a higher view
of Tradition, could commend Marsh's *Comparative View*.[28]

The Orthodox case against Dissent and its supposedly Evangelical allies in the 1810s revealed theological variations in attitudes to
antiquity and the rule of faith. But the substance of Orthodox
apologetic against the Church of Rome and Protestant Dissent
remained unimpaired.

THE TRACTARIANS AND ANTIQUITY

The Tractarian appeal to antiquity and the Fathers was not altogether the 'rediscovery' presented in later historiography. Tractarian rhetoric would seek to capitalise on the link with a select few
precursors such as Bishop Jebb, Routh,[29] Lloyd, Kaye[30] and even
Edward Hawkins. In fact, Hawkins's *Noetic* friends, Whately and
Arnold, were alarmed at the propaganda use which the Tractarians

---

[24] Varley, *Van Mildert*, pp. 58–9.
[25] T. Burgess, *A Charge Delivered to the Clergy of the Diocese of St. David's in the Month of September 1813* (Durham, 1813), pp. 26–8.
[26] Philodike, *Strictures on the Rev. G. Glover's 'Remarks on the Comparative View of Churches of England and Rome by Dr Herbert Marsh Lord Bishop of Peterborough'* (London, 1821), pp. 57, 62–3.
[27] Marsh, *Comparative View*, 2nd edn, p. 287. Marsh taunted Burgess (p. 288): 'surely a Bishop should not forget, that the rejection of the Prayer Book in the time of Charles I, was the very thing, which overturned the Church'.
[28] Varley, *Van Mildert*, p. 58.
[29] Newman dedicated his *Lectures on the Prophetical Office* to Routh.
[30] On Kaye's credentials as a patristic scholar, see Knight, 'John Kaye and the Diocese of Lincoln', ch. 1.

in the 1830s made of Hawkins's sermon *The Use and Importance of Unauthoritative Tradition* (1819). Arnold even felt that Hawkins's sermon had 'contributed to their mischief'.[31] After Keble's sermon extolling oral Tradition in 1836, Hawkins decided to follow Arnold's advice and to rewrite *Unauthoritative Tradition*.[32] The result was a new sermon, *The Duty of Private Judgment* (1838) and a series of Bampton Lectures in 1840 which, to the dismay of some Tractarians,[33] subtly modified the original argument.[34] Nevertheless, Newman in particular had been strongly influenced by Hawkins's 1819 sermon.[35] It was to that sermon and to the writings of Bishop Kaye that Newman appealed for the notion of a *disciplina arcani* or secret tradition within the bosom of the church which he expounded in his controversial *Arians of the Fourth Century* (1833),[36] though Kaye himself and other old High Churchmen repudiated the gloss which Newman put on their arguments.[37] In *Tract 85* Newman even appealed to Hawkins's sermon in his use of the *argumentum ad hominem* to justify doctrines such as the Trinity on the authority of Tradition alone because they were not explicitly enshrined in the letter of Holy Scripture. He directly echoed Hawkins's argument that 'the more fundamental the doctrine ... the more likely would it be rather implied than directly taught in the writings of the Apostles'.[38]

Certainly, there was nothing exceptionable in the Tractarian plan for a *Library of the Fathers* first formulated in 1836. Even moderate Evangelicals such as Edward Bickersteth lent their support. It was Bickersteth who actually encouraged Pusey to compose an intro-

31 T. Arnold to R. Whately, 4 May 1836, Stanley, *Life and Correspondence of Thomas Arnold*, vol. II, p. 34.
32 OCA, Hawkins Papers, Letterbook III, no. 218, E. Hawkins to R. Whately, 11 September 1836. For Edward Hawkins (1793–1882), Provost of Oriel College, Oxford, 1827-d, see *DNB*; J. W. Burgon, 'Edward Hawkins: The Great Provost', *Lives of Twelve Good Men*, vol. I, pp. 374–465.
33 OCA, Hawkins Papers, Letterbook VIII, no. 762, J. Keble to E. Hawkins, 26 July 1840.
34 E. Hawkins, *The Duty of Private Judgment: A Sermon Preached before the University of Oxford, November 11, 1838* (Oxford, 1838).
35 Newman, *Apologia*, pp. 65–6. For discussion of the nature of the influence, see L. Bouyer, *Newman: His Life and Spirituality* (London, 1958), p. 63; G. Biemer, *Newman on Tradition* (London, 1964), pp. 33–42.
36 J. H. Newman, *Arians of the Fourth Century* (London, 1833), pp. 147–9. See Newman's comment to Rose: 'I have no reason to change about it [i.e. *disciplina arcani*] – and ... the Bishop of Lincoln grants that Clement holds it.' J. H. Newman to H. J. Rose, 15 December 1836, *Letters and Diaries*, vol. V, p. 178.
37 R. Williams, 'Newman's *Arians* and the Question of Method in Doctrinal History', in I. Ker and A. G. Hill, eds., *Newman after a Hundred Years* (Oxford, 1990), p. 272.
38 [J. H. Newman], 'Lectures on the Scripture Proofs of the Doctrines of the Church', *Tract 85*, pp. 4–5. Cf. Hawkins, *Dissertation*, p. 64.

ductory address refuting eighteenth-century 'ultra-Protestant' disparagers of patristic testimony.[39] Here was a consensus on which the
Tractarians could have built. They chose not to. They had their own
agenda.

In the nature of their appeal to antiquity, the Tractarians were
not passive legatees of the Orthodox inheritance. That inheritance
might be a sound theological foundation, but was it enough? As
Newman made clear, the underlying Tractarian aim was to 'harmonise' and even 'complete' as well as 'catalogue' or 'sort' the 'vast
inheritance' of 'our treasures'.[40] At first, it was enough to display a
selection of the treasures and to pick and choose as circumstances
dictated. Thus, in *Tract 78*, the selection of extracts in the *catenae
patrum*, adducing testimonies to the Vincentian rule, by no means
accorded with one another. There was no differentiation. The point
of the extracts was to give historical support in a general way to the
Tractarian call for the contemporary Church of England to follow
antiquity. Yet it was to be a call which, for all the appearance of
similarity, would prove to be essentially different in method and
direction from that of the mainstream High Church tradition.

As T. M. Parker has demonstrated, Newman did not merely
rediscover the Fathers within 'the seventeenth-century tradition'.
Prior to 1834, when he embarked on his famous debate on Tradition
with the Roman Catholic Abbé Jager, Newman only had a 'nodding
acquaintance' with the Caroline Divines. His interest in patristic
theology had developed at a much earlier date.[41] H. D. Weidner has
questioned this view, pointing out that as early as 1828 Newman had
become thoroughly acquainted with the works of Pearson, Ussher
and Hooker. An early source of Newman's familiarity with the
Caroline Divines had been the Orthodox Bishop Mant's 1820 edition
of the Book of Common Prayer.[42] While such evidence might prove
that Newman's interest in the Fathers and the Carolines did not
develop separately as Parker suggests, the latter's conclusion – that
Newman did not approach or study the Fathers through the medium
or eyes of the Caroline Divines – remains intact.

[39] Liddon, *Life of Pusey*, vol. I, p. 435.
[40] Newman, *Lectures on the Prophetical Office*, p. 30.
[41] T. M. Parker, 'The Rediscovery of the Fathers in the Seventeenth-Century Anglican Tradition', in J. Coulson and A. M. Allchin, eds., *The Rediscovery of Newman* (London, 1967), pp. 41–5.
[42] H. D. Weidner, ed., *The Via Media of the Anglican Church by John Henry Newman* (Oxford, 1990), pp. xxi–xxv.

Parker's view squares with the opinion of Edwin Abbott. Abbott insisted that Newman's ambiguous later declaration that he read the Fathers 'through the eyes of' the Caroline Divines, was only one of his 'many self-deceptions'.[43] Certainly, Abbott tended to put the most hostile construction possible on any of Newman's statements. Nevertheless in the *Apologia* Newman provided credence for Abbott's argument when he conceded that when he came to read the Carolines, 'the doctrine of 1833 was strengthened in me, not changed'.[44]

The source of Newman's introduction to the Fathers and the history of the early church lay not in the Caroline Divines but as early as 1816, in his reading of the Evangelical Joseph Milner's *History of the Church of Christ*.[45] The seeds of Newman's divergence of approach to antiquity from that of the Caroline Divines and old High Churchmen lay precisely here. For while Newman's construct of the *via media* aimed to be a reassertion of the Caroline principle of vindicating the Church of England on the basis of antiquity, his view of antiquity was always coloured by the way in which his own historical imagination had been captivated by Milner's vivid portrait of the 'age of the martyrs'. As Stephen Thomas argues, like Milner, but unlike his Caroline mentors such as Bishop Bull, Newman responded to antiquity, 'not by the attempted extinguishment of his personal perspective, but existentially, imaginatively, and polemically'.[46]

An imaginative identification with antiquity, inspired by Milner's account, was partly evident in Newman's *Arians* but was more apparent in the highly coloured passages in his *Letters on the Church of the Fathers* relating to the popular election of St Ambrose as Bishop of Milan in the fourth century.[47] Newman's portrayal of the church of Ambrosian Milan had a polemical purpose. He appealed to antiquity not primarily for testimony to a particular disputed doctrine as had Mant, Kaye or Burton, 'as if the Church were some fossil remains of antediluvian era',[48] but in order to provide the model of a

43 Abbott, *Anglican Career of Cardinal Newman*, vol. II, pp. 329–30.
44 Newman, *Apologia*, p. 121.
45 *Ibid.*, p. 62.   46 Thomas, *Newman and Heresy*, p. 46.
47 See [J. H. Newman], 'Letters on the Church of the Fathers', *British Magazine*, 7 (June, 1835), 662–8; 8, (July–September 1835), 41–8, 158–65, 277–84.
48 [J. H. Newman], 'Burton's History of the Christian Church', *British Critic*, 20 (July, 1836), 211.

    Edward Burton (1794–1836). Regius Professor of Divinity, Oxford, 1827–d; Bampton Lecturer, 1828. *DNB*.

living church that could be reproduced in the nineteenth century. Yet there was a tension in Newman between on the one hand the need to prove himself a sound Anglican, and on the other hand his growing conviction that the Fathers went beyond Anglican teaching.

In the *Arians*, Newman himself adopted something of the same methodology which he criticised in divines such as Kaye and Burton. As Tom Mozley recalled, 'all the Fathers and all the Church Councils were to be marshalled in Anglican order and costume, and marched before us as we sat at our firesides'. But this approach was not natural to Newman, and Mozley suggested that 'possibly the iron, indeed the very rust of it, entered into Newman's soul'.[49] Certainly he eschewed it elsewhere. For Newman, Burton was 'better acquainted with the writings of Christian antiquity as historical records, or depositaries of facts, or again in their bearing upon one or two important modern questions, than in themselves, in their great fundamental principles, and their peculiar character and spirit, or what is sometimes called their ethos'.[50] Old High Churchmen, in Newman's eyes, for all their patristic learning and orientation, had a defective appreciation of the *ethos* or moral and spiritual character of the early church. The theological implications of this divergence in approach would be profound.

ANTIQUITY DISPUTED: THE OLD HIGH CHURCH AND TRACTARIAN THEOLOGICAL DIVERGENCE

A contrast between an essentially conservative High Church theory of Tradition and a more dynamic Tractarian theory was evident by the late 1830s.[51] Pre-Tractarian High Churchmen valued the Fathers primarily because their witness followed immediately after the period of Revelation. The early Fathers were deemed more likely to know the apostles' views of scriptural truth, and their real meaning, than modern commentators. In apologetic against Socinianism, Unitarianism, Protestant Dissent and Roman Catholicism, patristic witness had especial relevance as a means of vindicating

---

[49] Mozley, *Reminiscences Chiefly of Oriel College and the Oxford Movement*, vol. II, p. 400.
[50] [Newman], 'Burton's History of the Christian Church', 210.
[51] O. Chadwick, *The Mind of the Oxford Movement* (London, 1960), p. 39.

orthodoxy.[52] For the Tractarians, however, this was merely the starting-point. In their hands, antiquity became an absolute standard and final court of appeal, rather than as with most old High Churchmen, merely a corroborative testimony to the truth of the Church of England's formularies and the teaching of her standard divines. For Newman, the attempt of old High Church divines such as Kaye and Mant to force antiquity into an arbitrary conformity with 'modern' notions of scriptural truth, as enshrined in the Thirty-Nine Articles and other formularies, was misconceived and represented the exact opposite of the method he would come to employ in *Tract 90.* 'Whatever ... be the true way of interpreting the Fathers', he later observed, 'if a man begins by summoning them before him, instead of betaking himself to them, by seeking to make them evidence for modern dogmas, instead of throwing his mind upon the text ... he will to a certainty miss their sense.' Newman likened the presumption of such Orthodox divines in thus seeking to measure the Fathers by modern formulae, to an attempt 'to criticise Gothic architecture by the proportions of Italian'.[53]

For old High Churchmen, the appeal to antiquity could not supersede that which the Reformers and seventeenth-century divines had already made and which had been enshrined in the Church's authorised formularies. The guiding principle of their approach remained the distinction between fundamentals and non-fundamentals in doctrine and worship. As Van Mildert explained, Holy Scripture was 'the only Rule of Faith: and whatever benefit may be derived from other writings, reporting to us, as apostolical traditions, additional matters illustrative of our faith and worship; to them is to be assigned no more than a secondary rank, as being subsidiary, not essential to our Creed'.[54] Old High Churchmen such

---

[52] The emphasis was on a 'sober, rational estimate' of the writings of the Fathers. See F. Collinson, *A Key to the Writings of the Principal Fathers of the Christian Church, Who Flourished During the First Three Centuries. In Eight Sermons Preached before the University of Oxford, in the Year MDCCCXIII, At the Lecture Founded by the Late Rev. John Bampton* (Oxford, 1813), pp. 25–64.

[53] *British Critic,* 25 (January, 1839), 54.

[54] W. Van Mildert, *An Inquiry into the General Principles of Scripture-Interpretation. Considered in Eight Sermons Preached before the University of Oxford in the Year MDCCCXV, At the Lecture Founded by the late Rev. John Bampton, M.A.* (Oxford, 1815), p. 174. Van Mildert's approach drew heavily upon Waterland's 'Use and Value of Ecclesiastical Antiquity with Respect to Controversies of Faith'. See W. Van Mildert, ed., *The Works of Daniel Waterland ... To Which Is Prefixed a Review of the Author's Life and Writings, by William Van Mildert, D.D., Lord Bishop of Llandaff,* 10 vols. (Oxford, 1823), vol. v, ch. 7. The theological affinity between the two divines was highlighted by Van Mildert's editing of the ten-volume edition of

as Palmer of Worcester and William Sewell distinguished between matters of faith which could not be denied, and other doctrines which, though held by many, could only remain matters of opinion and of lesser importance. In the manner of Waterland, Palmer insisted that, apart from the necessity of an apostolical ministry, 'fundamentals' were limited to the Church's credal definitions as established by catholic consent. Palmer concluded, 'with reference to the doctrines actually supported by such judgments of the Universal Church ... it may be observed that they are by no means numerous, extending little beyond the Nicene Faith, the right doctrine of the Trinity, Incarnation and grace'.[55] On the other hand, from the dawn of the Movement, the Tractarians exhibited an impatience with such restrictions. They were privately critical of what they identified as 'the school of Waterland, from Waterland to Van Mildert' for a 'timid and apologetic tone when discussing the use and value of ecclesiastical antiquity',[56] even while Newman conceded that it was 'a more respectable school' than that of Hoadly.[57]

Initially, as in his controversy with the Abbé Jager in 1834–6, Newman had adhered to the notion of fundamental articles. Ironically in view of their later respective positions, in the Jager controversy in 1835 Newman's ally Benjamin Harrison criticised him for 'ultra-Protestantism' in his emphasis on 'fundamentals'.[58]

Waterland's works. See G. Best, 'The Mind and Times of William Van Mildert', *Journal of Theological Studies*, NS 14, (1963), 366. Cf. Varley, *Van Mildert*, p. 105. Waterland was also one of Joshua Watson's favourite divines, and 'in his opinion, one of the safest guides'. M. Watson, Ms 'Reminiscences', fol. 274.

55 Palmer, *Treatise on the Church of Christ*, vol. ii, p. 125. Yet there is an apparent ambivalence in Palmer's position on this question. According to Stephen Sykes, Palmer regarded 'fundamentals' as 'an ambiguous term ... conveying no definite notion', and drew attention to the internal inconsistency of the term in the works of Chillingworth, Laud and Waterland. S. Sykes, 'Fundamentals of Christianity', Sykes and Booty, eds., *Study of Anglicanism*, p. 241. See n. 58.

56 Liddon, *Life of Pusey*, vol. i, p. 413.

57 'Much might be said on the school of Waterland as well as of Hoadly, if you had time to read for it; a more respectable school, but inferior to that of the 17th century ... If you thought it worth while to read for it, I should gladly give you any hints which have struck myself. It was a favourite subject of dear Froude's.' Newman also stated that Froude 'said Waterland was the first and Van Mildert the last of the school'. J. H. Newman to R. I. Wilberforce, 25 September 1836, *Letters and Diaries*, vol. v, p. 363. See Froude's comment: 'I want a history of the Waterland school from Waterland to Van Mildert'. [Newman and Keble, eds.], *Remains of Richard Hurrell Froude*, vol. i, p. 434. See also Newman's rather disparaging reference to Edward Burton as a divine of 'the school of Waterland' which had 'succeeded to that of Bull' and had 'hitherto gone by the designation of high churchmen'. [Newman], 'Burton's History of the Christian Church', 211.

58 Allen, *John Henry Newman and the Abbé Jager*, pp. 158, 173; Sykes, 'The Fundamentals of Christianity', Sykes and Booty, eds., *Study of Anglicanism* , pp. 240–1. Ironically, given later

Nevertheless, as Stephen Thomas shows, there was ambiguity and a shifting quality in Newman's definition of what constituted fundamental articles.[59] For a time, his definition appeared to be still narrower than Palmer's, and he even suggested in his review of Palmer's *Treatise* that the latter over-extended its scope.[60] This was an example of Newman's ability to throw dust in the eyes of his readers.

Newman's adherence to the principle of fundamentals was only a temporary position provoked by the Jager controversy. Newman remained capable of using conservative rhetoric, insisting in his *Lectures on the Prophetical Office* that 'the "Rule of Faith"' was 'sole, unalterable, unreformable', the Church's duty merely being to transmit and not to remodel the faith.[61] Yet as he expounded the *via media* in those *Lectures*, he appears to have reacted against the static version of fundamentals being restricted to a few credal articles, and came to invest a whole range of doctrines and practices with a degree of dogmatic authority that ignored the distinctions on which old High Churchmen and he himself had earlier insisted. For Newman's introduction of the concept of a 'Prophetical Tradition' encompassing the doctrine of the first five centuries of the undivided church, in effect vastly widened the scope of what he regarded as matters 'of faith' and blurred any antithesis between essentials and non-essentials.[62] In the wake of the *Lectures*, even Newman's Tractarian friend, Samuel Wood, complained to Manning that Newman wished 'not merely to refer us to Antiquity, but to shut us up in it'.[63]

Newman's impatience with what he regarded as the selective view of antiquity common to the old High Church school increasingly surfaced in private correspondence. Thus in 1839, he confessed to his sister Jemima,

the question of the Fathers is getting more and more anxious. For certain persons will not find in them just what they expected. People seem to have

perceptions, Newman actually regarded Palmer's view of fundamentals as 'the first real nearing to Romanism which has in principle been made'. J. H. Newman to G. D. Ryder, [30 November] 1838, *Letters and Diaries*, vol. VI, p. 352. On the differences between Palmer's and Newman's views on faith and unity, see also n. 121; ch. 3, ns. 129, 130.

59 Thomas, *Newman and Heresy*, pp. 186–202.
60 [J. H. Newman], 'Palmer's Treatise on the Church of Christ', *British Critic*, 24 (October, 1838), 367–8. In contrast, see Froude's comment on the notion of 'fundamentals': 'I nauseate the word.' [Newman and Keble, eds], *Remains of Richard Hurrell Froude*, vol. I, p. 415.
61 Newman, *Lectures on the Prophetical Office*, pp. 297–300.
62 Thomas, *Newman and Heresy*, pp. 195–8.
63 Bodl. Lib, Manning Papers, Ms Eng Lett c. 654, fol. 447, S. F. Wood to H. E. Manning, 29 January 1836. Samuel Wood, barrister and one-time pupil of Newman at Oriel, has been described as one of that 'supporting cast of secondary figures' in the Oxford Movement 'which have remained in relative darkness'. J. Pereiro, 'S. F. Wood and an early theory of Development', *Recusant History*, 21 (1991), 524.

thought they contained nothing but the doctrines of baptismal Regeneration, Apostolical Succession, canonicity of Scriptures and the like. Hence many have embraced the appeal to them with this view. Now they are beginning to be undeceived.[64]

This drift in Newman's approach away from the old High Church method had by 1836, begun to alarm Hugh James Rose. Rose was disturbed by the underlying thrust of Newman's articles in the *British Magazine*. For Rose, Newman 'seemed to have killed Protestantism, and to have raised up on the other side an imposing figure of a church of Antiquity which many of his readers would identify with Rome'.[65] Rose spelled out his forebodings in a series of candid letters to Newman in May 1836. In one letter, he confided,

I am a little apprehensive of the effects of turning ... readers ... out to grass in the spacious pastures of Antiquity without very strict tether. All that is in Antiquity is not good; and much that was good for Antiquity would not be good for us ... I wish ... that Antiquity should be studied ... only with full, clear and explicit directions how to derive from it that good which is to be derived from it, and to avoid the ... quackery of affecting Antiquity.[66]

While old High Churchmen were content with a rearguard defence of their Orthodox inheritance, Newman and his followers were striving to supplement that inheritance, if not actually to create a new patristic norm for orthodoxy. Noting this divergence, Rose maintained that,

in any possible incursions into Antiquity, we are not like our own Reformers, looking for Truth and not knowing what will break upon us. We know exactly what the Truth is. We are going on no voyage of discovery. We know exactly the extent of the shore. There is a creek here, and a bay there, – all laid down in the charts; but not often entered or re-surveyed. We know all this beforehand, and therefore can lay down our plans, and not, (as I think), feel any uncertainty where we are going, or feel it necessary or advisable to spread our sails, and take our chance of finding a new Atlantis.[67]

Rose's plea fell on deaf ears. Newman had set sail on a voyage of discovery that ultimately would bring him to new shores.

Old High Churchmen accused Newman of countenancing a new

[64] J. H. Newman to Mrs J. Mozley, 17 November 1839, Mozley, ed., *Letters and Correspondence of Newman*, vol. II, p. 292.
[65] See Rose's candid letter of criticism to Newman dated 13 May 1836, reproduced in Burgon, *Lives of Twelve Good Men*, vol. I, pp. 214–20.
[66] H. J. Rose to J. H. Newman, 9 May 1836, *ibid.*, p. 210.
[67] H. J. Rose to J. H. Newman, 13 May 1836, *ibid.*, p. 219.

form of private judgment. On taking over the *British Critic* in 1838, Newman had confided to Churton, 'we think we have a notion of what is Catholic, if we can find to what it leads'. Much later, Churton confessed that this 'letter of his effectually kept me from writing a line in the "British Critic" afterwards. It is not for us to judge of the Church of England by our private notions of what is Catholic.'[68] Against such criticism, the Tractarians always sought to shelter behind the apparent authority provided by a Canon of 1571. This Canon enshrined the principle that preachers were to conform their teaching to 'the Catholic Fathers and Ancient Bishops'. Old High Churchmen insisted that the Tractarians claimed more latitude in their resort to antiquity on the basis of this Canon than was consistent with loyalty to the Church's formularies. They cited Waterland's and Van Mildert's careful definitions of the sense in which that Canon was to be understood.[69] The principle to be observed, they urged, was that, 'we should start with our formularies; we should suppose that they are right, and in studying the Fathers, take them for our guide, upon the ground that they are based on the decision, not of one learned or pious person, but of many'.[70] Moreover, old High Churchmen maintained the importance of deferring not only to a written authority enshrined in the formularies but to a living authority inherent in the episcopate. As William Sewell put it,

I do think it more than ever necessary to maintain that our access to the ancient church must be through the channel of our own English Church, and under the control of living rulers, as well as written rules. Our vitality must indeed be drawn from Apostolical sources, but only as the leaf is nourished from the root by adhering firmly to the branch on which it is growing.[71]

The contrast that emerged between Tractarian theoretical exaltation of episcopal authority and practical defiance of that same authority would give substance to Sewell's warning.

---

68 PH, Pusey Papers, LBV [Transcripts], E. Churton to E. B. Pusey, 23 January 1847; R. W. Jelf, *The Via Media: or the Church of England Our Providential Path between Romanism and Dissent* (Oxford, 1842), p. 37.
69 Van Mildert, ed., *Works of Daniel Waterland*, vol. v, pp. 317–18. Pusey justified his reception of prayers for the dead by recourse to the Canon of 1571. PH, Pusey Papers, LBV [Transcripts], E. B. Pusey to W. F. Hook, 8 November 1846.
70 W. F. Hook, *The Three Reformations: Lutheran – Roman – Anglican* (London, 1847), p. 67.
71 W. Sewell, *A Letter to Dr Pusey on No. 90 of the 'Tracts for the Times'* (Oxford, 1841), p. 9.

THEOLOGICAL IMPLICATIONS OF THE DIVERGENCE: THE TRACTARIANS AND THE SPECTRE OF THE NONJURORS

In his account of the Oxford Movement, A. P. Perceval outlined the theological implications of the divergent Tractarian approach to antiquity. Perceval was prepared to give a broader scope to his definition of essential doctrines than Pretyman-Tomline or Marsh would have conceded. But he complained that by abandoning the principle of fundamentals, the Tractarians began to confound together two distinct classes of doctrine. For Perceval, the first class were by no means confined to absolute credal 'fundamentals' such as the doctrines of original sin or the Trinity. On the contrary, they also comprised all those doctrines which had a clear warrant in Holy Scripture and had been witnessed to from the beginning, and taught authoritatively by all branches of the catholic church in its decrees, liturgies and rituals. These included the doctrine of apostolical succession as set forth in the Ordinal; baptismal regeneration as enshrined in the Catechism and Prayer Book's baptismal office; the eucharistic sacrifice and Real Presence as implied in the Prayer Book's communion office; and the principle of the appeal to antiquity itself, on the basis of the Vincentian rule, as supported by the Canon of 1571. Although not always explicit in Scripture alone, these doctrines were rendered authoritative since they could be confirmed by genuine apostolical tradition and a catholic consent of Fathers.

Perceval maintained that the Tractarians erred when they judged the existing Church of England by a direct appeal to antiquity as an absolute standard. In consequence, the Tractarians confounded with the acceptable first class of doctrines the equal necessity of other doctrines and practices which had never been considered binding. These doctrines may have been recommended by individual divines as 'counsels of perfection' but they had been taught neither uniformly, nor from the beginning, nor were they enshrined in the authorised formularies of the Church. This class of doctrine and practice included: the alleged necessity of turning to the east in prayer; the ideal and superiority of the celibate state; the absolute duty of fasting; the necessity of prayers for the dead; the concept of purification and growth in grace of souls in an intermediate state; notions of post-baptismal sin; reserve in communicating religious knowledge and the *disciplina arcani*; and theories of the mystical or allegorical scriptural interpretations of the Fathers. Perceval believed that it was the Tractarian 'attempt to propagate this latter class (of doctrine) by the same medium, apparently on the same ground, with the same force, and from the same quarter as the former, that gave rise to all the confusion, awakened suspicion, destroyed confidence'.[72]

Many of the doctrines listed by Perceval as being pressed by the Tractarians had been advocated by the Nonjurors Brett and Collier in controversy with Waterland and others and had fomented division between the so-called 'Usagers' and 'non-Usagers' within the Nonjuring camp itself. Similar differences over whether certain primitive practices were *de fide* or not, continued to separate later Nonjurors such as Thomas Deacon, Thomas Podmore and William Cartwright from mainstream High Churchmen from the 1730s till the 1780s.[73] The obvious parallel between the Tractarian theory of Tradition with that of the later Nonjurors, like the similar parallel of attitudes to establishment, was not lost upon the Hackney elders. As Edward Churton reminded Copeland in 1859, 'Mr Norris, as you will perhaps remember, at one time thought the Oxford men in danger of treading too much in the steps of the last Nonjurors, and he had for some time writings of some of them, Cartwright especially, in his hands, and talked and wrote to me about them, more than twenty years ago.'[74] It appears that Norris made extracts from the Cartwright–Boucher correspondence of the 1780s and decided to publish them, convinced that 'the tale they unfold' would prove a salutary and timely warning to the Oxford zealots.[75] The

---

[72] Perceval, *Collection of Papers*, p. 2.
[73] Broxap, *Later Nonjurors*, especially chs. 3 and 9; H. Broxap, *Thomas Deacon* (Manchester, 1911); Overton, *The Nonjurors*, pp. 290–308, 354–63, 373–5.
[74] SC, Churton Papers, E. Churton to W. J. Copeland, 27 September 1859.
[75] PH, Copeland Papers, H. H. Norris to W. J. Copeland, 7 February 1839. According to Edward Churton (*Memoir of Joshua Watson*, vol. I, p. 54), Norris was anxious 'to investigate the history of the decline and fall of the Nonjurors, more especially from his persuasion of its practical bearing upon the controversies of the day'. An article in the *British Magazine* in March 1838 ('The Prose Works of Bishop Ken') took a similar line. However, Copeland poured scorn on the implication that the Nonjurors were guilty of 'division for nothing'. [W. J. Copeland], 'Life and Works of Bishop Ken', *British Critic*, 24 (July, 1838), 179.

The correspondence to which Norris referred formed part of the Brett papers then in the possession of the High Churchman Thomas Bowdler, but loaned to Norris for the latter's controversial purpose. On Bowdler's death in 1856, the collection passed to Copeland, and thereafter into the hands of Canon Ollard, an Anglo-Catholic chronicler of the Oxford Movement. See Ollard's 'Preface' in Broxap, *Later Nonjurors*, pp. xvii–xxiii. However, in Ollard's preface to Broxap's study, Norris's use of the papers with Bowdler's blessing – to

Hackney fear was, as Joshua Watson expressed it, that like the later Nonjurors, the Tractarians by 'taking up practices of which they found some precedent or recommendation in the Primitive Church, and enforcing them as essential ... would come to prefer schism to charity ... losing their wisdom and their catholicity'.[76]

Norris's particular foreboding that history might repeat itself was heightened when his friend, the Manchester High Churchman, Richard Parkinson, sent him 'a very scarce book', Thomas Deacon's *Complete Book of Devotions* (1734). Parkinson had been struck by an apparent resemblence of Deacon's preface to the preface to the second part of Froude's *Remains*. For in the preface to the *Remains*, later attributed to Newman and Keble, the Nonjuring principle of an unreserved appeal to antiquity as normative was adopted. Parkinson even asked Norris whether Deacon's preface might be reprinted in the *British Magazine* so as to highlight the parallel.[77] The affinity was noted by other critics of the Movement. John Evans pointed out to C. P. Golightly in 1841 that there 'is a wonderful resemblance between the Tracts and a work which appeared in 1745 by Thomas Podmore of Manchester called "The Layman's Apology"'. Evans drew out the similarity with contemporary Tractarian claims, arguing that Podmore, 'in common with modern champions of Rome attempts to support by Bishop Brett's suicidal argument, the cause of tradition by comparing it to customs which are reckoned good ... when their beginning cannot be traced'.[78] Likewise, the Evangelical William Goode maintained 'that almost the only witnesses to whom they could properly refer us as at all supporting their system, are a few individuals, such as Brett, Hickes, Johnson and others, forming a small and extreme section of a small and extreme party in our church, namely the Nonjurors'.[79] Nonetheless, a few other isolated High Churchmen from the period of the 1780s to the 1820s, such as George Croft, John Oxlee and Samuel Wix, took a similarly exalted view of Tradition and the value of various

issue a warning from history to the Tractarians is overlooked and Bowdler is mistakenly claimed as being in entire sympathy with the Oxford Movement.

[76] M. Watson, Ms 'Reminiscences', fols. 36–7.
[77] Bodl. Lib, Ms Add d. 30, fol. 31, R. Parkinson to H. H. Norris, 13 March 1838.
[78] LPL, Ms 1805, fol. 164, J. Evans to C. P. Golightly, 11 December 1841; Bird, *Defence of the Principles of the English Reformation*, pp. 80–1.
[79] W. Goode, *The Divine Rule of Faith and Practice*, 3 vols. (London, 1842), vol. 1, p. xx. On the importance of John Johnson (1662–1725), Vicar of Cranbrook, Kent, in the history of High Church eucharistic theology, see chapter 5.

primitive practices which the Church of England had abandoned. In his controversy with Bishop Burgess in 1818–20, Samuel Wix closely identified himself with the later Nonjuring defence of disused primitive usages as set forth in Hickes's *Christian Priesthood*, Collier's *Reasons for Restoring*, Brett's *Tradition Necessary*, and Deacon's *Complete Collection of Devotions*.[80]

Old High Churchmen valued certain obsolete ancient customs but insisted that the Church of England had acted authoritatively and with good reason when it abandoned them. Article 34, it was claimed, ensured the right of a 'national church' to abolish or retain ceremonies. While prayers for the dead were 'primitive', they were not essential or 'fundamental'. Thus, Palmer of Worcester insisted that the Church's abandonment of prayers for the dead was justifiable. 'For those apostolical customs which are not necessary to salvation', he maintained, 'may be suspended or abrogated by the successors of the apostles, if there are good reasons for doing so'.[81] The Church was no slave to antiquity. Having made her own authoritative appeal, with its results enshrined in her formularies, this appeal could not be overturned or questioned by any subsequent exercise of private judgment by individuals, however learned. Therefore, even on 'open questions' the Church's mind should be respected. Joshua Watson, when 'speaking of questions on which the church has given no definite judgment ... said he thought we have no right to maintain opinions which lead to dangerous consequences'. Watson insisted that a 'practice which does not rest upon authority, should be abandoned, if, as a matter of fact, it leads to wrong, even though it may be adhered to harmlessly'.[82]

MORE IMPLICATIONS OF DIVERGENCE: THE TRACTARIANS, OLD HIGH CHURCHMEN AND THE REFORMERS

A consequence of the Tractarian approach to antiquity would be a growing critical unease with the English Reformers and Reforma-

---

[80] S. Wix, *Reflections Concerning the Expediency of a Council of the Church of England and the Church of Rome Being Holden with a View to Accommodate Religious Difficulties, and to Promote the Unity of Religion in the Bond of Peace* (London, 1818), pp. 40–78.

[81] W. Palmer, *Origines Liturgicae or Antiquities of the English Ritual*, 2 vols. (London, 1832), vol. II, p. 15; J. H. Pott, *The Rule of Faith Considered in a Charge Delivered to the Clergy of the Archdeaconry of London* (London, 1839), pp. 36–7.

[82] M. Watson, Ms 'Reminiscences', fol. 39; R. Mant, *The Laws of the Church. The Churchman's Guard against Romanism and Puritanism in Two Charges* (Dublin, 1842), pp. 5–10.

tion. Old High Churchmen had never felt any dichotomy between their respect for antiquity and veneration of the Reformers. The appeal of the pre-Tractarian High Church campaigners was to revive 'the principles of the Reformation'.[83] Cranmer was eulogised as an 'apostle of the reformed Church of England' who could 'truly be ranked with the greatest primitive bishops and the Fathers of the very first class'.[84] Even Bishop Bull could be cited as 'good authority for our calling our Bishops of Queen Mary's time "Martyrs"'.[85] Above all, the appeal of the English Reformers to antiquity was taken as axiomatic. The whole thrust of Orthodox apologetic was that Evangelical claims to be the true theological successors of the Reformers depended on the false assumption that Cranmer, Ridley, Latimer and their associates had sanctioned an unqualified right of private judgment and the principle of *sola scriptura*. On the contrary, insisted the Orthodox, the Reformers had appealed to antiquity and eschewed mere private judgment.[86] In fact, some moderate Evangelicals also took this line. While G. S. Faber would take issue with the Tractarian exaltation of Tradition, he yet could assure Newman in 1838, 'you and I quite agree in rejecting that modern absurdity, Insulated Private Judgment'.[87]

Nevertheless, as Peter Toon has shown, the presuppositions of many Evangelicals about the doctrine of private judgment being an essential principle of the Reformers, owed much to 'what we now know to be latitudinarian interpretations of the Reformation'.[88] But Evangelicals had some historical basis for their viewpoint. Certain individual Reformers such as Whitaker and Pilkington, who had

83 *Scholar Armed*, 2 vols. (2nd end, London, 1800), vol. I, p. 2.
84 *Orthodox Churchman's Magazine*, 2 (July, 1802), 8–9; C. Le Bas, *The Life of Archbishop Cranmer*, 2 vols. (London, 1833), vol. II, p. 301.
85 PH, Pusey Papers, LBV [Transcripts], B. Harrison to E. B. Pusey, 16 January 1839.
86 W. F. Hook, *A Call to Union on the Principles of the English Reformation* (London, 1838), pp. 7–8; Hook, *Three Reformations*, p. 55; W. F. Hook, *Our Holy and Beautiful House, the Church of England* (London, 1848), p. 18; W. E. Gladstone, *The State of Its Relations with the Church* (London, 1838), pp. 144–5; [J. F. Russell], *Tracts of the Anglican Fathers*, 2 vols. (London, 1841), vol. I, pp. iii–iv; F. W. Collison, *A Vindication of the Anglican Reformers in an Examination of Dr Scholefield's Discourses* Cambridge, 1841), pp. 30–3. Edward Churton maintained that Ridley upheld the Vincentian rule as the rule of faith. SC, Churton Papers, E. Churton to W. J. Copeland, 26 December 1862.
87 G. S. Faber to J. H. Newman, 9 April 1838, *Letters and Diaries*, vol. V, p. 229. Faber condemned 'ultra protestants' who 'throw the Fathers overboard ... and then steer us upon the quicksands of arbitrary judgment'. LPL, Golightly Papers, Ms 1805, fol. 232, G. S. Faber to C. P. Golightly, 21 June 1841.
88 Toon, *Evangelical Theology*, pp. 136–7. See Goode, *Divine Rule of Faith and Practice*, vol. I, p. xliii.

been in exile at Frankfurt under Queen Mary, countenanced the later Puritan approach whereby Scripture was the 'rule whereby we must try all things' and that 'whatever disagrees with Scripture should be rejected'. On the other hand, some of the Reformers such as Ridley accepted only a limited sense of *sola scriptura*. In contrast to the more extreme Protestants they adopted the principle of *adiaphora* which was enshrined in the Anglican formularies, whereby an Erasmian distinction was drawn between things necessary for salvation and things that were not.[89]

Initially, supporters of the Movement retained a respectful attitude to the Reformers, as witnessed by A. P. Perceval's sermon preached in Hadleigh, Essex, during the famous inaugural conference in July 1833 when the spirit of the Marian martyr of Hadleigh, Rowland Taylor was invoked.[90] As on other issues, however, latent divisions soon separated the Hadleigh 'conspirators'. From an early date, Froude was comparing Latimer to the extreme Evangelical and later Irvingite, H. B. Bulteel, labelling Bishop Jewell as 'what you would call in these days an irreverent Dissenter' and denouncing the Reformation as 'a limb badly set'.[91] Under Froude's influence, as on other points, Newman and Keble shifted ground. For a time, Newman practised 'economy'. For as Imberg suggests, Newman's praise of the Reformers even in the mid-1830s was not always sincere and was made for tactical purposes. This is clear from Newman's comment to Bowden in July 1835; 'your passages about the Reformers do not distress me at all – I am sure the more we can (conscientiously) praise them the better, and if another finds himself able to do so more than me, I am desirous to avail myself of his ability'.[92] By 1837, Newman was privately denouncing Cranmer and Jewell.[93] Some of Newman's followers would go further in public. For instance, Jewell was singled out for particular censure in

---

[89] This was the view of Alexander Knox. See *Remains of Alexander Knox*, 2 vols. (London, 1834), vol. II, p. 157.

[90] Perceval, *Collection of Papers*, p. 43.

[91] [Newman and Keble, eds.], *Remains of Richard Hurrell Froude*, vol. I, pp. 379, 251.

[92] *Letters and Diaries*, vol. V, p. 94. See Imberg, *In Quest of Authority*, p. 89. See Newman's admission to Thomas Henderson, Vicar of Messing, Essex: 'I should not have gone out of my way to attack them [the Reformers] – but now when through happy fortune, when I walk in the light of day and the free air, and no longer need all sorts of fictions and artifices to make our Cranmer or others Catholic ... it would have been sheer absurdity to bring myself again in the world of shadows.' PH, Ollard Papers, J. H. Newman to T. Henderson, March 1838 (copy).

[93] See Newman's comment in 1838: 'Cranmer will not stand examination ... the English Church will yet be ashamed of conduct like his.' PH, Ollard Papers, J. H. Newman to T. Henderson, *c.* March 1838 (copy).

a notorious article in the *British Critic* in 1841.

Keble also became disillusioned with the Reformers. Prior to 1833, Keble had identified with them unreservedly.[94] Yet by 1835, he was already maintaining that 'Hooker wrote many things in order to counteract in a quiet way the Ultra Protestantism of ... Cranmer and his school.'[95] By 1839, Keble was refusing to countenance the proposed Martyrs' Memorial at Oxford on the specific ground that 'anything which separates the present church from the Reformers I should hail as a great good'.[96] For as the preface to Froude's *Remains* made clear, Keble and Newman now insisted that churchmen had to make a choice between adherence to the principles of antiquity and catholic consent on the one hand, and to those of the Reformers on the other.[97] It was assumed that old High Churchmen who were critical of the Tractarians, lacked 'entire faith in Antiquity' because they wished 'to check the Fathers by the Reformers'.[98]

On the other hand, old High Churchmen insisted on drawing 'a broad distinction ... between what was done by the civil, and by the ecclesiastical powers' at the time of the Reformation. The latter could not be blamed for 'sacrilege'. Moreover, while maintaining that the Reformers had adhered to antiquity as well as Scripture, old High Churchmen approved of the selective nature of their appeal. Joshua Watson felt it to be 'a very important feature in the spirit of our best Reformers' that 'they did not hesitate sometimes to reject a practice of primitive christians, when it had been made on occasion of evil according to the example of Hezekiah with regard to the Brazen Serpent'.[99] Yet, though old High Churchmen generally regarded Cranmer as 'a good and holy man', it was not the Reformers as individuals or in their private opinions who were deemed infallible. On the contrary, as Alexander Knox's unfavourable comparison of Cranmer's theological views with those of Ridley reveals, individual Reformers were not beyond criticism.[100] It was the canonical status of the Reformation settlement alone that was

---

94 For example, see PH, Pusey Papers, LBV [Transcripts], J. Keble to A. P. Perceval, 16 February 1830.
95 PH, Pusey Papers, LBV [Transcripts], J. Keble to J. H. Newman, 21 January 1835.
96 PH, Pusey Papers, LBV [Transcripts], J. Keble to E. B. Pusey, 18 January 1839.
97 [Newman and Keble, eds.], *Remains of Richard Hurrell Froude*, vol. III, pp. xxi–xxxii.
98 BL, Gladstone Papers, Ms Add 44370, fol. 217, J. Keble to W. E. Gladstone, 30 July 1851.
99 M. Watson, Ms 'Remiscences', fols. 23 and 59.
100 *Remains of Alexander Knox*, vol. II, pp. 151–2. At an earlier date (1783), George Croft, in a public sermon at Oxford, had asserted: 'we enter into no undistinguishing and unqualified

sacrosanct. Hook was even prepared to concede, 'if any mistakes can be shown to have been made, any practices, not medieval, but really primitive and scriptural, omitted, let a Convocation be held to amend the error and correct the abuse'.[101] To conform one's private opinions and practice 'to some imaginary standard of perfection' culled out from 'some peculiar age or class of teachers' was but 'a repetition of Puritanism' or at best, 'Pseudo-Catholic'.[102] Old High Churchmen felt that the Tractarian disparagement of the Reformation merely played into the hands of 'ultra-Protestants' for whom it was associated with an absolute right of private judgment. Tractarian railing at the Reformers was deemed a betrayal of the historical perspective of generations of High Churchmen. For as Edward Churton lamented in 1860,

If Froude is right, Clarendon and Pearson, Bull and Waterland, and all our divines, 'whose footsteps I adore', down to good Bishop Jebb and Alexander Knox, are wrong. Who ever held such language about Ridley and Cranmer, before R. H. Froude? Unless they were some of the most peevish and narrowest intellects among the Nonjurors, of whom of course, Froude speaks with increasing admiration.[103]

Pusey adhered to a continued respect for the English Reformers which distinguished him from Keble as well as Newman. Far from advocating Keble's stark choice between the Fathers and the Reformers, as late as 1839 Pusey could insist to Keble, that it was to the Reformers that 'we owe our peculiar position as adherents to primitive antiquity'.[104] Even in 1841, in his defence of Newman's *Tract 90*, Pusey was citing Ridley and Cranmer's testimonies in favour of antiquity. Significantly, he confessed in the same year that he had never read the preface to the second volume of Froude's

vindication of our first Reformers'. G. Croft, *Sermons, Including a Series of Discourses on the Minor Prophets*, 2 vols. (London, 1811), vol. 1, p. 25. Edward Churton likewise insisted that he only commended the Reformers, more particularly Ridley, 'for what they preserved, rather than for what in many particulars they assisted in destroying'. SC, Churton Papers, E. Churton to T. T. Churton, 28 February 1845. See also Churton's comment: 'I quite feel with George Herbert, that the Reformation, with all its crimes, deserveth tears.' SC, Churton Papers, E. Churton to W. J. Copeland, 11 February 1842. Nonetheless, James Sack (*From Jacobite to Conservative*, pp. 221–4), overstates the lack of sympathy among pre-Tractarian High Churchmen for the Reformation. Sack fails to distinguish between their attitudes to the English and continental Reformation.
[101] PH, Pusey Papers, LBV [Transcripts], W. F. Hook to E. B. Pusey, 15 November 1846; Hook, *Three Reformations*, p. 68.
[102] [Sewell], 'Divines of the Seventeenth Century', *Quarterly Review*, 69 (March 1842), 452; Jelf, *Via Media*, p. 37.
[103] SC, Churton Papers, E. Churton to W. J. Copeland, 28 May 1860; PH, Pusey Papers, LBV [Transcripts], E. Churton to W. Gresley, 2 January 1860.
[104] PH, Pusey Papers, LBV [Transcripts], E. B. Pusey to J. Keble, 29 January 1839.

Remains in which the Reformers were disparaged.[105] Nevertheless, even Pusey slowly moved towards a more hostile view of the Reformers. In defining the distinctive tenets of 'Puseyism' in 1840, Pusey made clear how far the old High Church method of deferring to antiquity had become reversed in Tractarian theology. As Pusey explained, it was by antiquity 'that we interpret our own church when her meaning is questioned or doubtful; in a word, reference to the Ancient Church, instead of the Reformers, as the ultimate expounder of the meaning of our church'.[106] It was at the tribunal of antiquity that the Reformers had been tried and found wanting.

FURTHER IMPLICATIONS: THE TRACTARIANS, OLD HIGH CHURCHMEN AND THE SEVENTEENTH-CENTURY DIVINES

T. M. Parker's contention that Newman's knowledge of and interest in the Fathers predated that of the seventeenth-century divines is significant. The time sequence ensured that the latter would be subordinate to the Fathers as his ultimate point of reference. Of course, the Tractarians repeatedly cited and sheltered behind the testimony of the seventeenth-century divines, in whose footsteps they assumed they were but following. Even as late as 1851 in an impassioned defence of the Movement against its detractors, Pusey identified 'Tractarianism' as wholly bound up in lineal continuity with the Church's Caroline tradition: 'Tractarianism was entirely the birth of the English Church ... Tractarianism was not beheaded with Laud, nor trampled under foot in the Great Rebellion, nor corrupted by Charles II, nor expelled with the Nonjurors.'[107] Yet, how valid was the Tractarian claim to be the legitimate expositors of Caroline divinity? Old High Churchmen questioned the lineal continuity between the two, and asserted that they themselves represented the genuine 'Laudean party'.[108]

Old High Churchmen actually ascribed the divergence in the Tractarian approach to antiquity which they lamented, partly to a neglect and relative ignorance of the seventeenth-century divines by

---

[105] PH, Pusey Papers, LBV [Transcripts], E. B. Pusey to J. H. Newman, 8 January 1841; E. B. Pusey, *The Articles Treated on in Tract 90 Reconsidered and Their Interpretation Vindicated in a Letter to the Rev. R. W. Jelf* (Oxford, 1841), pp. 8–9.
[106] ECA, Phillpotts Papers, Spencer Gift, Ed/11/52/38, 'What Is Puseyism?' [1840].
[107] E. B. Pusey, *A Letter to the Rt. Hon. and Rt. Rev. the Lord Bishop of London in Explanation of Some Letters Contained in a Letter by the Rev. W. Dodsworth* (Oxford, 1851), pp. 258–9.
[108] [Sewell], 'Divines of the Seventeenth Century', 471–550.

the Movement's leaders. Charles Wordsworth later argued that the
Tractarians 'threw themselves into the study of the Fathers without
the steadying guidance which that study pre-eminently requires'.
Apart from Keble, in the case of Hooker, and Newman, in the case
of Bishop Bull, Wordsworth felt that the Tractarians made no deep
study or attempt to understand the true mind of the great seventeenth-century divines. Wordsworth found it significant that the
Library of Anglo-Catholic Theology, designed to increase familiarity
with those divines, was only set up in 1841, in response to the
anti-Tractarian Parker Society, five years after the commencement
of the *Library of the Fathers*.[109] The Tractarian leaders were less than
enthusiastic about the *Library of Anglo-Catholic Theology*. Newman
was always uninterested in it, conceding to Frederic Rogers in 1841
that 'it is no plan of mine, and neither Pusey nor I was warm about
it'.[110] In fact, Tractarian editors of the *Library of Anglo-Catholic
Theology*, such as Copeland and Charles Crawley, became increasingly dissatisfied with the content and tone of some of the works
they were supposed to be republishing. As Crawley explained to
Newman in 1841, Copeland's 'deeper study of the works in which
his editorial office engaged him made him acquainted with some
objectionable features in them which he had overlooked before and
which were too much for his sensitive mind to tolerate'. Crawley
himself sympathised, stating, 'I could not but respect his scruples
and agree with him in his opinion as to the character of some
passages which he pointed out to me in Bramhall for instance.'[111]
The message was clear. 'Copeland', Newman told Rogers, 'has
given up the editorship because our divines do not go far enough
for him.'[112] Clearly, when judged by antiquity, much seventeenth-century divinity could be deemed wanting. Moreover, the

---

[109] Cha. Wordsworth, *Annals of My Early Life*, p. 343.
[110] J. H. Newman to F. Rogers, 2 January 1841, Mozley, ed., *Letters and Correspondence of
Newman*, vol. II, p. 323. To Pusey, Newman was still more candid: 'I have never been for
it. Under the circumstances, the Parker Society urging, the subscriptions being collected,
and the first volume coming out, I suppose it must go on.' PH, Pusey Papers, J. H.
Newman to E. B. Pusey, 12 January 1841. Even Pusey was less than enthusiastic, telling
Newman: 'I should hardly be sorry, if the whole thing came to nothing.' PH, Pusey
Papers, E. B. Pusey to J. H. Newman, 8 January 1841. See also Keble's comment in 1838:
'I am sorry to say that Moberley disappoints us so far that he has made up his mind to edit
an English divine, Bishop Cosin, instead of translating St Ambrose.' KCA, Keble Papers,
J. Keble to J. H. Newman, 7 August 1838.
[111] Birmingham Oratory, Newman Papers, C. Crawley to J. H. Newman, 16 January 1841.
[112] J. H. Newman to F. Rogers, Mozley, ed., *Letters and Correspondence of Newman*, vol. II,
p. 323.

Tractarian editors were both anachronistic and selective in their approach. Historical context was ignored, and a spurious assumption of theological coherence was made in the very title 'Caroline Divines'.[113]

Newman's personal commitment to the ideal of Caroline Anglicanism which he expounded in the *Lectures on the Prophetical Office* was not half-hearted or insincere. On the contrary, in 1834–7, Newman had honestly sought to throw himself into the writings and spirit of the Caroline Divines as well as the early Fathers. Viewed in retrospect, Newman's *via media* phase might be seen as but a temporary staging-post in a long religious odyssey. Yet, at the time, it was held and propagated with a conviction, and even what he himself called a 'fierceness', that could not have been exceeded. Of course, some gaps in Newman's knowledge and understanding of Caroline divinity could be identified. Nevertheless, Newman was actually much better acquainted with the works not only of the Caroline Divines, notably Hammond and Stillingfleet as well as Bull, but also of select eighteenth-century High Churchmen such as Jones of Nayland, than some old High Church critics assumed.[114] Unpublished notes in the Birmingham Oratory Library reveal that Newman was well-versed even in the controversial divinity of Bishop Marsh, whose *Comparative View* he cited approvingly in his own *Lectures*, in spite of private misgivings about the work.[115] Therefore, it is not the genuineness of Newman's devotion to historic 'Anglicanism' that should be questioned, but rather the basis on which that commitment came to be erected and the manner in which it was expressed.

The key to Newman's ultimate loss of faith in Anglicanism lay in his attempt to erect a coherent dogmatic edifice on a structure never designed to support it. It has recently been maintained that Newman was opposed to theological 'system'.[116] Yet Newman's perennial complaint in 1836–7 was that 'Anglicanism' was but a 'paper theory', lacking in substance, existing only in outline. To Rose's profound dismay, Newman even doubted whether it represented a 'real religion' in the way that Calvinism or Roman

---

[113] Spurr, *Restoration Church*, pp. 394–5; N. Tyacke, *Anti-Calvinists: the Rise of English Arminianism, c. 1590–1640* (Oxford, 1990, paperback edn), pp. vii–viii.

[114] For the chronology of Newman's study of the Caroline Divines, see Weidner, ed., *Via Media*, pp. xxviii–xxxii.

[115] Newman, *Lectures on the Prophetical Office*, p. 80.

[116] Thomas, *Newman and Heresy*, p. 182.

Catholicism manifestly did.[117] In the *Prophetical Office*, Newman
sought consciously to recreate an 'Anglican system' from the scattered residue of seventeenth-century divinity. In this attempted
recreation, he sought to systematise as well as harmonise a body of
divinity that was intrinsically unsystematic, if not discordant. Ultimately, Newman's attempt to systematise Caroline divinity was
misconceived because, as was pointed out, the Caroline Divines
might have represented 'a school' but it was a school 'which never
has spoken as a school'.[118]

As Stephen Sykes has argued, Newman chose to overlook the
marked degree of underlying religious diversity within the High
Anglican tradition which Waterland, Van Mildert and most other
later apologists had conceded. In consequence, Sykes maintains,
Newman helped create 'the myth of a unique Anglicanism'.[119] In
this process, Newman sought not merely to reproduce, but to 'complete' the 'inheritance' of the seventeenth century. As he confided to
Rose in 1836, 'the Anglican system of doctrine is in matter of fact not
complete – there are hiatuses which have never been filled up – so
that, though one agrees with it most entirely as far as it goes, yet one
rather wishes for something more'.[120] By the nature of his appeal to
antiquity, Newman aimed to supplement the existing incoherent
'system' with precisely that 'something' he felt was lacking. For
Newman wished the Church of England literally to represent the
church of antiquity in doctrinal fullness if she was to compete with
the Church of Rome. Yet, Newman was seeking the impossible.

---

[117] Newman, *Lectures on the Prophetical Office*, p. 20. It was a perennial complaint of the
Tractarian Newman that even the soundest Anglican divinity was of an unsystematic
character, a controversial response to a particular challenge. See his comment to Keble in
1837: 'I do not like these unsystematic productions; they do not last. Who reads Horsley
against Priestley?' J. H. Newman to J. Keble, 20 November 1837, *Letters and Diaries*, vol.
VI, p. 167. Newman wanted the *via media* to be 'an integral system'. See n. 120. Likewise,
Newman told Pusey: 'Let us preach and teach, and develop our views into system.' J. H.
Newman to E. B. Pusey, 25 January 1836, *Letters and Diaries*, vol. V, p. 215.

[118] A. W. Haddan, 'English Divines of the 16th and 17th Centuries', in A. Weir and W. D.
Maclagan, eds., *The Church and the Age: Essays in the Principles and Present Position of the
English Church* (London, 1870), p. 230.

[119] S. W. Sykes, 'Newman, Anglicanism and the Fundamentals', *Newman after a Hundred Years*,
pp. 365–6.

[120] J. H. Newman to R. F. Wilson, 13 May 1836. *Letters and Diaries*, vol. V, p. 291. In the second
edition, the sentence, 'the Via Media has never existed', to which Rose objected, was
altered to, 'the Via Media viewed as an integral system has scarcely had existence'. For
the view that Newman was never an authentic intellectual disciple of the Caroline
Divines, see H. L. Weatherby, 'The Encircling Gloom: Newman's Departure from the
Caroline Tradition', *Victorian Studies*, 12, No. 1 (September, 1968), 57–82.

Caroline divinity, however blended, harmonised and supplemented, could never have fulfilled his expectation. Here Wilfrid Ward is misleading. For Ward implied that Newman always knew that he could never construct a coherent 'Anglican tradition', and that it was Palmer of Worcester who lived in the world of shadows, seeking the impossible. On the contrary, Palmer was always, like Rose, chiding Newman for striving for an unobtainable 'perfection' of the church.[121] 'Anglicanism', even if the word were new, was not something to be sought out or reconstructed; it was 'already found for us', and had long existed.[122] Yet it was not amenable to precise doctrinal formulation in the way which Newman for too long assumed. Unlike Newman, Palmer could live with the apparent inconsistencies of 'Anglicanism'. The aphorism ascribed by Ward to the Anglican Newman, 'let the dead bury their dead', only 'let the future be consistent'[123] represented only the despairing view of Newman the 'deathbed Anglican', whose dream of the *via media* already lay in ruins. Palmer had never sought consistency in such terms.

When Newman cited the Caroline Divines, he tended to extract only that which suited his rhetorical and controversial purposes, conveniently ignoring what did not. When, in his reading of the seventeenth-century divines, he found a discordant note, he privately expressed his dismay and disappointment. Newman's judgments on some of the Caroline Divines could be as harsh as any of Froude's in relation to the Reformers. For instance, he was convinced that Laud's friend, William Chillingworth, was the patron of later latitudinarianism, and an 'ultra-Protestant', on account of his maxim, 'the Bible only, the religion of protestants'.[124] It was in vain that Edward Churton, who was far better conversant with the nuances of Chillingworth's theology than was Newman, argued that 'the doctrine of Chillingworth ... is good Oxford divinity',[125]

---

[121] In contrast to Newman, Palmer denied that unity in doctrine was a note of the church, arguing that 'there may be a unity of error'. Palmer, *Treatise on the Church of Christ*, vol. 1, pp. 96–7.

[122] Bodl. Lib, Manning Papers, Ms Eng Lett c. 654, fol. 107, H. J. Rose to H. E. Manning, 20 March 1837.

[123] W. Ward, 'Some Aspects of Newman's Influence', *The Nineteenth Century*, 28, No. 175 (October, 1890), 569.

[124] [J. H. Newman], 'Le Bas's Life of Archbishop Laud', *British Critic*, 19 (April, 1836), 368.

[125] SC, Churton Papers, E. Churton to W. J. Copeland, 12 April 1836; E. Churton to W. J. Copeland, 21 May 1836. Churton insisted that in his *Religion of Protestants* (1637), Chillingworth 'again and again acknowledges the rule of Universal Tradition', *ibid.*, E. Churton to W. J. Copeland, 21 March 1836. For Churton, Laud's patronage of

and that Laud had 'something to do with this'. Similarly, Newman even found cause to fault such Caroline favourites as Hammond and Jeremy Taylor, asking Churton rhetorically in 1837, 'how comes Taylor to be so liberal in his "Liberty of Prophesying"? And how far is Hammond tinctured as regards the Sacraments with Grotianism?'[126]

Even as his faith in the *via media* began to wane in 1839–41, Newman found in the writings of the Caroline Divines a rich quarry to bolster his rearguard Anglican apologetic. Nowhere did Newman employ Caroline testimony to such subtle and controversial effect as in his celebrated *Tract 90* where he sought to give a 'catholic' interpretation to the Thirty-Nine Articles.

Dean Church himself admitted that Newman's citations of the Caroline Divines in *Tract 90* were somewhat one-sided.[127] For example, the manner in which Newman appealed to the testimony of Henry Hammond in favour of his interpretation of Article 20 seemed far-fetched and disingenuous. The authority is given where Newman cites Hammond as being in favour of the infallibility of General Councils, while the many statements of Hammond's suggesting that General Councils were indeed fallible are conveniently ignored.[128] Similarly, Bramhall is quoted out of context as being in favour of the doctrine of a 'comprecation of the saints', while other aspects of Bramhall's theology which contradicted cherished Tractarian tenets are studiously overlooked. Edwin Abbott later observed that Newman 'seemed to assume that every opinion, however extreme in the direction of Rome, that had been once expressed by any one High Church Bishop or Divine, and had not been authoritatively censured, at once became part of justifiable Anglican doctrine'.[129] Abbott might be considered incorrigibly biased against anything Newman was likely to say or do, but the

Chillingworth was no anomaly. Years later, he maintained: 'Laud was in truth a much more Broad Churchman, than the world seems yet willing to concede.' E. Churton, *A Legal Argument in the Case of Ditcher versus Denison* (London, 1856), p. 22.

[126] J. H. Newman to E. Churton, 14 March 1837, *Letters and Diaries*, vol. VI, p. 41.
[127] Church, *Oxford Movement*, pp. 286–7.
[128] Abbott, *Anglican Career of Cardinal Newman*, vol. I, p. 250.
[129] *Ibid.*, p. 247. One critic of the Tractarians conceded to Thomas Morris, a Tractarian tutor at Christ Church: 'Montagu and Thorndike ... may very possibly approach nearer to your [Tractarian] views than their contemporaries in general'. PH, Morris Papers, 1/13/2, J. D. Robertson to E. E. Morris, 14 August 1843. Christopher Wordsworth junior disapproved of the editing of Thorndike's works by the *Library of Anglo-Catholic Theology*, regarding him as a less safe guide than Bramhall. LPL, Wordsworth Papers, Ms 2147, fol. 162, C. Wordsworth (Jun.) to J. Watson, 14 February 1843.

testimony of Anne Mozley cannot be thus dismissed. According to her, in the heyday of the *via media*, Newman selected 'here a teacher, there an authority' but accepted 'them no further than they fell in with his views'. She felt that he snatched at 'every chance saying of any of our Divines', even though 'the whole tenor of the work has no weight with him'.[130]

It was J. B. Mozley (before he abjured Tractarianism) and Frederick Oakeley who perhaps perfected the method of Newman's selectivity of citation. In their skilful hands, the Caroline Divines were startlingly even made the vehicle of 'unprotestantising' the Church of England. In a debate with William Sewell, Mozley justified the Tractarian breach of earlier parameters of High Churchmanship by appealing to the precedent of the Caroline Divines themselves. In response to Sewell's conservative interpretation of seventeenth-century divinity, Mozley insisted that 'our church divinity has been ... a progressive, not a stationary one. The Laudian school was as clearly a new development of the church, in its day, as history can show it.'[131] Yet, while Mozley maintained that the Caroline Divines really went as far as the Tractarians if one but separated 'their real spirit from their controversial phraseology',[132] Oakeley made no such pretence, candidly admitting the difference. Thus, in his defence of *Tract 90*, Oakeley frankly acknowledged that citations from various seventeenth-century divines could just as easily be constructed to refute as to uphold aspects of Tractarian teaching. Yet, for him this did not matter. For as he explained, the object of Newman's citations was,

not to justify the Caroline divines, any more than to ground particular doctrines upon their authority, but merely to show what they have felt themselves at liberty to say without protest. And this fact has its own weight, whatever these divines may chance to have said elsewhere. Of course I do not here speak of reserves and qualifications made in the neighbourhood of the several passages.

The fact that contradictions between Caroline and Tractarian teaching on this or that doctrine might be found could safely be ignored, since there was no need to press the Carolines 'into our service beyond the point for which they are here claimed'.[133]

[130] 'Dr Newman's Apology', *Christian Remembrancer*, 48 (July, 1864), 178.
[131] [J. B. Mozley], 'Development of the Church of the Seventeenth Century', *British Critic*, 32 (July, 1842), 342.
[132] *Ibid.*, 345. [133] F. Oakeley, *The Subject of Tract 90 Examined* (London, 1841), pp. 3–4.

One can conclude that there was substance behind the accusation of critics of the Movement that the Tractarians used 'the delusive cover' of the seventeenth-century divines to advance their own distinctive cause.[134] In so doing, they bequeathed a tradition of one-sided interpretation which later Anglo-Catholic commentators would continue to propagate.[135]

In their Charges, various High Church bishops refuted Tractarian 'patristic fundamentalism' by appealing directly to the teaching of seventeenth-century Anglican divines and their Orthodox successors such as Waterland.[136] Some moderate Evangelicals such as G. S. Faber, James Garbett, Archdeacon Browne and C. S. Bird, also appealed to the same historical and doctrinal sources in order to challenge the Tractarians on their own chosen ground.[137] Faber's own earlier appeal to the *'Recorded consent of primitive antiquity'*[138] almost matched the Tractarian method, though he found 'Protestant' doctrine in the early Fathers which the Tractarians did not. Noting this discrepancy, other Evangelicals such as William Goode shunned any such reliance on the Vincentian canon.[139] Yet even

[134] H. Fish, *Jesuitism Traced in the Movements of the Oxford Tractarians* (London, 1842), p. 61.
[135] More and Cross, eds., *Anglicanism*, pp. xix, xxx, 307–16; J. Booty, 'Standard Divines', Sykes and Booty, eds., *Study of Anglicanism*, pp. 168–71.
[136] For example, see E. Denison, *Obligations of the Clergy in Preaching the Word of God. A Charge to the Clergy of the Diocese of Salisbury* (London, 1842), pp. 22–3. See also, *Testimonies to Church Principles, Selected from Episcopal Charges and Sermons* (London, 1843).
[137] G. S. Faber, *Letters on Tractarian Secessions to Popery* (London, 1846), pp. 20, 59–60; J. Garbett, *Christ as Prophet, Priest and King: Being a Vindication of the Church of England from Theological Novelties. Considered in Eight Sermons Preached before the University of Oxford ... At the Lecture Founded by the Late John Bampton M.A.*, 2 vols. (Oxford, 1842), vol. II, pp. 3–129. Keble commented: 'Garbett's admissions in his Bampton Lectures [are] being said to go the full extent of our doctrine.' KCA, Heathcote Papers, J. Keble to W. Heathcote, 25 February 1842. Significantly, the Evangelical Archdeacon Browne based his view on the relative value of antiquity in confirming the canonicity of Holy Scripture on the argument advocated by Bishop Kaye. J. H. Browne, *Strictures on the Oxford Tracts. A Charge Delivered to the Clergy of the Archdeaconry of Ely, at a Visitation held in the Parish Church of St. Michael's, Cambridge, on Thursday June 7, 1838* (London, 1838), pp. 130–2; C. S. Bird, *A Defence of the Principles of the English Reformation from the Attacks of the Tractarians; or, a Second Plea for the Reformed Church* (London, 1843), pp. 53–72.
[138] For example, see G. S. Faber, *The Difficulties of Romanism* (London, 1826); In his response to Tractarianism, Faber distinguished between 'Aboriginal antiquity' which he commended, and what he regarded as the more corrupt teaching of the later Fathers. G. S. Faber, *Provincial Letters from the County-Palatine of Durham Exhibiting the Nature and Tendency of the Principles of the 'Tracts for the Times', and Their Various Allies and Associates* (London, 1842), pp. 58–60. Faber even commended Palmer of Worcester's *Treatise on the Church of Christ* for maintaining this distinction. G. S. Faber, *The Primitive Doctrine of Regeneration* (London, 1840), p. xiv.
[139] For Evangelical criticism of Faber for 'paying too great deference' to antiquity, see *Christian Observer* New Series, No. 1 (April, 1838), 263.

Goode did not neglect the value of patristic or earlier Anglican testimony in attempting to turn the tables on the Tractarians.[140] Goode's *Divine Rule of Faith and Practice* (1842), according to one reviewer, exposed the Tractarians as guilty of 'a convenient process of misquotation, and accumulating "catenas" of later Divines, simply by detaching passages from the context and applying them in a manner diametrically opposite to that which their authors designed'.[141] Even Laud and Heylin, *bête-noires* of Low Churchmen, were defended by Garbett and Goode in their anti-Tractarian polemic. As Garbett maintained, Laud and Heylin and their 'school, rejected, honestly, the Roman doctrine, and still venerated the scriptural founders of the Reformed Church'.[142] The implication was that the Tractarians did not. Moreover, like Faber and Bird, Goode could fairly appeal even to the anti-Evangelical school of Marsh and Pretyman-Tomline in support of a repudiation of Tradition.[143] However, Goode's attempt to prove that divines such as Jackson, Ussher, Stillingfleet, Patrick, Waterland and Van Mildert were also opposed to the authority of Tradition, even in a qualified non-Tractarian sense, was disingenuous and mistaken in the eyes of most old High Churchmen. For the latter, Goode's controversial method was no less unscrupulous and biased in one direction than was Tractarian polemic in another.[144]

Yet old High Churchmen were troubled by the plausibility of Goode's evidence and argument. Archbishop Howley was led to question whether the Tract writers could any longer claim either patristic or Caroline testimony as conclusive in their favour. After anxious consultation with Howley, Dean Lyall conveyed to Bishop Bagot the Archbishop's concern that 'if Dr Pusey and Mr Newman believe their opinions to be founded on the authority of the Ancient and Anglican Fathers ... it is for them to make good their opinions

---

[140] Goode, *Divine Rule of Faith and Practice*, vol. III, pp. 404–5. Goode also cited (pp. 513–14) Van Mildert's 1814 Bampton Lectures as testimony in his critique of Tractarianism. See also, W. Goode, *Tract XC Historically Refuted* (London, 1845), pp. 151–90.

[141] Fish, *Jesuitism of the Oxford Tractarians*, pp. 61–2.

[142] J. Garbett, *The University, the Church, and the New Test. A Letter to the Lord Bishop of Chichester* (London, 1845), p. 73.

[143] Goode asserted: 'the reader will find the Protestant view well laid down by Bishop Marsh in his *Comparative View of the Churches of England and Rome*'. W. Goode, *The Case as It Is: or, a Reply to the Letter of Dr Pusey to His Grace the Archbishop of Canterbury* (London, 1842), p. 73.

[144] *Christian Remembrancer*, 23 (June, 1840), 394–411; *British Magazine*, 18 (July, 1840), 34–9; *Church of England Quarterly Review*, 7 (April, 1840), 307–8.

by showing that Mr Goode is guilty of the fault with which he charges others'.[145] Tractarian polemicists did step forward, but the waters had been muddied, and the controversy was not conclusively resolved.

Some High Churchmen who seceded to the Church of Rome also conceded that on this subject, as on that of church and state, Evangelicals such as Goode had the better of the historical argument – a view shared by some recent writers.[146] To the delight of Evangelicals but the dismay of High Churchmen, in 1850 William Maskell admitted that the Caroline Divines ultimately failed in the controversial purposes to which the Tractarians had put them. As Maskell candidly conceded, 'catenae are useful enough, within their proper and reasonable limits; they create difficulties sometimes, whilst they seldom suffice to establish a conclusion: employed, however, as they have been, of late years by our own [i.e. High Church] party, they are not merely a packed jury, but a jury permitted only to speak half their mind'.[147] By 1845, Newman himself had reached a similar conclusion, his earlier confidence in the seventeenth-century divines evaporating as 'he read the Fathers more carefully, and used his own eyes in determining the faith and worship of their times'.[148] Both Maskell and Newman, while journeying to Rome by very different routes, would feel a profound sense of disappointment and betrayal, of having been 'taken in' by the Caroline Divines.

THE CRISIS OF THE *VIA MEDIA*: NEWMAN'S *TRACT 90* AND THE OLD HIGH CHURCH REACTION

Newman's quest to prove Anglicanism's literal identity with antiquity led to an increasing concern to delineate a 'primitive' version of doctrines or practices which Protestants had hitherto deemed

[145] PH, Bagot Papers, W. R. Lyall to Bp R. Bagot, 14 January 1842 (copy).
[146] Toon, *Evangelical Theology*, p. 159; Bennett, 'Patristic Tradition in Anglican Thought'.
[147] W. Maskell, *A Second Letter on the Present Position of the High Church Party in the Church of England* (London, 1850), p. 16.
[148] PH, Pusey Papers, LBV [Transcripts], J. H. Newman to E. B. Pusey, 19 February 1844. As a Roman Catholic, Newman would conclude: 'They [the Anglo-Catholic divines] had reared a goodly house, but their foundations were falling in. The soil and the masonry both were bad. The Fathers would "protect" Romanists as well as extinguish Dissenters.' J. H. Newman, *Lectures on Certain Difficulties Felt by Anglicans in Submitting to the Catholic Church* (London, 1850), p. 125.

corrupt or erroneous.[149] It was *Tract 90*, in its ambitious endeavour
to show that, while the product of an 'uncatholic age', the Thirty-
Nine Articles were 'patient' of a 'catholic' sense,[150] that represented
the apogee of the process. Newman was aware that, for some of his
followers, the 'Protestant' nature of the Articles was becoming a
stumbling-block in their allegiance to the Church of England. As
early as 1835, he had confessed to being 'no friend' of the Articles,
even privately complaining that they countenanced 'a vile Protestantism'.[151] Yet as long as Newman was otherwise secure in his
conviction that the Church of England was the church of antiquity,
such misgivings could be brushed aside.

The 'stomach-ache' induced in Newman by the Roman Catholic
Nicholas Wiseman's likening of the Church of England to the
Donatists, increased his personal need to come to terms with an
acknowledged source of tension. He felt his theory of the *via media*
to have been 'absolutely pulverised'.[152] Newman's stronghold
had been antiquity. But in the 'face' of the 'mirror' of antiquity
itself, for the first time he felt that Rome's claim to identity with
antiquity might be vindicated at the expense of Anglicanism. As
Thomas argues, Newman had 'a sickening intuition' which placed
his own *via media* position of allegiance to antiquity 'in an analogical
relation to the spectrum of ancient theological opinion', i.e.
Monophysitism.[153] In short, the so-called 'patristic fundamentalism'
of the Tractarians was even echoed in the theological traditionalism
of the Monophysites. Might not the very 'traditionalism' of
Anglicanism be no more than mere ecclesiastical antiquarianism,
after all? In this personal religious crisis, Newman sought to salvage
his own flagging Anglican allegiance as well as to check the
Romeward drift of his younger followers. The result was a self-styled
experimentum crucis[154] to show that, when interpreted in the light of
antiquity, the Articles were not the anomaly or difficulty that they
might otherwise appear to a 'Catholic Christian'.

It was not the attempt to establish a compatibility between the
Thirty-Nine Articles and Catholic truths as enshrined in antiquity,

149 *Tract 79*, p. 3.
150 [J. H. Newman], 'Remarks on Certain Passages in the Thirty-Nine Articles', *Tract 90*
(2nd edn, Oxford, 1841), p. 4.
151 J. H. Newman to R. F. Wilson, 13 May 1835, *Letters and Diaries*, vol. v, p. 70.
152 Newman, *Apologia*, p. 212.
153 Thomas, *Newman and Heresy*, pp. 204–5.   154 Newman, *Apologia*, p. 232.

138 *The Oxford Movement in context*

that primarily troubled critics of *Tract 90*. There had been several historical precedents for Newman's attempt, such as that of Christopher Davenport in 1634 and Samuel Wix in 1818.[155] Nonetheless, most of these earlier precedents had presupposed that Rome would in effect have to abjure the Council of Trent and return to 'primitive' models of faith and order. In *Tract 90*, no such reorientation on the part of the Church of Rome was insisted upon.[156]

Old High Churchmen were concerned at the ambiguity of Newman's meaning. Newman claimed that it was only what he called the 'dominant errors' or 'the actual popular beliefs and usages sanctioned by Rome in the countries in communion with it' rather than 'the Catholic teaching of early centuries' which was condemned in the Articles.[157] In a complete reversal of earlier Tractarian apologetic wherein the Council of Trent was deemed to have enshrined error that had previously been only 'floating',[158] Newman now attempted to distinguish the so-called 'dominant errors' or popular abuses, from a legitimate 'official' teaching of Rome as established by that same Council. Critics of the Tract eagerly seized on this glaring inconsistency.[159] Moreover, Newman's argument – that only the 'Romish' and not the 'Tridentine' versions of particular Roman Catholic doctrines had been condemned in the Articles – entailed a degree of historical inaccuracy and special pleading as to dates and chronology, which not only Evangelicals such as the Bishop of Ossory but also old High Churchmen such as Bishop Phillpotts disproved with ease.[160]

What was the clear principle in Newman's sifting of the wheat of

[155] For discussion of these precedents, see G. Tavard, *The Quest for Catholicity: a Study in Anglicanism* (London, 1963), pp. 149–60.

[156] J. R. Page, *The Position of the Church of England in the Catholic World Suggested by a Perusal of No. XC of the 'Tracts for the Times'* (London, 1844), p. 10; J. T. Tomlinson, *The Prayer Book, Articles and Homilies: Some Forgotten Facts in Their History of Which May Decide Their Interpretation* (London, 1897), p. 285.

[157] Newman, *Apologia*, pp. 159–60.

[158] *Tract 15*, p. 10; [Newman and Keble, eds.], *Remains of Richard Hurrell Froude*, vol. 1, pp. 306–7.

[159] Wiseman pointed out Newman's inconsistency regarding the status of the Tridentine decrees: 'you now blame us for departure from them. Why not suspect your judgments if you find they vary?' N. Wiseman, *A Letter Respectfully Addressed to the Rev. J. H. Newman upon Some Passages in His Letter to the Rev. Dr. Jelf* (London, 1841), p. 30.

[160] J. T. O'Brien, *A Charge Delivered to the Clergy of the United Dioceses of Ossory, Ferns and Leighlin at His Primary Visitation in September 1842* (2nd edn, London, 1843), pp. 165–8; Goode, *Tract XC Historically Refuted*, pp. 76–7; H. Phillpotts, *A Charge Delivered to the Clergy of the Diocese of Exeter, at the Triennial Visitation in June, July, August and September 1842* (London, 1842), pp. 37–8.

'Catholic' teaching from the chaff of 'dominant errors'? The term 'Catholic' was overworked by Newman and other Tractarians, but was rarely satisfactorily explained. 'What a useful weapon that word "Catholic" is!', observed William Goode, 'with three syllables it settles everything ... It is a magic word that turns everything it touches into gold.'[161] Likewise, Newman's embittered brother, Francis, later argued that, in *Tract 90*, his use of three epithets, 'Roman', 'Catholic' and 'Papal', enabled him 'to play his own game on simple minds'.[162] Even Liddon felt that Newman's use of the phrase, 'doctrine of the Old Church' with which he sought to render the Articles compatible, was an ambiguous expression, open to misunderstanding.[163] Certainly, there was a suspicion that, by 'Catholic', Newman meant not only the teaching of antiquity alone but also part of the Tridentine teaching of the Church of Rome. Herein lay a source of growing divergence between Newman, now attracted by Rome's method of discerning antiquity, and Pusey, who remained locked in a 'patristic fundamentalism' that was no less essentially 'static' than Palmer's more selective traditionalism. For according to Pusey's conservative defence of Newman's principle of interpretation of the Articles, Newman only meant by 'Catholic', that which was 'ancient', not elements of 'the later definite system in the Church of Rome'.[164] As Liddon later admitted, the two were now at cross purposes. Pusey was mistaken about or ignorant of Newman's real position by 1841.[165]

For old High Churchmen, *Tract 90*, even with the gloss provided by Pusey, entailed a dangerous misapplication of a legitimate principle. The church's formularies were being tried by a merely private judgment as to what was and was not antiquity. The very ambiguity of Newman's use of the term 'Catholic' gave a superficial plausibility to the central argument of *Tract 90*. For, as Bishop Phillpotts admitted, the statement in the Canon of 1571 that preachers should uphold the doctrines of the primitive church appeared to assert the very principle propagated in *Tract 90*, 'namely, that the Articles

---

[161] Goode, *The Case as It Is*, p. 59.
[162] F. W. Newman, *Contributions to the Early History of the Late Cardinal Newman*, p. 97.
[163] Liddon, *Life of Pusey*, vol. II, pp. 162–3. As Brilioth observed: 'here already occurs a shadow, which falls ever thicker upon the path of progressive Anglo-Catholicism right down to the present day, the absence of any clear content in the idolised formula of catholicity'. Brilioth, *Anglican Revival*, p. 155; Tavard, *Quest for Catholicity*, ch. 7.
[164] E. B. Pusey, *The Articles Treated on in Tract 90 Reconsidered and Their Interpretation Vindicated* (Oxford, 1841), p. 5.
[165] Liddon, *Life of Pusey*, vol. II,. pp. 225–9.

were to be understood in the Catholic sense'. Nonetheless, as Phillpotts argued, the Canon of 1571 would,

be found on consideration to be utterly irreconcilable with the application of that principle, as contended for in the Tract, for it is there maintained, that any man will satisfy the duty incurred in subscribing the Articles, if he assents to them, not in their plain, and obvious, and grammatical sense, but in that sense which he, of his own mere opinion, shall determine to be "Catholic", whereas the Canon shows that the plain, and obvious, and grammatical sense, is also the Catholic sense.[166]

Phillpotts's High Church critique of *Tract 90* was widely echoed. Palmer of Worcester took a similar line in spite of his private expressions of approval to Newman. Adams is mistaken in tracing a theological congruity between Newman's method in *Tract 90* and Palmer's in his *Treatise on the Church of Christ*. Adams likens Palmer's attempt to reconcile Henry VIII's *King's Book* and the Articles, with Newman's attempt to reconcile the Articles and the Tridentine decrees.[167] But the analogy is not convincing. Clearly Palmer implied something very different from Newman by primitive doctrine.

A comparison of the relevant sections of the first and second editions of Palmer's *Treatise*, published in 1838 and 1842, is instructive. In the 1838 edition of the *Treatise*, Palmer had simply stated as one of the rules of interpretation of the Articles, that they were to be understood in 'the sense most conformable to Scripture and to Catholic Tradition, which she [the Church] acknowledges to be her guides'.[168] Significantly, four years later, in the light of *Tract 90*'s assumption as to what constituted 'Catholic Tradition', Palmer felt that he needed to be more precise. Thus, in the enlarged 1842 edition of his *Treatise*, Palmer added an important note of caution, explaining precisely what he meant by interpreting the Articles in the 'most catholic sense'. In the additional passage, the implied rebuke of the key principle of *Tract 90* is clear. For Palmer made clear that,

the rule of interpreting the Articles in the most catholic sense, is one which must not be vaguely and indiscriminately applied to all the Articles, as if we were at liberty to affix to them whatever meaning seems to us most consistent with Scripture or with Tradition. The principle thus applied

166 Phillpotts, *A Charge to the Clergy of the Diocese of Exeter ... 1842*, p. 28.
167 Adams, 'William Palmer's *Narrative of Events*', p. 88.
168 Palmer, *Treatise on the Church of Christ*, vol. I, p. 204.

would lead to a most dangerous tampering with the authorised formularies of the church; would open the way for evasions of their most evident meaning, and thus render them wholly useless as tests of belief or persuasion.

On the contrary, such a rule of interpretation could only apply to 'particular cases where a legitimate doubt of the meaning of any Article exists, and where it cannot be solved either by the language of other parts of the Articles, or of other formularies of the church'.[169] An example of such a legitimate case was the perennial dispute that had long divided the Orthodox and some Evangelicals over whether Article 17 relating to election and predestination should be interpreted in an Arminian or Calvinist sense. Here, a certain latitude was permissible, and it was precisely with this particular dispute in mind that Laud had declared the Articles to be 'articles of peace'. But, as Protestant High Churchmen such as Faussett as well as Evangelicals such as Goode pointed out, this precedent did not support Newman's own peculiar theory of 'catholic latitude'. For the points of doctrine in the Articles for which Newman claimed such a 'catholic latitude' were precisely those 'points on which Luther, Calvin and Arminius are agreed'; in short, they embodied 'the great verities distinguishing the orthodox Protestant theology from the corrupt creed of Rome'.[170]

Certainly in the wake of the rise of Arminian interpretations of the Articles as sanctioned by public authority after the 1620s, it was not always easy to determine where the bounds of a latitude of interpretation should lie. During the eighteenth century heterodoxy sometimes sheltered under cover of the broader reaction against Calvinism. Arians and Deists took advantage of the relative freedom on disputed points which Laud won for the Church. Against this trend, the Orthodox rallied. Waterland, Thomas Sherlock, Secker and others rebutted what they regarded as the abuse of such freedom by heterodox divines such as Samuel Clarke and Francis Blackburne.

Newman touched a raw nerve of Protestant orthodoxy when he argued that if there could be latitude on certain points in

---

[169] Palmer, *Treatise on the Church of Christ* (3rd edn, London, 1842), vol. II, p. 214; C. R. Elrington, *Subscription to the XXXIX Articles* (Dublin, 1842), p. 15.

[170] W. Goode, ed., *Two Treatises on the Church. The First by Thomas Jackson ... the Second by Herbert Sanderson* (London, 1843), p. iii. Godfrey Faussett used almost the same words: 'Unfortunately for his [Newman's] object, the very questions he feels interested in leaving open, are for the most part those which our Reformers were especially careful to close.' G. Faussett, *The Thirty-Nine Articles Considered* (Oxford, 1841), p. 97.

interpreting the Articles, why not on others? In response, Oxford Protestant High Churchmen such as Faussett and Charles Ogilvie likened Newman's principle of 'catholic' subscription to that of the 'Arian' theories of subscription advocated by Clarke, Blackburne and others in the preceding century. Significantly, Ogilvie cited Waterland's and Van Mildert's later arguments against 'Arianising' as no less applicable to the principles of *Tract 90*.[171] For if the Articles could be thus rendered 'patient' of a 'Catholic' interpretation, they could as easily be subject to an unorthodox one.[172] Certainly, old High Church forebodings on this point seemed borne out by the way in which many contemporary latitudinarians such as Stanley would rally in defence of *Tract 90* on the ground that the latter was a blow against all creeds and tests. Stanley would even use the precedent of *Tract 90* as a justification for the latitude enshrined in the later Gorham Judgment and for his own campaign in 1863–4 for the abolition of subscription altogether.[173] Newman and Pusey may have repudiated any such inferences and consequences, but the damage to the dogmatic integrity of Protestant High Church orthodoxy cannot be overestimated. It was left to Edward Churton to reassert what old High Churchmen insisted was the true 'catholic' principle of interpreting the Articles as 'articles of peace' in the manner upheld by Laud, Taylor and Bramhall. For Churton, this Laudian interpretation was opposed alike to the rival theories of Tractarian, Evangelical and latitudinarian subscription. Thus, while the principles of subscription advocated in *Tract 90* were evasive, Evangelicals no less erred by making all the Articles matters of faith, and latitudinarians adopted an equally false principle in depriving the Articles of all doctrinal application. In short, the Articles meant both more than latitudinarians allowed, and less than Evangelicals maintained, but also represented 'catholic' principles in a sense different from that advocated by the Tractarians.[174]

---

171 C. A. Ogilvie, *Considerations on Subscription to the Thirty-Nine Articles* (Oxford, 1845), pp. 11–12; Faussett, *Thirty-Nine Articles*, p. 8.

172 E. A. Knox, *Reminiscences of an Octogenarian, 1847–1934* (London, 1935), p. 66.

173 A. P. Stanley, *A Letter to the Bishop of London on the State of Subscription* (London, 1863), p. 23; [A. P. Stanley], 'Subscription', *Macmillan's Magazine*, 43 (January, 1881), 209–11.

174 E. Churton, *The Church's Law of Doctrine: A Charge Delivered to the Clergy of the Archdeaconry of Cleveland, at the Annual Visitation, 1864* (London, 1864), pp. 14–24.

The emergence of a genuinely 'Romanising' wing to the Movement in the early 1840s, associated with Newman's followers such as W. G. Ward, Frederick Oakeley, J. D. Dalgairns and F. W. Faber, marked an ideological watershed. For the Wardites, with the exception of Oakeley, jettisoned the historical rhetoric and preoccupations of early Tractarianism. A new source of divergence within the Movement itself opened up.[175] Pusey and Palmer differed markedly as to how far Antiquity should be used in deciding on the interpretation of particular doctrines and practices. However, for Ward, with his ethical priorities and philosophical cast of mind, antiquity was almost irrelevant because by the early 1840s he had already come to regard the living, modern Church of Rome as the ultimate repository of doctrinal truth.

Newman's *Tract 90* was written with followers like Ward in mind. Yet Ward always seemed to be one step ahead of his nominal leader, extending and developing what was but latent in Newman's mind. Ward's defence of *Tract 90* well illustrated this. Newman had been manifestly unclear as to what he actually meant by the phrase, 'the authoritative teaching of the Church of Rome'. Pusey had sought to sidestep the question of the precise status of the Tridentine decrees by lamely arguing that 'this part of the question relates rather to the hope of future repentance and restoration of Rome than to any thing which concerns ourselves at the moment'.[176] Sensing that Newman meant more than this, Ward had no such reticence. He admitted that Newman's terminology had been ambiguous, but sought to draw out what he felt were legitimate inferences. In two pamphlets, Ward further extended Newman's argument that the Articles should be subscribed to without regard to the known opinions of their compilers or even of the 'imponens' or authority enjoining subscription. Ward insisted that the Articles had to be interpreted in a 'non-natural' sense if they were to be accommodated to 'Catholic' truth.[177] In effect, as F. L. Cross has argued, Ward was maintaining that we

---

[175] See Ward, *William George Ward and the Oxford Movement*, ch. 4.
[176] Pusey, *The Articles Treated on in Tract 90 Reconsidered*, p. 5.
[177] Ward, *William George Ward and the Oxford Movement*, p. 173. See W. G. Ward, *A Few Words in Defence of Tract 90* (Oxford, 1841). Copeland later remarked to Pusey that the whole 'disturbance' over *Tract 90* had been due 'to Ward's stealing a march upon you and

interpret the Articles right when we make them mean the very reverse of what they appear to say! Whereas Newman had expressed his readiness to withdraw the phrase which he had used of the Articles, viz. 'ambiguous formularies', Ward held that the only means of giving them a Catholic sense at all was to defend their ambiguity.[178]

Yet while Newman denied the principle of a 'non-natural sense', in practice he had come close to advocating it. Moreover, his private correspondence in 1841–2 reveals a growing sympathy with Ward's position and divergence away from that of Pusey.[179] Nevertheless, Ward's *Ideal of a Christian Church* (1844), in which he maintained the startling proposition that it was possible to hold 'the whole cycle of' Roman Catholic doctrine within the Church of England[180] had only a limited influence on Newman. Ward's ethical points of reference contrasted with Newman's primarily historical outlook. The difference in approach ensured that Newman's reasons for his own ultimate secession to Rome in 1845 remained quite distinct from those of his younger followers.

Newman's loss of faith in the *via media*, sealed by the response to *Tract 90*, entailed no decline of interest in antiquity. On the contrary, his patristic and historical research was fuelled by the quest for the true principle of determining the sense of antiquity. Ultimately, he was to find the key to his dilemma in the construction of a theory of the development of religious doctrine, by which the apparent discrepancies in the Fathers, along with the supposed 'corruptions' of the later Church of Rome, could be explained and accounted for.[181]

Newman's shift in theological perspective in 1843 when he formulated the theory was important. Yet there was continuity as well as change. Contemporary critics and later commentators have noted seeds of the idea of 'development' in his *Arians* as early as 1833 and, above all, in *Tract 85*.[182] Moreover, it can be argued that, in

getting a first hearing for a false gloss'. PH, Pusey Papers, LBV [Originals], W. J. Copeland to E. B. Pusey, 15 November 1865.
[178] F. L. Cross, *John Henry Newman* (London, 1933), p. 125.
[179] For example, see Birmingham Oratory, 'Tract 90 Correspondence', no. 115, J. H. Newman, 7 April 1863.
[180] W. G. Ward, *The Ideal of a Christian Church Considered in Comparison with Existing Practice* (2nd edn, London, 1844), pp. 47–92.
[181] J. H. Newman, *An Essay on the Development of Christian Doctrine* (London, 1845), pp. 11–12.
[182] Greenfield, 'The Attitude of the Early Tractarians to the Roman Catholic Church', vol. II, p. 255. See also, Pereiro, 'S. F. Wood and an early theory of Development', 524–53.
Examples of the High Anglican response to Newman's doctrine of Development

embracing 'development' Newman simply modified the rhetoric of history which had supported his discarded *via media* theory. As Thomas shows, Newman had already formulated a rhetoric of the 'development of heresy' in his *Arians*. This helped ease him into the idea of the 'development of orthodoxy' in the early 1840s. Newman's later patristic research convinced him that his earlier high Tractarian correlation of heresy with innovation had been misplaced. Theological 'conservatism' was no necessary bulwark against heterodoxy as he had once assumed.[183] On the contrary, the new lesson he found in antiquity was that heresy could coexist with precisely that 'shutting' of oneself up in antiquity of which he had earlier been accused, and of which he would feel those Tractarians who rallied around Pusey after 1845, were guilty. In short, antiquity must not become antiquarianism. Patristic fundamentalism, unleavened by engagement with a 'living' church, was no more a touchstone of right belief than the biblical fundamentalism he had assailed in the 1830s. Study of the Fathers had led Newman to Rome, but it was the Fathers viewed in that peculiarly personal, imaginative way which had gripped him on his first reading of their heroic exploits in the pages of Milner.

include: W. Palmer [of Worcester], *The Doctrine of Development and Conscience Considered in Relation to the Evidence of Christianity and of the Catholic System* (London, 1846); W. J. Irons, *The Theory of Development Examined* (London, 1846); W. Gresley, *The Theory of Development Briefly Considered* (London, 1846). See also, C. L. Brown, 'Newman's Minor Critics', *Downside Review*, 89 (1971), 13–21; D. Nicholls, 'Newman's Anglican Critics', *Anglican Theological Review*, 47 (1965), 377–95.

183 Thomas, *Newman and Heresy*, chs. 16, 17. See also Ker, *Newman and the Fullness of Christianity*, ch. 6.

CHAPTER 3

Ecclesiology: the apostolic paradigm

APOSTOLICITY OF ORDER AND HIGH CHURCHMANSHIP, 1760–1840

A belief in the divine basis of a threefold ministerial order, an episcopal system of church government and a lineal succession of the episcopate, represented a key component of traditional High Churchmanship. Notwithstanding the Reformation, the Church of England was deemed to have preserved apostolicity of ministerial order. This claim figured prominently in the apologetic of the Caroline Divines in controversy with both Presbyterian and Roman Catholic opponents, and found classic expression in the celebrated *Three Letters to the Bishop of Bangor* (1717–19) by the Nonjuror, William Law.

A reassertion of the doctrine of the necessity of an apostolic ministerial commission was integral to early Tractarian polemic. The *catenae patrum* in the Tracts in favour of apostolical succession was in this case conclusive proof that the Tractarian advocacy was no novelty, since eighteenth-century witnesses such as Horne and Jones of Nayland were cited as well as their predecessors from the Stuart era.[1] Yet, as on other questions, it suited the purposes of Tractarian rhetoric to portray their advocacy of apostolical succession as the recovery of an ancient truth lost sight of in the 'deadness' of eighteenth-century Anglicanism. The assumption was made that the focus on apostolical succession in the early Tracts had roused discussion 'on points which had long remained undisturbed'.[2] This assumption deserves questioning.

The testimony of both Gladstone and Bishop Blomfield supported the Tractarian view. Blomfield 'is said to have remarked that after

[1] *Tracts for the Times*, vol. III for 1835–6, No. 74 (London, 1836) pp. 1–55.
[2] *Tracts for the Times*, vol. II for 1834–5 (London, 1839), p. iii.

William Law's *Letters to the Bishop of Bangor*, no writer asserted the doctrine of apostolical succession until the Tractarians arose'.[3] In response to Blomfield's flippant remark that the number of those who believed in the doctrine could be counted on the fingers of two hands, Joshua Watson equally loosely asserted, in an allusion to the faithful remnant in 1 Kings 19, v. 18, 'my Lord, there are a good seven thousand'.[4] Certainly, it had suited Whig latitudinarian divines of the Hanoverian era such as Hoadly and Blackburne, as well as Protestant Dissenting polemicists, to belittle contemporary High Church support for *jure divino* ecclesiastical principles. This was the context for Warburton's self-serving argument that the apostolical succession in the Church of England had been lost at the Revolution in 1689 with the lay deprivations of those bishops who refused to swear the Oath of Allegiance to William of Orange in 1689. It was an argument that proved serviceable for Rational Dissenters such as Joseph Priestley and Samuel Heywood, anxious to rebut revived High Church 'apostolical' claims being made by Horsley and others in the 1780s and 1790s.[5] When highlighting their own contribution, Warburton's testimony bolstered the Tractarian contention that the Hanoverian divines had allowed church principles to fall into a decay which only the Movement of 1833 had reversed.

The mere quantity of literary testimony is no sure guide to the scale of support for the doctrine among clergy or laity. On the contrary, the number of publications advocating it can be regarded as a response to a perceived want. Certainly, contemporary sources point to a degree of lay ignorance on the subject. When Daubeny's *Guide to the Church* first appeared in 1798, a friendly reviewer noted that the

nature of the Christian church, by what its unity is constituted, and in what the offence of schism consists, are subjects, by long neglect, rendered so obscure, to perhaps the majority of persons in this country, that acknowledgments are justly due to a writer, who, at the present period, undertakes to elucidate them.[6]

---

[3] J. H. Overton, *The Evangelical Revival in the Eighteenth Century* (London, 1886), p. 159. The remark had been attributed to Blomfield as early as 1843 by Gladstone. See, BL, Gladstone Papers, Ms Add 44360, fol. 250. [Draft of article for *Foreign and Colonial Review* by W. E. Gladstone, 1843.]

[4] Webster, *Joshua Watson*, p. 19.

[5] [Heywood], *High Church Politics*, pp. 6–7; R. Apsland, *A Plea for Unitarian Dissenters. In a Letter of Expostulation, to the Rev. H. H. Norris* (London, 1813), p. 10.

[6] Daubeny, *An Appendix to the Guide to the Church*, pp. 106–7; ESCRO, Locker-Lampson Papers, B/5/19 (copy), C. Daubeny to Lord Kinnoul, November 1800.

According to other testimony, the climate had scarcely improved by 1820. When John Oxlee's *Sermon on the Christian Priesthood* was published in that year, a reviewer sadly observed that, 'men of this generation are scarcely prepared for the reception of such ancient and primitive truths. We apprehend that its perusal will have an effect similar to putting new wine into old bottles.'[7]

Some contemporary testimony, contrary to the above evidence, revealed a growing popularity of the doctrine of apostolical succession.[8] Certainly, in the era of the Movement, the older generation of High Churchmen resented the Tractarian monopolisation of credit for reviving the doctrine. In his episcopal Charge of 1843, Bishop Bethell questioned Tractarian presuppositions from a Hackney Phalanx perspective and clerical career dating back to the 1800s. Referring to the doctrines of church authority and succession, Bethell complained that Tractarian 'encomiasts have spoken of them as truths which had been forgotten and lost to the church till they were rescued from oblivion by the authors of the Tracts'. Bethell admitted 'that they were kept much in the background' but insisted that 'they never ceased to be held and avowed'.[9] In similar vein, Rose had complained to Newman, after reading his *Tract 71*, 'I wish that you had somewhat more represented the Apostolical Succession as a regular, undoubted doctrine, held undoubtingly by all true Churchmen, and only a little neglected, – than as a thing to which we were to recur as a sort of ancient novelty – a truth now first recovered.'[10] Even Newman's apparently radical suggestion in the 1830s that the Articles should be amended so as to include a protest on behalf of the doctrine of apostolical succession,[11] had precedents in earlier complaints by George Horne, J. H. Spry and Godfrey Faussett about the absence of any explicit enunciation of the doctrine in the Church's formularies.[12]

---

[7] *Anti-Jacobin Review*, 58 (January, 1820), 425; 59 (February, 1821), 530. Oxlee provided 'a continued and uninterrupted list of Christian Bishops from the Blessed Apostles Peter, Paul and John, down to the present prelates of Canterbury, York and London'. Oxlee, *Claim of the Protestant Dissenters*.

[8] *Christian Remembrancer*, 3 (March, 1821), 157.

[9] C. Bethell, *A Charge to the Clergy of the Diocese of Bangor ... in 1843* (London, 1843), pp. 15–16.

[10] H. J. Rose to J. H. Newman, 9 May 1836, J. W. Burgon, *Lives of Twelve Good Men*, vol. I, p. 108.

[11] *Tract 41*, 'Via Media II', pp. 3–4.

[12] J. H. Spry, *Christian Unity Doctrinally and Historically Considered, in Eight Sermons Preached before the University of Oxford, in the Year MDCCCXVI, at the Lecture Founded by the Late Rev. John Bampton* (Oxford, 1817), p. 189; Faussett, *Claims of the Established Church*, pp. 9–12.

Although there was a widespread perception that by the end of the eighteenth century 'Hoadlyite' principles had 'sunk into very general dis-esteem',[13] divines of the 'Cambridge intellectual party' such as Paley or Balguy, whom some consider within the Orthodox umbrella, retained an old Low Church antipathy to the claims of a commissioned priesthood.[14] Even the more genuinely Orthodox such as Pretyman-Tomline and Marsh did not dwell on 'apostolical descent'.[15] Nonetheless, the new political climate of the 1760s in the wake of George III's accession proved conducive to a revival of *jure divino* High Church claims. The Hutchinsonians were at the forefront of this revival. Thus in 1765, George Berkeley junior preached an uncompromising defence of apostolical succession from the pulpit of St Mary's, Oxford.[16] Moreover, Francis Blackburne was complaining in the late 1760s that, in response to his 'Hoadlyite' polemic *The Confessional* (1765), churchmen once more 'skirmished in the old posture prescribed in the ancient system of church authority', reviving what he called 'exploded doctrines' such as apostolical succession.[17] The published works in which such doctrines were upheld in the pre-Tractarian era included: Stevens's *Nature and Constitution of the Christian Church* (1773), Jones of Nayland's *Essay on the Church* (1780), Daubeny's *Guide to the Church* (1798) and *Appendix to the Guide* (1804), Sikes's *Discourse on Parochial Communion* (1812), John James Watson's *Divine Commission and Perpetuity of the Christian Priesthood* (1816), Burgess's *Primary Principles of Christianity* (1829), and the Bampton Lectures of Le Mesurier (1807), J. H. Spry (1816) and Faussett (1820). Of these, the Tract writers only took notice of Daubeny's *Guide*, which was cited in *Tract 74*. Newman had a copy of the work, of which a new edition had been published in 1830.[18] Yet the kinship between Tractarian and earlier Hackney restatements of the doctrine was made evident at the time of the re-publication in

---

[13] The verdict of Jonathan Boucher in the *Anti-Jacobin Review*, 4 (November, 1799), 253.

[14] For example, see Balguy, 'On Church Authority', Discourse VI [1769], *Nine Discourses*, pp. 104–5.

[15] See G. Pretyman-Tomline, *Elements of Christian Theology*, 2 vols. (London, 1799), vol. II, pp. 367–401.

[16] E. Berkeley, ed., *Sermons by the Late Rev. George Berkeley* (London, 1799), No. 1.

[17] *Works Theological and Miscellaneous of Francis Blackburne*, vol. I, p. xxxv.

[18] In 1833, Pusey asked Newman for his copy of the 1830 edition of Daubeny's *Guide to the Church*. PH, Pusey Papers, LBV [Transcripts], E. B. Pusey to J. H. Newman, December 1833.

1839 of Archdeacon Watson's treatise on the Christian Priesthood first published in 1816.[19]

The anti-Low Church credentials of Evangelicals prior to 1833 primarily rested on their relatively high views of apostolical authority and order. In 1820, the Evangelical Daniel Wilson insisted that a firm belief in 'the authority and purity of our national church' was a view common to both Evangelical and Orthodox alike.[20] Sometimes exception was taken to the full *jure divino* episcopal edifice erected by divines such as Daubeny,[21] but it is noteworthy that the writings of Jones of Nayland which the *Christian Observer* commended as worthy of instruction in 1804, were precisely those on the constitution of the church.[22] Moreover, even the bitter controversy involving Daubeny on the one hand and John Overton and Sir Richard Hill on the other between 1798–1805, focused much more on doctrinal issues such as grace, free will and Justification, than on ecclesiological principles of church order. Comparisons with the Tractarian era are instructive. The *Christian Observer* of the 1830s was to be more antipathetic to the appearance of High Church claims in favour of apostolical succession than it had been in the 1800s.[23] Apostolical succession in Tractarian hands would be divisive in a way that it had not been prior to 1833. Yet even in the late 1830s the Tractarian appeal to apostolicity struck a chord with some Evangelicals. For some High Churchmen this was a hopeful sign. As Edward Churton remarked to H. H. Norris in 1838, 'one encouraging feature in these days, is that we find many clergymen, who though given to favour the Calvinistic doctrines, as fancying they have more "unction", are not unwilling to add to them more strict notions of Apostolical Succession etc. If we can separate these from the wilder class, they may do us much good.'[24] With discreet handling, the Tractarians might have used the doctrine as a basis of union within the church. But instead, division ensued. Why?

For all the continuity, differences between the Tractarian and much of the older High Church presentation of the doctrines of

[19] J. J. Watson, *The Divine Commission and Perpetuity of the Christian Priesthood as Considered in a Charge to the Clergy of the Archdeaconry of St Albans at His Primary Visitation, 1816* (new edn, London, 1839), p. vi.
[20] Quoted in J. Bateman, *The Life of Daniel Wilson*, 2 vols. (London, 1860), vol. 1, pp. 205–6.
[21] R. Hill, *Reformation-Truth Restored: Being a Reply to the Rev. Charles Daubeny's 'Appendix' to His 'Guide to the Church'* (London, 1800), pp. 15–20.
[22] *Christian Observer*, 3 (November, 1804), 680; 6 (October, 1807), 677.
[23] *Christian Observer*, 38, No. 2 (March, 1838), 184.
[24] SC, Churton Papers, E. Churton to H. H. Norris, 12 May 1838.

episcopacy and the succession can be identified. According to W. N. Molesworth, apostolical succession had been 'indeed familiar to the clergy, not only of the Orthodox, but of the Evangelical schools', but it tended to be regarded as 'a sort of esoteric doctrine about which they were discreetly silent, or at which they just tacitly hinted in their discourses'.[25] In the advertisement to the second volume of the *Tracts for the Times*, Newman highlighted his own sense of the difference between the two. Hitherto, it was alleged, churchmen had maintained the doctrine merely for order's sake. Of course, church order was a vital principle for the Tractarians, but there was a deeper, sacramental dimension to their restatement of the doctrine. For Newman, the doctrine was 'to be approached joyfully and expectantly as a definite instrument, or rather the appointed means of spiritual blessings'. Viewed in this light, prevailing views on the subject were inadequate. Therefore, for all its outward support, apostolical succession, Newman explained, was

a doctrine which is as yet but faintly understood among us ... The particular deficiency here alluded to [i.e. lack of a sense of spiritual blessings] may also be described by referring to another form under which it shows itself, viz. the a priori reluctance in those who believe in the apostolical commission, to appropriate to it the power of consecrating the Lord's Supper, as if there were some antecedent improbability in God's gifts being lodged in particular observances and distributed in the particular way.[26]

In their high sacramental understanding of the doctrine, the early Tractarians were in accord with the emphasis of Nonjuring divines such as William Law and Leslie and a few later exponents such as Daubeny who regarded episcopacy as the *esse* of the church. However, as critics of the Movement pointed out, much Orthodox apologetic for the doctrine had entailed only a negative appeal to the Church's 'title deeds' and historical pedigree, and defence of episcopacy as the *bene esse* of the church. As Toon has demonstrated,

25 W. N. Molesworth, *The History of England from the Year 1830–1874*, 2 vols. (London, 1879), vol. 1, p. 281.
26 *Tracts for the Times*, vol. 1, No. 4 (London, 1834), p. v. Froude and Keble also enunciated this view. See KCA, No. 62, R. H. Froude to A. P. Perceval, 14 August 1833; J. Keble to J. Davison, 13 August 1833. Keble conceded that Hooker had not drawn from the doctrine of apostolical succession the inference that episcopacy was the sole divinely-appointed channel of sacramental grace, on which he himself insisted. Keble, ed., *Works of Richard Hooker*, vol. 1, p. lxxxi.

the stress of many Evangelicals on episcopal order and succession was at one with this line of Anglican apologetic.[27] Apostolical succession could be valued in terms of historical continuity but the Tractarian view that special grace was communicated in the succession of bishops was repudiated because, for Evangelicals, grace was related to the truth of the Gospel and the power of the Holy Spirit.[28] For this reason, Evangelical assailants of Tractarian interpretations of the doctrine could happily appeal to the testimony of both Marsh and Pretyman-Tomline to defend their case. The Movement's Evangelical critics maintained that the Tractarians added their own superstructure to the basic premise of Orthodox apologetic, when they tied the actual derivation of sacramental grace and mystical union with Christ to the necessity of the apostolical commission. Goode marshalled an array of Caroline testimonies to prove that the Tractarian position went well beyond that of the mainstream seventeenth-century divines.[29]

The Tractarian linkage of the validity of sacraments to the succession was also rejected by many moderate High Churchmen such as Edward Hawkins and Bishop Blomfield. Hawkins drew a distinction between 'the more cautious language' of a consensus of the Caroline Divines and the 'more rigid principles of the Succession' advocated by William Law and the Nonjurors, and in the earlier numbers of the *Tracts for the Times*. The distinction in application of the same doctrine between the two was important. Moderate supporters of apostolical succession, Hawkins explained,

do not run into the two mistakes common with those who uphold the extreme doctrine; neither assuming, for it is only an assumption, the necessary connexion between the office of the minister and the efficacy of the sacraments; nor supposing that the arguments which prove Episcopacy, or an Episcopal Succession to be right, and much more than right, prove it also to be essential.[30]

[27] Toon, *Evangelical Theology*, pp. 184–6. In correspondence with Pusey, the Evangelical Anne Tyndale conceded the value of the doctrine. PH, Tyndale Papers, A. Tyndale to E. B. Pusey, 20 November 1833. Other Evangelicals repudiated the doctrine. See P. Maurice, *The Popery of Oxford Confronted, Disavowed and Repudiated* (London, 1837), p. 16.
[28] Goode, *The Case as It Is*, pp. 17–18.
[29] W. Goode, *The Divine Rule of Faith and Practice*, 3 vols. (3rd edn, London, 1853), vol. II, pp. 270–322.
[30] E. Hawkins, *Apostolical Succession: a Sermon* (London, 1842), p. 31.

CATHOLICITY OF ORDER AND HIGH CHURCHMANSHIP, 1760–1833

Catholicity encompassed more than apostolicity alone. As fully formulated by the Caroline Divines in response to the dual challenge of Rome and Geneva, the theory of Anglican catholicity was based on scriptural and Cyprianic testimonies in favour of unity being a mark or note of the true church. On the one hand, the Roman Catholic interpretation of unity which was deemed to represent usurpation was repudiated. On the other hand, Geneva was considered to err in an opposite direction by interpreting unity primarily in terms of an invisible body of true believers.

For pre-Tractarian High Churchmen, following the lead of the Caroline Divines, catholicity did not imply a dogmatic centre of unity embodying the universal church as Roman Catholic controversialists asserted. Catholicity implied a federation of separate territorial entities that each upheld certain notes or 'fundamentals' of catholic faith and apostolic order. The Church of England was not itself *the* Catholic or universal church, as the Church of Rome professed to be, but rather, a branch of that universal church. The Church of England's claim to be a true branch of the church universal stood or fell by its preservation of apostolic order through the succession. The claim of other branches to true catholicity rested on the same basis. As Daubeny put it,

Every Christian society, possessing the characteristic marks of the Church of Christ, I consider to be a separate branch of the Catholic or Universal visible Church upon earth. The Church of England, the Church of Ireland, and the episcopal church of Scotland and America possess these marks. In the same light, the churches of Denmark, Sweden and Rome, are to be considered, not to mention the great remains of the once-famous Greek church, now to be found in the empire of Russia and in the East.[31]

High Churchmen insisted that unity of the church did not entail the dependence of one branch church upon another, but rather a coexistence on an equal basis. As Isaac Barrow had put it, 'all churches which have a fair settlement in several countries, are co-ordinate; neither can one challenge a jurisdiction over the other'.[32] Absolute uniformity and submission was no necessary part

---

[31] Daubeny, *An Appendix to the Guide to the Church*, pp. 106–7.
[32] A. Napier, ed., *Theological Works of Isaac Barrow*, 9 vols. (Cambridge, 1859), vol. VIII, p. 749.

of catholicity. Unity did not even need entail a 'necessary communion between all branches' of the catholic church as Roman Catholics argued.[33] On the contrary, as Palmer of Worcester put it, 'the principle of obedience to the Roman Pontiff, as the true test of catholic unity, was a principle tending to schism. It was never taught by the Gospel, and it was injurious to the catholic communion of churches.'[34] Within the limits prescribed by adherence to the notes of apostolic order, catholicity implied the widest possible terms of communion.[35] 'As Christian unity', explained J. H. Spry, 'is not merely a union of hearts and opinions, so neither does it consist in, or require an entire union of opinion ... or we shall destroy the possibility of unity, by making that essential to it, which never can be obtained.'[36]

For pre-Tractarian High Churchmen the Anglican theory represented a *via media* between rival theories of unity represented by Rome and Geneva. The Church of England was not 'merely Protestant' and thus not on the same level as non-episcopal foreign reformed or Dissenting churches. But at the same time it was not, as later Tractarians would have it, the natural 'sister' or even dependent child of the Church of Rome. The Church of England was both Catholic and Protestant and the two were perfectly compatible. Pre-Tractarian High Churchmen were proud of the title 'Protestant'. Yet echoes of a later Tractarian preference for the former of the two titles can be found, and some High Churchmen were most at ease with the epithet 'Reformed Catholic'. As Henry Handley Norris confided in 1812,

If names had any weight, I much more highly prize the title of a Catholic than that of a Protestant which later appelation I am by no means proud of, as it confounds one with those from whom Christianity I verily believe has suffered more outrages than from the Papists themselves. The distinguishing title of a member of the Church of England is a Reformed Catholic – and this places him in a central position from which the Papist and the larger portion of that mixed multitude known by the name of Protestant diverge, in opposite directions indeed but to equal distances.[37]

[33] Daubeny, *Guide to the Church*, p. 150.
[34] Palmer, *Treatise on the Church of Christ*, vol. 1, p. 454.
[35] W. Cave, *A Discourse Concerning the Unity of the Catholic Church Maintained in the Church of England* (London, 1684), p. 29; [W. Stanley], *The Faith and Practice of a Church of Englandman* (London, 1688), p. 3.
[36] Spry, *Christian Unity*, pp. 10–11.
[37] SC, Churton Papers, H. H. Norris to R. Churton, 30 September 1812.

HIGH CHURCHMANSHIP AND PROTESTANT DISSENT

The logic of High Church ecclesiology was that churches which stood in breach of apostolic order by having disavowed episcopal government lacked an essential note or mark of a true church and were in a state of formal schism from the church catholic. Protestant Dissenters in England manifestly fell into this category. High Churchmen were adamant that episcopacy was 'not to be disputed from without such a necessity as does not exist in this kingdom'.[38]

On this point, pre-Tractarian High Churchmen were no less rigid than their successors. From the 1790s onwards, in the wake of the rise of Methodism and Evangelical Dissent coupled with the anti-Jacobin reaction, the Orthodox became increasingly inclined to brand Dissenters as 'schismatics' rather than merely 'separatists'. In the Bible Society controversy, the High Church protagonists insisted upon the inherently schismatical nature of any schemes of formal co-operation with Dissenters as proposed by the Society's Evangelical friends.[39]

In their concern for church order, many Evangelicals in principle distanced themselves from the political cause of Protestant Dissent. Yet in practice, the degree of doctrinal common ground between the two and the Evangelical readiness to co-operate with Dissenters in the Bible Society, gave credence to Orthodox charges that Evangelicals sanctioned schism. The High Church identification of Evangelicals with Protestant Dissenters was a factor in the gradual deterioration of relations between the Orthodox and Evangelicals from the 1800s onwards.[40] Moreover, while even Overton and Sir Richard Hill had sought to present themselves as friends of ecclesiastical order in their controversy with Daubeny in the 1800s, the former's rejection of Daubeny's taunt of being 'schismatical' entailed an acceptance of 'Hoadlyite' arguments which Dissenters themselves sheltered behind. For instance, Hill rejected Daubeny's 'unchurching' of Dissenters, by insisting that the charge of schism against Dissent had not been applicable since the Toleration Act of 1689. In short, because the civil power had ensured religious toleration for

---

38 Le Mesurier, *Nature and Guilt of Schism*, p. 437.
39 For example, see H. H. Norris, *A Practical Exposition of the Tendency and Proceedings of the British and Foreign Bible Society* (2nd edn, London, 1814), p. 359; 'Norris on the Bible Society', *British Critic*, New Series, 2 (July, 1814), pp. 4–9.
40 T. Belsham, *The Present State of Religious Parties in England, Represented and Improved in a Discourse* (London, 1813), p. 12.

Dissenters, therefore *jure divino* grounds of objection had lost their force.[41] For High Churchmen insistent that episcopal claims were inherent and not based on civil authority, such arguments were irrelevant. In the writings of John Oxlee, Dissenters were portrayed as wilful rebels to the divine ordinance, whose 'forward and impious conduct' deserved 'the just vengeance of God' and 'the severity of hell torments'.[42] Tractarian rigidity towards Protestant Dissent, as exemplified in Newman's attitude in the Jubber case, thus had a long pedigree.[43]

HIGH CHURCHMANSHIP, THE CONTINENTAL PROTESTANT AND EASTERN CHURCHES

In traditional High Church ecclesiology, the abandonment of episcopal government by most of the foreign reformed churches in the sixteenth century was deemed highly regrettable, but unavoidable in the circumstances of those times. It had not been possible to assert purity of doctrine alongside continued adherence to the episcopal system. A clear line of demarcation was drawn between their case and that of the dissenting bodies in England and even the established Presbyterian Church of Scotland, for whom no such plea of necessity could be made.[44] Even Laud had accepted the validity of German Lutheran orders, maintaining that their system of superintendency preserved the substance, though not the name, of episcopacy. As Norman Sykes argued, by formulating such an accommodation to their theory, High Churchmen were able to affirm their solidarity with the rest of the Reformation world, and to avoid the potentially embarrassing isolation that would have resulted from its unqualified application.[45]

Eirenicism towards continental Protestantism characterised divines of the school of Pretyman-Tomline and Marsh. For Pretyman-Tomline, the claim to recognition of such churches rested on the 'grand fundamentals' of Christianity as enshrined in their

---

[41] Hill, *Reformation-Truth Restored*, pp. 17, 200.

[42] Oxlee, *Claim of the Protestant Dissenters*, p. 71.

[43] For an account of the Jubber episode, see Gilley, *Newman and His Age*, pp. 128–30.

[44] *The Works of Joseph Hall*, 10 vols. (Oxford, 1837), vol. x, p. 147; *The Works of the Most Rev. Father in God, John Bramhall*, 5 vols. (Oxford, 1842–5), vol. II, pp. 42–3. Palmer, *Treatise on the Church of Christ*, vol. I, p. 361, 377, 458.

[45] N. Sykes, *Old Priest and New Presbyter* (Cambridge, 1956), pp. 30–84; J. Pinnington, 'Historical Necessity of the Lambeth Quadrilateral', *Heythrop Journal*, 11 (1970), 127–47.

state-authorised confessions. The 'Church of Holland' and 'Church of Geneva', he maintained, 'were as much parts of the visible Church of Christ as were the apostolic churches of Jerusalem, Antioch, or Alexandria, because, although not perfect in that they lacked the episcopal regimen, they yet adhered to the fundamental principles of the Gospel'.[46] Yet even High Churchmen such as Daubeny who upheld episcopacy *jure divino* as the *esse* of the church, maintained the liberal Caroline distinction in favour of the continental non-episcopal churches. In short, while some of the foreign Reformers 'did vary from the Apostolical Succession, they still acknowledged the sacredness of the principle'.[47]

In some of the early numbers of the *Tracts for the Times*, residual traces of such eirenicism can be detected. For instance, in *Tract 4*, Keble hinted at the old distinction, arguing, 'it is one thing to slight and disparage this holy succession when it may be had, and another thing to acquiesce in the want of it when it is (if it be anywhere) really unobtainable'.[48] Even the anti-Tractarian Christopher Benson approvingly noted that in *Tract 15*, the Lutheran churches were regarded not as deliberately 'at variance with the Apostolical usage' but 'as Episcopal churches, sede vacante, or with the Episcopate in commission'.[49] As late as 1839, Pusey still upheld the more charitable view of the status of the foreign reformed churches maintained by Bramhall and other Caroline divines.[50] On the other hand, as early as 1836, Newman was expressing private dismay at the apparent concessions when judging heresy and schism which the early eighteenth-century canonist Bingham had made. Not liking what he found in Bingham, Newman's dismissal of his testimony was characteristically off-hand. 'Ever since the "Glorious" [i.e. 1688]', he assured Henry Wilberforce, 'we of the Church have been in an unutterable stupor – so do not be surprised at Bingham.'[51] Newman turned to more congenial authorities, admitting to Rose that he and his followers differed from the Caroline Divines in their view of continental Protestants.[52] The Jerusalem bishopric controversy in

46 Pretyman-Tomline, *Elements of Christian Theology*, vol. II, pp. 396–7.
47 Nott, *Religious Enthusiasm*, pp. 84–5.
48 *Tracts for the Times*, vol. I for 1833–4, No. 4 (New edn., London, 1838), p. 6. Nonetheless in this Tract (p. 7), Keble maintained: 'it would be wrong to allow such necessity, without proof quite overwhelming'. See Imberg, *In Quest of Authority*, pp. 146–53.
49 Quoted in Benson, *Discourses upon Tradition and Episcopacy*, p. 110.
50 Pusey, *A Letter ... to the Bishop of Oxford*, pp. 163–73.
51 J. H. Newman to H. W. Wilberforce, 14 September 1836, *Letters and Diaries*, vol. v, p. 357.
52 J. H. Newman to H. J. Rose, 23 May 1836, *Letters and Diaries*, vol. v, p. 302.

1841–2, which helped complete his loss of allegiance to the Church of England, marked an outpouring of unqualified Tractarian hostility towards the continental reformed churches hitherto unparalleled in the history of the Church of England.

The Jerusalem bishopric scheme which partly originated with the King of Prussia, entailed mutual co-operation between German Lutherans and members of the Church of England.[53] The aim was to promote conversions among the Jews, but the enthusiasm of Evangelicals such as Lord Shaftesbury as well as liberal churchmen fuelled Tractarian suspicions. For the Tractarians, the implied solidarity and equality envisaged between the Church of England and a non-episcopal body, amounted to collaboration with 'schismatics', and was subversive of the status of the Eastern Orthodox churches. In short, it represented 'a flag of allegiance held out to Zurich and Geneva from Lambeth'.[54]

The disdain for the foreign Protestant churches elicited in the Tractarian reaction to the Jerusalem bishopric can be contrasted with the eagerness of High Churchmen in the reign of Queen Anne to support apparently similar projects to introduce episcopacy into the churches of the Prussian territories.[55] Even Evangelical critics of the Tractarians, such as Goode, made a telling comparison between a Tractarian readiness to 'unchurch' the foreign reformed, and the eirenic attitude of 'their favourite witnesses' from the seventeenth century such as Bishop Cosin who when in exile had communicated 'rather with Geneva than Rome'.[56] Nevertheless, there is evidence to suggest that the more hardline position of the Tractarians was rather the outcome of a gradual trend among earlier High Churchmen than a sudden *volte-face*. The force of the contrast drawn by

---

[53] On the controversy, see R. W. Greaves, 'Jerusalem Bishopric', *EHR*, 44 (1949), 328–52; P. J. Welch, 'Anglican Churchmen and the Establishment of the Jerusalem Bishopric', JEH, 8 (1957), 193–204.

[54] BL, Gladstone Papers, Ms Add 44358, fol. 359, Lord John Manners to W. E. Gladstone, Feast of St John, 1841; Liddon, *Life of Pusey*, vol. II, p. 249.

[55] Sykes, *Old Priest and New Presbyter*, p. 213.

[56] Goode, *The Case as It Is*, p. 17. To refute the Tractarians, Goode drew up his own *catenae patrum* of High Church divines opposed to the absolute necessity of episcopal orders for valid ordination. See, W. Goode, *A Reply to Archdeacon Churton and Chancellor Harrington on the Term, 'Church of Scotland' in the Fifty-Fifth Canon, and on Non-Episcopal Ordinations* (London, 1852), pp. 31–2; W. Goode, *A Vindication of the Doctrine of the Church of England on the Validity of the Orders of the Scotch and Foreign Non-Episcopal Churches* (London, 1852), pp. 11, 26–7; W. Goode, *Brotherly Communion with the Foreign Protestant Churches Desired and Cultivated by the Highest and Best Divines of the Church of England* (Cambridge, 1859), pp. 17–34.

Goode, and highlighted by Norman Sykes, is offset by a growing questioning of the validity of the traditional plea of necessity. That plea might have been conclusive in the era of the Reformation. Yet, though still conceded in theory, the subsequent history of the continental churches meant that by the late eighteenth century it had become less of an extenuating factor. Opportunities for the reintroduction of episcopacy had not been followed up. In consequence, High Church acceptance of the validity of non-episcopal foreign orders became more grudging;[57] the status of their churches coming to be seen as increasingly doubtful and, in some cases, even invalid.[58] Moreover, many pre-Tractarian High Churchmen, including Hugh James Rose, linked the rising heterodoxy among the German Lutheran and Genevan churches to a failure to re-establish apostolical discipline.[59] Ironically, in his 'German war' with Rose in 1829, it was Pusey who, to his later regret, adopted the more liberal and eirenic position.[60]

There was an element in Newman's outraged response to the Jerusalem bishopric that was entirely novel when viewed in the context of earlier High Churchmanship. Tractarian objections went beyond a conviction that the continental reformed churches were schismatical or even tainted with Socinianism. Ultimately, the real

[57] On evidence of an increasingly negative attitude to non-episcopal Protestant bodies among pre-Tractarian High Churchmen, see Nott, *Religious Enthusiasm*, pp. 84–7; *British Critic*, 8 (July, 1817), 32; Daubeny, *Guide to the Church to Which Is Prefixed Some Account of the Author's Life and Writings* (1830), p. xviii.

For a critique of Norman Sykes's argument that the Tractarians departed from earlier High Church apologetic in questioning the validity of non-episcopal orders, see A. L. Peck, *Anglicanism and Episcopacy: a Re-examination of the Evidence with Special Reference to Professor Norman Sykes's 'Old Priest and New Presbyter'* (London, 1958), pp. 40–1; J. Pinnington, 'Anglican Openness to Foreign Protestant Churches in the Eighteenth Century: a Gloss on the Old Priest and New Presbyter Thesis of Norman Sykes', *Anglican Theological Review*, 51 (1969), 133–40; J. Pinnington, 'Church Principles and the Early Years of the Church Missionary Society: the Problem of the German Missionaries', *Journal of Theological Studies*, 20 (October, 1969), 320–32; R. A. Norris, 'Episcopacy', in Sykes and Booty, eds., *Study of Anglicanism*, pp. 300–7.

[58] John Oxlee attacked the 'Calvinistic Protestant churches of France, Holland, Germany and Prussia' for having 'impiously discarded the legitimate form of church government'. J. Oxlee, *A Sermon in Which It Is Unanswerably Proved . . . that the Christian Priesthood Is a Perfect Hierarchy* (York, 1821), pp. 97–8.

[59] H. J. Rose, *A Letter to the Lord Bishop of London, in Reply to Mr Pusey's Work on the Causes of Rationalism in Germany* (London, 1829), p. 144.

[60] Liddon, *Life of Pusey*, vol. I, p. 170; L. Frappell, 'Science in the Service of Orthodoxy: the Early Intellectual Development of E. B. Pusey', in Butler, ed., *Pusey Rediscovered*, pp. 14–19; Imberg, *In Quest of Authority*, p. 166.

focus of hostility was Protestantism.[61] As Newman maintained in his own highly coloured Protest, the intrinsic fault in the scheme was its proposed admission of 'maintainers of heresy to communion, without formal renunciation of their errors'.[62] Newman was explicit that it was Lutheranism and Calvinism itself, not merely heterodox corruptions of those creeds, which merited anathematisation. Here the gulf with historic High Churchmanship was unbridgeable.

Julius Hare condemned Newman's 'audacity' in calling 'those doctrines heretical which almost all the great divines of our Church' had always regarded as 'among the best expositions of truth'.[63] Hare was a Coleridgean Broad Churchman who hero worshipped Luther,[64] but his expression of dismay was widely shared by old High Churchmen.

A. P. Perceval was able to meet the disparagers of the scheme on their own ground. Perceval was no uncritical apologist of German Lutheranism in the manner of Julius Hare. He shared Rose's earlier correlation of heterodox trends with non-episcopacy in Lutheran Germany, and lamented lost opportunities for its reintroduction.[65] In full accordance with Anglican theory, he denied Palmer of Magdalen's suggestion that Lutherans were heretical because they lacked bishops. Roman or Greek anathemas had no authority for a member of the Church of England. Short of an Ecumenical Council being convened, English bishops could not allow them. 'And until they have done so', he observed, 'for individual members of our Church to treat such anathemas as binding, or to promulgate them within the British dioceses, seems to be a simple violation of the first principles of ecclesiastical order'.[66] For according to traditional High Church theory, one branch of the church catholic had no right to excommunicate another branch.

---

61 W. Palmer [of Magdalen], *A Letter to a Protestant-Catholic* (Oxford, 1842), pp. 36–7; J. R. Hope, *The Bishopric of the United Church of England and Ireland at Jerusalem* (London, 1841), pp. 42–3. See also n. 161.

62 Newman, *Apologia*, pp. 251–2.

63 Bodl. Lib, Manning Papers, Ms Eng Lett c. 653, fol. 210, J. Hare to H. E. Manning, 30 December 1841.

64 Julius Hare (1795–1855). Rector of Hurstmonceaux, Sussex, Archdeacon of Lewes. For Hare's critique of Tractarian misrepresentations of Luther, see J. Hare, *A Vindication of Luther* (London, 1855). See also, Avis, *Anglicanism*, pp. 253–8; W. P. Haugard, 'A Myopic Curiosity: Martin Luther and the English Tractarians', *Anglican Theological Review*, 66 (October, 1984), 399.

65 A. P. Perceval, *Results of an Ecclesiastical Tour in Holland and Northern Germany* (London, 1846), p. 11.

66 A. P. Perceval, *A Vindication of the Proceedings Relative to the Mission of Bishop Alexander in Jerusalem* (London, 1843), p. 17.

Old High Churchmen disputed the interpretation of the branch theory on which Palmer of Magdalen's and Newman's antipathy to the Jerusalem bishopric partly rested. According to Palmer's interpretation, the whole church in its fullness consisted of its 'Anglican, Greek, and Latin' branches. In consequence, 'whenever any one of the three was present, the other two, by the nature of the case, were absent, and therefore the three could not have relations with each other, as if they were three substantive bodies, there being no real difference between them except the external accident of place'.[67] Yet when Palmer sought to put this theory into practice he was rebuffed.

At Oxford, Palmer had embarked on a correspondence with the Russian Orthodox divine M. Komiakhoff which he hoped would strengthen ties between the Anglican and Eastern churches.[68] Palmer's overtures to the Russian church mirrored attempts at reconciliation with the Greek church made by Anglican divines in the seventeenth century. He aimed to restore contacts broken during the course of the eighteenth century. For as C. J. Abbey pointed out, during the latter period the 'Eastern Church, after attracting a faint curiosity through the overtures of the later Nonjurors, was as wholly unknown and unthought of as though it had been an insignificant sect in the furthest wilds of Muscovy'.[69]

Palmer's view of the branch theory was tested in 1844 by reports of a Russian lady being received into the Church of England by an Anglican chaplain in St Petersburg. If Palmer's theory was correct, the chaplain had been guilty of a schismatical act. Palmer, who was in Russia at the time, asserted his right as an 'English Catholic' to communicate with the Russian church on his own terms. The Russian Orthodox response exposed the fragility of Palmer's claim

---

[67] W. Palmer [of Magdalen], *Notes of a Visit to the Russian Church in the Years 1840, 1841.* Edited by Cardinal Newman (London, 1882), pp. vi–vii; W. Palmer [of Magdalen], *Aids to Reflection on the seemingly double character of the Established Church, with reference to the Foundation of a 'Protestant bishopric' at Jerusalem* (Oxford, 1841), pp. 6–8.
   William Palmer (1811–79). Magdalen College, Oxford, 1826; Fellow, and Deacon, 1832; Tutor, 1838–43. Sought admission into the Greek church at various times, 1842–53; received into the Roman Catholic church, 1855. A profoundly learned theologian.

[68] See W. J. Birkbeck, ed., *Russia and the English Church during the Last Fifty years*, vol. I, *Containing a Correspondence between Mr William Palmer, Fellow of Magdalen College, Oxford, and M. Komiakhoff, in the Years 1844–1854* (London, 1895).

[69] C. J. Abbey and J. H. Overton, *The English Church in the Eighteenth Century*, 2 vols. (London, 1878), vol. I, pp. 157–62.

of a harmony of doctrine subsisting between the Anglican and Eastern Churches.[70] The Russians only granted Palmer's request on condition that he anathematise forty-four 'heretical' propositions in the Thirty-Nine Articles.[71] Palmer did as he was asked but then tried to make out that he made no such doctrinal compromises in a 704-page *Appeal* to the Scottish bishops whom, as 'primitive High Churchmen', he regarded as likely to be sympathetic to his scheme. But Palmer found little consolation in this quarter, with the bishops privately puzzled by his 'strange book' and pitying his 'monomania on the subject of the Church'.[72]

For old High Churchmen, the Russian Church's response was not surprising. In their view, the fallacy in Palmer's interpretation of the branch theory, which the later Newman mistakenly regarded as 'the formal teaching of Anglicanism', was glaring. The refinements of Caroline ecclesiology were overlooked, and Bramhall's distinction between a 'true' and a 'perfect' church ignored. The Roman and Greek Churches were 'true' in terms of order but in their modern form they were 'corrupt' in terms of doctrine. Bishop Kaye expressed the distinction with characteristic clarity: 'I consider the Reformed Episcopal Church to be the true representative of the primitive Church; the Roman and Greek Churches to be branches, but erring branches of the Catholic Church. If the unity of the Church is to be restored, they must renounce their errors and join us: we must not go over to them.'[73] From this perspective, only if the Roman Catholics and Greek Orthodox reformed themselves on the 'primitive' basis of the English Reformation, could an Anglican episcopal presence within their branches of the church be regarded as a schismatical act. Thus, a limited mission on the territory of the Eastern churches could be justified on the ground of the latter's supposed 'corruption'. As Edward Churton observed to Copeland in 1842, 'you cannot make things as they were in the first four centuries ... I do not see why our veneration for St James and St Symeon is to make us blind to the more than half-barbarous condition of the church which may, for what I know, still preserve a succession from

70 R. Palmer, *Memorials. Family and Personal*, p. 408.
71 J. M. Neale, *The Life and Times of Patrick Torry, D. D. Bishop of St Andrews, Dunkeld and Dunblane* (London, 1856), p. 225.
72 BL, Gladstone Papers, Ms Add 44300, fol. 174, Bp W. Skinner to W. E. Gladstone, 4 April 1849.
73 PH, Copeland Papers, BP J. Kaye to J. Beaven, 27 October 1841; Bethell, *Charge to the Clergy of the Diocese of Bangor ... 1843*, p. 36.

them.'[74] Yet while such an attitude dismayed later Tractarians, Pusey himself in the earlier stages of the Movement had taken precisely the same line. Thus, in 1834 he had expressed the hope that 'it may please God, that the Greek, including the Russian, Church may be purified by its contact with the Reformed Churches of the West'.[75] Eight years later, Pusey was sounding a very different note.

Traditional High Church defenders of the Jerusalem bishopric regarded it as a unique opportunity to assert the Church of England's claim and vocation to be a standard or model of catholicity, in the best tradition of Laudianism rather than mere 'pan-protestantism'.[76] According to Bishop Blomfield, the scheme was 'eminently calculated ... to advance the boundaries of Christ's Church'.[77] The beneficial object, Perceval insisted, was that 'our Apostolic character and our Catholic faith be notified and made known by the presence of one of the apostolic order from among us, as our ambassador to Apostolic churches'.[78] On 'Catholic principles', the Church of England surely had a 'duty to give an Episcopate to all communities of Christians which may seek it, if their belief is orthodox'.[79] Tractarian comparisons of the scheme's proposed comprehension of Lutherans and Anglicans with attempts to establish Presbyterianism in Scotland under William III were rejected. 'By the one act', observed F. D. Maurice, 'the English church would have proclaimed Episcopacy to be of no value; by the other, she proclaims it to be of the greatest.' Moreover, 'by the one she must have reduced herself to the level of those with whom she was negotiating; by the other, she does what in her lies to raise them to her level'.[80] Maurice was a Broad Churchman who did not

---

[74] SC, Churton Papers, E. Churton to W. J. Copeland, 1 February 1842. When resident in St Petersburg in the early 1770s, Charles Daubeny formed the view that the Greek church was 'in a state of equal degradation with the Latin'. Daubeny, *Guide to the Church to Which Is Prefixed Some Account of the Author's Life and Writings*, p. vii.

[75] E. B. Pusey to B. Harrison, 8 April 1834, Liddon, *Life of Pusey*, vol. I, p. 289.

[76] Hook, *Reasons for Contributing towards the Support of an English Bishop at Jerusalem*, p. 4.

[77] BL, Gladstone Papers, MS Add 44356, fol. 202, Bp C. J. Blomfield to W. E. Gladstone, 3 November 1841.

[78] Perceval, *Vindication*, p. 7.

[79] SC, E. Churton to W. J. Copeland, 11 February 1842; PH, Pusey Papers, LBV [Transcripts], E. Churton to A. P. Perceval, 1 May 1843; W. Palmer [of Worcester] to A. P. Perceval, 2 May 1843.

[80] F. D. Maurice, *Three Letters to the Rev William Palmer, Fellow and Tutor of Magdalen College, Oxford, on the Name 'Protestant'; on the Seemingly Ambiguous Character of the English Church; and on the Bishopric at Jerusalem* (London, 1842), p. 55.

conceive the unity of the church in visible terms. His concept of catholicity was altogether more nebulous than that of High Churchmen. However Maurice's arguments in defence of the Jerusalem bishopric against Palmer of Magdalen were in accord with those of traditional High Church ecclesiology.

The old High Church concern to extend the boundaries of Anglican episcopalianism took practical forms, and included Perceval's plan for an Anglican bishopric on Heligoland to counteract the rationalism of the German Lutheran church.[81] In contrast to what has been called an old High Church 'longing for latter-day Reformations' and 'Catholic Reform' as the basis of a new ecclesiological settlement,[82] Tractarian antipathy to the Jerusalem bishopric could easily be portrayed by critics as closed and insular. It was a mentality well exemplified by James Hope when he maintained, 'I had rather that our church should wait upon the good providence of God within her present narrow limits, for centuries to come, than that it should gather in whole nations at the expense of even a single Catholic principle.'[83]

HIGH CHURCHMANSHIP AND THE ROMAN CATHOLIC CHURCH

Anti-Roman Catholicism was intrinsic to traditional High Church ecclesiology. For as J. C. D. Clark has explained, 'anti-Romanism was a marked feature of pre-Tractarian High Churchmanship for this reason: Anglicanism was justified not on principles of private judgment, or of the expediency of any establishment, but ultimately, because its doctrine was true'.[84] This High Church strand of anti-Roman Catholicism was distinct from the eighteenth-century latitudinarian variant with its primary objection to 'priestcraft'. For Daubeny, the latitudinarian reluctance to dwell on the 'apostolical' features of the Church of England had handed the Church of Rome an undeserved advantage. As a result, Daubeny's anti-Romanist polemic sought to demonstrate 'that the Faith, which the Church

[81] A. P. Perceval, *The Result of a First Endeavour to Re-establish in Germany, the Ancient Ecclesiastical Missions from England and Ireland, in 1846–47* (London, 1847); G. E. Biber, *The English Church on the Continent* (London, 1845).
[82] J. Pinnington, 'The Longing for Latter-day Reformations: Anglican Preoccupations with Catholic Reform in Europe before Vatican I', *Heythrop Journal*, 11 (1970), 17–31.
[83] Hope, *Bishopric of the United Church of England and Ireland at Jerusalem*, pp. 58–9.
[84] Clark, *English Society*, p. 272.

has in her keeping, stood upon ... broader ground than that of mere human opinion'.[85]

Not only contemporary Protestant Dissenters and Roman Catholic controversialists, but also later Anglo-Catholic writers, pointed to the apparent contradiction implied in High Church polemic. For it seemed to 'play the papist' against Dissent by inveighing against the 'sin of schism', and then to 'play the Protestant' against Rome, by denouncing papal tyranny.[86] For contemporary High Churchmen, there was no contradiction. Against both sets of opponents, they refuted the claim that the Church of England's separation from Rome at the Reformation had been a separation of the same kind or on the same principles as the subsequent separation of Dissenters from the Church of England.

The 'wide disparity' of the two cases was insisted upon. Thus, on the one hand, Ralph Churton argued, 'Dissenters ... leave us upon such slight grounds and pretences, as even if they were true, do by no means authorise them in breaching the unity of the church.' On the other hand, Churton insisted, 'the points which compelled us to separate from the Church of Rome, were matters not merely wrong, but highly sinful, and ... obtruded upon as articles of faith, and indispensable terms of communion'.[87] Unlike Dissenters, the Church of England, High Churchmen argued, had not withdrawn from the universal, visible Church of Christ, but only from a corrupt branch of that church. Unlike Dissenting communities, the Church of England had retained the vital notes of apostolic order and catholic unity.

At the root of High Church anti-Roman apologetic lay a conservative defence of the English Reformation. Caroline controversialists such as Bramhall had made a clear distinction between a right of judgment by individuals in the case of Dissent and the public judgment made by the Church of England at the Reformation.[88] The Reformers had not only preserved the essentials of apostolic faith as noted above, but had preserved the essentials of

---

85 C. Daubeny, *A Charge Delivered to the Clergy of the Archdeaconry of Sarum, 1821* (London, 1821), pp. 14–15; C. Daubeny, *On the Nature, Progress and Consequences of Schism* (London, 1818), p. 156.

86 J. G. Rogers, *Anglican Church Portraits* (London, 1876), pp. 205–7.

87 R. Churton, *An Answer to a Letter from Francis Eyre of Warkworth* (London, 1796), p. 12; R. Churton, *A Short Defence of the Church of England* (London, 1795); Palmer, *Treatise on the Church of Christ*, vol. I, p. 160.

88 *Works of Bramhall*, vol. II, pp. 34–5, 580–99.

apostolic order and catholic unity. For old High Churchmen, the English Reformation was orderly and regular. No precedent had been set for the radical sectarian principle of individual protest against ecclesiastical authority or 'mob-Reformations'. On the contrary, the protest of the English Reformers had been a collective act legitimised by the church in Convocation. The aim was to conserve and restore, not destroy or impair unity. Of course, the Church of England was 'Protestant', but she did not thereby cease to be 'Catholic'. As Daubeny explained, her 'Protestantism' consisted in 'the right which one independent branch of the Church of Christ claims, of protesting, in its collective character, against the errors of another branch of it; with which, from local circumstances, it may, or may not hold communion'.[89] In short, the unity of the church was as much imperilled by 'those overweening pretensions of popery which would place the whole of christendom, except itself, in a state of schism', as by the subversive and 'licentious' spirit of the Protestant sectaries.[90]

To strengthen the claims of the English Reformation to continuity and conservatism, some Orthodox churchmen such as Bishop Burgess developed the theme of the original independence and self-sufficiency of the British churches. In breaking with Rome, the Church of England had 'merely resumed her primitive character'.[91] It was precisely because of the High Church claim that the British churches possessed apostolic continuity that 'Romanism' within the British Isles could be portrayed as an alien 'usurpation' and schism. Perceval, Palmer of Worcester and Hook all propagated the rigidly High Church notion of the Church of Rome being the 'new Church' in Britain, or, as Palmer put it, 'a body of dissenters from our churches', having 'no succession from the founders of our churches, or from the ancient bishops'.[92] In contrast, it was claimed, the bishops of the Church of England were 'the only

---

89 Daubeny, *Guide to the Church*, pp. 149–50; W. Palmer [of Worcester], *Remarks on Dr Arnold's 'Principles of Church of Reform'* (Oxford, 1833), pp. 31–2.

90 'Life and Writings of Archdeacon Daubeny', *British Critic*, 9 (April, 1832), 308.

91 T. Burgess, *Primary Principles of Christianity: a Charge Delivered to the Clergy of the Diocese of Salisbury* (Salisbury, 1829); T. Burgess, *Tracts on the Origin and Independence of the Ancient British Church and on the Supremacy of the Pope* (London, 1815); T. Burgess, *The English Reformation and Papal Schism* (London, 1819).

92 W. Palmer [of Worcester], *The Apostolical Jurisdiction and Succession of Episcopacy in the British Churches Vindicated against the Objections of Dr Wiseman in the 'Dublin Review'* (London, 1840), p. 197; Palmer, *Treatise on the Church of Christ*, vol. I, p. 454; Oxlee, *Christian Priesthood*, pp. 101–2.

representatives of the bishops of the Celtic and Anglo-Saxon churches'.[93]

In spite of an ecclesiological consensus, there were differences of emphasis in attitude to the Church of Rome among pre-Tractarian High Churchmen. A closeness between the two churches, in terms of common apostolic foundation, was conceded even by the most 'Protestant' of Orthodox apologists such as Burgess. This very closeness in terms of the 'foundations', however, only fuelled the need of High Churchmen to justify and show the causes for the separation with Rome. As Ralph Churton explained, 'it was necessary to bring forward one or more instances of sinful corruption in the church we quitted; for, short of this, nothing could exempt us from what is in the eye of scripture, a very heinous crime, the sin of schism'.[94] In short, it was necessary to denounce 'Romish corruption' as loudly as possible, 'because', as Bishop Barrington put it, 'we are not contending for trifles; because they are not slight matters which first separated the Church of England from the Romish church'.[95] It is in this context that not only the charges of 'idolatry' but also the application of Mede's Antichrist prophecies to the Church of Rome by High Churchmen such as Jones of Nayland, Daubeny, Ralph Churton and Van Mildert, need to be set.[96] Moreover, the apocalyptic atmosphere of the 1790s, by fuelling prophetical theories of Antichrist, may have bolstered and prolonged the more virulent strain of High Church antagonism to Rome.[97]

The French Jacobinical persecution of the Gallican church and the subsequent experience of contact with French émigré clergy in

[93] A. P. Perceval, *The Roman Schism Illustrated from the Records of the Catholic Church* (London, 1836), p. xxvii.

[94] R. Churton, *Answer to Francis Eyre of Warkworth*, p. 14; C. Daubeny, *A Charge Delivered to the Clergy of the Archdeaconry of Sarum, 1827* (London, 1827), p. 13; Faussett, *Claims of the Established Church*, p. 7; H. Phillpotts, *Letters to Charles Butler Esq. on the Theological Parts of his 'Book of the Roman Catholic Church'* (London, 1825).

[95] S. Barrington, *Grounds of Union between the Churches of England and of Rome Considered in a Charge* (London, 1811), p. 8. See also W. J. Baker, 'The Attitudes of English Churchmen towards the Reformation, 1800–1850', unpublished Ph.D thesis, University of Cambridge, 1966, p. 140.

[96] See P. Misner, 'Newman and the Tradition Concerning the Papal Antichrist', *Church History*, 42 (1973), 375–88. For High Church examples of the genre, see R. Churton, *Antichrist or the Man of Sin. A Sermon Preached before the University of Oxford at St Mary's, on Sunday, May 23, 1802* (Oxford, 1804) *Anti-Jacobin Review*, 55 (September, 1818), 69.

[97] Murray, 'Influence of the French Revolution on the Church of England', p. 68. However, linking Antichrist with Jacobinism helped weaken its identification with the Papacy. See Olliver, *Prophets and Millennialists*, pp. 50–1. But for evidence to the contrary, see Sack, *From Jacobite to Conservative*, pp. 244–5.

England may have encouraged the growth of more eirenical attitudes among High Churchmen such as Bishop Horsley.[98] Protestant Dissenters complained that Horsley appeared to adopt a more lenient tone in controversy against Roman Catholics than against themselves.[99] D. A. Bellenger suggests that it was the political need to exalt the Gallican Church as 'a bulwark against chaos' rather than any theological reorientation as such that prompted the numerous examples of Anglican charity to the exiled clergy in the 1790s.[100] The Roman Catholic John Milner's suggested alliance with Anglican High Churchmen at this time played on such priorities.[101] In his response to Milner's overtures, Horsley was sympathetic and conciliatory, but cautious. In fact, Horsley's ecumenical preferences had already been evidenced prior to the case of the French émigré clergy by his intervention in 1791 over the Catholic Relief Bill and, as F. C. Mather suggests, were the product of more than mere political calculation.[102] Certainly, Horsley's speeches in the House of Lords in favour of the Relief Bill breathed an eirenical spirit. Moreover, it is significant that Horsley's prophetical writings in the era of the French Revolution entailed a decisive repudiation of Mede's 'unwarrantable, monstrous supposition, that Christian Rome is Antichrist'.[103] In Horsley's case, it would seem that

98 H. T. Brandreth, *Oecumenical Ideals of the Oxford Movement* (London, 1947), p. 20; B. and M. Pawley, *Rome and Canterbury through Four Centuries* (London, 1974), p. 79; D. Bellenger, 'The Émigré Clergy and the English Church, 1789–1815', *JEH*, 35 (July, 1983), 392–410. For an example of High Church sympathy for the plight of the French émigré clergy, see R. Nares, *Man's Best Right: a Solemn Appeal in the Name of Religion* (London, 1793), p. 29. For Bishop Horsley's sympathy for Pope Pius VI at the hands of his French captors, see S. Horsley, *Critical Disquisitions on the Eighteenth Chapter of Isaiah in a Letter to Edward King* (London, 1799), pp. 107–8. Sack, *From Jacobite to Conservative*, ch. 9, argues that High Church eirenicism towards Rome peaked in but predated the 1790s and was commonplace in the period of the American Revolution.
99 *A Welsh Freeholders' Address to the Rt Rev Samuel Horsley, Lord Bishop (lately of St David's), now of Rochester* (London, 1794), pp. 11, 15; R. Hall, *An Apology for Freedom of the Press* [1793] (4th edn, London, 1819), p. xiv.
100 Bellenger, 'Émigré Clergy and the English Church', 392–410.
101 See Milner, *Letters to a Prebendary*. Milner's projected High Church–Roman Catholic alliance against Low Church Latitudinarianism, 'aimed to secure those bishops who are termed orthodox: particularly Dr Horsley & Dr Cleaver of Chester'. Quoted in Mather, *Horsley*, p. 107.
102 Mather, *Horsley*, ch. 6. Horsley appears to have relished Milner's broadsides on 'Hoadlyism'. Significantly, Milner's *Letters to a Prebendary* was 'generously defended and highly extolled' by his friend Bishop Horsley in a speech in the House of Lords. F. C. Husenbeth, *The Life of the Rt. Rev. John Milner D. D. Bishop of Castabala* (Dublin, 1862), pp. 74–5.
103 *British Magazine*, 4 (1833), 718–41. Horsley's *Critical Disquisitions on the Eighteenth Chapter of Isaiah* (1799), with its denial that the Pope was Antichrist, attracted keen 'no popery' criticism. On this, see A. Robinson, 'Identifying the Beast: Samuel Horsley and the

portraying the Revolution as Antichrist involved a rejection of the eschatological basis of anti-Roman Catholicism. On the other hand, some Orthodox churchmen such as Daubeny and Pretyman-Tomline interpreted the events of Revolutionary France and especially the Irish Rebellion of 1798 so as to bolster rather than soften anti-Roman polemic,[104] while even Jones of Nayland's attitude towards Rome hardened in the later 1790s.[105]

While one group of High Churchmen, including Burgess, the later Daubeny and Ralph Churton, employed violently anti-Roman Catholic rhetoric, another group, including George Croft, Samuel Wix, John Oxlee, George Glover, William Harness and Noel Ellison, used the common 'apostolical foundations' of the two churches as the basis for a proposed reunion.[106] The divergence in attitude resurfaced in a sharp controversy in 1818–20 between two High Churchmen, Wix and Bishop Burgess. To the dismay of Burgess, Wix maintained that 'no solid objection prevails against the Church of England attempting a union with the Church of Rome; since the Church of Rome is acknowledged by the Church of England to be a true apostolical church'.[107] Moreover, the eirenicists pointed out that Latin Christendom had greatly depended upon Rome for many centuries. The Church of England was indebted to Rome, not only for the reconversion of England by St Augustine, but for the lineal transmission of the apostolic succession. As one High Churchman put it, those 'who would thus disclaim our Romish parentage seem to forget that the further they remove ... from the Roman Catholic Church, the lower they sink us, and the nearer they cause us to approach to the degraded and precarious condition of dissenters'. Pride, rather than embarrassment, was the proper response to the taunts of Dissenters that the Church of

Problem of the Papal AntiChrist', *JEH*, 43 (October, 1992), 592–607; Oddy, 'Eschatological Prophecy', pp. 75–83, 174–9.

104 G. Pretyman-Tomline, *A Sermon Preached at the Cathedral Church of St. Paul . . . on December 19, 1797* (London, 1798), pp. 12–13. Daubeny's attitude towards Rome notably hardened after 1798. Sack (*From Jacobite to Conservative*, p. 219) rightly maintains that 'the level of anti-Romanism rose as the confidence of a renewed High Church Anglicanism waxed.'

105 In 1797 Jones of Nayland explained his own revived anti-Romanism on the grounds that he could not find that 'their [papists'] late troubles have lessened their pride or mended any of their doctrines, so have not assumed what I suppose to have been the purpose of divine providence against them'. Magdalen College Archives, Oxford, Horne Papers, D.G.1. W. Jones to Mrs G. Horne, 5 December 1797.

106 J. Oxlee, *Three Letters Addressed to Mr C. Wellbeloved* (York, 1824), pp. 42–3.

107 S. Wix, *Christian Union without the Abuses of Popery* (London, 1820), pp. 16–17.

England's orders derived from the source of 'the venerable see of Rome'.[108]

The eirenic overtures of Wix and Oxlee in favour of reconciliation between Rome and Canterbury might be regarded as a precedent for later Anglo-Catholic reunionists in the 1850s and 1860s. But the reunionist High Churchmen of the 1820s differed in emphasis rather than substance from their more Protestant High Church colleagues. Oxlee and Wix looked forward to reunion on the basis of a mutual intercommunion of episcopal churches of the various Patriarchates. As with Montague, Laud and Wake, who had made similar proposals in the seventeenth century, the essential precondition was that the Church of Rome renounced her later corruptions and returned to her supposedly 'primitive' condition. For Wix, as much as for Daubeny or Burgess, 'Popery, in its usurped supremacy, and its doctrinal errors' was 'utterly incapable of reunion with a protestant church'.[109]

NEWMAN, THE TRACTARIANS AND THE CHURCH OF ROME, 1833–41

The context of the Oxford Movement's birth – the protest against Catholic Emancipation and on behalf of the 'Protestant' Church of Ireland – initially seemed to identify it with traditional High Church anti-Romanism. Bishop Burgess's early support was symbolic of the apparent link.[110] Moreover, the early involvement of Palmer of Worcester and Perceval fostered the expectation that the Oxford divines would share their concern to assail the 'Roman schism' in Ireland. This inspired Hurrell Froude's misgivings about what he called 'Tract Protestantism'.

Newman retained a degree of residual anti-Roman Catholicism which Froude and even Keble found uncongenial.[111] Newman's

---

[108] S. H. Cassan, *Lives of the Bishops of Winchester*, 2 vols. (London, 1827), vol. II, p. 16.

[109] Wix, *Christian Union*, p. 3; C. Daubeny, *The Protestant Companion; or, a Seasonable Preservative against the Errors, Corruptions, and Unfounded Claims of a Superstitious and Idolatrous Church* (London, 1824), pp. vii–viii. Ralph Churton privately poured scorn on 'Mr Wix's rash project'. SC, Churton Papers, R. Churton to H. H. Norris, 13 July 1818. On pre-Tractarian Anglican reunionist schemes, see V. A. McClelland, 'Corporate Reunion: a Nineteenth-Century Dilemma', *Theological Studies*, 43 (1982), 3–7.

[110] On Bishop Burgess's regard for the early numbers of the *Tracts for the Times*, see Liddon, *Life of Pusey*, vol. I, p. 282.

[111] Greenfield, 'Attitude of the Early Tractarians to the Roman Catholic Church', vol. I, pp. 81–2, 212.

earlier view of Rome as Antichrist was in the prophetical tradition associated not only with John Foxe, Joseph Mede and Thomas Newton, but also with the High Churchmen Daubeny and Van Mildert as well as later Evangelical commentators. This view died only slowly.[112] Moreover, in constructing his *via media* in the mid-1830s, Newman honestly set out to make the Anglican theory of catholicity his own grounds for refutation of Roman Catholic claims. This was the purpose of his first thorough study of the Caroline Divines and even of Bishop Marsh, in 1834–5, when he was compiling his 'Tracts against Popery'. As he told Robert Wilberforce in 1835, 'I still recommend Laud – and if you can buy it separate, Stillingfleet's comment thereupon. Also get Marsh's (Bishop of Peterborough) "Comparative View of the Churches of England and Rome" – a work of miserable tone, but clear, and useful to a certain point.'[113] In the early Tracts, in his controversy with Jager and in his *Prophetical Office*, the broad outlines of classic Anglican ecclesiology are evident. The breach of the Anglican theory of unity by the claims of papal supremacy is singled out for censure in the catalogue of 'Romish' errors which Newman compiled in conscious imitation of the example of Bishop Hall in *Tract 38* and *Tract 41*.[114] Yet the Tracts did not fulfil the anti-Romanist expectations which some old High Churchmen had of them. Newman privately admitted that 'it would be a great comfort to wash one's hands of the whole controversy, and say "settle it among yourselves Gentlemen"'.[115] Certainly, 'ultra-Protestantism' was assailed in a way which 'Romanism' ultimately was not. Even Manning felt moved to tell Newman in 1839 that he had 'promised some foreigners in Italy to tell you that you had not done enough polemically against Romanism ... I do not like the tone of our James the Second divines, but their books could be very useful if reprinted.'[116]

---

112 Misner, 'Newman and the Tradition Concerning the Papal Antichrist', pp. 375–88. In *Tract 20* (p. 3), Newman explicitly linked Rome with Antichrist. In the *Apologia* (p. 219), Newman cited passages from his *Tract 85*, 'Advent Sermons on Antichrist', to show that, though he was 'feeling after some other interpretation of prophecy instead of his [Newton's] ... Bishop Newton was still upon my mind even in 1838'. See also Oddy, 'Eschatological Prophecy', pp. 129–37.

113 J. H. Newman to R. I. Wilberforce, 10 September 1835, *Letters and Diaries*, vol. v, p. 158.

114 Imberg, *In Quest of Authority*, p. 92.

115 J. H. Newman to R. I. Wilberforce, 10 September 1835, *Letters and Diaries*, vol. v, p. 158.

116 Bodl. Lib, Manning Papers, Ms Eng Lett c. 654, fol. 43, H. E. Manning to J. H. Newman, 23 October 1839. Joshua Watson lamented: 'no Jeremy Taylor or Bishop Bull is to be found amongst their [i.e. Tractarian] prophets, no Dissuasives from Popery, no statements

Before Wiseman's raising of the spectre of 'Donatism', there emerged an underlying hesitation or reticence in Newman's vindication of the Church of England in controversy with Rome. He could expound the grounds for the separation but found it increasingly hard to accommodate the fact of separation. Imberg argues that Newman never accorded to catholicity the same weight he gave to apostolicity as an attribute of the Church; and that as early as 1836 he gave indications of an 'emotional inclination towards Rome'.[117] For instance, in *Tract 20*, Newman curiously understated Anglican claims to catholicity. In *Tract 71* he conceded that the *sacramentum unitatis* which he deemed essential for purity of faith had been 'shattered in the great schism of the sixteenth century'. In consequence, Newman argued that 'since that era at least, Truth has not dwelt simply and securely in any visible Tabernacle'. Moreover, it was even allowed that the Church of England was 'in a measure in that position which we fully ascribe to her Latin sister, in captivity'.[118] Contradicting the traditional High Church defence of the independence of 'branch' churches, Newman's earliest private complaint against the Reformers was that far from merely conserving, they had, by compiling the Thirty-Nine Articles, actually 'added to the Faith'. Therefore, Newman believed that the Reformers had committed the very fault of which High Churchmen always accused the Council of Trent.[119]

As early as 1836, Newman criticised Archbishop Wake as a symbol of 'Revolution-Protestantism'. It was in vain that Rose protested Wake's loyalty to an earlier Caroline mode of treating with Rome.[120] Significantly, Newman disparaged even Jeremy Taylor with the comment, 'he is a writer essentially untrustworthy ... The necessity, for example, of seeming an anti-Papist will draw all his nails out.'[121]

According to Rose, *Tract 71* left the disquieting impression that

of the corruptions of Rome to alarm and restrain them'. Churton, *Memoir of Joshua Watson*, vol. II, p. 275.

[117] Imberg, *In Quest of Authority*, pp. 64–6, 104–5. Rose privately complained of Newman's *Lectures* for contending 'that our system never had a wide practical influence'. Bodl. Lib, Manning Papers, Ms Eng Lett c. 654, fol. 40, H. J. Rose to H. E. Manning, 20 March 1837.

[118] *Tracts for the Times*, vol. III for 1835–6, No. 71 (London, 1836), pp. 29–31.

[119] Newman put these views into the mouth of 'Clericus' in a dialogue in *Tract 38*, but clearly identified with the statements.

[120] H. J. Rose to J. H. Newman, 13 May 1836, Burgon, *Lives of Twelve Good Men*, vol. I, p. 215.

[121] J. H. Newman to Mrs J. Mozley, 4 June 1837, *Letters and Diaries*, vol. VI, p. 81.

there was safety in the Church of England but nothing more. Allegiance merely rested on the principle of 'any port in a storm'.[122] As Bishop Bethell later argued, the Tract 'represents us as standing on low ground, and remaining in the church, not because we think our church a purer and better church than that of Rome, but simply because we are in it'.[123] Newman was rebuked for 'instilling a habit of viewing our church ... from above, and from without'.[124] Even Pusey in 1836 shared these grounds of misgiving, and repeatedly urged Newman to adopt a more confident, belligerent tone. 'You will recollect', he told Newman in one letter, 'that (I think) in almost every paper you have shown me, I have wished some changes where you have spoken of the English church; and on this occasion, I [say] ... the ground taken seemed low ... you should bear in mind the effect which Rose anticipates.'[125]

Tract 71, composed in 1835, revealed that Newman no longer accepted the Anglican notion of unity comprising co-equal 'branch churches' untrammelled by doctrinal uniformity. This divergence in ecclesiology paralleled his divergence on establishment and rule of faith. All three interlocking themes surfaced together in his anguished letters to Rose in May 1836. Yet as long as Newman's allegiance to Anglicanism could be defined as allegiance to 'our portion of the church universal' rather than to the 'particular' 'Church of England', his loyalty was not in doubt. Yet the tension in his own mind between 'national' or 'particular' and 'Catholic' or 'universal' grew rather than abated. As Edward Churton later lamented, from this time onwards Newman 'could no longer speak of attachment to the Church of England but as what he called an insular theory, a national fancy, or a hankering after the privileges of Judaism'.[126] The gulf between Newman's own distinctive vision of Anglican Catholicity and that of the old High Churchmen was revealed in his review of Palmer of Worcester's *Treatise* in the *British Critic* in 1838.

Newman concluded that the unity of the church required more than the mere 'notes' of apostolic order and a doctrinal allegiance restricted to fundamentals. He faulted Palmer's statement of the

122 H. J. Rose to J. H. Newman, 13 May 1836, Burgon, *Lives of Twelve Good Men*, vol. 1, pp. 215–16.
123 Bethell, *Charge to the Clergy of the Diocese of Bangor ... 1843*, pp. 45–6.
124 Poole, *Present State of Religious Parties*, p. 22.
125 PH, Pusey Papers, LBV [Transcripts], E. B. Pusey to J. H. Newman, May 1836.
126 Churton, *Memoir of Joshua Watson*, vol. II, p. 141.

traditional theory precisely because of its apparent detachment of
the idea of catholicity from doctrinal considerations. 'What',
Newman asked, 'becomes of the Notes of the Church? What purpose
do they serve? What relief and guidance is afforded to the inquiring
mind, if the church thus indicated preaches Popery in Rome and
Zwingli-Lutheranism in England? The difficulty is certainly considerable.'[127] Yet it was a difficulty for Newman, not Palmer or the
old High Churchmen. For what Newman was already searching for
was a catholicity comprising an absolute 'harmony of parts' as 'the
external test of a view being real'. He wanted a theory that was
'self-balanced and self-sustained and entire'.[128] The 'attraction' of
the Roman and Calvinistic theories lay in their apparent fulfilment
of this ideal; the latent implication was that the territorial nature of
the Anglican theory offered no such fulfilment. Wiseman's intervention only heightened a tension that already existed.

Newman's 'stomach-ache' induced by Wiseman's famous article
in 1839 in the *Dublin Review* was the result not only of the blow it
struck against the Anglican theory of antiquity, but also of the 'hit'
made at its theory of catholicity. The charge of 'Donatism' proved to
be as unsettling as that of Monophysitism. Wiseman had engaged
with the High Church theory as early as 1836. He had then likened
its notion of a unity in diversity that did not depend on formal
external communion with that held by the Donatists who, 'seem to
have wished to maintain the independence of the African Church, as
requiring no direct connexion with the Churches of Asia'.[129] It was
Wiseman's application of the analogy in his 1839 article that gave
Newman such a fright. Wiseman's recalling of St Augustine's
dictum against the schismatical Donatists, *securus judicat orbis terrarum*, seemed to provide the solution to the conundrum he had
wrestled with in his own review of Palmer's *Treatise* a year earlier.
Newman's nerves steadied and Wiseman's explanation was rejected,
but the 'shadow' remained 'on the wall'. Newman's subsequent
apologetic revealed that his conviction of the 'catholicity' of Anglicanism had taken an even harder knock than that of his faith in its
'antiquity'.[130] The rhetorical questions which he posed in another
article in the *British Critic* in 1840 again reveal the old tension in

---

[127] [Newman], 'Palmer's Treatise on the Church', 363.   [128] *Ibid.*, 349.
[129] N. Wiseman, *High Church Claims: or, A Series of Papers on the Oxford Controversy, the High
Church Theory of Dogmatical Authority, Anglican Claim to Apostolical Succession etc. No. 5
Occasioned by the Publication of the 'Tracts for the Times'* [1836] (London, [1838?]), p. 87–117.
[130] Thomas, *Newman and Heresy*, pp. 219–21.

more acute form. The 'difficulty', Newman posed, was that 'the
church being "one body", how can we, estranged as we are from
every part of it except our own dependencies, unrecognised and
without intercommunion, maintain our right to be considered part
of that body?'[131]

Old High Churchmen did not feel the difficulty which Newman
experienced, because for them unity did not depend on intercommunion. Edward Churton never understood the force which Wiseman's article could have had on Newman. Churton felt that, in
raising the charge of 'Donatism', Wiseman had employed, 'a
favourite old commonplace of Roman Catholic controversialists, on
which I cannot well suppose that Wiseman could say anything
particularly new or striking. If it was so, it is only a further proof
how a fine subtle mind may be taken captive by a bold and coarse
one.'[132] Yet for Newman, the answers provided by Anglican controversialists no longer sufficed. He now admitted that, while the
charge of 'want of primitiveness' could be effectively alleged against
Rome, that of 'want of catholicity' alleged by Rome against the
Church of England was at least plausible.[133] As a later writer
observed of Newman's *British Critic* article, 'the Roman ground has
settled immoveably into the writer's mind. The body of thought
which runs through it is Roman: scattered portions of the Anglican
argument hang upon it or float around it, but the body is Roman; it
moves through the light opposition which is made to it, as a ship
moves through floating pieces of timber.'[134]

TRIUMPH OF THE ROMAN CATHOLIC THEORY OF CATHOLICITY, 1841–5

Wiseman's article not only unsettled Newman but his argument in
favour of 'the exclusive catholicity of the Roman Communion' also
proved 'dangerously effective' with Newman's younger follower-
s.[135] These 'Romanising' followers such as Faber, Dalgairns,
Morris, Ward and Oakeley, had tired of the argument from mere
apostolicity. The preoccupations of the early Tracts would no
longer suffice. The gap between theory and reality seemed too

131 [J. H. Newman], 'Catholicity of the Church', *British Critic*, 27 (January, 1840), 53.
132 SC, Churton Papers, E. Churton to W. J. Copeland, 28 February 1860.
133 [Newman], 'Catholicity of the Church', 49.
134 *Christian Remembrancer*, 11 (January, 1846), 190.
135 Palmer, *Memorials. Family and Personal*, p. 313.

great.[136] They regarded catholicity as a living idea, not an antiquarian debating point. 'Catholicity', observed Faber, 'cannot be realised without considerable approach to Catholic communion; and the nearest approach we have made is to communion with Catholic antiquity. We make neither head nor tail of the present church.'[137] The Church of England was deemed to possess 'catholicity without union or unity with Christendom', which Dalgairns condemned as 'absurd'.[138] From this perspective, when viewed against the awful, looming reality of Latin Christendom, the Church of England seemed but a puny portion cut off like a limb from its parent body, while foreign travel confirmed a sense of the insularity of Anglicanism.[139]

The void which Newman's younger followers sensed was not immediately filled by Rome. At first, the Church of England's isolation, while lamented, was not deemed a conclusive refutation of her claims. As Dalgairns put it, 'we can only consider ourselves to be a portion of the Church Catholic by looking upon our separation as an accident, a temporary state of things for which we mourn as a sin'.[140] In answer to Newman's pertinent question in 1842, 'where is the Church?', his followers, like their leader, could only answer that it was in partial eclipse, because 'the Church only is, where it is one'.[141] Yet this was an uneasy resting place. In the present day, the church must be somewhere.

Newman's younger followers were quicker than himself in reaching a final answer. Their craving for a united visible church embodying an external dogmatic centre of authority could only be realised within the Roman Catholic communion. As Dalgairns argued,

Of all communities, the Roman is the only body which is visibly one in such a sense that it cannot possibly be two. The Anglican theory does not admit of the church being one in that sense ... In order to be the body of the Lord

136 Robert Wilberforce later admitted that these themes were dwelt upon in the early Tracts 'with a technicality which was not unnaturally disliked by those who felt the overwhelming importance of personal religion'. Wilberforce, *Evangelical and Tractarian Movements. A Charge* (London, 1851), p. 11.
137 Quoted in R. Addington, *Faber: Poet and Priest* (London, 1974), pp. 81–2.
138 KCA, 'Miscellaneous Letters', J. B. Dalgairns to J. M. Gresley, 6 January 1843.
139 J. Pinnington, 'The Debate on the Continental Churches: Some Late Twentieth-Century Reflections on a Mid-Nineteenth-Century Anglican Crisis of Identity', *Downside Review*, 91 (1977), 49–61.
140 KCA, 'Misc. Letters', J. B. Dalgairns to J. M. Gresley, 6 January 1843.
141 Bodl. Lib, Ms Eng Lett d. 102, fol. 80, J. H. Newman to W. R. Lyall, 16 July 1842 (copy).

it must be visibly and invisibly one in the same sense in which a human body is one.[142]

Yet while the logic of the ecclesiology of Faber, Ward and Dalgairns was realised in enthusiastic acceptance of the theory of papal supremacy, for Newman personally the conclusive factors lay elsewhere. Arguments about the nature of catholicity, like antiquity, played an essentially negative role in his conversion. Anglican catholicity, like antiquity, had 'failed' him, but this induced only a negative retreat from Anglicanism. The idea of development of doctrine provided a positive intellectual pull, but there would be a positive spiritual motivation too.

High Churchmanship and eschatology: a key to Newman's conversion

As Sheridan Gilley has demonstrated, it was eschatology as much as ecclesiology that provided the essential ingredient in Newman's conversion. For Rome could hardly represent 'the centre of unity' so long as Newman remained convinced, as he did until well into the 1830s, that she was Antichrist.[143] A shift in Newman's ecclesiological perspective was facilitated by an abandonment of this view by the late 1830s. Newman's recoil from the theory of Rome as Antichrist owed much to its apparent conflict with his understanding of the doctrine of apostolical succession. He felt that the theory destroyed the Anglican claim to apostolicity, dependent as it was on a succession of orders through Rome.[144] Yet in taking this line, as Faussett triumphantly pointed out in his controversy with Newman in 1838, the latter overlooked the important distinction between Rome as metaphysically a 'true' church in its foundation, and as apostate and anti-Christian in its later teaching; a distinction which High Churchmen as reputable as Jones of Nayland and Van Mildert had upheld.[145] Significantly, in 1841 the testimony of such

---

[142] KCA, 'Misc. Letters', J. B. Dalgairns to J. M. Gresley, 16 January 1846; J. B. Morris to J. M. Gresley, 1 February 1846.

[143] Gilley, *Newman and His Age*, p. 190.

[144] J. H. Newman, *A Letter to the Rev. Godfrey Faussett D. D. Margaret Professor of Divinity on Certain Points of Faith and Practice* (Oxford, 1838), p. 31. Keble had reached this view as early as 1824. See Misner, *Papacy and Development*, p. 14.

[145] G. Faussett, *The Revival of Popery. A Sermon Preached before the University of Oxford, at St Mary's ... 20 May 1838* (2nd edn, Oxford, 1838), p. vi. Faussett appealed to Jones of Nayland who had asserted: 'the succession of church offices is no more affected by the errors of Popery, than a man's pedigree is affected by his bodily distemper, or the distempers of his parents'. W. Jones, 'A Short View of the Present State of the Argument

High Churchmen to the notion that Rome was idolatrous and anti-Christian in her teaching was cited as telling evidence of 'the singular discrepancy which exists between the present Oxford school of high churchmanship, and that of a more old-fashioned and a purer school'.[146] The younger Christopher Wordsworth kept alive this strand of prophetical anti-Roman Catholicism in earlier High Churchmanship, devoting a lengthy treatise published in 1850 to proving that the Church of Rome was the Babylon of the Apocalypse.[147] Nevertheless, some old High Churchmen denied that the Church of Rome represented the embodiment of Antichrist. For example, Edward Churton distanced himself from the view of his father Ralph on this point. Thus, in a rare break with filial allegiance, Edward maintained, 'my father had no good reasons for his dread of new Smithfield burnings and I know what beside, – and . . . in his following of Mede's view about the Great Apostacy, he followed the multitude without examination'.[148]

The significance of eschatology in Newman's secession to Rome lay in his reinterpretation, rather than outright rejection, of the prophetical theories propounded by Mede and others. Newman simply turned his earlier interpretation of Antichrist prophecies on its head. Ultimately, Newman was thereby able to regard the Church of Rome and the Papal Supremacy as the true fulfilment of the 'Imperial image' portrayed in the Book of Revelation.[149] In short, Newman's journey to Rome followed a Protestant prophetical route as well as a High Anglican ecclesiastical one.

REALIGNMENT: KEBLE, PUSEY AND ANGLO-CATHOLIC ECCLESIOLOGY, 1845–51

The ecclesiology formulated by Keble, Pusey and the Tractarian loyalists who did not secede to Rome, represented a position distinct

between the Church of England and the Dissenters', *Scholar Armed*, 2 vols. (London, 1795), vol. II, p. 66. The Bisley school sought to persuade Newman that holding the Church of Rome to be Antichrist was compatible with the High Church notion of apostolical succession. See Birmingham Oratory, Newman Papers, J. F. Christie to J. H. Newman, 2 August 1838; T. Keble to J. H. Newman, 24 August 1838.

146 *British Magazine*, 10 (December 1841), 828–9.

147 C. Wordsworth, *Is the Church of Rome the Babylon of Revelation? An Essay Derived in Part from the Author's Lectures on the Apocalypse* (London, 1850), p. 104.

148 SC, Churton Papers, E. Churton to T. T. Churton, 28 February 1845. Palmer of Worcester also refrained from identifying the Church of Rome with Antichrist. See W. Palmer [of Worcester], *A Fifth Letter to N. Wiseman* (Oxford, 1841), p. 4.

149 Misner, 'The Imperial Image of the Church', *Papacy and Development*, pp. 50–7; Gilley, 'Newman and Prophecy, Evangelical and Catholic', 160–88.

both from that of old High Churchmen and that of the later Anglican Newman and the Romanisers. Their position remained similar to that outlined in *Tract 71*, with their allegiance focused on the universal rather than their own particular church. Pusey had criticised Newman for adopting this standpoint in 1836, but within a few years he had made it his own. As he explained to Isaac Williams,

a great difference, really, between what are called Anglicans, and such as myself, is, that they are quite contented that things should remain as they are; they think our Church is 'toto feres atque rotunda' in herself; I can only look upon this as a provisional state, that we are as we are, because we cannot help ourselves, but that we ought really to desire to be otherwise, i.e. not thus insulated.[150]

Like Newman at an earlier date, Pusey's eventual loss of faith in the English Reformers stemmed from his doubts that a particular, branch church could reform itself by itself, 'still more with such allies as the Lutherans and Zwinglians'.[151] It was not the abstract necessity of the Reformation that he questioned, but its mode. Such questioning put Pusey no less at odds than Newman had been with the whole tenor of Caroline and later Anglican apologetic. But the source of Pusey's change of heart was different from Newman's.

Among the Caroline Divines, the Tractarians felt especial devotion for Herbert Thorndike, on account of his having 'seen further than others'.[152] 'It was Thorndike', Pusey explained, who 'first broke in upon the acquiescence which I had ever yielded to our hereditary maxim that a particular church had a right to reform itself. A misgiving, expressed by him, raised the question in my mind.'[153] Such misgivings, long held by Keble, did not lead either to question the Church of England's catholicity, in the manner of Newman. For them, the ancient undivided church, and not the modern Church of Rome, was the only legitimate centre of unity. The true and unerring voice of current, divided catholic Christendom could only be expressed in an Ecumenical Council. As Keble put it, 'we stand as orthodox Catholics upon a constant virtual appeal to the Ecumenical voice of the church'.[154]

If Keble and Pusey were not Romanisers in their ecclesiology,

---

[150] LPL, Williams Dep 3/28, E. B. Pusey to I. Williams, 27 July 1842.
[151] PH, Pusey Papers, LBV [Transcripts], E. B. Pusey to H. E. Manning, 9 July 1844.
[152] *Idem.*
[153] PH, Pusey Papers, LBV [Transcripts], E. B. Pusey to H. E. Manning, 12 August 1845.
[154] Quoted in A. O. J. Cockshut, *Anglican Attitudes* (London, 1959), p. 44.

they adopted a position of official 'neutrality'. They gave an ecumenical gloss to the old 'branch theory'. For, according to Keble, 'both the churches of England and Rome, being branches of the church, as our theory asserts, they cannot really be enemies to each other'.[155] This eirenicism put Keble and Pusey at odds with Palmer of Worcester and the old High Churchmen, preventing them from signing Palmer's Declaration against the Gorham Judgment in 1850, because it 'puts our adherence to the church on the ground that the English Church reformed itself in the sixteenth century and says there can be no intercommunion until Rome reforms herself'.[156]

The position of Keble and Pusey was not without its own difficulties. The later Roman Catholic convert, Thomas Allies, related that Pusey had admitted that

as soon as you give up violent anti-Roman statements and feelings, and admit Rome to be a church, our position becomes a weak one. It was easier to deny her catholicity (this may account perhaps for the strong anti-Roman tone generally taken by our divines), but that being admitted, our position becomes strictly defensive and lies in points not easily stated.[157]

REASSERTION: THE OLD HIGH CHURCH REACTION

Pusey's candid admission to Allies echoed what Rose had vainly sought to impress upon Newman in 1836. Faced with the Tractarian abandonment of the old ecclesiology and the adoption of new models of catholicity, old High Churchmen in the 1840s were provoked into a reassertion of the traditional position. In works such as Biber's *Standard of Catholicity* (1840), Palmer of Worcester's *Letters to Dr Wiseman* (1842), Christopher Wordsworth's *Theophilus Anglicanus* (1843), R. W. Jelf's *Via Media* (1844), William Gresley's *Anglo-Catholicism* (1844) and William Barter's *English Church Not in Schism* (1845), the Newmanite challenge was taken up and met on High Church ground. Thus for Biber, there was no apostolical basis for the much-vaunted notion 'that the visible branches of the church militant upon earth were to be comprehended together in one great

155 PH, Pusey Papers, LBV [Transcripts], J. Keble to E. B. Pusey, 7 September 1845; J. Keble to E. B. Pusey, 15 January 1844.
156 LPL, Keble Dep 2/17, J. Keble to W. J. Copeland, 19 September 1850.
157 M. Allies, *Thomas William Allies, 1813–1903* (London, 1924), p. 45.

body forming a visible church catholic'.[158] The Tractarian antipathy to the name 'Protestant' was also disposed of. For old High Churchmen, 'Protestant' and 'Catholic' were not mutually exclusive terms.[159] According to R. W. Jelf, the Church of England was 'best defined perhaps by the term "Protestant-Catholic-Church"' ... The Protestant character of her teaching may be called an accident, the Catholic her essence.'[160]

The contrast between Palmer of Worcester's and Newman's responses to Wiseman's writings revealed a widening gulf in their respective ecclesiologies. Unlike Newman, Palmer was supremely untroubled by Wiseman's application of St Augustine's *orbis terrarum* dictum. Palmer confidently resorted to the traditional Anglican view that it was the Roman and not the English church that was schismatical. For Palmer, as for the Caroline Divines, the Church of Rome had separated from the communion of the Eastern as well as the British churches, and 'the mere fact of not being in communion' with Rome was no proof of schism.[161] It was argued that 'unity in error is not Christian unity', so that 'by imposing the necessity of

---

[158] G. E. Biber, *The Standard of Catholicity; or an Attempt to Point in a Plain Manner Certain Safe and Leading Principles, Amidst the Conflicting Opinions by Which the Church Is at Present Agitated* (London, 1840), p. 298.

[159] Much was made in Tractarian rhetoric of the fact that the term 'Protestant' nowhere appeared in the Church's formularies. For example, see National Library of Scotland, Hope-Scott Papers, Ms 3670, fol. 21, J. R. Hope to Sir R. Inglis, 10 January 1842. However, old High Churchmen showed that earlier Anglican divines had gloried in the title. See Bethell, *Charge to the Clergy of the Diocese of Bangor ... 1843*, p. 49. On the other hand, Edward Churton conceded: 'I think you will find that writers before the time of the Troubles [i.e. Great Rebellion] use the word Protestant in a different sense from what it now must necessarily bear. They had no sects at home to include in the term.' SC, Churton Papers, E. Churton to W. J. Copeland, 12 April 1836. There were pre-Tractarian High Church precedents for expressions of dislike of the term. See N. Ellison, *Protestant Errors and Roman Catholic Truths* (London, 1829), p. 66.

[160] Jelf, *Via Media*, p. 28; [Sewell], 'Divines of the Seventeenth Century', 505–23; C. Wordsworth (Jun.), *Theophilus Anglicanus* (London, 1843), p. 171. Jelf's definition was based on Laud's avowal in his *Conference with Fisher the Jesuit* (1622) cited by Wordsworth: 'the Protestants did not get their name by protesting against the Church of Rome, but by protesting (and that when nothing else would serve) against her errors and superstitions. Do you remove them from the Church of Rome and our Protestantism is ended, and the separation too.'
    Bishop Phillpotts echoed the classical Laudian 'middle way' when he maintained: 'I should esteem any act a poor, and worse than worthless, compliment to the *Protestant* character of our Church, aye, and a real weakening of that Protestant character, rightly understood, which tends to make that character less *Catholic*, and less worthy of the confidence of the sound portion of the Catholic Church throughout the world.' H. Phillpotts, *A Reply to Lord John Russell's Letter to the Remonstrance of the Bishops against the Appointment of Rev. Dr Hampden to the See of Hereford*, (London, 1847), p. 24.

[161] Palmer [of Worcester], *Treatise on the Church of Christ*, vol. 1, pp. 325–52.

erring as a term of union, Rome became guilty of a breach of unity, and so the sin of schism lies at her door'.[162]

Palmer of Worcester retained a very different understanding of the 'branch theory' from that of his namesake of Magdalen. He was later criticised for a 'Donatist' exposition of the ecclesiastical status of the Church of England.[163] Certainly there was truth in C. J. Abbey's contention in 1878 that in 'all the course of its long history, before and after the Reformation, the National Church of England' had 'never perhaps, occupied so peculiarly isolated a place in Christendom as at the extreme end of the last century, and through the early years of the present one'.[164] Tractarian-inspired fraternisation with continental Roman Catholics and, to a lesser extent, under Palmer of Magdalen's aegis, with the Eastern churches, opened up a new chapter in Anglican ecumenical relations. However, for the school of Palmer of Worcester, Tractarian openness to the wider church was one-sided. For the example of the Jerusalem bishopric affair showed that Tractarian openness could be very selective. Moreover, it was the school of Palmer of Worcester and Perceval, rather than the more extreme Tractarians, which ultimately was concerned to extend the boundaries of the Anglican communion. It was the old High Churchmen rather than advanced Tractarians who espoused a pan-Anglicanism associated with the rise of colonial churches.[165]

Old High Churchmen did not regard isolation as a mark of disfavour. On the contrary, 'isolation may', observed R. W. Jelf, 'be one natural characteristic of the middle way; a sign of God's favour, as Israel was'.[166] Size of communion was no test of truth. On the contrary, even if the Church of England, argued Barter, was to 'find herself alone, but still contains the perfection of the faith which has been held from the beginning, it is her glory and honour'.[167] Old

---

[162] Wordsworth, *Theophilus Anglicanus*, pp. 169–71.

[163] Neale, 'The Laudian Reformation', pp. 181–3. For later Anglo-Catholic criticism of Palmer of Worcester's theory as 'Donatist', see T. A. Lacey, *Unity and Schism* (London, 1917), p. 46; P. E. Shaw, *The Early Tractarians and the Eastern Church* (London, 1930), pp. 20–1. I am indebted to Mr Roger Turner for the Lacey reference.

[164] Abbey and Overton, *English Church in the Eighteenth Century*, vol. I, p. 443.

[165] It was at Joshua Watson's house in Westminster, that 'was first fostered the good design of sending bishops to the British colonies'. E. Churton, *The Gifts of God to the Good. A Sermon Preached in the Parish Church of St John's, Hackney, on Sunday, February 11, 1855, being the Sunday after the Funeral of Joshua Watson Esq.* (London, 1855), pp. 18–19.

[166] Jelf, *Via Media*, p. 31.

[167] W. B. Barter, *The English Church Not in Schism, or, a Few Words on the Supremacy of the Pope and the Progress of Antichrist* (London, 1845), p. 55.

High Churchmen opposed what they called the 'purely Occidental theology' of the later Tractarians.[168] Old High Churchmen might regard the modern Eastern churches as scarcely less corrupt than Rome, but they still appealed to the example of those churches in their own repudiation of the later Tractarian assumption that Latin Councils could legislate for all Christendom.

The younger Wordsworth's *Theophilus Anglicanus*, it was felt, did not get the credit it deserved in the polarisation that took place in the middle of the century. Although adapted for use in America and translated into French and even modern Greek, Charles Wordsworth later lamented that it, 'was not taken up by either the friends, or the adversaries of the Movement, being, I suppose, too decidedly Anglican to please the former, and too decidedly Catholic to please the latter'.[169] The comment was an appropriate verdict on the dilemma facing old High Churchmanship in the 1840s.

---

[168] *Anglo-Catholic Principles Vindicated*, p. 5.
[169] Cha. Wordsworth, *Annals of My Early Life*, p. 350. The author's father hailed *Theophilus Anglicanus* because he thought nothing 'more likely to arrest the progress of the evils threatened to us from Newman and Newmanism'. LPL, Ms 2149, fol. 285, C. Wordsworth (Sen.) to C. Wordsworth (Jun.), 6 July 1844.

CHAPTER 4

Spirituality, liturgy and worship

HIGH CHURCHMANSHIP AND ASCETICISM

The Oxford Movement was primarily a spiritual force, a quest for holiness through self-denial and mortification of bodily and worldly appetites. Included in the 'ascetic motive' were strict notions of prayer, alms-giving, fasting, the ideal of poverty, voluntary retirement, repentance and penance. Asceticism was practised by the Movement's leaders, notably Froude, Pusey and Newman in his Littlemore years. An abiding Tractarian fear was 'for people to be made high churchmen in a great hurry as high as steeples and be no better for it'.[1] Yet there was continuity with at least an element of the High Church tradition. As a writer in the Evangelical *Record* conceded in 1838, contemporary High Churchmanship had 'formed a compact with fasting, long prayers, observance of days, great show of devotion', but these were 'no strangers to it; they have been its supporters many times before'.[2]

The ascetical strain in High Church spirituality had found appealing expression in seventeenth-century figures such as George Herbert, Nicholas Ferrar, Thomas Ken and Ambrose Bonwicke, and, in the eighteenth century, Robert Nelson, William Law and Bishop Wilson.[3] When Pusey advocated fasting in *Tract 18* and *Tract 66*, he drew on this testimony.

Law's spirituality influenced the young John Wesley and the Oxford Methodists in the early 1730s.[4] In the middle years of the eighteenth century, it left its mark on the Hutchinsonians. Horne's

---

[1] LPL, Williams Dep 9/19, I. Williams to T. Keble, 21 May 1838.
[2] *Record*, No. 1068 (22 March, 1838).
[3] For an example of Newman's imaginative identification with Caroline Anglican spirituality, see [J. H. Newman], 'Taylor versus Nicholas Ferrar', *British Critic*, 26 (October, 1839), 440–57.
[4] J. B. Green, *John Wesley and William Law* (London, 1845), pp. 32–49.

and Stevens's habits of fasting and regard for the ideal of celibacy owed much to Law's example.[5] According to Edward Churton, there was a religious motivation in Stevens having 'made a single life his choice'.[6] Law's ascetic influence also left its mark on members of the Hackney Phalanx. Dean Rennell was 'profoundly acquainted' with Law's spiritual writings. It was Rennell who passed on the *Serious Call* to the young W. F. Hook in the 1820s.[7]

A severe strain of pre-Tractarian High Churchmanship was counterbalanced by another strand akin to the ethical and pruden-tial tone of latitudinarian spirituality. The spiritual temper that characterised many Orthodox as well as latitudinarian churchmen has been called 'Tillotsonian',[8] though Canon Overton, followed by recent scholars, suggested that Tillotson's personal spirituality was much more concerned with such demands of the gospel as the duty of self-denial than many eighteenth-century exponents of his teach-ing as well as Evangelical critics assumed.[9] A better epithet to describe the spiritual temper unfairly associated with Tillotson's name might be that of 'Warburtonian', preferred by some con-temporaries.[10] This spiritual emphasis embodied an aversion to extravagant devotional austerities as 'useless' and anti-social, if not 'popish'. The objection was not so much a Protestant repudiation of any implied doctrine of merit, but a dislike of the 'irrational', 'fanatical' or 'enthusiastical'. 'Warburtonian' rhetoric lumped together 'Methodism' and Calvinist Evangelical examples of what it regarded as ascetical excess, with those of Roman Catholics and some Nonjurors such as Law.[11] Conflict between the two strands was exemplified in a controversy involving the 'Warburtonian' Joseph Trapp and William Law.[12] For Trapp, the essence of spirituality was to be sober, moral, attentive in worship and duties. Against Law, Trapp argued, 'to eat nothing but bread and herbs, and drink

[5] Jones, *Memoirs of Horne*, p. 44.   [6] Churton, *Memoir of Joshua Watson*, vol. 1, p. 24.

[7] Stephens, *Life and Letters of Walter Farquhar Hook*, vol. 1, p. 97.

[8] Thomas Mozley popularised the term 'Tillotsonian'. T. Mozley, *Reminiscences Chiefly of Towns, Villages and Schools*, p. 119.

[9] A. C. Clifford, *Atonement and Justification. English Evangelical Theology, 1640–1790: an Evalu-ation* (Oxford, 1990), pp. 33–49. See also n. 44.

[10] Johnson Grant, *Summary History*, vol. IV, p. 35.

[11] For an example of the genre, see Bishop Lavington's *The Enthusiasm of Methodists and Papists Compared* (London, 1749).

[12] For Victorian High Churchmen, the Hanoverian Church 'was in danger of suffering far more from the mistaken defence of advocates than from the eccentricities of the zealous revivalists'. G. C. Perry, *A History of the English Church. Third Period. From the Accession of the House of Hanover to the Present Time* (London, 1887), p. 67.

nothing but water, unless there be a particular reason for it, is folly at best'.[13]

Anti-asceticism remained a feature of one element of Orthodox spirituality up to the eve of the Oxford Movement and beyond. It found expression in the High Churchman Thomas Le Mesurier's Bampton Lectures in 1807. Le Mesurier castigated the Church of Rome for the 'peculiar and extraordinary honour which she ascribes to virginity' and for her penances and 'unnecessary mortifications'.[14] The same 'Warburtonian' spiritual temper prompted a reviewer of new editions of Thomas à Kempis's *Imitation of Christ* and Jeremy Taylor's *Holy Living and Holy Dying* in the High Church *British Critic* in 1820, to insist that such works were 'not suited to all readers, and above all, were likely to produce an injurious effect upon the ardent and enthusiastic mind of such a youth as Wesley'.[15] Robert Southey, in his *Book of the Church* (1824), combined with political glorification of Laud and antipathy to Puritanism a similar anti-ascetical tone that was directed against Roman Catholics and Methodists alike. Even primitive martyrs as well as Anglo-Saxon saints like Dunstan[16] did not escape Southey's ridicule. Whereas for Newman, 'St Simeon upon his pillar' was a model of primitive sanctity,[17] Southey poured scorn on those pilgrims of the early church who went

to behold and reverence, like a living idol, a maniac in Syria, who, under that burning climate, passed his life upon the top of a lofty column, and vied with the yoguees in India in the folly and perseverance with which he inflicted voluntary tortures upon himself.[18]

The Tractarian ascetical emphasis rekindled these tensions within High Churchmanship. Tractarian strictures on the supposedly self-indulgent lifestyle of the Oxford Heads of Houses in the 1830s and 1840s and Froude's depiction of the 'Z' clergy as 'two bottle

---

[13] J. Trapp, *The Nature, Usefulness, and Regulation of Religious Zeal. A Sermon Preached at St Mary's, Oxford, August 2, 1739* (Oxford, 1739), p. 7.

[14] Le Mesurier, *Nature and Guilt of Schism*, p. 205.

[15] 'Southey's Life of Wesley', *British Critic*, New Series, 14 (January, 1820), 4.

[16] R. Southey, *The Book of the Church*, 2 vols. (London, 1824), vol. 1, p. 88. See S. Gilley, 'Nationality and Liberty, Protestant and Catholic: Robert Southey's *Book of the Church*', *SCH*, 18 (1982), 409–32, especially 420–2. Southey's Roman Catholic antagonist Joseph Lingard maintained that *The Book of the Church* had 'plainly been written for a purpose, to please the high-church party' (cited, p. 422). See n. 32.

[17] [Newman], 'Taylor versus Nicholas Ferrar', 324.

[18] Southey, *Book of the Church*, vol. 1, p. 16.

Orthodox' or 'pampered aristocrats',[19] paralleled a similar line of critique employed by the young Wesleys and the Oxford Methodists a century earlier. Likewise, the tone of Godfrey Faussett's public attack on the Tractarians in a university sermon in 1838 recalled the strictures made by Trapp on Law a hundred years previously. Faussett's extreme High Church credentials in the 1820s are beyond challenge, but he found Froude's exemplification of Tractarian asceticism offensive. The echoes of eighteenth-century 'Warburtonian' rhetoric in his sermon are clear. Trapp had denounced one of Law's works for containing 'monstrous enthusiastical absurdities' and 'raving dreams', and had warned him of 'the nature, and tendency of that baneful plague, that many-headed monster, *Enthusiasm*'.[20] In similar vein, Faussett castigated Froude's *Remains* as containing 'the wild and visionary sentiments of an enthusiastic mind'.[21] Like Law, Froude was also attacked for 'rigid mortifications and painful penances', and for being 'righteous overmuch'.[22] Other moderate High Church critics of the Tractarians employed the same language. Edward Hawkins commonly referred to the Tractarians as 'the fanatical party',[23] while Hook confided to Pusey in 1840 that, while his own mother was a staunch High Churchwoman, 'she has the old notions of the last century, considers all that you are doing as enthusiasm'.[24]

The Tractarians ascribed this line of opposition from those who 'have hitherto professed High Church principles as they are called' to their alienation 'at bottom by the strictness and severity implied in the more searching parts of church discipline'.[25] Newman responded with satire as well as indignation to Faussett's charges against Froude. Aware that Faussett was a stickler for order and rubric, Newman pointedly informed him, 'I think your tone as regards mortifications and penances, is such as to discourage persons from obeying certain rules of the church respecting them'. Moreover, while Faussett had censured 'rigid mortifications and painful penances', Newman observed, 'you have not given us to

[19] See [Newman and Keble, eds.], *Remains of Richard Hurrell Froude*, I (1838), p. 329.
[20] J. Trapp, *A Reply to Mr Law's Earnest and Serious Answer* (London, 1741), pp. 41, 117. The Hutchinsonians had also been accused of being 'Fanaticks' and 'Enthusiastic New-reformers'. See [B. Kennicott], *A Word to the Hutchinsonians* (London, 1756), p. 8.
[21] Faussett, *Revival of Popery*, p. 13.   [22] *Ibid.*, pp. 16–17.
[23] OCA, Hawkins Papers, Letterbook IV, No. 425, E. Hawkins to R. Whately, 21 December 1843. Mark Pattison later referred to his own 'fanatical instincts' at this time. Pattison, *Memoirs*, p. 207.
[24] PH, Pusey Papers, LBV [Transcripts], W. F. Hook to E. B. Pusey, 10 October 1840.
[25] PH, Copeland Papers, W. J. Copeland to J. Bowdler, 6 December 1841.

understand whether . . . you object to them in toto, or only in excess'.[26]
Criticism of the apparent want of asceticism in old High Churchmanship repeatedly surfaced in later Tractarian rhetoric.
Newman parodied the 'High and Dry' churchman who 'amongst
the fasting "Fathers of the English Church" . . . fasted retro-
spectively and was at peace' but whose embarrassment was total 'at
being called upon to patronise the actual abstinence laid down so
unmercifully in the Book of Common Prayer'.[27] Similarly, in his
Ideal of a Christian Church, W. G. Ward singled out 'the school of
Tomline' for an utter want of reverence for saintliness, celibacy or
earnest and habitual prayer.[28] Pusey even faulted the younger 'Z'
allies of the Movement in these terms. As he patronisingly informed
Hook in 1843, 'the ascetic principle seemed to me that which was
wanting in your writings and those of your school (I mean Palmer,
Gresley, Jelf) if I may so call it, and now I trust, God is leading you
on to it'.[29]

Some 'Zs' identified with the Tractarian ascetic *ethos*. Edward
Churton deplored the 'mode' of Faussett's attack ('an offence
against ecclesiastical order'), 'his style, coarse, dull and irreverent,
and the want or moral feeling displayed throughout'. He congratu-
lated Newman on his robust reply. 'If I had attacked you', Churton
assured Newman, 'there is not one sentence I could have borrowed
from the Professor'.[30] Moreover, Churton's regard for Anglo-Saxon
saints such as Bede, Alcuin and Dunstan,[31] contrasted with the tone
of some Protestant High Church polemic such as Southey's *Book of
the Church*. Churton did not sympathise with Southey's 'church
principles generally. In his *Book of the Church* he follows the ultra-
Protestant views much too closely . . . He follows the absurd vulgar
trash about St Dunstan, and follows no system of distinguishing
between the age of credulity and the age of imposture'.[32]

Tractarian asceticism manifested itself not only in a restatement
of the monastic ideal of retirement from the world. Under Pusey's

[26] Newman, *Letter to the Rev. Godfrey Faussett*, pp. 91–2.
[27] [J. H. Newman], 'Geraldine', *British Critic*, 24 (July, 1838), 66–7.
[28] Ward, *Ideal of a Christian Church*, p. 425.
[29] PH, Pusey Papers [Transcripts] LBV, E. B. Pusey to W. F. Hook, 27 September 1842.
[30] Birmingham Oratory, Newman Papers, No. 44, E. Churton to J. H. Newman, 18 September 1838.
[31] PH, Gresley Papers, GRES 3/7/32, E. Churton to W. Gresley, 10 May 1842.
[32] PH, Gresley Papers, GRES 3/7/19, E. Churton to W. Gresley, 7 April 1840. According to
Gilley, 'Southey had the rationalist temper which ascribed miracles to sacerdotal fraud.'
Gilley, 'Robert Southey's *Book of the Church*', 421.

aegis, it took the practical form of the reintroduction of sisterhoods into the Church of England from the 1840s onwards. Tractarian antipathy towards the English Reformers focused on their apparent abandonment of the ascetical dimension of spirituality. The comparison drawn with the Fathers was telling. As the preface to Froude's *Remains* asserted, 'compare the sayings and manner of the two schools on the subject of fasting, celibacy, religious vows, voluntary retirement and contemplation ... and ... any sort of self-denial ... but ... there can be little doubt that ... the tone of the fourth century is so unlike that of the sixteenth ... that it is absolutely impossible for the same mind to sympathise with both'.[33] In reintroducing the conventual life and emphasising the monastic ideal, Pusey felt that he was but restoring to the Church of England an essential element of the spiritual inheritance of 'ancient' Christianity.[34]

The monastic and contemplative ideal had never lacked exponents among pre-Tractarian High Churchmen. The ideal of community life had first been put into practice by Nicholas Ferrar at Little Gidding in the early seventeenth century. Proposals for a revival of a form of female community life dated back to Mary Astell's proposals in 1694, while in 1761 William Law established a community of ladies bound by vows of celibacy at King's Cliffe. Even Southey, for all his strictures on Roman Catholic ascetical practice, had advocated the revival of a 'Reformed' version of religious sisterhoods in the Church of England.[35] Moreover, in a sermon at Oxford in 1783, the High Churchman George Croft urged the Church of England to learn from the ascetical standards set by the Church of Rome. Croft singled out monasticism, in which 'though pregnant with so many mischiefs, and filled with so many instances of avarice and sensuality, we find no other purpose than that of retiring from the world, and being devoted to the study of religion and learning'.[36] Edward Churton later took a similar view. 'It is impossible', he maintained, 'for a serious mind to suppose that

---

[33] [Newman and Keble, eds.], *Remains of Richard Hurrell Froude*, vol. III, p. xix.
[34] Pusey, *Letter to the Lord Bishop of London* (1851), p. 221.
[35] Gilley, 'Robert Southey's *Book of the Church*', 420. For Southey's advocacy of Anglican nunneries, see R. Southey, *Sir Thomas More; or Colloquies on the Progress and Prospects of Society*, 2 vols. (London, 1829), vol. I, pp. 93, 154–5, 339–40; vol. II, pp. 37, 228. A reviewer of the *Book of the Church* in the High Church *British Critic* criticised Southey's 'remarkable ... partiality' for the founders and reformers of 'monkery'. 'Southey's Book of the Church', *British Critic*, 21 (May 1824), 453.
[36] Croft, *Sermons*, vol. I, p. 21.

a rule of life so early introduced into the Christian church, so approved by the most eminent Fathers and confessors of those early times, and so long kept up in almost every Christian country, can have been allowed without some providential purpose'.[37]

Hackney did not disapprove of initial Tractarian efforts at revival of the religious life. After visiting Joshua Watson in retirement at Daventry in 1842, the Tractarian Charles Marriott proudly informed Newman, 'I was desirous to know what he thought of the monastic life ... I found the good old man ... spoke decidedly in favour of some institution of the kind. I told him what you were doing at Littlemore, and he seemed to like the notion of it much'.[38] The objection which old High Churchmen such as the sympathetic Bishop Phillpotts would raise against Pusey's sisterhoods was not disapproval of the idea as such, but of his apparent turning of a 'counsel of perfection' into a 'Romish' vehicle of virtue or merit in itself.[39]

HIGH CHURCHMANSHIP AND SPIRITUAL TEMPER

The most commonplace Tractarian assumption about the Orthodox churchmanship of the Georgian era concerned its devotional 'coldness' and 'formalism'. 'Serious religion' was deemed to be concentrated on the Evangelical side, so that 'orthodoxy without warmth made but a feeble battle against piety without orthodoxy'.[40] For Frederick Oakeley, Georgian High Churchmen were utterly 'un-Apostolical': 'their too great prejudices against singularity, enthusiasm or intensity of any kind', he observed, 'make it exceedingly doubtful what kind of a reception a person like St Augustine or St Bernard would have encountered from some of them'.[41] Later writers have further propagated these presuppositions of Tractarian historiography. According to Brilioth, 'the weakness of that kind of High Churchmanship which was preached by Daubeny and his likes' was 'that they so entirely cut themselves off from the spiritual

---

[37] E. Churton, *Biography of the Early Church* (London, 1840), p. vi.
[38] PH, Ollard Papers, C. Marriott to J. H. Newman, 10 January 1842 (copy).
[39] See Edward Hawkins's marginalia on p. 234 of his copy of Pusey's *Letter to ... the Lord Bishop of London* (1851). See also *Letters on the Plymouth Sisters Suggested by the Recent Pamphlets and Letters of ... Miss Sellon and the Bishop of Exeter* (London, 1852), pp. 14–21; S. Gill, 'The Power of Christian Ladyhood: Priscilla Lydia Sellon and the Creation of Anglican Sisterhoods', in S. Mews, ed., *Modern Religious Rebels. Presented to John Kent* (London, 1993), pp. 154–5.
[40] *British Critic*, 25 (April, 1839), 471.   [41] *British Critic*, 32 (July, 1842), 230.

well which streamed forth from the Evangelical revival of the eighteenth century'.[42] Such assumptions can be questioned by contrary evidence.

The perennial Evangelical critique of contemporary Anglican preaching in the late eighteenth and early nineteenth centuries was its apparent neglect of doctrinal content such as Justification and the Atonement and its extolling of the 'all-sufficiency of mere morality'.[43] The critique was aimed primarily at the 'Warburtonian' school rather than at the 'Orthodox' as a whole.

Recent reappraisal of Tillotson's spirituality noted above has questioned the view that he was a preacher of mere moralism. It has been suggested that in reaction to the 'solifidianism' of the Puritan sectaries, Tillotson merely strove to reconnect morality to godliness, and by no means sought to undervalue the Atonement as Evangelical critics suggested.[44] Nevertheless, the devotional temper of those who regarded themselves as Tillotson's spiritual successors in the eighteenth century was colder than that of both earlier High Churchmen and Evangelicals.[45] Moreover, this devotional temper also characterised some of the Orthodox. The devotional rhapsodies characteristic of Evangelical writers such as the poet, William Cowper, were alien to this school. The Orthodox divine, Thomas Randolph, Oxford's Margaret Professor of Divinity in the 1760s, was not untypical in condemning an over-dependence on inward feelings in prayer as a dangerous reliance on 'the false bottom of fancy and imagination'.[46]

There was a tendency for some Orthodox churchmen in the forefront of campaigns of 'refutation of Calvinism' in the 1800s and 1810s, such as Pretyman-Tomline and Marsh, to embrace the moral preaching as well as anti-asceticism of the 'Warburtonian' school. For the Arminian controversialist Richard Warner, the model of pulpit instruction in the reigns of the first two Georges remained the ideal. Warner stressed the 'clear reasoning, sober argument, and

---

[42] Brilioth, *Anglican Revival*, p. 45.
[43] See Overton, *The True Churchman Ascertained*, pp. 289–90.
[44] Clifford, *Atonement and Justification*, pp. 33–49; I. Rivers, *Reason, Grace and Sentiment: a Study of the Language of Religion and Ethics in England, 1660–1780*, vol. 1: *Whichcote to Wesley* (Cambridge, 1991), pp. 37–59. Cf. N. Sykes, 'Sermons of John Tillotson', *Theology*, 58 (1955), 297–302.
[45] Abbey and Overton, *English Church in the Eighteenth century*, vol. 1, pp. 279–338.
[46] T. Randolph, *The Witness of the Spirit. A Sermon Preached before the University of Oxford at St Mary's* (Oxford, 1768), p. 13.

touching exhortation' of this standard of preaching,[47] citing Tillotson and even the Arian Samuel Clarke, as well as Taylor, Barrow
and Butler as his spiritual mentors.[48] Warner's reference to 'touching exhortation' showed that even churchmen of his mould did not
discount the cultivation of the feelings. Warner considered that
'the orthodoxy of the Establishment has been happily preserved,
till of late years' by holding the mean between 'the fervour of
enthusiasm on the one hand, and the coldness of a merely ethical
system on the other'.[49] For Warner, this model of orthodoxy was
threatened by 'the style adopted by that new and numerous class of
Church-of-England Divines, who either by assumption or nomina-
tion, are known as Evangelical Preachers!'[50] The latter were castigated for 'engrafting the errors of Calvinism, and the follies of
fanaticism, on the truths of Scripture, by substituting the harsh,
dissociating and wild speculations of the Tabernacle, for the con-
solatory and amiable, and reasonable tenets of the Church'.[51]
Significantly, in the 1840s Warner would denounce 'Puseyism'[52]
on very similar grounds to his assault on 'Calvinism' in the pre-
Tractarian era.

Such attitudes only confirmed the readiness of some Calvinistic
Evangelicals to divide the Church on the basis of a rival spirituality,
into 'Rational Divines' on the one hand, and 'Evangelical Divines'
on the other.[53] Into the former 'unspiritual' category, John Overton
would place not only avowed 'Latitudinarians' and Socinians such
as Richard Fellowes but 'Arminian' High Churchmen such as
Daubeny.[54] Overton's categorisations, however, were not represen-

47 R. Warner, *Evangelical Preaching (Commonly So Denominated): Its Character, Errors and Tendency in a Letter to ... the Bishop of Bath and Wells* (London, 1828), pp. 7–8.
   Richard Warner (1763–1857). St Mary Hall, Oxford, 1787; ordained 1790; various
curacies in the Bath area, 1796–1809; Rector of Great Chalfield, Wilts., 1809–17; Vicar of
Norton St Philip, Somerset, 1817–18; Rector of Chelwood, Somerset, 1827-d; FSA.
48 R. Warner, *A Letter to the Hon and Rt. Rev. Henry Ryder D.D. Lord Bishop of Gloucester on the
Admission to Holy Orders of Young Men Holding (What are Commonly Called) Evangelical
Principles* (Bath, 1818), p. 16.
49 R. Warner, *Considerations on the Doctrines of the Evangelical Clergy and on the Probable Effects of
Evangelical Preaching: A Sermon Preached at Frome, Somersetshire, on Monday June 2nd, 1817 at the
Visitation of the Rev. Richard Sandiford, Archdeacon of Wells* (London, [1817]), p. 24.
50 Warner, *Evangelical Preaching*, p. 9; R. Warner, *Old Church of England Principles: in a Series of
Plain, Doctrinal and Practical Sermons*, 3 vols. (London, 1817), vol. 1, p. vi.
51 Warner, *Letter to Rt. Rev. Henry Ryder*, p. 19.
52 [R. Warner], *Anti-Puseyism* [from Keene's *Bath Journal* of 25 September, 1843]; R. Warner,
Apostacy from Christ: May England Be Charged with It? (London, 1843).
53 Hill, *Reformation-Truth Restored*, pp. i–xvii.
54 Overton, *Four Letters to the Editor of the 'Christian Observer'*, p. 24.

tative of Evangelicals as a whole. On the contrary, many Evangelicals and Orthodox, for all their differences of doctrinal emphasis on issues such as Justification, conversion, and baptism, were united by a common devotional fervour, even if the expression of their spirituality took different forms.

The Evangelical commentator J. W. Middelton was more generous in distinguishing the 'Orthodox' from 'Paley and his school', and acknowledging a spiritual basis to his categories of 'Orthodox', 'Latitudinarian' and 'secular'. Middelton's praise was especially directed towards the Hutchinsonian High Church divines such as Horne and Jones of Nayland who, he insisted, deserved to 'be enumerated as individuals who stood in the gap in that season of latitudinarianism and heterodoxy'.[55] The spiritual affinities between the Hutchinsonians and leaders of the Evangelical Revival[56] have not always been fully recognised.

Although Hutchinsonian relations with Evangelicals cooled after the 1760s,[57] the closeness in spiritual tone was such that the former were often accused of 'enthusiasm' and of being 'Methodistical'.[58] Even after Hutchinsonians such as Horne had sought 'deliverance ... from all danger of fanatical infection',[59] they continued to make common cause with Evangelicals in campaigning against mere moralism in popular preaching. They had an especial distaste for what Jones of Nayland called the 'empirical divinity' and the 'rash reasoners of the Warburtonian school'.[60] Echoing the standard Evangelical complaint that many contemporary clergy could be faulted for 'not preaching the whole Gospel', Horne lamented in 1791, 'that by delivering cold inanimate lectures on moral virtue, independent of Christianity, many of our clergy of late years have

[55] Middelton, *Ecclesiastical Memoir*, p. 31.
[56] Bebbington, *Evangelicalism in Modern Britain*, p. 57; A. S. Wood, *Thomas Haweis* (London, 1957), pp. 46–7; G. H. Tavard, *The Seventeenth-Century Tradition: a Study in Recusant Thought* (Leiden, 1978), pp. 254–5. As late as 1833, the Evangelical *Christian Observer* defended Hutchinsonianism. *Christian Observer*, 33 (April, 1833), 219–21; E. Sidney, *The Life of Sir Richard Hill* (London, 1839), pp. 189–30.
[57] Jones, *Memoirs of Horne*, pp. 64–5.
[58] Ralph Churton later recalled the remark commonly made in his early years, 'that a Hutchinsonian is a Methodist with learning and a Methodist is a Hutchinsonian without learning'. SC, Churton Papers, R. Churton to T. T. Churton, 29 May 1828.
[59] Jones, *Memoirs of Horne*, p. 65. In 1766, William Stevens privately condemned Methodists for 'propagating the same pestilential notions now, that the Puritans did then [i.e. early seventeenth century]'. *Memoirs of William Stevens* (new edn, 1859) p. 157.
[60] *Ibid.*, p. 45.

lowered themselves much in the estimation of the religious part of the laity'.[61]

A spiritual High Churchmanship that had affinities with Evangelicalism in this period cannot be limited to the Hutchinsonians alone. For it was the non-Hutchinsonian Orthodox churchman, Archbishop Secker, who had been the very first to lament the 'want of Evangelical preaching' as early as the 1760s.[62] It is true that by 'Evangelical', Secker did not mean just the particular doctrinal shibboleths that would distinguish the so-called 'Evangelical' party from their Orthodox brethren. Although regarded by latitudinarian critics such as Blackburne as a disciple of Laud and rigid adherent of 'the maxims of High-Church government',[63] Secker was also hailed as an 'Evangelical Divine' and as one than whom 'few men, it may be presumed, have worn the Mitre with more lustre'.[64] Above all, it was the non-Hutchinsonian High Churchman, Samuel Horsley, likewise regarded by some as 'another Laud', who won the keenest Evangelical plaudits; his episcopal charges earning more Evangelical and even Methodist respect than some historians have allowed.[65] Horsley's openness and neutrality over the Calvinist–Arminian controversy distinguished him from most Orthodox divines. Moreover, while Horsley the High Churchman might rebuke Methodism's 'disorderly zeal for the propagation of truth', he admired its spiritual fervour. He also impressed Evangelicals with his view that 'an over-abundant zeal to check the frenzy of the Methodists first introduced that unscriptural language which confounds religion and morality'.[66] Such sentiments led Middelton to extol Horsley's Charge of 1790 as having 'caused a greater

---

[61] Horne, 'A Charge Intended to Have Been Delivered to the Clergy of the Diocese of Norwich', p. 14.

[62] Grant, *Summary History*, vol. IV, p. 160.

[63] [F. Blackburne], *Memoirs of Thomas Hollis*, 2 vols. (London, 1780), vol. I, p. 227. On Secker's churchmanship, see J. S. Macauley and R. W. Greaves, eds., *Autobiography of Thomas Secker, Archbishop of Canterbury* (Lawrence, Kans, 1988), pp. ix–xvi; J. Downey, *The Eighteenth-Century Pulpit: a Study of the Sermons of Butler, Berkeley, Secker, Sterne, Whitefield and Wesley* (Oxford, 1969), ch. 4.

[64] Overton, *True Churchman Ascertained*, p. 36.

[65] For example, see [J. Benson], 'Observations on Bishop Horsley's Charge to the Clergy of the Diocese of St Asaph' [1806], *Miscellaneous Papers in Defence of Evangelical Religion, and of the Methodists* (Hull, 1827), pp. 59–65.

[66] *The Charge of Samuel, Lord Bishop of St David's to the Clergy of His Diocese, Delivered at His Primary Visitation in the Year 1790* (London, 1801), p. 28.

sensation among the friends of religion, than had been produced by any similar event since the best age of the English Church'.[67] The contemporary High Church writer, Johnson Grant, admitted a spiritual affinity between the Orthodox and latitudinarians in a mutual repudiation of the Evangelical emphasis on an inward, sensible perception of the Holy Spirit as test of faith. One of Pusey's later complaints about the 'High and Dry' of earlier generations was that they were too dismissive of the need for an inward change of heart in their 'mechanical', 'objective' and 'chilly' representation of the plan of salvation.[68] His own presentation of 'Catholic' baptismal teaching sought to avoid this tone and give an 'Evangelical' emphasis on the experiential. Grant himself acknowledged this weakness in contemporary Orthodox apologetic, but denied that it was general. He insisted that, on the whole, the Orthodox acknowledged the importance of inward feelings which could be cultivated in the devotional life. He complained that many divines of what he called the anti-Methodist 'Warburtonian school' such as Joseph Trapp had failed 'to distinguish between the fancies of the visionary, and that inward witness which is the blessed privilege of those who truly believe'.[69] Grant was frankly critical of the Marsh–Tomline variant of Orthodox divinity emanating from the anti-Calvinist controversy of the 1800s for being 'blind to the promotion of spiritual religion'. He commended the Orthodox George Nott's Bampton Lectures of 1802, however, for allowing spiritual 'influence its due extent, both in the understanding and on the will'.[70]

Even the combative Daubeny could refer positively to the religious witness of moderate Evangelicals such as William Wilberforce and Hannah More, in spite of his often severe strictures on their theological opinions.[71] In the preface to his *Guide to the Church*, Daubeny stressed that both he and Wilberforce 'look to the same Cross as our only hope and title to salvation'. He even expressed the hope that Wilberforce might 'become the blessed instrument in God's hand of raising the dead to life, by bringing back the soul of

---

[67] Middelton, *Ecclesiastical Memoir*, p. 328.
[68] E. B. Pusey, *Parochial Sermons*, 2 vols. (London, 1852), vol. i, p. viii.
[69] Grant, *Summary History*, vol. iv, p. 35; Middelton, *Ecclesiastical Memoir*, p. 30.
[70] Grant, *Summary History*, vol. iv, pp. 160, 565.
[71] ESCRO, Locker-Lampson Papers, b/5/20, C. Daubeny to J. Boucher, 3 March 1801; C. Daubeny to J. Boucher, 16 April 1800.

Christianity to that body from which it has long since disappeared'.[72]

Evangelicals had no monopoly of devotional intensity. The Orthodox could match their spiritual fervour, although Brilioth was right to claim that the Orthodox devotional temper did not draw on the 'well' of the Evangelical Revival.[73] But the fact that divines such as Daubeny and Bishop Burgess drew on distinctively High Church and Nonjuring sources of spirituality is hardly an index of their coldness. On the contrary, the evidence of the private devotional reading and practice of such churchmen sharply contradicts Brilioth's somewhat caricatured portrait.

Certainly, there was a restraint in High Church spirituality that could be mistaken for dryness. In fact, Orthodox rhetoric against 'enthusiasm' has been subject to as much later misrepresentation as its rhetoric in defence of 'establishment'. For example, many Victorian commentators overlooked the fact that, whereas the term 'enthusiasm' acquired a decidedly favourable sense in the nineteenth century, denoting a contrast to lukewarmness or indifference, in the previous century the term had possessed genuinely negative connotations. In the eighteenth century, enthusiasm implied not religious zeal, but a dangerous abuse of spiritual influences, 'a misconceit of inspiration', an 'afflatus of the Deity'.[74]

Nevertheless, Tractarian perceptions of the 'High and Dry' nature of Orthodox spirituality can partly be explained by a certain declension towards 'chilliness' discernable from the 1800s onwards, in the wake of the demise of the Hutchinsonians and especially the death of Horsley in 1806. Sheridan Gilley has argued that one aspect of the reaction in the Church of England to the French Revolution was a discrediting of the Evangelical appeal to subjective spiritual feelings and imagination with which earlier High Churchmen such as the Hutchinsonians had up to a point also indulged.[75] Emotional fervour in devotional language and practice became more suspect in High Church circles than it had previously been. This fear of emotional excess in devotion characterised the tone of the Hackney-controlled *British Critic* in the 1810s and 1820s, and is borne out by

[72] Daubeny, *Guide to the Church*, pp. v–vi.   [73] Brilioth, *Anglican Revival*, p. 45.
[74] Abbey and Overton, *English Church in the Eighteenth Century*, vol. I, pp. 530–1.
[75] S. Gilley, 'John Keble and the Victorian Churching of Romanticism', in J. R. Watson, ed., *An Infinite Variety: Essays in Romanticism* (London, 1983), pp. 228–9; R. W. Greaves, 'On the Religious Climate of Hanoverian England', inaugural lecture, University of London, November 1963, p. 17.

the less than flattering impressions of the Phalanx leaders at this date which their friend Bishop Jebb drew.[76] In short, the representatives of High Churchmanship with which the rising Tractarians had contact in the late 1820s and early 1830s, and which Newman witheringly satirised as 'condescending and pompous', stiff and 'priggish', were arguably more deserving of the 'High and Dry' label than their later eighteenth-century predecessors. Moreover, there were several children of traditional High Church households who would embrace Evangelicalism in the era *c.* 1800–25 precisely because, as the example of John Bowdler the Evangelical son of the High Churchman Thomas Bowdler showed, there was a perception that religious feelings were no longer given an adequate outlet within contemporary High Churchmanship.[77] In the next generation the spiritual attraction of Tractarianism in this same quarter would ensure that this trend would be reversed.

The harnessing of the force of Romanticism by the future Tractarian John Keble in his *Christian Year* (1827) can be viewed as spiritually liberating for High Churchmanship.[78] For Keble's 'churching of Romanticism' injected a poetic and restrained emotional quality into the spirituality of High Churchmanship which had been evident in the Hutchinsonians as well as the seventeenth-century divines and religious poets, but which had declined over succeeding decades. The result was that High Churchmanship imbued with Keble's Romantic colouring and note of moral seriousness would have an appeal for the rising generation, especially those from Evangelical households, which it might otherwise have lacked. While a new and idealistic generation in the 1830s might despise the 'miserable tone' of the 'school of Marsh and Tomline', Keble enabled them to associate High Churchmanship no longer with mere 'formalism' but once more with that 'heart religion', 'play of mind, and elasticity of feeling' which Newman later defined as vital

[76] Bodl. Lib, Ms Eng Lett d. 123, fol. 141, J. Jebb to C. A. Ogilvie, 16 June 1820; C. Forster, ed., *Thirty Years Correspondence between John Jebb and Alexander Knox*, vol. II, p. 4.

[77] C. Bowdler, *The Religion of the Heart as Exemplified in the Life and Writings of John Bowdler* (London, 1857), pp. 77–8. Manning also criticised the old High Church school for 'its stiff, formalistic, sectarian, intolerant temper'. Bodl. Lib, Manning Papers, Ms Eng Lett c. 658, fol. 25, H. E. Manning to W. Dodsworth, 13 June 1844.

[78] Gilley, 'John Keble and the Victorian Churching of Romanticism', pp. 236–7. On links between Tractarianism and Romanticism, see G. B. Tennyson, *Victorian Devotional Poetry: the Tractarian Mode* (London, 1981), especially chs. 2 and 3; S. Prickett, *Romanticism and Religion* (Cambridge, 1976). By 1837, there had been sixteen editions of the *Christian Year* published. Brian Martin suggests that half a million copies were sold by 1877. B. Martin, *John Keble. Priest, Professor and Poet* (London, 1976), p. 110.

elements of the Tractarian *ethos*. On the other hand, it has been rightly pointed out that the very popularity and influence of the *Christian Year* showed that Keble had mined a rich and enduring vein of traditional High Anglican spirituality.[79]

There was to be a marked contrast, however, between the emotional and ecstatic spirituality of the later 'Romanising' school among the Tractarians and the more sober and restrained temper of Keble's High Churchmanship. The former would find expression in extravagant hagiographies and martyrologies of medieval and Counter-Reformation as well as early Christian saints. For old High Churchmen, the 'Liguorian' spirituality expressed in Pusey's meditations on the Passion entailed 'the same indulgence of feeling with which one looks and weeps over a tragedy or a novel'.[80] They considered such spirituality to be morbid as well as superstitious. This difference in devotional tone was an important ingredient in the breach between old High Churchmanship and later Tractarianism. Although Pusey tried to bolster Anglican allegiance among the disaffected by importing Roman Catholic devotional forms, the appeal of the Roman model of sanctity was what ultimately drew Newman and some of his followers to the Church of Rome. It was the test of holiness that proved conclusive.

HIGH CHURCHMANSHIP AND THE DOCTRINE OF RESERVE

The revived High Church spirituality of Keble's *Christian Year* exemplified a restraint and self-effacement that was in constructive tension with the warmth and feeling it also embodied. Reserve became a distinctive element of the Tractarian spiritual *ethos*. For the Tractarians, this signified more than a spiritual temper. In his *Arians of the Fourth Century*, Newman identified the notion of reserve or 'economy' in communicating religious knowledge as a theological principle, the *disciplina arcani*, employed by the early Fathers.[81] The doctrine of Reserve counselled an adaptation of imparted revealed truth to the capacities and understanding of the receiver. As William Copeland explained in 1836,

[79] S. Baring-Gould, *The Church Revival. Thought Thereon and Reminiscences* (London, 1914), p. 75.
[80] Bodl. Lib, Ms Eng Misc e. 117, fol. 310, J. C. Crosthwaite to E. B. Pusey, *c.* April 1842.
[81] Newman, *Arians*, pp. 47–58. See R. T. Selby, *The Principle of Reserve in the Writings of John Henry Newman* (Oxford, 1975), pp. 1–43; G. B. Tennyson, 'Tractarian Aesthetics: Analogy and Reserve in Keble and Newman', *Victorian Newsletter*, No. 55 (Spring, 1974).

there is a deep and awful spirit in the Fathers which quite strikes one to the ground and forms a strange contrast to that heatless, flippant spirit in which so stupendous a doctrine as the Atonement is spoken of by persons who would fain believe themselves better Christians for talking so. People have got to learn that true piety lies too deep to be always in the tongue, and is too sublime to be talked about.[82]

The Tractarians sympathised with the Evangelical emphasis on 'heart religion' and religious feeling. But the Tractarian dislike of the Evangelical tendency to regard subjective feelings as a test of truth became a source of conflict between the two parties. In contrast to the Evangelical style of 'popular religion', the Tractarians emphasised awe, reverence and an avoidance of show. There was a consciously anti-Evangelical animus to the Tractarian presentation of the doctrine of Reserve. Evangelicals responded to the challenge. For them, Reserve was a principle which struck at the very root of the Gospel, and amounted to the imposition of a moral thraldom to sacerdotal power.[83] Old High Churchmen also reacted against the Tractarian application of the theory, though their line of critique was sometimes distinct from that of Evangelicals. Bishop Phillpotts condemned the doctrine because he felt that it was inconsistent with the ministerial duty to inculcate the people in the truths of sacramental religion.[84] Even the later Roman Catholic convert, William Maskell, was led to contrast Evangelical 'plain speaking' favourably with High Church reticence and reserve in communicating doctrinal truth.[85]

Yet at the level of devotional temper, the Tractarian adherence to the notion of Reserve was in tune with early High Churchmanship. William Copeland recognised that Keble's teaching on Reserve, 'was mainly in the spirit of Bishop Butler', and that 'Butler's dislike of excessive talkativeness was in harmony with his own'.[86] There were other eighteenth-century witnesses to this spirit beside Butler. As the nineteenth-century biographer of the Hutchinsonian William Kirby observed, it was precisely the fact that 'those whose minds were wont to find a centre of action at Nayland Parsonage looked not for earthly applause' but rested content with a 'humble, secret,

[82] PH, Copeland Papers, W. J. Copeland to M. A. Copeland, 4 November 1836.
[83] Toon, *Evangelical Theology*, pp. 133–5.
[84] H. Phillpotts, *A Charge Delivered to the Clergy of the Diocese of Exeter, at the Triennial Visitation in ... August, September and October 1839* (London, 1839), pp. 14–15.
[85] Maskell, *Second Letter on the Present Position of the High Church Party*, pp. 65–6.
[86] PH, Copeland Papers, W. J. Copeland, Ms 'Narrative of the Oxford Movement'.

unaffected, unaspiring practice of piety', that accounted 'for so little being known of their labours'.[87] A Victorian biographer of Jones of Nayland maintained a similar perspective in the face of contemporary assumptions of Tractarian novelty. Thus, Jones of Nayland was proudly cited as an example of the fact 'that English churchmen had condemned the irreverent admixture of things sacred and profane long before some late assailants of the same offences against decorum and religious feeling were born to denounce them to the world as the results of the English Reformation'.[88] Particularly striking was the precise way in which the message of Isaac Williams's *Tract 80* was prefigured by Daubeny in a Charge of 1824, when he attacked what he called 'the unreserved and indiscriminate application of strong evangelic language to Christians who might be in the infancy of their growth' and therefore could not 'be supposed to have attained in any degree to that state of spiritual proficiency, to which that language originally belonged'.[89]

The *ethos* of Reserve was also central to the spirituality of members of the Hackney Phalanx. It lay at the root of their opposition to Evangelical propagation of Holy Scripture among the unlearned without any comment or guidance. Hackney's implacable resistance to the activities of the Bible Society was more than the merely 'High and Dry' aversion to breaches of order and decorum that it is sometimes presented as. A vital theological principle, often regarded as peculiar to Tractarianism, was at stake. For it was in the very spirit and language that the Tractarian leaders would later employ, that Norris in 1813 asserted as his primary ground of opposition to the Bible Society, that Scripture was 'not in the purpose of God, the instrument of conversion – but the repository of divine knowledge for the perfecting of those already converted. I mean that it is the children's bread and not to be cast to dogs'.[90]

HIGH CHURCHMANSHIP AND ANTI-RATIONALISM

A feature of Hanoverian Anglican apologetic, as set forth by Warburton and Paley, was an emphasis on the reasonableness of Christianity, and an exaltation of the claims of human reason and

[87] J. Freeman, *The Life of the Rev. William Kirby* (London, 1852), p. 36.
[88] W. Teale, 'William Jones', in *Lives of English Divines* (London, 1846), p. 363.
[89] C. Daubeny, *A Charge Delivered to the Clergy of the Archdeaconry of Sarum ... 1824* (London, 1824), p. 8.
[90] SC, Churton Papers, H. H. Norris to R. Churton, 4 March 1813.

intellect in the discernment of divine truth. According to Gascoigne, this emphasis was encouraged by the nature of church–state ties in the period.[91] It represented a shift in the old balance between reason, scripture and tradition as maintained by the Caroline Divines.

The overlap between Latitudinarians and elements of the Orthodox in terms of spiritual temper was paralleled by a similar overlap in terms of theological temper. According to Edward Churton, 'it was a misfortune of many English divines of the period which followed the Revolution, that they thought they could teach and maintain Catholic doctrine while they departed from Catholic terms, and that the more divine mysteries were made level to what they called right reason, the more benefit would accrue to the Christian Faith'. Churton cited the example of 'the unfortunate terminology' of the High Churchman William Sherlock as well as of the latitudinarian Tillotson.[92] At a later date, the Orthodox apologetic of Bishop Marsh and others of the Cambridge 'intellectual party' remained rooted in the evidence theology propounded by Paley.[93] Moreover, Pietro Corsi has suggested an intellectual basis to the *rapprochement* between the Oriel *Noetics* and High Church Hackney Phalanx in the 1820s. Both emphasised reason and natural theology. Corsi concludes that the 'philosophy of John Locke admitted of more traditional and conservative uses in High Church circles'.[94]

For the Tractarians, the defect of Orthodox apologetic of the generation preceding their own, was that 'religion seemed to be placed in the understanding, rather than in the affections'.[95] Newman's personal reaction against the Orthodox consensus of the

---

[91] Gascoigne, *Cambridge in the Age of the Enlightenment*, p. 307.

[92] E. Churton, ed., *A Supplement to Waterland's Works. Fourteen Letters from Daniel Waterland to Zachary Pearce. Edited, with an Historical and Critical Preface by Edward Churton* (Oxford, 1868), p. xiv.

[93] Braine, 'Life and Writings of Herbert Marsh', p. 4; Waterman, 'A Cambridge Via Media'.
    Richard Warner (see n. 47), whose spiritual mentors remained Paley and Paley's patron 'the learned and enlightened' Edmund Law, Bishop of Carlisle, was an exponent of the 'rational' strain in Arminian apologetic characteristic of Hanoverian Low Churchmanship. Warner's later censures on Tractarianism mirrored his earlier strictures on Calvinism. As in his attack on Evangelicalism, Warner's broadside on the Oxford Tracts rested on an appeal to 'Chillingworth, Hoadley, S. Clarke, Tillotson, Jortin, Paley, and a crowd of other enlightened English divines ... opposed, *toto coelo*, to such notions'. [R. Warner], *The Simplicity and Intelligible Character of Christianity. In a Series of Four Sermons ... With a Postscript on the Evidences of Christianity* (Bath, 1839).

[94] Corsi, *Baden Powell*, p. 73. [95] Pusey, *Parochial Sermons*, vol. i, p. viii.

1820s is well attested. In a striking passage in his *Autobiographical Memoir*, Newman observed, 'a cold Arminian doctrine, the first stage of liberalism, was the characteristic ... both of the high and dry Anglicans of that day and of the Oriel divines'.[96] The significance of this passage was, as Thomas points out, that 'the potential slide into liberalism was here not presented as so often, via Evangelical Protestantism, popular or otherwise, but via the upholders of the creed, liturgy, establishment, Arminianism and orthodoxy – the Zs, who are lumped together with Noetics such as Whately and Hawkins'.[97] The point was reinforced by Newman's admission that he was only 'saved' from the cold intellectualism of 'Arminianism' by the 'imaginative devotion' to the Fathers he learned from the Evangelical Milner.[98] Elsewhere, Newman traced the origins of the Latitudinarian and rationalist 'virus' in the Church of England to the influence of the Dutch Arminians, the Erasmian Hugo Grotius and Episcopius on Laud's liberal acolytes, Chillingworth and Hales. Newman considered the 'Arminian school' of Marsh and Tomline to be tinctured by this influence.[99]

In challenging the supremacy of the *Noetics* at Oxford, the Tractarians reacted against the 'presumptious turn of mind, the reliance on intellectual ability, supposed to result from instruction addressing itself to the intellect alone', in favour of 'formation of moral character by habit' and the inculcation of the deeper ethical and spiritual truths of moral philosophy.[100] Learning was not disparaged. On

---

[96] H. Tristram, ed., *John Henry Newman: Autobiographical Writings* (London, 1956), p. 83.
[97] Thomas, *Newman and Heresy*, pp. 14–15.
[98] Tristram, ed., *Newman: Autobiographical Writings*, p. 83.
[99] [Newman], 'Le Bas's Life of Archbishop Laud', 368.

On Newman's prompting, his friend Samuel Wood proposed an article in which he would 'point out that the Arminianism ... which succeeded the Calvinism of the reformation and was its reaction, and which assumes to itself ... the name of *Orthodoxy*, is just as non-catholic and more Rationalistic, and as far removed from the Mysterious and True system as Calvinism'. S. F. Wood to J. H. Newman, 29 May 1837, *Letters and Diaries*, vol. VI, p. 77.

Newman regarded the Orthodoxy of the Hanoverian era as at one with latitudinarianism in its rationalising tendency. See his comment in 1835: 'The fashionable high Church (so to call it!) divinity of the last century was the divinity of the Revolution – of which the great Masters range from the latitudinarians Tillotson and Burnet down to the Socinianizing or Socinian Hoadley – a chilling, meagre, uncompassionate, secular divinity indeed – of which Paley's shallowness, Warburton's coarse ingenuity, and the present Bishop of Peterborough's [Herbert Marsh] deadness, are representatives in the three provinces of Argument, Philosophy, and Orthodoxy.' J. H. Newman to Sir J. Stephen, 16 March 1835, *Letters and Diaries*, vol. V, pp. 45–6.

[100] Nockles, 'An Academic Counter-Revolution', 100.

the contrary, even liberal critics acknowledged that the Tractarians presented a favourable contrast with Evangelicals in this respect.[101] But true learning consisted of more than mere cultivation of the intellect. The prerequisites for the reception of the truth of the Gospel were not intellectual attainment or rational enquiry, but the simplicity and teachable disposition of little children. An emphasis on the study of evidences as popularised by Paley was repudiated because, in Newman's words, it encouraged an 'evil frame of mind' whereby 'the learner is supposed external to the system'. For all his dissatisfaction with the Protestant content of the Articles, Newman was a staunch advocate of subscription at Oxford precisely because it impressed upon the minds of the young subscriber 'the teachable and subdued temper expected of them. They are not to reason, but to obey; – and this quite independently of the degree of accuracy, the wisdom etc. of the Articles themselves'.[102]

The Oxford liberal Baden Powell recognised that the Tractarian repudiation of natural theology lay squarely in the tradition of the Hutchinsonian divines.[103] Recently, Brian Young has demonstrated how the anti-rationalism of the Hutchinsonians represented a profound reaction, by a section of the Orthodox whom he aptly labels the 'dogmatist' party, against Latitudinarians best described as 'anti-dogmatist'; a line of cleavage, Young argues, which the subscription controversy debate in the Church of England in 1772–3 sharpened.[104]

Hutchinsonian High Church rhetoric against the contemporary cult of human reason strikingly prefigured that of the Tractarians. In words closely akin to those of Newman's, George Horne argued that Christ had taken a little child, and 'set him forth as a pattern to show with what temper of mind His doctrine must be received, and that men, even the greatest and wisest of them, must become as little children, before they can be His disciples'.[105] Like Froude and

101 Baden Powell, *Tradition Unveiled: or an Exposition of the Pretensions and Tendency of Authoritative Teaching in the Church* (London, 1839) pp. 12–14.
102 J. H. Newman to A. P. Perceval, 11 January 1835, Liddon, *Life of Pusey*, vol. 1, p. 301.
103 Baden Powell, *Oxford Essays: the Burnett Prizes. The Study of Natural Theology* (Oxford, 1857), pp. 178–80.
104 Young, '"Orthodoxy Assailed"', ch. 2. Young argues (p. 364) that anti-French *philosophes* and Counter-Enlightenment ideas 'assumed the status of orthodoxy in late eighteenth century Anglican thought', allowing the Hutchinsonian divines to enjoy 'a late flowering of mainstream success'; Aston, 'Horne and Heterodoxy', 896–8.
105 W. Jones, ed., *Works of the Rt. Rev. George Horne D.D. Late Lord Bishop of Norwich*, 4 vols. (2nd edn, London, 1818), vol. II, 'Discourse IV', 'The Tree of Knowledge', p. 70.

Newman, Horne asserted the absolute supremacy of faith over verifiable 'experience' or external evidence. Reason, Horne insisted,

can no more find out, without the help of Revelation, the original state and constitution of man, the changes that have happened in his nature, and the counsels of God, that have taken place in consequence of these changes ... than she can prove metaphysically, that William the Conqueror vanquished Harold, at Hastings, in Sussex.[106]

Samuel Horsley modified his early Newtonianism in favour of a similar emphasis;[107] arguing in 1790 that on some mysterious subjects, 'it is not expected that we comprehend, but that we believe; where we cannot unriddle we are to learn to trust; where our faculties are too weak to penetrate, we are to check our curiosity and adore'.[108]

A major aim of the *Society for the Reformation of Principles* was to resist the pretensions of natural religion and rationalism. Several of the works reprinted in the *The Scholar Armed* were devoted to this end. Nevertheless, Jones of Nayland and his friends represented only one arm of the Orthodox reaction to the French Revolution. As Sheridan Gilley has shown, just as that reaction ultimately helped foster a trend towards coldness in spirituality, so this was paralleled by an actual strengthening of the evidential approach in Orthodox apologetic;[109] a trend from which, according to Corsi's evidence, even the Hackney Phalanx was not immune. For example, in 1802 one of the Hackney circle, the Scottish bishop George Gleig, assailed those Hutchinsonian 'blockheads' who regarded Bull as a Deist and Newton an atheist 'merely because the former conceived of the Trinity in Unity in a way somewhat different from Hutchinson and because the latter made use of terms in science which Hutchinson did not approve'.[110]

Paley remained something of a model in much Orthodox theological discourse, and it took the Oxford Movement to finally dethrone him.[111]

[106] Horne, *An Apology for Certain Gentlemen in the University of Oxford*, p. 14; G. Watson, *A Seasonable Admonition to the Church of England. A Sermon Preached before the University of Oxford at St Marys ... 1751* (Oxford, 1751), p. 14. George Watson (1723?–73), Fellow of University College, Oxford. Tutor and mentor of Horne. Watson's writings, ignored by the Tractarians, were rediscovered by the Victorian literary antiquarian, J. M. Gutch. See J. M. Gutch, ed, *Watson Redivivus. Four Discourses Written between the Years 1749 and 1756* (London, 1860). *DNB*.
[107] Mather, *Horsley*, chs. 3 and 4.
[108] S. Horsley, *An Apology for the Liturgy and Clergy of the Church of England* (London, 1790), pp. 66–89.
[109] Gilley, 'John Keble and the Victorian Churching of Romanticism', p. 229.
[110] Quoted in Churton, *Memoir of Joshua Watson*, vol. I, p. 21.
[111] Gascoigne, *Cambridge in the Age of Enlightenment*, p. 306. See also, G. A. Cole, 'Doctrine, Dissent and the decline of Paley's reputation 1805–1825', *Enlightenment and Dissent*, 6 (1987), 19–30; D. L. LeMahieu, *The Mind of William Paley: a Philosopher and His Age* (London, 1976), ch. 6.

Certainly, it is significant that even Rose felt that Newman's 'rejection of what are commonly called "the Evidences"' was dangerous, in that it 'excludes wholly all consideration of Unbelievers and of faint Believers'.[112] Rose's lectures on the *Evidences of the Christian Religion* delivered at King's College, London, in 1836–7, illustrate his difference of emphasis from Newman. Similarly, even Edward Churton, who remained very sympathetic to the Hutchinsonian spiritual temper, considered that certain Hutchinsonian writings such as John Ellis's *On the Knowledge of Divine Things* went too far in 'seeming to deny that man could, by rightly exercising the gift of reason, arrive at a first cause. Justin Martyr saw no necessary antagonism between a traditional and a rational religion'.[113] Hackney upheld the confirmatory value of 'Evidence Theology' which the Tractarians, like the Hutchinsonians, disdained.

The difference of emphasis between the Hackney Phalanx and the Tractarians was reflected in contrasting estimates of Hanoverian Anglican apologetic against Socinianism and Deism. Churton was exceptional among the Orthodox in sharing the Tractarian critique of the Hanoverian divines, Butler excepted, for rationalising tendencies. One of Churton's own mentors, Van Mildert, had taken a different view. Van Mildert, himself the champion of Waterland as the model of Anglican orthodoxy, contended that the Hanoverian divines had not neglected the essentials of the Christian faith or overlooked miracles, prophecy, scriptural history and mystery, as later critics alleged.[114]

This difference in historical perspective later resurfaced in the Orthodox reaction, shared by Evangelicals, to Mark Pattison's contribution to *Essays and Reviews* in 1860. By that date, Pattison had abandoned his earlier Tractarianism, but his historical estimate of Augustan divinity as rationalistic in tendency and strictures on 'the nakedness of Orthodox theology' in that age remained in accord with Tractarian rhetoric.[115] In his response to Pattison, Thomas Candy stressed a link between the Tractarian reaction against

112 H. J. Rose to J. H. Newman, 11 October 1838, Burgon, *Lives of Twelve Good Men*, vol. 1, p. 262.
113 Churton, *Memoir of Joshua Watson*, vol. 1, p. 37.
114 Van Mildert, ed., *Works of Daniel Waterland*, vol. 1, p. 219. On the qualified nature of Van Mildert's adherence to the Hutchinsonian tradition of opposition to the claims of natural theology and the religion of evidences, and his modified acceptance of Paley's version of the Argument from Design, see Varley, *Van Mildert*, pp. 41–3. Norris also criticised the Hutchinsonians for disparaging Reason. Churton, *Memoir of Joshua Watson*, vol. 1, p. 58.
115 Pattison, 'Tendencies of Religious Thought in England, 1688–1750', pp. 259–60.

'Evidence Theology' exemplified in Newman's *Tract 85* and the 'Germanizing' rationalism of the later Pattison. Pattison, Candy complained, had put 'the Orthodox estimate of revealed religion lower than he has any right to do',[116] but the source of the mistake was traced to the baneful influence of the *Tracts for the Times*:

> The 'Tracts for the Times' – an authority with Mr Pattison – have perhaps been the main cause of leading him into his erroneous view of facts. Had he been proof against their dogmatism and un-English spirit of religious bondage, he would not have discovered rank Rationalism in the works of which the Church is, I Hope, still justly proud; nor by implication made the same Tracts its conqueror.[117]

HIGH CHURCHMANSHIP, MYSTICISM AND THE SACRAMENTAL PRINCIPLE

The Tractarians believed that Paley's argument from design and evidence was superficial because it failed to engage with those deeper moral truths that lay above and beyond nature, in the unseen world. In contrast, the Tractarians stressed the limitations of human reason and intellect in perceiving religious truth. There was another method of perceiving such truths, vouchsafed to him who possessed the eyes of faith and which was beyond the focus of the 'sight' of the merely 'carnal man'. This typological or sacramental principle, expounded in the Fathers, but which was also part of the High Church spiritual inheritance, enabled a man of faith to be ready, as Thomas Mozley put it, 'to admit other modes of being, operation, presence, extension, continuance, growth, production, union, and incorporation, besides those we are permitted to discern in the visible creation'.[118] In short, material phenomena were both the types and instruments of things unseen.

In his unpublished *Lectures on Types and Prophecies* (1836), Pusey argued that God had created 'a sort of sacramental union between the type and the archetype, such that the type is meaningful only to the extent that it expresses the archetype, and the archetype can be

---

116 T. H. Candy, *The Antidote; or, an Examination of Mr Pattison's Essay on the Tendencies of Religious Thought* (Cambridge, 1861), p. 21; C. Gooch, *Remarks on the Grounds of Faith Suggested by Mr Pattison's Essay on the Tendencies of Religious Thought* (Cambridge, 1862), p. 11. I am indebted to Dr Brian Young of Sussex University, for both these references.
117 Candy, *The Antidote*, p. 30.
118 [T. Mozley], 'History of the "Evidences"', *British Critic*, 26 (July, 1839), 24.

grasped only by means of embodiment within the type'.[119] In *Tract 89, On the Mysticism attributed to the Early Fathers of the Church* (1841), Keble emphasised the patristic basis of an allegorical understanding of external or material things. Keble concluded that it was the positive teaching of the Fathers that 'the works of God in creation and providence' were intended to assure 'us of some spiritual fact or other, which it concerns us in some way to know'. These intimations 'fulfilled half at least of the nature of sacraments' and 'were pledges to assure us of some spiritual thing, if they were not means to convey it to us'.[120]

Keble valued Hooker because, like the early Fathers, he considered as sacraments of a sort 'all those material objects which were any how taken unto the service of religion: whether by Scripture, in the way of type or figure; or by the Church, introducing them into her ritual'. Keble argued that Hooker was imbued with a 'kind of theory, pervading the whole language and system of the Church', by which it was understood that 'all sensible things may have other meanings and uses than we know of, apt to assist men in realizing Divine contemplations'. The Church 'selected a certain number and order of' these 'sensible things; certain actions of the body, such as bowing at the name of Jesus, and turning towards the east in prayer'.[121]

Besides Hooker, Bishop Butler was the only other figure from the High Church tradition to whom the Tractarians appealed as testimony to this principle. For Newman, Butler's 'wonderfully gifted intellect caught the idea which had actually been the rule of the Primitive Church, of teaching the more sacred truths by rites and ceremonies'.[122] But the Tractarians overlooked the valuable witness of other eighteenth-century High Churchmen.

The patristic theory of sacramental symbolism was implicit in the writings of numerous pre-Tractarian High Churchmen. It found its most explicit application in the works of Horne and Jones of Nayland. In a sermon by Jones in Nayland parish church in 1786, the argument of Pusey's *Lectures on Types* of half a century later was strikingly prefigured. Like Pusey, Jones argued that the language of

[119] PH, Pusey Papers, E. B. Pusey, Ms 'Lectures on Types and Prophecies' [1836]. On Tractarian typology, see Tennyson, *Victorian Devotional Poetry*, pp. 145–8; A. Louth, 'The Oxford Movement, the Fathers and the Bible', *Sobornost*, 6: 1 (1984), 30–45.
[120] *Tracts for the Times*, vol. vi for 1838–40, No. 89 (London, 1840), p. 148.
[121] Keble, ed., *Works of Richard Hooker*, vol. i, pp. xci–xcii.
[122] CUL, Ms Add 7349, fol. 138, J. H. Newman to J. Stephen, 16 March 1835.

Scripture consisted not merely of words, 'but of signs or figures taken from visible things'. Similarly, he maintained that Revelation made use of natural things as the signs of spiritual truth, 'on consequence of which the world which we now see becomes a sort of commentary on the mind of God, and explains the world in which we believe'.[123] For Jones, as for the Tractarians, rites and ceremonies were divinely-ordained types of 'things unseen'. As he explained,

> priests and singers in our church wear a white linen garment as a sign of purity, and to give them a nearer alliance to the company of heaven. Chanting by responses ... in the first ages, was intended to imitate the choir of angels, which cry out one to another with alternate adoration. The primitive Christians turned towards the east, in their worship, to signify their respect to the true Light of the world. They set up candles as a sign of their illumination by the gospel; and evergreens are still placed there at Christmas, to remind us that a new and perpetual spring of immortality is restored to us, even in the middle of winter, by the coming of Jesus Christ.[124]

Edward Churton did much to keep alive the memory of this Hutchinsonian teaching among his Tractarian friends. It was he who first drew up a patristic theory of scriptural allegory with reference to earlier Hutchinsonian notions.[125] Keble, in favour of whom Churton dropped the subject,[126] developed the theme in *Tract 89*. Keble did not mention the Hutchinsonian witness in his writings on the subject, but the Tractarian Frederic Rogers stressed the link. In his review of Keble's edition of Hooker's works in the *British Critic* in 1837, Rogers observed, 'if ... [in Keble's Preface] any of our readers should imagine they see anything of the Hutchinsonian system, as it has been called, those who know anything about it, will see what Bishop Horne, and Jones of Nayland, turned to good use'.[127] Precursors of Hutchinsonian biblical typology are to be found in the writings of some earlier Evangelicals but also in Horsley's works on the Psalms and on prophecy.[128] Nevertheless, the climate of

123 W. Jones, *A Course of Lectures on the Figurative Language of Holy Scripture, and the Interpretation of it from Scripture Itself. Delivered in the Parish Church of Nayland in Suffolk in the Year 1786* (London, 1786), p. 9.
124 *Ibid.*, p. 318–19.
125 PH, '*British Critic* Papers', E. Churton to J. H. Newman, 9 December 1837.
126 PH, '*British Critic* Papers', E. Churton to J. H. Newman, 6 January 1838.
127 *British Critic*, 21 (April, 1837), p. 375. On links between Tractarian and Hutchinsonian mysticism, see Tavard, *Seventeenth-Century Tradition*, pp. 254–9.
128 On Horsley's typology and emphasis on prophecy, see Mather, *Horsley*, pp. 206–7, 265–6; Oddy, 'Eschatological Prophecy', pp. 174–9.

anti-Jacobin reaction inspired a dread of popular millennarianism among the Orthodox. This reaction also induced a reaction against the mystical and typological in the same quarters. The Hackney divines became more wary of mysticism than the Hutchinsonians had been. Even Rose warned Newman against making 'religion mysterious, in such an age as this'. For Rose, the Tractarian tendency to recommend mystery 'as a counterpoise to Utilitarianism' was mistaken. Rose warned, 'can we, have we the right to introduce any mystery for which we have not authority?'[129] In short, truth did not require such an aid.

The main opposition to Tractarian mysticism came from remnants of the Oriel *Noetics*, who retained a Hanoverian mistrust of mysticism. Thus Richard Whately assailed the Oxford divines for affecting 'a sort of mystical, dim, half-intelligible kind of sublimity', and cited the moderate High Churchman Edward Copleston's disparaging description of them as 'the Magic-Lantern school'.[130]

HIGH CHURCHMANSHIP, RITUAL AND CEREMONIAL

Tractarian sacramentalism found practical expression in forms of worship. In a university sermon in 1830, Newman argued that Christians 'must receive the Gospel literally on their knees, and in a temper altogether different from that critical and argumentative spirit which sitting and listening engender'.[131] Accordingly, he always made a point of kneeling or bowing to the altar in St Mary's for long periods. Here there was continuity with earlier High Churchmanship, for this had been the accustomed practice of George Horne and Martin Routh in Magdalen College chapel.[132]

Preaching and listening to sermons had their place, Newman argued, but prayers were not sermons, though the 'Puritans etc. wished to make them so'. On the other hand, the truly primitive way was when 'the worshipper did not think of himself – he came to God

---

[129] Burgon, *Lives of Twelve Good Men*, vol. 1, p. 145. See also Norris's comment: 'Hutchinson's notions in philosophy are very fanciful and mysterious, his notions in religion pious in the extreme; he makes everything in the material world furnish him with some type of heaven, and finds mystery in all parts of the history of the sacred scriptures'. Churton, *Memoir of Joshua Watson*, vol. 1, p. 58.

[130] R. Whately, *Miscellaneous Lectures and Reviews* (London, 1851), p. 86.

[131] See J. H. Newman, 'The Influence of Natural and Revealed Religion Respectively', *Sermons Chiefly on the Theory of Religious Belief Preached before the University of Oxford* (London, 1843).

[132] R. D. Middleton, *Magdalen Studies* (London, 1936), p. 15.

– God's house and altar were the sermon which addressed him and roused him'.[133] Newman's rationale was also behind the reverential practice of pre-Tractarian High Churchmen. According to William Stevens's biographer, it was 'a point of duty' for him, 'not to turn his back upon the Lord's table, when spread for the reception of those who were religiously and devoutly disposed'.[134] Thomas Sanders had made precisely the same point as Newman in a sermon preached before the University of Oxford at St Mary's in 1801. Sanders condemned the modern practice of congregations sitting when they should kneel. Sanders argued, like Newman at a later date, that it was 'essentially necessary that our outward deportment should indicate humility, and correspond with the inward disposition of the soul'.[135] A similar conviction led the young Daubeny, after a tour of the continent in 1788, to lament that the Swiss Reformed were not 'kneeling Christians', but rather, 'peripatetic Christians'.[136]

Sacramentalist theory also found expression in the adornment and decoration of church interiors and in a reverence for holy places. For old High Churchmen, making the visible into 'a type of the invisible' meant a decent chancel, altar-hangings, communion-rails, etc. in the restrained Laudian tradition of 'the beauty of holiness'. Thus, following the example of Bishop Butler in his private chapel in the 1740s, Daubeny erected a plain cross over the altar and pulpit of his church at Bath in the 1800s.[137] Like Butler, Daubeny contended 'that the objection to forms and ceremonies must chiefly depend upon the idea of the party engaged in them; and that, consequently, they may be not only very innocent, but very advantageous assistances to religious worship.'[138] He regretted that among Evangelicals, the figure of the cross had fallen 'a sacrifice to the intemperate paroxysms of reforming frenzy, and puritanical fanaticism'.[139] Indeed even some notably Protestant-minded divines could be cited in defence of the use of crosses and devotional pictures. For example, for Thomas Tenison, Archbishop

---

[133] J. H. Newman to Mrs J. Mozley, 4 June 1837, Mozley, ed., *Letters and Correspondence of Newman*, vol. II, p. 233.

[134] [Park], *Memoirs of William Stevens* (1812), p. 54. This had also been the practice of Stevens's friend Thomas Calverley. *Ibid.*, p. 30.

[135] T. Sanders, *A Practical Sermon on the Nature of Public Worship* (Oxford, 1801), pp. 11–12.

[136] Daubeny, *Guide to the Church to which is Prefixed Some Account of the Author's Life and Writings*, p. xviii.

[137] J. Butler, *The Analogy of Religion ... with a Preface and Memoir by Samuel Halifax, Lord Bishop of Gloucester* (London, 1802), p. xlviii.

[138] Daubeny, *Protestant Companion*, p. 125.   [139] *Ibid.*, p. 293.

of Canterbury under William III, devotional pictures were not idolatrous but rather, 'mute Poems' and 'useful as Monitors'.[140]

Sacramentalism was likewise reflected in ceremonial practice. George Horne's favouring of external forms as aids to faith extended as far as the then unusual practice of placing lighted candles on the altar during celebrations of the eucharist in Magdalen College chapel in the 1780s[141] – a practice which in 1761, Thomas Wilson, Prebendary of Westminster, had advocated for parochial churches as well as cathedrals.[142] Horne was self-consciously Laudian in his ceremonialism. In 1788, he complained to his fellow Hutchinsonian, George Berkeley, after protests against ceremonial in Canterbury cathedral, 'the anti-Laudian spirit on the subject of caps, hoods, and surplices, I find, is not yet extinct'.[143] Another Hutchinsonian, Samuel Glasse, lamented the neglect of Holy Days and the daily service, and advocated stricter observance of the fasts and festivals of the church on the lines set forth by Robert Nelson in his influential *Companion for the Festivals and Fasts of the Church of England* (1704).[144] As F. C. Mather has demonstrated, the Hutchinsonians were not the only purveyors of a ritualist and sacramental churchmanship in the Georgian era. Mather shows that a richer Laudian tradition of worship lingered on in the conservative practice of several collegiate churches, notably Manchester with its Nonjuring history.[145] At the parochial level this tradition, as manifest in observance of saints' days, the daily service and weekly communions, tended to be strongest in parts of the North and West.[146] In Cornwall, a High Church revival in the late eighteenth century has been linked to a revival of interest in Cornish antiquities.[147]

While the architectural setting and ceremonial ingredients of Anglican worship should fittingly have represented High Church sacramentalism, the gap between theory and practice had been

[140] Wickham Legg, *English Church Life*, p. 145.

[141] R. D. Middleton, *Newman and Bloxam* (London, 1947), p. 28.

[142] T. Wilson, *The Ornaments of Churches Considered: a Sermon Preached before the University of Oxford, at St Mary's ... 1761* (Oxford, 1761), p. 97.

[143] BL, Berkeley Papers, Ms 39312, fol. 79, G. Horne to G. Berkeley, 13 October 1788.

[144] S. Glasse, *A Course of Lectures on the Holy Festivals of the Church* (London, 1797), pp. x–xi. See n. 180. Glasse revived observance of Ascension Day in Wanstead parish church. In 1788, he had a congregation of over two hundred worshippers. BL, Althorp Papers, Poyntz Letters, E. 16, S. Glasse to C. Poyntz, March 1788.

[145] Mather, *Horsley*, p. 15. Visiting Manchester in 1823, the Bishop of Ohio, Philander Chase, noted 'prayers are read and the psalms chanted every day in the old cathedral church'. *Bishop Chase's Reminiscences*, 2 vols. (Boston, 1848), vol. 1, p. 218.

[146] Mather, *Horsley*, p. 16.

[147] H. Miles Brown, 'The High Church Tradition in Cornwall, 1662–1831', *Church Quarterly Review*, 150 (1950), 69–80.

evident long before the Cambridge Ecclesiologists drew attention to
the fact. Newman could be mockingly satirical on the point. 'Who
would ever recognise', he observed in 1839, 'in a large double cube,
with bare nails, wide windows, high pulpit, capacious reading desk,
galleries projecting, and altar obscured, an outward emblem of the
heavenly Jerusalem, the font of grace, the resort of angels?'[148]

Later depictions of the lack of reverence in worship and barren-
ness of church interiors in the century prior to the Oxford Movement
owed something to Cambridge Camdenite exaggeration. Nevertheless, old High Churchmen at a later date also noted a contrast in
standards of ritual observance with the days of their youth. As R. W.
Evans, who had been a member of the Hackney Phalanx, informed
the clergy of his Westmorland archdeaconry in 1857,

I do see both here and everywhere our public worship much more carefully
conducted than heretofore within my own memory; so much so, that, even
under the regulations of one who is said to hold what are called Low
Church principles, it is more solemn and closer to the rubric than it was
according to the performance of many, if I may not say almost all those
who professed to belong to the High Church party at the beginning of the
century.[149]

Many pre-Tractarian High Churchmen had reason to lament the
general lack of splendour in either worship or interior decoration of
churches. In 1721, Thomas Lewis had complained that 'no images
but lions and unicorns must now be the embellishment of our
churches, and the Arms of the Civil Magistrate may stand with
Applause where the Cross, the Arms of a Crucified Saviour, must be
defaced as Popish and Idolatrous'.[150] In his Bampton Lectures in
1786, George Croft called for the reintroduction of a richer ceremonial into Church of England worship. Croft commended Laud's
efforts in this direction in the previous century, but lamented a subsequent decline in standards. Croft observed that 'many wise and
good men little inclined to vexatious animadversion have been of the
opinion that somewhat more of the Romish ritual, or of outward
decoration, might have been retained without injury to religion'.[151]
Similarly, in 1825, the Orthodox churchman Johnson Grant com-

148 [J. H. Newman], 'The American Church', *British Critic*, 26 (October, 1839), 324.
149 R. W. Evans, *A Charge Delivered to the Clergy of the Archdeaconry of Westmorland, at the Visitation in May 1857, at Ulveston, Whitehaven, and Kendal* (London, 1857), p. 24. Robert William Evans (1789–1866). Vicar of Tarvin, Cheshire, later Archdeacon of Westmorland. *DNB*.
150 Wickham Legg, *English Church Life*, p. 130.   151 Croft, *Sermons*, vol. 1, p. 22.

plained, 'our churches are too bare of ornaments ... if we admit of stained glass, when it can be procured, in the windows, wherefore not of frescoes on the walls and ceiling? To speak of the danger of colouring is ridiculous, for who worships the picture over a communion table?'[152]

The Tractarians gave priority to doctrine over ritual and architectural decoration. Pusey complained to Bishop Tait in 1860, 'I am in this strange position, that my name is made a byword for that with which I never had any sympathy, that which the writers of the Tracts, with whom in early days I was associated, always deprecated, – any innovations in the way of conducting the Service, anything of Ritualism, or especially any revival of disused Vestments'.[153] Pusey later explained this caution: 'we felt that it was very much easier to change a dress than to change the heart, and that externals might be gained at the cost of the doctrines themselves'.[154] Apart from minor incidents in Oxford in the late 1830s such as an outcry over the wearing of a liturgical scarf by a deacon, William Palmer of Magdalen, and complaints over Newman's bowings and crossings during eucharistic celebrations at St Mary's, few criticisms of the Tractarians focused on ceremonialism. Liturgical innovations such as turning to the east in prayer were defended as being strictly in conformity with the rubric or as recommended by Caroline liturgists such as Bishop Sparrow in his *Rationale of Common Prayer*.[155]

It was not the Tractarians but the Ecclesiologists, under the auspices of the Cambridge Camden Society, who applied the principles of the Catholic Revival to church architecture, furnishings and rubrical observance. Prominent among Camdenite concerns was the pre-eminence given to the relationship of the altar to the pulpit, the breaking up of the traditional composition of pulpit, reading-desk and clerk's desk, and the removal of pews. As Nigel Yates has shown, contrary to common perceptions, 'significant developments had taken place during the two or three decades before the Oxford Movement in the ordering of church interiors'.[156]

[152] Grant, *Summary History*, vol. IV, p. 440; H. Best, *Four Years in France* (London, 1826), p. 27.
[153] Liddon, *Life of Pusey*, vol. IV, pp. 211–12.
[154] *Ibid.*, pp. 212–13. Pusey explained in 1839: 'It seems beginning at the wrong end for the ministers to deck their own persons: our own plain dresses are more in keeping with the state of our church, which is one of humiliation'. E. B. Pusey to J. F. Russell, 9 October 1839, Liddon, *Life of Pusey*, vol. II, p. 142. See n. 165.
[155] PH, Pusey Papers, LBV [Transcripts], E. B. Pusey to Bp R. Bagot, 26 September 1837.
[156] N. Yates, *Buildings, Faith and Worship: the Liturgical Arrangement of Anglican Churches, 1600–1900* (Oxford, 1991), p. 115.

Some old High Churchmen disputed the extent of Camdenite claims of architectural and rubrical neglect in the pre-Tractarian Church of England. Joshua Watson observed, 'the impertinence of these Camdenians is perfectly unendurable ... they would almost seem to take to themselves the language of the prophetess, and say that the highways were unoccupied, and the people wandered in byways, until the Camdenians arose, masters in Israel'.[157] In contrast to Archdeacon Evans's later testimony, Watson insisted in the 1840s that 'much of the evil we now deprecate arises from those who are now agitators not having seen the church in her beauty in their own early days'.[158]

Hackney High Churchmen such as Joshua Watson, Norris, Sikes and Archdeacon Lyall, strove to enforce rubrical observance as early as the 1810s and 1820s. Watson helped restore the print of the Communion Office in the Book of Common Prayer to large, bold type.[159] Moreover, according to Joshua Watson's nephew John David Watson in 1842, his predecessor at Guilsborough, Thomas Sikes, 'was ever in advance of those around him in almost all such points as those to which endeavour has been made of late to call attention'.[160] Even one of the Camdenites, Beresford-Hope, later conceded that it was a member of the Hackney Phalanx, Dean Chandler, who in that period emerged as 'a fostering father of the new life of English worship'.[161]

The ritual controversy of the 1840s had little direct connection with Tractarianism, but was the product of the long-standing efforts of the High Church bishops, Blomfield and Phillpotts, to enforce the rubrics. Bishop Blomfield's controversial Charge on the subject in 1842 was largely a restatement of a sermon he had preached as early as 1818 at Saffron Walden when Archdeacon of Colchester.[162] As is clear from Frances Knight's study of the diocese of Lincoln, many of the liturgical changes being introduced into parishes in the early 1840s which were decried as 'Puseyite' innovations, represented a

157 Churton, *Memoir of Joshua Watson*, vol. II, pp. 201–2. On the Camden Society, see J. F. White, *The Cambridge Movement* (Cambridge, 1962); A. G. Lough, *The Influence of John Mason Neale* (London, 1962).
158 Churton, *Memoir of Joshua Watson*, vol. I, pp. 139–40; vol. II, p. 131. Mather dates the nadir of Anglican liturgical standards at around 1800. Mather, 'Georgian Churchmanship reconsidered', 261.
159 PH, Copeland Papers, W. J. Copeland, Ms 'Narrative of the Oxford Movement'.
160 Bodl. Lib, Norris Papers, Ms Eng Lett c. 790, fols. 103–6, J. D. Watson to H. H. Norris, 27 January 1843.
161 A. J. B. Beresford-Hope, *The Worship of the Church of England* (London, 1874), p. 9.
162 A. Blomfield, ed., *A Memoir of Charles James Blomfield, Bishop of London with Selections from His Correspondence*, 2 vols. (London, 1863), vol. I, pp. 330–1.

restoration of obsolete rubrics once insisted upon by the Laudians in the 1630s rather than those late medieval practices associated with advanced Ritualism.[163] Similarly, the ceremonial alterations introduced by Hook at Holy Trinity, Coventry, between 1828 and 1837 conformed to a Laudian pattern.[164] Pusey himself, in seeking to distance the Tractarians from charges of formalism, later maintained that there 'was at that time, a school – a somewhat stiffer school [than the Oxford divines] – who were anxious on all occasions to bring out all the details of the rubrics, and that even in matters which were of no importance whatever, and which had no definite meaning; though they created not only tumults, but an idea of clerical tyranny'. Yet Pusey admitted that that for which Phillpotts and Blomfield contended, represented but 'a low uniformity of ritual' when compared to Camdenite and Ritualist standards.[165]

Although old High Churchmen had a greater share than Tractarians in the initial revival of public worship and in the arrangement of church buildings, they deplored the later Camdenite manifestations of that revival. When Charles Drury in 1852 enumerated to G. A. Denison what he regarded as the negative features of 'the movement of 1833', his keenest satire was reserved for the Camdenites. 'The movement', Drury maintained,

has given us more painted glass – I admit it. Has decorated more churches in the style of the twelfth century, I admit it. Has sent a number of people to sing, usually very badly, instead of to pray, I acknowledge it. Has taught more clergymen to stick out their heads in very painful angles from their shoulders during service, and keep them so – I have witnessed it. Has

---

163 Knight, 'John Kaye and the Diocese of Lincoln', pp. 257–8. Knight calculates (p. 280) that as early as 1828, three out of eleven Lincoln churches had monthly communion. On the pre-Tractarian return to 'liturgical orthodoxy', see Yates, *Buildings, Faith and Worship*, pp. 108–23.

164 For examples of Hook's liturgical innovations at Coventry, see PH, Pusey Papers, LBV [Transcripts], W. F. Hook to A. P. Perceval, 1 September 1830; 6 September 1830. Even Palmer of Worcester, while an opponent of later Ritualism, had conceded in his *Origines Liturgicae* that the English ritual as confirmed in the Elizabethan Injunctions (1564) and the canons of 1603, not only permitted a bishop to wear a cope in public ministrations but 'gave the same liberty to presbyters in celebrating the eucharist'. W. Palmer, *Origines Liturgicae*, vol. II, p. 313. See also Edward Churton's later defence of the use of incense in public worship. E. Churton, *Unity and Truth in Catholic Toleration. A Charge Delivered at the Annual Visitation of the Archdeaconry of Cleveland ... 1867*, (2nd edn, London, 1867), p. 23.

165 Liddon, *Life of Pusey*, vol. IV, p. 213; E. B. Pusey, *The Proposed Ecclesiastical Legislation: Three Letters to 'The Times'* (Oxford, 1874), p. 35. In his last years, however, Pusey became sympathetic to the Ritualist cause and claimed the Caroline Divines as its forerunners: 'they saw what it was good to do, and what could not be done *then*, and laid up a provision for the future, when minds should be suited to it'. E. B. Pusey, *Unlaw in Judgments of the Judicial Committee ... A Letter to H. P. Liddon* (London, 1881), pp. 26–7.

engaged them in several very queer historical devices ... I am far from denying it.[166]

The gulf between the Camdenites and earlier advocates of rubrical conformity was clear. The early Ritualists demanded not only the revival of daily prayers and weekly communion for which the Orthodox had also contended, but for the restoration of full eucharistic vestments and lighted and vested altars.[167] In advocating fuller ceremonial, the Camdenites and their advanced High Church supporters were careful to base their case on the supposed authority of the Ornaments Rubric of the second year of the reign of Edward VI.[168] For the Ritualist R. F. Littledale, every ornament and rubric in the Missal not abolished by Henry VIII in 1545 or by Edward VI in 1547 remained lawful, 'unless it contradicts some express statement of the Prayer Book. Thus, censers were used in 1548, and therefore incense is lawful now, though it is not mentioned in the Prayer Book'.[169] Some old High Churchmen regarded this as a spurious argument which overlooked other later rubrical precedents such as the statements in the 1549 rite as well as Archbishop Parker's *Advertisements* (1566) and the addition to the rubric in the Act of Uniformity in 1662. Even A. P. Perceval, like Hook a keen advocate of a Laudian standard of decorum in public worship, by the middle of the century had reacted strongly against what he regarded as Ritualist excess. In 1851 Perceval revealed that at Oxford in the 1810s he had supported the custom of placing candles on the communion table on the principle of reverence for sacred things. He now drew a sharp contrast between this and W. J. E. Bennett's placing of lighted tapers in broad daylight on a vested altar at St Barnabas, Pimlico, which he condemned as a practice 'directly connected with the doctrine of Transubstantiation'.[170] Against Bennett's appeal to the 1548 Edwardine Injunctions, Perceval countered with patristic testimony and later Angli-

---

[166] PH, Denison Papers, 2/24/12, C. A. Drury to G. A. Denison, 26 May 1852.

[167] *Hierurgia Anglicanae: Documents and Extracts Illustrative of the Ceremonial of the Anglican Church after the Reformation. Edited by Members of the Ecclesiological, Late Cambridge Camden Society A.D. 1848. Revised and ... Enlarged by W. Stanley* (new edn, London, 1901), Pt. I, p. xvii.

[168] See W. J. E. Bennett, *The Principles of the Book of Common Prayer Considered. A Series of Lecture-Sermons* (London, 1845), p. 156, 335.

[169] R. F. Littledale, *Catholic Ritual in the Church of England Scriptural, Reasonable, Lawful* (London, 1865), p. 11.

[170] A. P. Perceval, *On the Use of Lights on the Communion Table in the Day Time* (London, 1851), pp. 3–4.

can authorities such as the liturgist Nicholls and canonist Bingham.[171]

For old High Churchmen, Ritualism represented no less a breach of Anglican rubrical order than had earlier Evangelical irregularities. By the late 1850s old High Churchmen feared that Ritualist excesses were discrediting the liturgical and rubrical renewal which they themselves had inspired – a renewal, they insisted, which had made progress even among Low Churchmen and could have acted as a bond of union within the Church. In 1858 a representative of the school of 'consistent Anglicans' maintained not only that the churches and services of 'the "Low" Church party ... have much improved since we commenced our labours' but that they had become

more in accordance with the letter and spirit of the English Church's laws and usages than are some of the churches and services of Romanizers and semi-Romanizers, who have gone beyond what they once pleaded for, as though they perversely wished to preserve the same relative distance between themselves and all below them, and thus to discourage and prevent any approach to union.[172]

The essential difference between the old High Church and later Ritualist rubrical campaigns, apart from the degree of ceremonial practice and interior decoration deemed permissible, lay in the fact that the former still contended for the Laudian ideal of uniformity and order in a way which the latter, for all their appeal to the legality of the Ornaments Rubric, ultimately did not. Ritualism represented the logical outcome of the sectarian tendency in Tractarianism to pursue that which was deemed catholic even at the expense of submission to episcopal authority.

HIGH CHURCHMANSHIP AND LITURGY

If the Oxford Tractarians, as opposed to their Camdenite counterparts, did not much differ from old High Churchmen in ceremonial practice, they came to diverge markedly in their liturgical preferences.

[171] *Ibid.*, p. 7. On the survival of altar candlesticks in eighteenth-century Anglican worship, see Wickham Legg, *English Church Life*, pp. 139–44. In the ritual case of Westerton v. Liddell (1855), Dr Lushington in the Consistory Court ruled that while candles might be placed on the altar, they could only be lit when needed for light.

[172] 'Church Parties in 1858', *English Churchman* (August 26, 1858), 191. On the gulf between Ritualism and early Tractarianism, see G. W. Herring, 'Tractarianism to Ritualism: A Study of Some Aspects of Tractarianism outside Oxford from the Time of Newman's Conversion in 1845, until the First Ritual Commission in 1867', unpublished D.Phil thesis, University of Oxford, 1984, pp. v–xiii, 274–83.

A hallmark of the Orthodox had always been liturgical conservatism. At various times, as in the 1580s, 1689 and 1772–3, there had been either 'Puritan' or 'latitudinarian' attempts to reform the Prayer Book in a more Protestant direction. It was only from about 1790–1830, coinciding with the conservative reaction to the French Revolution, that there occured a lull in such moves.[173] The Orthodox could feel thankful that the Prayer Book had been preserved in its integrity.

For pre-Tractarian High Churchmen, this conservatism proved a unifying factor that offset differences of emphasis in Orthodox liturgical apologetic. The Marsh–Tomline school tended to defend the Prayer Book in terms of legal status or as a 'badge of establishment' bequeathed by the 'fathers of the English Reformation', observance of which was enjoined by civil as well as canonical authority.[174] On the other hand, the school of Horsley, Daubeny and Van Mildert emphasised the apostolicity of the Prayer Book and its conformity with Catholic antiquity. This difference of theological emphasis was reflected in a difference of private liturgical preference.

Most of the Orthodox regarded the idea of liturgical alteration even in a 'primitive' direction as abhorrent. Bishop Pretyman-Tomline considered the second, more Protestant, Edwardine rite of 1552 to have been a distinct 'improvement' on the first rite of 1549.[175] At the other extreme of the High Church spectrum, the later Nonjurors found doctrinal defects, such as the absence of prayers for the dead, in the existing Prayer Book in comparison with the 1549 rite and the Scottish Prayer Book of 1637 – their own liturgical ideal being represented by the ancient Clementine liturgies.[176] While the latter viewpoint found no general favour among establishment High Churchmen, divines such as Horsley, Daubeny and some members of the Hackney Phalanx privately conceded their personal preference in favour of the 1549 rite as more primitive.[177] Their difference from the later Nonjurors was in their denial that the alterations invalidated the catholic integrity of the existing Prayer Book. Such High Churchmen took comfort in the later

[173] G. J. Cuming, *A History of Anglican Liturgy* (London, 1969), p. 191.
[174] Marsh, *Inquiry into the Consequences of Neglecting to Give the Prayer Book with the Bible*, p. 50.
[175] Pretyman-Tomline, *Elements of Christian Theology*, vol. II, pp. 22–3.
[176] See T. Podmore, *A Layman's Apology for Returning to Primitive Christianity* (Leeds, 1747); Broxap, *Thomas Deacon*; Broxap, *Later Nonjurors*.
[177] Mather, *Horsley*, p. 204.

modifications in 1559 and 1662 as having been in a catholic direction and restorative of any damage inflicted in 1552. They blamed the alterations made in 1552 on to the malign influence of foreign Reformers such as Martin Bucer and Peter Martyr.[178] At the same time, Orthodox churchmen such as Marsh, not in sympathy with this more High Church liturgical position, were prepared to defend the soundness of even the 1637 Scottish rite from extreme Protestant charges of 'popery'.[179] Moreover, throughout the eighteenth century, a continued catholic understanding of the Prayer Book was aided by the wisespread use of liturgical commentaries by divines in the Caroline tradition, such as L'Estrange, Comber, Sparrow, Robert Nelson and Charles Wheatley.[180]

The liturgical revival of the 1840s was not the product of Tractarian endeavour alone. The roots of revival can be dated back to at least as early as the first decades of the century, in the sermons and lectures of Van Mildert, and in the historical editions and ritual manuals of John Reeves, Charles Lloyd and William Palmer of Worcester. The aim was to emphasise the 'catholic' and 'primitive' liturgical continuity of the Church of England. As early as 1797 in a sermon, revised and enlarged in 1817, Van Mildert had pointed out that the 'Ritual of the Romish Church, though composed in the Latin tongue, and clogged with many superstitions and exceptionable forms, was yet in many parts of it, truly Scriptural, and well calculated for the comfort and edification of pious worshippers'. Van Mildert reminded contemporaries that 'some of the most admired parts of our Book of Common Prayer are taken almost literally from the Romish Ritual: and this, far from being any just objection to it, proves that the compilers were guided by the genuine spirit of moderation and Christian candour'.[181] Palmer adopted a similar line in his learned *Origines Liturgicae* (1832) in which he insisted that, 'although our liturgy and other offices were corrected and improved ... the greater portion of our prayers have been

---

[178] Daubeny, *An Appendix to the Guide to the Church*, pp. 195–6.
[179] H. Marsh, *A Reply to the Strictures of the Rev. Isaac Milner* (Cambridge, 1813), pp. 97–8.
[180] W. K. Lowther, *Eighteenth-Century Piety* (London, 1944), pp. 2–3; C. J. Stranks, *Anglican Devotion: Studies in the Spiritual Life of the Church of England between the Reformation and the Oxford Movement* (London, 1961); McAdoo, *Spirit of Anglicanism*, p. 198.
[181] W. Van Mildert, 'On the Liturgy of the Church of England', in C. Ives, ed., *Sermons on Several Occasions and Charges, by William Van Mildert, Late Bishop of Durham, to Which is Prefixed a Memoir of the Author*, 6 vols. (Oxford, 1838), vol. I, pp. 167–8; Varley, *Van Mildert*, pp. 37–8.

continually retained and used by the Church of England for more than twelve hundred years'.[182]

Tractarian liturgical writings should be set within the context of the influence of Palmer's earlier contribution. As Adams shows, Palmer himself drew heavily on earlier Anglican liturgists. In the composition of his *Origines*, Palmer was able to make full use of the earlier research of Bishop Lloyd. The partly derivative nature of Palmer's labours[183] did not diminish the impact of the *Origines*. According to Thomas Mozley, 'when this work came out, it made a great sensation. Its simple statement of facts and documentary evidence took with people who were wearied with logic and jaded with style.' To 'most Oxford men', Mozley recalled, 'it was like an accident of continental travel before railways – the sudden view of a vast plain full of picturesque objects and historical associations'.[184] Tractarian liturgists would owe an enormous debt to Palmer.

The Tractarians initially appeared in the guise of defenders of the liturgical *status quo*, in the face of renewed attempts at revision supported even by Blomfield and J. B. Sumner.[185] There was a tactical reason for the Tractarians' temporary alliance with the 'Zs' in defence of the existing Prayer Book. As Newman made clear in *Tract 3*, *Tract 38* and *Tract 41*, any further revision was likely to be in a Protestant or latitudinarian direction,[186] so that the rhetoric of conservation rather than restoration served a useful purpose. The Tractarian identification with the later Nonjurors, however, became reflected in the adoption of a more critical attitude to the Prayer Book.

Palmer's adherence to the principle of 'fundamentals' enabled

---

[182] Palmer, *Origines Liturgicae*, vol. 1, p. 189.

[183] For a critique of Palmer's writings for lack of originality, see [P. Le Page Renouf], *The Character of the Rev. William Palmer, M.A. of Worcester College, as a Controversialist* (London, 1843), pp. 50–1.

[184] Mozley, *Reminiscences Chiefly of Oriel College and the Oxford Movement*, vol. 1, pp. 321, 293. William Copeland insisted that, with the exception of the eighteenth-century liturgist Nicholls, nobody prior to Palmer had 'yet published any part of the English offices in their original language'. PH, Copeland Papers, W. J. Copeland, Ms 'Narrative'. Palmer acknowledged his debt to earlier liturgists such as L'Estrange, Nicholls, Wheatley, Shepherd, and Mant, as well as the materials collected by the late Bishop Lloyd while Regius Professor of Divinity at Oxford. Palmer, *Origines Liturgicae*, vol. 1, pp. iii–v. Both Hurrell Froude and William Maskell owed a debt to Palmer's liturgical labours, though it has been suggested that Newman's liturgical thought owed little to Palmer. See n. 199.

[185] C. F. Barmann, 'The Liturgical Dimension of the Oxford Tracts, 1833–1841', *Journal of British Studies*, 7 (May, 1968), 94; D. A. Withey, *John Henry Newman: the Liturgy and the Breviary: Their Influence on His Life as an Anglican* (London, 1992), pp. 9–12.

[186] *Tracts for the Times*, vol. 1, No. 3 (London, 1834), p. 5.

him to accommodate and justify the removal of primitive doctrines such as prayers for the dead in the revision of the 1549 rite.[187] It also determined his opposition to Manning's plan in 1838 to reprint the Nonjuror Brett's collected liturgical works, which he felt would prove divisive.[188] On the other hand, for the Tractarians, as for the later Nonjurors, such omissions amounted to serious 'wants and imperfections' in the Prayer Book.[189] Even in Isaac Williams's *Tract 86*, while comfort was taken in a 'superintending providence' having preserved much 'primitive' doctrine in the Prayer Book, it was lamented that 'the sanctity of the ancient forms of worship' had been seriously impaired by the liturgical changes of the Reformation.[190] In Newman's *Tract 71* and *Tract 75*, a tone of deep regret for what the Church of England had apparently lost superseded the note of thankfulness for what had been preserved. While actual 'projects of change and reform' were disavowed, there was the seed of later Anglo-Catholic liturgical licence in the assertion that 'the omissions . . . or rather obscurities of Anglican doctrine, may be supplied for the most part by each of us for himself'.[191] Increasingly envious eyes were cast upon the Roman Breviary, described as 'a treasure which was ours as much as' of Roman Catholics. The Church was urged to 'recover . . . what we have lost through inadvertence',[192] with Bucer and 'the foreign party' blamed for damaging alterations to King Edward's first Prayer Book.[193]

The private opinions of the Tractarian leaders were still more extreme. In a letter to Mary Giberne in 1836, Newman bluntly denied that 'the Prayer Book is or ever was intended to be a repository of the perfect Gospel', its form having been entirely 'decided', he claimed, 'by a number of accidents'.[194] Likewise, Froude's relatively restrained criticisms in *Tract 63* were not matched in private, where he maintained, 'I can see no other claim which the Prayer Book has on a layman's deference, as the teaching of the Church, which the Breviary and Missal have not in a far

[187] Palmer, *Origines Liturgicae*, vol. II, p. 16.
[188] Bodl. Lib, Manning Papers, Ms Eng Lett c.654, fol. 20, H. E. Manning to J. H. Newman, 2 March 1838.
[189] *Tracts for the Times*, vol. III for 1835–6, No. 71 (London, 1836), p. 30.
[190] *Tracts for the Times*, vol. IV for 1836–7, No. 86 (London, 1838), p. 5.
[191] *Tract 71*, p. 35.   [192] *Ibid.*, p. 1; *Tracts for the Times*, vol. III, No. 75, p. 11.
[193] *Tracts for the Times*, vol. I for 1833–4, No. 38, pp. 5–6.
[194] J. H. Newman to Miss M. Giberne, 19 April 1836, Mozley, ed., *Letters and Correspondence of Newman*, vol. II, p. 193.

greater degree.'[195] Old High Churchmen criticised the tone of Tractarian comment on the liturgy as undutiful and likely to raise dangerous longings in favour of Rome. Even Isaac Williams's *Tract 86* was privately deplored by Edward Churton. Although Churton wished that 'Bucer had never advised those alterations' to the 1549 rite, he regretted that the Tract gave the impression that the communion was not 'a soul-satisfying service'.[196] It 'was an error in judgment', Churton commented years later, 'to publish such a sickly train of reflections'.[197]

The contrast between the Tractarian approach and that of earlier liturgists such as Wheatley and Palmer, was highlighted in contemporary discourse. For instance, in 1847, a writer in the then moderate Tractarian *Christian Remembrancer* observed, 'hitherto, the existing liturgy was appealed to as a standard, and all other liturgies were used in illustration of it, and in subordination to it. Now it was demanded that the de facto Church herself should descend to a comparison with something "ab extra".' Whereas, according to the reviewer, Palmer's *Origines* assumed 'the absolute infallibility and perfection of the Prayer Book', the Tractarian argument was 'that we are deficient'.[198] Even Froude's restrained *Tract 63* effectively turned Palmer's *Origines* on its head by using his primitive liturgical evidence as proof of the limitations of the existing Prayer Book.[199]

The Tractarians had no monopoly of the flowering of liturgical scholarship and interest in the 1840s. The most learned liturgist of the period, William Maskell, while an admirer of the 1549 rite and Nonjurors, did not himself support the Tractarian and Camdenite efforts at liturgical restoration. While the tone of Maskell's *Ancient Liturgy of the Church of England* (1844) was not uncritical of the Prayer Book as it was, Maskell eschewed the counter-reforming liturgical animus of the Camdenite John Fuller Russell's *Hierurgia Anglicanae* (1848). Maskell insisted that the 'essentials of a valid consecration are to be found in the liturgy of 1552: much more then after the improvements, few though they may be, which from time to time

[195] Quoted in L. M. Guiney, *Hurrell Froude, Memoranda and Comments* (London, 1904), p. 171.
[196] PH, Pusey Papers, LBV [Transcripts], E. Churton, to E. B. Pusey, 13 December 1841.
[197] SC, Churton Papers, E. Churton to W. J. Copeland, 26 December 1862.
[198] 'Maskell on the Ancient English Ritual', *Christian Remembrancer*, 13 (January, 1847), 89.
[199] Brendon, *Hurrell Froude*, p. 143. Froude described his contribution in *Tract 63* as an 'analysis' of Palmer's *Origines Liturgicae*. In contrast, Newman took little notice of Palmer's work. According to Withey, Newman did not even possess a copy of *Origines Liturgicae*. See Withey, *Newman: the Liturgy and the Breviary*, p. 156n.

have been made in it, by the Bishops in the reigns of Elizabeth, and James, and Charles'.[200] To the evident puzzlement of the above Tractarian reviewer of Maskell's work in the *Christian Remembrancer*, Maskell did not obviously use the 'primitive' liturgical materials which he unearthed primarily in order to assail defects in the existing Prayer Book. His method was closer to that of Palmer of Worcester, whom he cited favourably, than to that of the Ecclesiologists; his tone more 'Anglican' than later Nonjuring, still less 'Romanising'. Thus for Maskell, it was not only axiomatic that 'none would wish to be restored the trifling observances and the doubtful rites which the rubrics of the old service enjoin', but that 'it is our duty to ... express our dislike to much still retained in the present Roman liturgy, but which we have not in our own'.[201]

HIGH CHURCHMANSHIP AND DEVOTIONAL MANUALS

Charles Lloyd's lectures on the Breviary at Oxford in the mid-1820s made a profound impression on the future Tractarians who heard them.[202] A distinction can be drawn between the Tractarian exaltation of the Roman Breviary primarily as a devotional model to satisfy spiritual longings, and the primarily antiquarian approach of even later Nonjurers as well as the traditional High Church liturgiology of Lloyd and Palmer. Frederick Oakeley drew attention to this source of difference when in 1840 he expressed, 'great satisfaction that the ancient services are coming to be studied, not merely as a matter of literature ... but for the purposes of private devotion'.[203] One of Newman's earliest complaints against the English Reformers had been that they aimed 'to Lutheranise our devotions'.[204] The emergence of a genuinely 'Romanising' spirituality among the advanced wing of the Movement was built upon such assumptions. W. G. Ward's *Ideal of a Christian Church* took this line of critique to its logical limit.[205] For the school of Ward, Faber and Dalgairns, not only the Breviary but also other Roman Catholic manuals became

200 W. Maskell, *The Ancient Liturgy of the Church of England According to the Uses of Sarum, Bangor, York, and Hereford, and the Modern Roman Liturgy in Parallel Columns*, 2nd edn (London, 1846), p. xcvii.
201 *Ibid.*, p. xliii.   202 See ch. 2, n. 2.
203 [F. Oakeley], 'The Church Service', *British Critic*, 27 (April, 1840), 251. On Newman's motivation in translating the Roman Breviary, see Withey, *Newman: the Liturgy and the Breviary*, chs. 3–5.
204 LPL, Williams Dep 3/26, J. H. Newman to I. Williams, 13 December 1838.
205 Ward, *Ideal of a Christian Church*, p. 428.

the ultimate devotional standard by which traditional Anglican spirituality as well as her liturgy was judged and ultimately found wanting. As Frederick Faber confided to Newman in 1845, he had been 'feeding ... penitents with Roman devotion, Roman rules, lives of Saints, because I really did not know, Bishop Taylor failing, where to look in my own church for what I wanted'.[206]

The logical result of the Tractarians' devotional motivation in extolling the Breviary at the expense of the Prayer Book was Pusey's systematic policy in the 1840s of republishing 'adapted' Roman Catholic devotional works. Pusey's aim was to supply spiritual wants not realised in classical Anglican spirituality; not with the aim of 'Romanising' the Church of England in the way Ward conceived, but 'to save persons from the temptation of seeking out of the Church where God had placed them, what might be applied to them within her'. As Pusey insisted, there were precedents for such adaptations, including that of the young John Wesley, as well as the example of seventeenth-century liturgists such as Cosin, Stanhope, Nichols and Hickes. The Prayer Book itself, Pusey reminded his critics, was but an 'adaptation of the Breviary and Missal'.[207] It was Richard Mant, one-time member of the Hackney Phalanx and later opponent of the Tractarians, who was responsible for the translation and editing of a selection of hymns from the Roman Breviary published in 1837.[208]

Old High Churchmen held that Pusey's adaptations were dangerous, and that they followed an entirely different principle from those of Mant. As Edward Hawkins explained in a marginal note on his copy of Pusey's *Letter to the Bishop of London* (1851), 'no one blames Dr Pusey for adapting good foreign books, tinctured with error, to English uses, but for the manner in which he has done this; inculcating some errors, and seducing unstable minds towards error'.[209] Hawkins pointed out that Pusey's principle for selecting and adapting was not that of the Church of England. Pusey was not content with even English pre-Reformation manuals but chose for

---

206 F. W. Faber to J. H. Newman, 28 October 1845; quoted in Addington, *Faber: Poet and Priest*, p. 128. Pusey made the same point, commenting in 1844: 'with a few great exceptions (as Bp Andrewes, some of J. Taylor etc.) I am dissatisfied with the run of our books'. PH, LBV [Transcripts] E. B. Pusey to W. K. Hamilton, 19 December 1844.

207 Pusey, *Letter to the Lord Bishop of London ... 1851*, p. 103.

208 Richard Mant (1775–1848). Bishop of Down and Connor, 1821–d. Author of *The Holydays of the Church* (1828–31) and *Ancient Hymns from the Roman Breviary* (1837).

209 Taken from Hawkins's pencil marginalia on p. 107 of his copy of Pusey's *Letter to the Bishop of London*.

his adaptations several works in the continental Counter-Reformation spiritual tradition such as Surin's *Foundations of the Spiritual Life*, and Avrillon's *Guide to Passing Lent Holily*.[210] As shown above, old High Churchmen faulted the 'Romish Methodist' character of such spirituality.[211] Thus, Phillpotts's practical support for Pusey during the 1840s did not preclude him in 1851 from expressing a staunchly Protestant disapproval of the policy of distributing books of devotion 'in which all but divine honour is ascribed to the Virgin Mary'. Phillpotts even expressed dismay that those guilty of such proceedings 'have not been proceeded against'.[212]

Pusey's spiritual rationalisations also conflicted with basic High Church notions of order and authority, in a way parallel to earlier Evangelical defences of joining the Bible Society. The Irish High Churchman John Crosthwaite in 1842 complained that Pusey's main defence, that 'some may feel edified by using such a book' was nothing 'but the very argument by which the Evangelical party have for thirty years been defending their Prayer meetings and other schismatical proceedings'.[213] For Crosthwaite, Pusey's policy revealed the kinship of the Tractarian mentality with that of Puritan followers of the notorious slanderer of the late-Elizabethan episcopate, 'Martin Mar-Prelate'.[214] Likewise for Edward Churton, it was the neo-Evangelical manner of putting imagined spiritual good before the principle of order and submission to the Church's own rules that, as he told Pusey, 'compelled me, most unwillingly to foresake that entire union with you in which I found so much comfort'.[215]

Such criticisms were not confined to Protestant High Churchmen. Manning made a similar point, questioning Pusey's defence of his adaptations on the ground that 'to claim impressions, and to call

210 On Pusey's identification with 'the tradition of holy folly' in Roman Catholic and Eastern Orthodox spirituality, see J. Saward, *Fools for Christ's Sake: Holy Folly in Catholic and Orthodox Spirituality* (London, 1981), pp. 207–9.
211 Hook coined the term 'Romish Methodism' to describe Pusey's spirituality in the 1840s. PH, Pusey Papers, LBV [Transcripts], W. F. Hook to E. B. Pusey, 6 February 1845.
212 H. Phillpotts, *A Pastoral Letter to the Clergy of the Diocese of Exeter on the Present State of the Church ... 1851* (London, 1851), p. 51.
213 Bodl. Lib, Ms End Misc e. 117, fol. 310, J. C. Crosthwaite to E. B. Pusey, April 1842.
    John Crosthwaite (1800–74). Trinity College, Dublin; BA 1823; Vicar of St Mary-at-Hill, London, 1844-d; editor of *Irish Ecclesiastical Journal*, 1840–4; editor of *British Magazine*, 1844–9.
214 *British Magazine*, 29 (January 1846), 236.
215 PH, Pusey Papers, LBV [Transcripts], E. Churton to E. B. Pusey, 9 December 1841.

them spiritual is really to say nothing more than every Protestant says, who believes his private judgment to be guided or absorbed into a spiritual light'.[216] The 'Bisley school' of moderate Tractarians also disapproved. John Keble's brother, Thomas, Isaac Williams and George Prevost, though they had known and admired the Parisian Breviary since 1829 and in the case of Williams already translated some Breviary hymns, all pleaded with Newman in 1836–8 to refrain from publishing even an expurgated edition of the Breviary offices.[217]

Some of those who later seceded to Rome, such as William Dodsworth and William Maskell also criticised Pusey for his policy of adaptations. Maskell was the most consistent, having always espoused a very 'Anglican' disapproval of adapting Roman devotions,[218] thereby earning Palmer of Worcester's approbation[219] and dismaying Pusey's supporters, who maintained that Maskell's strictures, would seem 'in any one else' like 'a sop to the Cerberus of the day'.[220] On the other hand, Newman's and Dodsworth's criticism of Pusey's policy entailed the reversal of an earlier position. In contrast to his earlier enthusiasm, by 1843 Newman regarded devotional adaptations as 'like sewing a new piece of cloth on an old garment'.[221] As a Catholic, he became even more convinced that Pusey's drawing on foreign devotions was essentially sectarian in

216 PH, Pusey Papers, LBV [Transcripts], H. E. Manning to E. B. Pusey, 25 July 1845. See also Gladstone's comment: 'I have been seriously troubled by some of the things which he [Pusey] has left in his Avrillon's Advent; though he calls it "adapted", I fear I am not quite adapted to it'. BL, Gladstone Papers, Ms Add 44247, fol. 241, W. E. Gladstone to H. E. Manner, 2 January 1845.
217 G. Prevost to J. H. Newman, 2 November 1838, *Letters and Diaries*, vol. VI, p. 336. See also, Jones, *Isaac Williams and His Circle*, p. 45; Withey, *Newman: the Liturgy and the Breviary*, pp. 33–6. Withey (p. 25) shows that the project was initiated by London Tractarian laymen such as Samuel Wood, Robert Williams and Robert Hope-Scott, with Newman only becoming involved later.
218 Maskell, *Ancient Liturgy of the Church of England*, p. cxlv.
   Withey (pp. 67–8) suggests that the translation of the Sarum Breviary, first mooted by Bowden and others in 1839–40, was more acceptable to High Churchmen than the Roman Breviary because it was English and not 'Romish'. Maskell, however, repudiated not only the continental Roman Catholic manuals of the Counter-Reformation epoch but also English medieval psalters and *Horae*. W. Maskell, *Monumenta Ritualia Ecclesiase Anglicanae or Occasional Offices of the Church of England According to the Ancient Use of Salisbury, the Prymer in English and Other Prayers and Forms with Dissertations and Notes*, 2 vols. (London, 1846), vol. I, pp. clxxxiv–v.
219 *English Review*, 8 (September, 1847), 195–6; (September, 1846), 180–7.
220 'Maskell on the Ancient English Ritual Books', *Christian Remembrancer*, 13 (January, 1847), 102. The reviewer complained (p. 101), that, in his second edition of the *Ancient Liturgy*, Maskell had made 'some additions, which display a more loyally Anglican direction'.
221 PH, Pusey Papers, LBV [Transcripts], J. H. Newman to E. B. Pusey, 2 December 1843.

principle.[222] After a similar volte-face, Dodsworth by 1850 regarded Pusey as disingenuous in seeking 'to satisfy persons out of the pale of the [Roman Catholic] Church with devotions designed for her own children', and in quoting an author 'partially, either in defect or excess, in order to accommodate his writings to a purpose which he himself never contemplated'.[223] In short, the converts to Rome echoed earlier old High Church warnings that the importation of adapted Roman devotions would act rather as an enticement than a bulwark against secession.

[222] 'While you stick to the old Church of England ways you are respectable ... [But] he does not appeal to any but his own interpretation of the Fathers ... There is a tradition of High Church and Low Church – but none of what now is justly called Puseyism.' J. H. Newman to H. W. Wilberforce, 20 January 1848, C. S. Dessain, ed., *Letters and Diaries*, vol. XII (London, 1962), p. 155.
[223] W. Dodsworth, *Further Comments on Dr Pusey's Renewed Explanation* (London, 1851), p. 7. William Dodsworth (1798–1861). Trinity College, Cambridge, BA 1820; MA 1823; Perpetual curate of Christ Church, St Pancras, 1837; Joined Church of Rome, 1851. *DNB*.

CHAPTER 5

The economy of salvation: sacraments and Justification

HIGH CHURCHMANSHIP AND THE SACRAMENTS IN CONTEXT

It was not immediately clear that Evangelicals as a body would react against the exaltation of sacraments and ordinances in the early numbers of the *Tracts for the Times*. Differences between the Orthodox and Evangelical parties were primarily confined to the nature of the spiritual effects of the sacraments, though even on this point eirenic voices on both sides were not lacking. One Orthodox churchman in 1833 even asserted in relation to the position of both schools, 'are not our sentiments upon the efficacy of Baptism, and the sacred obligation of the body and blood of Christ, cast exactly in the same Gospel-mode?'[1] On the subject of baptism, however, the controversies involving Richard Mant and Thomas Scott in the 1810s and again in the late 1830s between Pusey and Evangelical critics, showed that this was not the case.

High Churchmen faulted Evangelicals for holding that sacraments were little more than that which they signified rather than effectual means of grace.[2] A repudiation of this position was an important element in the theological evolution of both the young Gladstone and Samuel Wilberforce from Evangelicalism to High Churchmanship. According to Gladstone, it was a closer examination of the Occasional Offices of the Prayer Book which 'opened my eyes'.[3] As Gladstone later recalled, 'it imparted to the framework of my Evangelical ideas a shock from which they never recovered. I found that in regard to the priesthood and to sacramental doctrine

[1] J. B. James, *Remarks on Party Distinctions in Religion; Advanced to the Orthodox and Evangelical Clergy of the Church of England* (London, 1833), p. 8.
[2] Phillpotts, *A Charge to the Clergy of the Diocese of Exeter . . . 1839*, pp. 64–5; Phillpotts, *A Charge to the Clergy of the Diocese of Exeter . . . 1842*, pp. 18–25.
[3] G. W. E. Russell, *Mr Gladstone's Religious Development: a Paper Read in Christ Church, May 5, 1899* (London, 1899), p. 17.

in its highest essence, we remained upon the ground of the pre-reformation period, and stood wholly apart from the general mass of Protestantism.'[4]

Gladstone's and Samuel Wilberforce's religious development was related to a changed doctrinal understanding of the sacrament of baptism. It was the Baptismal Office in the Prayer Book rather than the opinions of individual Reformers on which the High Church interpretation of baptismal doctrine rested.

HIGH CHURCHMANSHIP AND BAPTISMAL REGENERATION

The sacrament of baptism notoriously divided Orthodox and Evangelicals in the pre-Tractarian era. The exposition of the doctrine of baptismal regeneration by Richard Mant, Richard Laurence and Christopher Bethell in the 1810s was made in the context of the anti-Calvinist controversy spearheaded by the Orthodox and directed against Evangelicals.[5] This Orthodox apologetic provoked a vigorous Evangelical response from Thomas Scott and others, and was a factor in the Evangelical secession from the Church of England in 1815 known as the 'Western Schism'. The seceders who adhered to the Calvinist notions of indefectible grace and election denied baptismal regeneration outright as unscriptural.[6] While most Evangelicals regarded baptism as little more than an initiation into the visible church, Scott and others readily conceded that baptism was at least a sign of regeneration as laid down in Article 23.[7] Moreover, some moderate Evangelicals accepted a modified version of the doctrine of baptismal regeneration, as in the case of J. B. Sumner. In Sumner's treatise *Apostolical Preaching* (1815) directed against the doctrine of high Calvinistic preaching, not only Bishop Thomas Wilson's and Bishop Horsley's writings[8] but even Mant's

---

[4] BL, Gladstone Papers, Ms Add 44790, fols. 160–1, 'Autobiographica'.

[5] For example, see C. Bethell, *An Apology for the Ministers of the Church of England Who Hold the Doctrine of Baptismal Regeneration in a Letter Addressed to the Rev. George Stanley Faber* (London, 1816); R. Laurence, *The Doctrine of Baptismal Regeneration Contrasted with the Tenets of Calvin* (Oxford, 1815).

[6] G. Carter, 'Evangelical Seceders from the Church of England, *c.* 1800–1860', unpublished D.Phil thesis, 2 vols., University of Oxford, 1990, vol. 1, ch. 4.

[7] T. Scott, *An Inquiry into the Effects of Baptism, According to the Sense of Holy Scripture, and of the Church of England* (London, 1815), p. 17.

[8] J. B. Sumner, *Apostolical Preaching Considered in an Examination of St Paul's Epistles* (London, 1815), pp. 7, 247.

views on regeneration were not unfavourably cited.[9] The young Gladstone's acceptance of the doctrine was partly owing to the influence of Sumner's work.[10]

Even moderate Evangelicals such as Sumner differed markedly from High Churchmen on the spiritual effects which the latter insisted inseparably accompanied baptism. While rejecting the extreme Calvinist basis of a denial of baptismal regeneration,[11] Sumner was also insistent, on the authority of various Elizabethan divines, that the grace of spiritual regeneration could often be separated from the sacrament of baptism.[12] Sumner protested his own consistency when the issue came to a head in the Gorham controversy in 1847–50. Sumner, like William Goode, personally did not entirely share Gorham's covenant theology whereby it was argued that God bestowed on an infant an antecedent or prevenient grace separate from the rite of baptism itself. They both, however, denied that this doctrine was heretical, as Phillpotts maintained in his action against Gorham. On the contrary, Sumner argued, Gorham's view had been maintained by some of the church's 'worthiest members' such as Bullinger and Ussher and was a matter about which 'Scripture does not speak definitively'.[13] For another moderate Evangelical, E. A. Litton, the Calvinist and High Church positions represented mutually unacceptable rival extremes: the one falsely maintaining 'that regeneration takes place previously to, and irrespectively of, baptism; while another affirms that that sacrament is the sole and exclusive instrument of the new birth, everything that has taken place previously being only of a preparatory nature'.[14] Similarly, Goode did not deny that baptism was 'the rite in and by which the gift of remission of sins is formally made over to mankind'. He merely questioned 'whether it is made over necessarily and absolutely to everybody in and by that rite'.[15] Yet from the High Church perspective, there was an anti-sacramental animus and a rejection of the spiritual prerogatives of priesthood in

---

[9] *Ibid.*, p. 165.   [10] P. J. Jagger, *Gladstone: the Making of a Christian Politician*, pp. 177–8.

[11] Sumner, *Apostolical Preaching*, (9th edn, London, 1850), pp. iii, vi.   [12] *Ibid.*, p. vii.

[13] *Ibid.*, p. x; J. B. Sumner, *A Charge Delivered to the Clergy of the Diocese of Chester in 1849* (London, 1849), p. 13.

[14] E. A. Litton, *A Sermon on John III 5, Preached in the Church of St Thomas, Appleton on Sunday April 7, 1850, in Reference to the Recent Legislative Decision in the Case of Gorham versus the Bishop of Exeter* (London, 1850), p. 21.

[15] W. Goode, *A Letter to the Bishop of Exeter, Containing an Examination of His Letter to the Archbishop of Canterbury* (London, 1850), p. 11.

Goode's denial that 'God's acts are dependent upon those of the minister'.[16]

Belief in baptismal regeneration was common to both old High Churchmen and Tractarians. Bishop Bethell, the leading Orthodox theologian of the Hackney school on the episcopal bench, welcomed Pusey's 'Scriptural views of Baptism' as expounded in *Tract 67*. In 1836 Bethell expressed satisfaction at finding Pusey confirming 'the views which I have long ago taken'.[17] Both Orthodox and Tractarians were united in assailing those Evangelicals who appeared to them to deny or explain away and qualify a doctrine enshrined in the Prayer Book. Moreover, Evangelical critics of what they called the 'Tract-school doctrine of Regeneration being identified with Baptism' in the 1840s were also assailing the doctrine long propagated by the Orthodox school of Mant.[18] Yet in an attempt to detach the more moderate Evangelicals such as Litton from the more extreme element, a few Orthodox churchmen adopted a conciliatory line on the baptismal issue in 1850. Francis Massingberd, for example, complained that William Goode appeared to take it for granted, 'that there is no intermediate position between the very highest doctrine on the sacrament of Holy Baptism, and that novel notion of hypothetical grace by which Mr Gorham has endeavoured to make his denial of the grace of the sacrament'.[19]

The only difference between the Orthodox and the Tractarian attitude to the sacrament of baptism lay in the latter's attempt under Pusey's aegis to give a more 'purely sacramental' and patristic interpretation of the doctrine compared to the 'chilly' and 'objective' formulations preferred by Mant, Bethell, Marsh and Pretyman-Tomline.[20] Bishop Bethell himself sensed a different tone and language from his own in Pusey's writings on baptism. Significantly, Bethell baulked at Pusey's 'Evangelical' phraseology, complaining that Pusey had applied to the sacrament of baptism the

---

[16] *Ibid.*, p. 27.

[17] C. Bethell, *A General View of the Doctrine of Regeneration in Baptism* (4th edn, London, 1845), preface to the 2nd edn [1836], pp. xxvii–xxviii.

[18] *A New Tract for the Times: the 'Church Principles' of Nice, Rome and Oxford, Compared with the Christian Principles of the New Testament* (London, 1842), pp. 1–49.

[19] F. C. Massingberd, *A Letter to the Rev. William Goode, M. A. Showing that the Opinions of Cranmer, Ridley, and Bucer, Concerning Holy Baptism Were Opposed to Those Contained in a Letter of Peter Martyr, Lately Published by Him. With Comments on His Inferences from That Letter* (London, 1850), p. 6; C. J. Blomfield, *A Charge Delivered to the Clergy of the Diocese of London at the Visitation in November 1850* (London, 1850), p. 26.

[20] Brilioth, *Anglican Revival*, pp. 307–14.

language of Calvinistic divines regarding the necessity of a change of affections and inward feelings. For Bethell, this was to confound the renovation which accompanied baptism, with conversion, repentance and faith – which were strictly only fruits of baptism.[21]

On the other hand, for Pusey, the Orthodox presentation of the truths of the doctrine of baptismal regeneration bore out his conviction that they had placed religion too much 'in the understanding, rather than in the affections'. Pusey's criticism of the Orthodox for lack of asceticism was paralleled by his complaint that baptismal regeneration had been used 'as a skreen to hide from themselves the necessity of the complete actual change of mind and disposition necessary to them'.[22] His emphasis on the heinousness of post-baptismal sin challenged the Orthodox quite as much as the Evangelicals, and was consequently resisted. There was no sharper critic of Pusey's teaching on this point than Bishop Phillpotts. For Phillpotts, Pusey's view robbed the sacrament of baptism of its 'full and genuine efficacy'.[23]

The Gorham controversy was not provoked by Tractarianism, though Gorham's advertisement for a curate 'free from Tractarian error' had helped to provide a spark and Goode sought to discredit the High Church case by drawing attention to the link.[24] In fact, some old High Churchmen urged the Tractarians to stay out of the controversy altogether; being convinced that they were just as guilty of a 'non-natural' interpretation of Anglican formularies as were Evangelicals regarding baptism. Thus, the hope was expressed that 'all who have in any way tried the forbearance of the Church by extravagances in an opposite direction to those of Mr Gorham ... would show their discretion by taking a place as little conspicuous as possible'.[25] Old High Churchmen provided the fiercest combatants on the anti-Gorham side. Evangelical sensitivities were sometimes derided, with one Orthodox churchman protesting that the *opus operatum* 'in the present day has become the Buonaparte of the

---

[21] Bethell, *Doctrine of Regeneration in Baptism*, pp. xxix–xxxii.

[22] Pusey, *Parochial Sermons*, vol. I, p. viii.

[23] Phillpotts, *A Charge to the Clergy of the Diocese of Exeter ... 1839*, p. 83.

[24] W. Goode, *The Doctrine of the Church of England as to the Effects of Baptism in the Case of Infants* (London, 1850), pp. 2–3.

[25] J. C. Robertson, *The Bearings of the Gorham Case: a Letter to a Friend* (London, 1850), pp. 19–20; [F. Mitford], *Observations on the Judgment in the Gorham Case: and the Way to Unity* (London, 1850), pp. 25–7.

Evangelical nursery'.[26] Phillpotts argued that, by taking Gorham's side in 1850, J. B. Sumner had abandoned his own earlier views on baptism as expressed in *Apostolical Preaching*.[27] Exponents of the High Church interpretation argued that Evangelical supporters of Gorham such as Goode had departed from the more moderate ground occupied by Scott and others against Mant in an earlier generation. According to Robert Wilberforce, Calvinism had not been an issue for Scott in the way it appeared to be for Goode.[28] On the other hand, it can be argued that baptismal regeneration was an issue forced upon Evangelicals in 1850 by those High Churchmen who wanted to make a particular interpretation of the doctrine an Anglican shibboleth. Had the Gorham Judgment gone the other way, a large Evangelical secession might have ensued.

In contrast to Phillpotts's polemics, Pusey struck a relatively eirenic note in the Gorham controversy. Pusey regarded denial of baptismal regeneration as heresy. But he remained more sensitive than had the Orthodox to the underlying Evangelical concern that baptismal regeneration should not lessen the necessity of a personal change of heart.[29] Moreover those such as Maskell, for whom the Gorham Judgment was a catalyst for their own crisis of Anglican allegiance, came to agree with Evangelicals such as Goode that a consensus of Elizabethan divines, many of whom were Calvinist, no more conclusively favoured an exclusive interpretation of baptismal regeneration supported by High Churchman than it favoured a purely ecclesiastical interpretation of Royal Supremacy.[30] In abandoning Tractarianism for a more Protestant position, James Mozley reached a similar conclusion while drawing a different inference. Mozley's research uncovered 'statements made sometimes, which, if

---

[26] R. F. Lawrence, *A Letter to a Friend upon Certain Suggestions Recently Made by Archdeacon Hare, as to the Measures to Be Adopted for the Removal of Doubts on the Doctrine of Regeneration* (Oxford, 1850), p. 13.

[27] H. Phillpotts, *A Letter to the Archbishop of Canterbury* (London, 1850), p. 4.

[28] R. I. Wilberforce, *The Doctrine of Holy Baptism: with Remarks on the Rev. W. Goode's 'Effects of Infant Baptism'* (2nd edn, London, 1849), pp. 1–8.

[29] Forrester, *The Young Doctor Pusey*, p. 192; J. C. S. Nias, *Gorham and the Bishop of Exeter* (London, 1951), pp. 9–10. Pusey's reluctance to take a stronger line was a source of dismay for some of his erstwhile followers who seceded to Rome in the wake of the Gorham crisis. See, W. Dodsworth, *A Letter to the Rev. E. B. Pusey, on the Position Which He Has Taken in the Present Crisis* (2nd edn, London, 1850), pp. 4–16. On Pusey's sensitivity to Evangelical concerns over baptismal regeneration, see also P. Cobb, 'Leader of the Anglo-Catholics?', in Butler, ed., *Pusey Rediscovered*, pp. 350–1. Pusey was convinced that on the issue, Evangelicals 'believe better than they speak'.

[30] Maskell, *Second Letter on the Present Position of the High Church Party*, pp. 11–33.

put into easy English and placed before our orthodox friends, would be set down at once as heresy, but which occur in undoubtedly orthodox authorities'.[31]

Mozley's conclusion was deeply unpalatable to many High Churchmen. Yet not only High Church Evangelicals such as Archdeacon Sinclair but also moderate High Churchmen such as Bishop Kaye, to the dismay of Phillpotts took a detached view of the doctrinal bearings of the Judgment.[32] Even Joshua Watson, perhaps mellowing in old age, while firmly holding the doctrine of baptismal regeneration, distanced himself from Phillpotts's position. For Watson, the verdict 'merely testified to the fact that scope is allowed for different opinions and interpretations of her [i.e. the Church's] formularies'. Unlike many of the High Church partisans in the controversy, Watson quietly insisted that there was 'no new heresy to condemn'[33] – a view with which W. F. Hook and Palmer of Worcester also concurred, in spite of their conviction of the dire constitutional consequences of the Judgment.[34] In the last resort, such High Churchmen took the line which Phillpotts himself ultimately also shared – that the Judgment did not 'unchurch' the Church of England in the way that Maskell and Manning assumed,

---

[31] J. B. Mozley, *The Primitive Doctrine of Baptismal Regeneration* (London, 1856), especially pp. v–vi; J. B. Mozley, *A Review of the Baptismal Controversy* (London, 1850). Mozley argued that the 'Gorham judgment simply sanctioned a *de facto* state of things which had existed from the first – there being too, nowhere, any dogmatic statement the other way in the formularies'. J. B. Mozley to A. Mozley, 2 December 1862, A. Mozley, *Letters of J. B. Mozley*, p. 254.

[32] H. Phillpotts, *A Letter to the Clergy of the Diocese of Exeter, on Certain Statements of the Archdeacon of Middlesex in his 'Prefatory Epistle' to the Second Edition of His Charge . . . 1851* (London, 1851), p. 2. For private criticisms of Bishop Blomfield's line by Phillpotts, see PH, Pusey Papers, LBV [Transcripts], Bp H. Phillpotts to E. B. Pusey, 20 February 1850. For Phillpotts's critique of Bishop Kaye's line, see Phillpotts, *A Pastoral Letter to the Clergy of the Diocese of Exeter . . . 1851*, pp. 51–60. In 1862, J. B. Mozley defended his own moderate position on the ground that he had 'said nothing but what recognised moderate High Church divines have said, such as the late Bishop Kaye'. J. B. Mozley to A. Mozley, 2 December 1862, A. Mozley, ed., *Letters of J. B. Mozley*, p. 254.

[33] Churton, *Memoir of Joshua Watson*, vol. II, p. 279.

[34] LPL, Mill Papers, Ms 1491, fol. 45, W. Palmer [of Worcester] to W. H. Mill, 22 April 1850; W. F. Hook, *Gorham v. the Bishop of Exeter: a Letter . . . on the Present Crisis of the Church* (London, 1850), pp. 12–13. Churton likewise criticised the line taken by Maskell and Manning: 'They say the Church cannot abide two contradictory doctrines. I must hold them to the logical meaning of their term. She may abide two contradictory interpretations, however inconvenient.' Gorham was 'very heterodox, but not absolutely heretical. I should say on Catholic principles, he ought to be tolerated, though not approved.' PH, Gresley Papers, GRES 3/7/90, E. Churton to W. Gresley, 26 March 1850. Churton privately regretted 'the wisdom and expediency of Henry of Exeter's course' and complained of 'a want of moral propriety in baiting an old parson like Gorham'. E. Churton to R. I. Wilberforce, 18 July 1849, PH, Churton Papers, CHUR 2/4/23.

precisely because the formularies remained unaltered. The moderate High Church position was voiced by Bishop Blomfield when he maintained that there was little 'to fear from the diversity of opinions which may from time to time arise in the Church. A clergyman may sometimes preach strange doctrines; but he must formally contradict them as often as he reads the Liturgy in his church.'[35]

The force of the Orthodox argument was conceded by some Evangelicals in the Gorham controversy. Thus Gorham's counsel maintained that 'the Book of Common Prayer is to be considered simply as a guide to devotion, not as defining any doctrine'.[36] Goode also conceded the point, arguing that the Prayer Book was 'carefully drawn up so as to give as little offense as possible to Romish prejudices'. Goode asked rhetorically, 'is such a Book calculated to serve the purpose of a standard of faith?'.[37] Although the Judgment accommodated their views, latent Evangelical unease with the doctrine apparently enshrined in the Baptismal Office forced some among their ranks to push for the ultimate goal of liturgical revision.[38]

HIGH CHURCHMANSHIP AND EUCHARISTIC DOCTRINE

Prior to the rise of Tractarianism there was near consensus between Orthodox and Evangelical churchmen regarding eucharistic doctrine. This consensus survived the early phase of the Oxford Movement, but thereafter, the Tractarians diverged.

In an episcopal Charge in 1843, Bishop George Murray criticised the Tractarians for implying that the High Church doctrines of the Real Presence and eucharistic sacrifice had been jettisoned over the preceding century. Murray cited in evidence the works of Daniel Waterland, Archdeacon Sharp and Bishop Cleaver.[39] Certainly, Tractarian assumptions as to the supremacy of Zwinglian notions

---

[35] G. E. Biber, *Bishop Blomfield and His Times: a Historical Sketch* (London, 1857), p. 380; M. W. Mayow, *A Letter to the Rev. William Maskell* (2nd edn, London, 1850), pp. 20–2.

[36] Biber, *Bishop Blomfield and His Times*, p. 378.

[37] W. Goode, *A Vindication of the 'Defence of the Thirty-Nine Articles' as the Legal and Canonical Test of Doctrine in the Church of England in All Points Treated in Them, in Reply to the Recent 'Charge' of the Lord Bishop of Exeter* (2nd edn, London, 1848), p. 35; *Revise the Liturgy; by a Peer* (London, 1845), p. 6.

[38] Carter, 'Evangelical Seceders', vol. I, p. 27; E. Peaston, *The Prayer Book Revisions of Victorian Evangelicals* (London, 1963).

[39] G. Murray, *A Charge Delivered by the Rt. Rev. George, Lord Bishop of Rochester, to the Clergy of His Diocese, at the Visitation . . . 1843* (London, 1843), p. 22.

popularised by Hoadly, of the Lord's Supper as a mere commemorative ceremony without any particular promise of grace attached to it, were exaggerated. The opinions of Hoadly did not prevail generally among the clergy, but the separation of the Nonjurors encouraged for a time a leaning towards lower views of the sacrament.[40] Orthodox eucharistic teaching continued to be witnessed to and propagated. The Roman Catholic John Milner maintained in controversy with the Latitudinarian John Sturges in 1798, that 'Hoadlyite' eucharistic teaching had never constituted representative Anglicanism and had almost died out.[41] In 1857 H. C. Grove corroborated this view. Grove pointed out that in the seventeenth century the highest doctrine of the eucharist emanated from Calvinist divines as well as classical Laudians. He traced the rise of Zwinglian notions to the influence of Arminian rather than Calvinist divines.[42] Certainly at a later date there were divines such as Richard Warner, renowned for anti-Calvinism, who held eucharistic views that can be classed as Low Church and rationalistic.[43] Pusey did not sufficiently recognise the gulf between Calvinist or 'Genevan' and Zwinglian eucharistic doctrine. Newman was less inclined to confound the two. He often expressed an aversion to 'a cold Arminian doctrine' and maintained an intellectual respect for the integrity of the Calvinist system. He was convinced that it was not Calvinists but Dutch Arminian divines such as Grotius who had fostered lower and more rationalistic sacramental views among English churchmen.[44]

The two main interpretations of eucharistic doctrine shared by the Orthodox were virtualism and receptionism. The former view was held not only by the Nonjurors but also by establishment High Churchmen such as John Johnson, Vicar of Cranbrook and author of *The Unbloody Sacrifice* (1714–18); Thomas Wilson, Bishop of Sodor and Man; Bishop William Cleaver; and Alexander Knox. Virtualists maintained that the bread and wine, once set apart by

---

[40] T. Bowdler, *A Memoir of the Late John Bowdler Esq. to Which Is Added Some Account of the Late Thomas Bowdler Esq.* (London, 1825), pp. 85–6.

[41] J. Milner, *Letters to a Prebendary* (2nd edn, London, 1802), p. 384.

[42] H. C. Grove, *The Teaching of the Anglican Divines of the Time of King James I and King Charles I, on the Doctrine of the Holy Eucharist, Extracted from Their Writings, with an Introduction, Containing Remarks on the Late Works on That Subject by Dr Pusey and Mr Keble* (London, 1858), pp. 6–7, 15–16.

[43] R. Warner, 'Disunion among Christians: in a Letter to the Editor of the Bath Journal' (November 1, 1843). The Catholic Bishop Milner unfavourably contrasted the eucharistic teaching of divines of this school with that of their Laudian predecessors such as John Cosin. [J. Milner], *A Vindication of the End of Religious Controversy* (London, 1822).

[44] [Newman], 'Le Bas's Life of Archbishop Laud', 369.

consecration, while not changed physically into the body and blood of Our Lord, became so in *virtue*, power and effect. A 'proper' and propitiatory sacrifice based on an offering of the elements to God was presupposed. The Real Presence was taught, but that presence was not located in the elements of bread and wine. The doctrine as espoused by Johnson was popularised by the later Nonjurors.[45] It won favour among devotees of the 1549 Prayer Book such as Horsley and Daubeny in his earlier years, even if not all Johnson's opinions were subscribed to.[46] The high demand for Nonjuring eucharistic literature continued in the early years of the nineteenth century.[47] The Hackney divines came under its influence, although the effect on them was not permanent – they came to prefer the rival doctrine of receptionism.[48]

Receptionists, who included Orthodox and Evangelicals alike, taught that the Real Presence was subject to the worthiness of the recipient of the eucharist. It has been suggested by some later Anglo-Catholic writers such as Darwell Stone that receptionism derived mainly from the seventeenth-century Cambridge Platonist, Ralph Cudworth, and that it represented a 'central' rather than 'High Church' position.[49] This view is debatable. Certainly, as the High Church Bishop Cleaver maintained, receptionism held 'the most general suffrage among our divines' in the century preceding Hoadly.[50] Its main Orthodox exponents such as Van Mildert, the later Daubeny, Phillpotts, and most of the Hackney school, drew inspiration from the Church's formularies and such divines as Hooker and Waterland. In pre-Tractarian Anglicanism, it was Waterland's *Review of the Doctrine of the Eucharist* (1737) rather than Hoadly's *Plain Account of the Sacrament of the Lord's Supper* (1735) which had most influence on standard eucharistic teaching and practice.[51] Caroline

---

[45] T. Brett, *The Life of the Rev. Mr Johnson, Late Vicar of Cranbrook, Kent* (London, 1748), pp. xxiv–xxvi.

[46] Mather, *Horsley*, pp. 204–5.

[47] For example, see *Orthodox Churchman's Magazine*, 7 (1804), 37; *Anti-Jacobin Review*, 54 (1818), 276.

[48] W. H. Mackean, *The Eucharistic Doctrine of the Oxford Movement: a Critical Survey* (London, 1933), pp. 1–7.

[49] Darwell Stone, *A History of the Doctrine of the Holy Eucharist*, 2 vols. (London, 1909), vol. II, pp. 315–16; Holtby, *Daniel Waterland*, pp. 206–7.

[50] W. Cleaver, *A Sermon on the Sacrament of the Lord's Supper, Preached before the University of Oxford at St Mary's on 25 November, 1787* (Oxford, 1789), p. 3.

[51] Mackean, *Eucharistic Doctrine of the Oxford Movement*, pp. 10–15; W. R. Crockett, 'Holy Communion', in Sykes and Booty, eds., *Study of Anglicanism*, pp. 272–83. On Hooker's teaching, see J. E. Booty, 'Hooker's Understanding of the Presence of Christ in the

devotional literature such as Taylor's *Worthy Communicant* and Comber's *Companion to the Altar* was concerned with spiritual preparation for a 'worthy receiving' of the sacrament. Such manuals remained popular in the eighteenth century. Waterland's view of the eucharist as 'a feast upon a sacrifice' was a more Protestant position than Johnson's. Robert Wilberforce even regarded Waterland as 'quite a Zwinglian'.[52] Nonetheless, Waterland's insistence that the eucharist was a commemorative sacrifice set him apart not only from Hoadly, but also from advocates of a 'central' position such as Warburton who, while opposing Hoadly's memorialist teaching, also denied any sacrificial character to the sacrament.[53]

Receptionists such as Phillpotts and Charles Lloyd pointed out that the term 'Real Presence' appeared nowhere in the Church's formularies. Although Christ was present in the sacrament, this did not mean *in* the elements, but in the celebration.[54] In asserting a 'heavenly' Real Presence, the advocates of receptionism were at one with virtualists. According to both views, the bread and wine were set aside for a new purpose by means of consecration while not altering in nature or substance. The main difference was that receptionism attached less instrumental efficacy or *virtue* to the eucharistic symbols than did the virtualist doctrine. Thus, Horsley took a higher view of the sacramental efficacy of the words of consecration than did Waterland and others of his receptionist school.[55]

Initially, the Tractarians were concerned only to exalt the importance of the sacrament and did not engage in doctrinal speculation. Tractarian antipathy to the doctrine of Transubstantiation was marked, being grounded on a conviction that it represented a form of rationalism.[56] The *catenae patrum* which they drew up in support of the Real Presence in *Tract 74* and *Tract 81* included as many representatives from the receptionist school of Hooker and Waterland as from the virtualist school of Brett, Johnson and

Eucharist', in J. E. Booty, ed., *The Divine Drama in History and Liturgy* (Alison Park, Pa., 1984), pp. 131–48.

[52] LPL, Mill Papers, Ms 1494, fol. 40, R. I. Wilberforce to W. H. Mill, n.d. [1850].

[53] Mather, *Horsley*, p. 19. See W. Warburton, *A Rational Account of the Lord's Supper* (London, 1761).

[54] Phillpotts, *Letters to Charles Butler*, pp. 231–58; Churton, *Memoir of Joshua Watson*, vol. 1, p. 275.

[55] Mather, *Horsley*, pp. 204–5.

[56] Keble, *Sermons, Academical and Occasional*, p. 380. For a survey of Tractarian eucharistic doctrine, see A. Hardelin, *The Tractarian Understanding of the Eucharist* (Uppsala, 1965).

Alexander Knox. Much to Froude's dismay, Newman even reprinted Cosin's *History of Popish Transubstantiation* in *Tract 27*. For Froude, this was another example of 'Tract Protestantism'.[57]

Newman's early eucharistic views were moderate,[58] apart from some unguarded expressions in the early Tracts. It was only in his *Letter to Dr Faussett* in 1838 that Newman was provoked into a more explicit statement of eucharistic theology. There are hints in this work that, under the influence of Froude's more advanced views, Newman was moving towards acceptance of an 'objective' or 'local' presence,[59] but there is no evidence to suggest that he as yet defined the Real Presence in anything but a spiritual sense. Where Newman did provoke latent tensions in High Church attitudes was in his use of the word 'altar' rather than holy table. Some old High Churchmen such as Hook and Churton, following earlier divines,[60] took Newman's side against Faussett on this point.[61] Others joined Faussett in emphasising the purely symbolic sense of the term for earlier Anglican divines, in their anxiety to deny any notion of a 'propitiatory' as well as material or 'proper' sacrifice in the eucharist.[62]

As was evident in *Tract 81*, Pusey for some while did not diverge from the pre-Tractarian consensus.[63] It was his famous sermon on the eucharist at Oxford in 1843 that first attracted opposition from the Oxford camp. Pusey's representation of his teaching as fully in tune with that of a consensus of seventeenth-century divines such as Overall, Andrewes, Hammond and Taylor, was repudiated

[57] R. H. Froude to J. H. Newman, January 1835, *Letters and Diaries*, vol. v, p. 18. Froude's eucharistic views received their fullest expression in his 'Essay on Rationalism' (1834), later published in the *Remains*. On Froude's teaching, see Brendon, *Hurrell Froude*, pp. 158–62.

[58] Mackean, *Eucharistic Doctrine of the Oxford Movement*, pp. 72–6.

[59] Newman, *Letter to the Rev. Godfrey Faussett*, pp. 45–91. Yet Faussett accepted a 'Real Presence' in the sense understood by Hooker and Waterland, i.e. 'not in the sacrament, but in the worthy receiver of the sacrament'. Faussett, *Revival of Popery*, p. 44 n. Newman came closest to defining his view of the eucharist in a private letter in 1838 wherein he maintained that the eucharist was 'not only ... a real and proper sacrifice of the bread and wine, but a sacramental presence of Christ crucified'. He commended Johnson's *Unbloody Sacrifice* as 'a standard work on the subject', but cautioned that it was 'badly put together'. J. H. Newman to Miss Holdsworth, 6 February 1838, *Letters and Diaries*, vol. vi, p. 198.

[60] For example, see Croft, *Sermons*, vol. i, pp. 20–1.

[61] Charles Daubeny had earlier warned churchmen against 'being frightened at the words altar, priest'. Daubeny, *Appendix to the Guide to the Church*, p. 311.

[62] Faussett, *Revival of Popery*, 'Preface' to 2nd edn (3rd edn, Oxford, 1838), pp. vi–vii; Bethell, *Charge to the Clergy of the Diocese of Bangor ... 1843*, p. 42; T. Lathbury, *A History of the Convocation of the Church of England from the Earliest Period to the Year 1742* (2nd edn, London, 1853), p. 487.

[63] Mackean, *Eucharistic Doctrine of the Oxford Movement*, pp. 61–5.

by many old High Churchmen, including Norris of Hackney, as well as by six of the Oxford Heads of Houses, who formally condemned the sermon.[64] Pusey was deemed guilty of the Tractarian fault of citing the Caroline Divines selectively and out of context.[65] It has been suggested not only that Pusey misrepresented the eucharistic teaching of Bishop Andrewes but also that he ascribed to Overall the authorship of a treatise never written by that divine.[66] Pusey was criticised for garbling the Fathers, and the Vincentian rule of catholic consent was even applied to confute his interpretation of patristic teaching.[67]

Yet opinion among High Churchmen was divided over whether or not Pusey had taught unsound doctrine. Edward Churton, Hook and Bishop Phillpotts defended Pusey against his more strident accusers, maintaining that they themselves only differed from him in expression.[68] In fact no one from the High Church camp accused Pusey of propagating Transubstantiation or even of any doctrinal error of substance. The most common charge was that Pusey had been guilty of misty exaggeration of the truth. Pusey's sermon was too vague to provide a forum for general attack. It was never intended to be a precise doctrinal statement. Pusey himself was anxious to repudiate suggestions of 'Romish' bias. He insisted that he had only meant, in line with the Orthodox position, to teach a commemorative view of the eucharist.

One of Pusey's supporters portrayed his opponents as taking a

---

64 PH, Pusey Papers, LBV (Transcripts), H. H. Norris to A. P. Perceval, 28 July 1843. Likewise, Joshua Watson approved of the formal condemnation of Pusey's sermon at Oxford: 'it passes no judgment upon doctrine, but silences the preacher, not as an unsound, but as an unsafe, teacher of the youths committed to his academical care'. Churton, *Memoir of Joshua Watson*, vol. II, p. 153.

65 J. S. Edison, *The Doctrine of Dr Pusey's Sermon* (London, 1843), pp. 72–3; S. Lee, *Some Remarks on the Sermon of the Rev. Dr Pusey Lately Published at Oxford* (London, 1843), pp. 10, 97; J. Garbett, *A Review of Dr Pusey's Sermon; and the Doctrine of the Eucharist According to the Church of England* (London, 1843), p. lxxxix; J. T. Tomlinson, *The Prayer Book, Articles and Homilies: Some Forgotten Truths in Their History* (London, 1897), p. 285.

66 Mackean, *Eucharistic Doctrine of the Oxford Movement*, pp. 85–6.

67 F. W. Miller, *Dr Pusey and the Fathers; or, a Comparison of the Doctrine in the Sermon of the Former with Writers of the First Five Centuries* (London, 1843), pp. 53–5.

68 PH, Pusey Papers, LBV [Originals], E. Churton to E. B. Pusey, 6 June 1843. Churton described Pusey's sermon as 'a solemn earnest devotional oration, scarcely containing a sentence for which there is not a warrant almost to the very letter in the Fathers and the Divines of Bishop Andrewes' school'. PH, Pusey Papers, LBV [Transcripts], E. Churton to A. P. Perceval, 22 June 1843. For Gladstone's defence of Pusey's sermon, see PH, Pusey Papers, LBV [Transcripts], W. E. Gladstone to E. B. Pusey, 30 June 1843. Bishop Bagot of Oxford and Bishop Murray of Rochester also declared Pusey's sermon to be 'unimpeachable'. PH, LBV [Transcripts], E. B. Pusey to H. E. Manning 19 July 1843.

'low and rationalizing' view of the sacraments. They were 'at the bottom Zwinglians', offended by 'any strong statement of the supernatural virtue of the Eucharist'. Pusey's opponents were described as 'a mixed body: – Evangelicals and Establishment men, the latter of various shades, some mere successors of the Hoadley and Tillotson school, most pure liberals as regards church principle, others of a rather better, but still weakened and attenuated church views'. The same Tractarian writer warned of an 'alliance which has been forming of late between the Evangelicals and the old misnamed High Church'. It was asserted that all 'these parties agree together up to a certain point: Evangelicals, Liberals, Establishment men, may have more or less of moderation or indifference, and not know exactly what statements on the Eucharist they would like; but they know very well what they dislike'.[69] Certainly by the later 1840s, Pusey, like other Tractarians such as Robert Wilberforce and W. J. E. Bennett, regarded both the virtualist and receptionist doctrines as wholly inadequate expressions of patristic teaching. As Pusey confided to Manning in 1845,

The Eucharist Sacrifice alas! is not a doctrine which it can be assumed that a High Churchman holds. Do you think that to above one in a hundred so called, S Chrysostom's words ... would represent what they felt, or even conceived or aimed at? Would the idea of it, as a solemn act, distinct from Holy Communion itself, occur to them?[70]

Similarly, in his influential treatise on the eucharist in 1853, Robert Wilberforce conceded 'that the importance of consecration has been little dwelt upon by many English [High Church] writers'. Wilberforce explained this away by referring to 'the popular unwillingness to break altogether with the Foreign Protestants'. He justified his own more advanced doctrine on the principle that he was 'only bringing out those truths, which the circumstances of a former generation withheld it [the Church] from expressing'.[71]

---

[69] 'Dr Pusey's Sermon', *British Critic*, 34 (October, 1843), 474–5.

[70] PH, Pusey Papers, LBV [Transcripts], E. B. Pusey to H. E. Manning, 20 October 1845. In 1867, Bennett contrasted High Church eucharistic teaching of that date with the period of his youth in the 1820s. See, W. J. E. Bennett, *A Plea for Toleration in the Church of England in a Letter to the Rev. E. B. Pusey* (London, 1867), p. 2.

[71] R. I. Wilberforce, *The Doctrine of the Holy Eucharist* (London, 1853), pp. 18–20. Wilberforce (p. 312) assailed the virtualist doctrine of Johnson's *Unbloody Sacrifice* for holding that the *res sacramenti* did not represent 'the actual Body of Christ born of the Virgin' but rather, 'a kind of impanation of the Spirit'. For Wilberforce, Johnson's theory was subversive of 'the whole economy of the Gospel', and cut off 'the relation of the Holy Eucharist to the Incarnation of Christ'. Unlike earlier Anglican divines, Wilberforce argued that, as a direct result of consecration, Christ was objectively present in relation to the elements. Crockett, 'Holy Communion', Sykes and Booty, eds., in *Study of Anglicanism*, p. 279.

Such Tractarian rhetoric entailed a certain misrepresentation of old High Church eucharistic theology. Terminology proved a source of misunderstanding. By the 'Real Presence', Tractarian apologists increasingly implied an Objective if not material presence in the sacrament itself, rather than one confined to the heart of the recipient. This view marked a divergence from the understanding of the Real Presence held by Hooker and the consensus of Caroline Divines which the Tractarians were reluctant to admit. The divergence was most painfully exhibited when R. D. Hampden, Regius Professor of Divinity at Oxford, in 1844 refused to pass one of the exercises for the BD degree submitted by the Tractarian R. G. Macmullen of Corpus Christi College. Macmullen was failed specifically because he had not, like Hooker, disowned a presence in the elements apart from their reception by the faithful communicant. On the contrary, Macmullen had interpreted the 'very order and rite of consecration itself in our Book of Common Prayer' as 'a presumption in favour of the view that the Church of England does teach that the sacramental elements are themselves changed into the body and blood of Christ'.[72]

In the 1850s, this divergence fully surfaced in the so-called Denison case. In the Bath Judgment of 1856, the Archdeacon of Taunton, G. A. Denison, after being prosecuted in the Archbishop of Canterbury's court by the Reverend Joseph Ditcher, was condemned and given a sentence of deprivation, subsequently reversed on appeal, for having preached a sermon in Wells cathedral in 1853 upholding doctrine 'directly contrary and repugnant to Articles 28 and 29'. Denison taught an Objective understanding of the Real Presence, while condemning Transubstantiation. In contradiction to the main tenet of receptionism, he insisted that the logical conclusion of the High Church theory of sacramental efficacy implied that the grace of the sacrament did not depend on the worthiness or otherwise of the individual recipient. If High Churchmen could accept objective sacramental efficacy in the case of baptism, why not in the case of the eucharist?[73]

Though never a close ally of the Tractarian leaders in earlier years and best identified as an advanced old High Churchman, Denison was supported by Pusey and Keble. Keble, who now advocated the adoration of Christ in the sacrament, helped Pusey

---

[72] R. G. Macmullen, *Two Exercises for the Degree of B. D.* (Oxford, 1844), p. 277.
[73] Denison, *Notes of My Life*, p. 233.

draw up a protest against the Bath Judgment.[74] As early as 1841 Keble had taken a stand against his own diocesan bishop, Charles Sumner, when the latter blocked the ordination candidature of Keble's curate, Peter Young, on the grounds that Young refused to deny any Real Presence 'excepting to the faithful receiver'.[75] Keble's dissatisfaction with the doctrinal position of old High Churchmen on this point was already clear at that time. For as Keble informed Pusey, though he conceded that Archbishop Howley's answer to his 1841 protest against Sumner's treatment of Young had been kind, he regarded it as 'very unsatisfactory on the point of doctrine as held by our Church'.[76]

Neither the Laudians nor even the Nonjurors had held Robert Wilberforce's or Pusey's later eucharistic doctrines of an objective presence and eucharistical adoration.[77] There was also a gulf between the authentic Nonjuring doctrine and that of Pusey's leading Scottish episcopalian follower, Alexander Penrose Forbes, Bishop of Brechin. While defending the Scottish Communion Office as more primitive than the English rite, Bishop Forbes maintained that virtualist doctrine was 'rationalistic' as well as inadequate.[78] Bishop Forbes's own teaching was opposed by his brother, George Hay Forbes, who represented the genuine Nonjuring tradition in Scottish episcopalianism.[79] From the later Tractarian perspective, the Nonjuring doctrine amounted, in Newman's words, to the 'real absence'.[80] Moreover, Keble's later views also diverged from earlier Anglican eucharistic teaching. Keble conceded that Hooker did not interpret the Real Presence in his own sense.[81] Yet Keble was not

---

[74] Mackean, *Eucharistic Doctrine of the Oxford Movement*, p. 111.

[75] Liddon, *Life of Pusey*, vol. II, p. 231. Newman later accused Bishop Blomfield of rejecting a candidate for ordination on similar grounds while admitting that he could not prove this. Newman, *Apologia*, p. 272.

[76] PH, Pusey Papers, LBV [Originals], J. Keble to E. B. Pusey, 11 March 1842. As early as 1839, Keble had denied Cranmer's credentials as 'a *bona fide* martyr' partly on the grounds that Cranmer had died professing the view of the sacrament expressed in his answer to Stephen Gardiner. Keble queried whether Cranmer's doctrine was not 'such as the ancient church would have called heretical'. KCA, J. Keble to E. B. Pusey, 18 January 1839.

[77] Mackean, *Eucharistic Doctrine of the Oxford Movement*, pp. 156–7.

[78] A. P. Forbes, *A Primary Charge to the Clergy of His Diocese at the Annual Synod* (London, 1857), pp. 23–6.

[79] W. Perry, *George Hay Forbes* (London, 1927), pp. 106–7, 118–19; *An Analysis and Refutation of Certain Erroneous Views Recently Promulgated with Regard to the Doctrine of the Holy Eucharist* (Edinburgh, 1858), pp. 5–9.

[80] Newman, *Lectures on Anglican Difficulties*, pp. 185–6.

[81] J. Keble, *On Eucharistical Adoration* (Oxford, 1857), pp. 124–5. See Keble's explanation (p. 124) of what he considered Hooker's defective eucharistic views: 'The truth is, if one

averse to one-sided quotations from Anglican authorities to support his altered views, as when he admitted: 'I see no disingenuousness in adopting words, from Ridley (e.g.) or any other, to express one's own view without stopping to inquire whether, on other occasions, the same author might not have employed different or even contradictory language.'[82]

Old High Churchmen regarded the eucharistic views of Robert Wilberforce, Pusey and Keble in the 1850s as incompatible with the Church's formularies.[83] It was argued that the Fathers had employed figurative language on the subject which could only be reproduced with qualifications in the light of 'Romish' corruptions of patristic teaching.[84] Nevertheless, Phillpotts commended Pusey's *Doctrine of the Real Presence* (1855) as a 'well-sustained and triumphant statement of the doctrine of the Church'.[85]

When eucharistic controversy flared up in the Scottish episcopal church in 1857, the moderate High Church party among the bishops led by William Trower and Charles Wordsworth, took a lead in publicly condemning the views of Bishop Forbes of Brechin which were akin to those of Denison.[86] In contrast, their High Church counterparts in the Church of England were reluctant to condemn Denison. Bethell, as one of the last Hackney Phalanx voices on the bench, put Denison's teaching into historical perspective. Following Waterland, Bethell insisted on a 'relative' rather than 'real' or 'substantial' change in the elements effected by consecration. He concluded that Denison's position was not irreconcilable with this doctrine.[87] Bethell admitted that the term 'real' or 'really'

may venture to say it of one so wise, holy, and venerable, that on this subject, as on the apostolical succession, and some others, Hooker was biased by his respect for Calvin and some of his school, in whose opinions he had been educated, and by sympathy with the most suffering portion of the foreign Reformers, so as instinctively and unconsciously to hide his eyes from the unquestionable consent of antiquity, and to make allowances which, logically carried out, would lead to conclusions such as the ancient church never could have endured.'

82 Quoted in Mackean, *Eucharistic Doctrine of the Oxford Movement*, p. 126.
83 PH, Denison Papers, B/5/69/ii, Bp R. Bagot to G. A. Denison, 10 June 1853; H. Phillpotts, *A Pastoral Letter to the Clergy of His Diocese, before His Triennial Visitation ... 1857* (London, 1857), pp. 66–7. Phillpotts conveyed his criticisms to Denison in a letter dated 4 December 1856. See Davies, *Henry Phillpotts*, p. 373.
84 Bethell, *Charge to the Clergy of the Diocese of Bangor ... 1843*, pp. 42–3.
85 Liddon, *Life of Pusey*, vol. III, p. 433.
86 *The Brechin Charge and the Six Bishops. A Provincial Letter by Pascal* (Edinburgh, 1858); W. Perry, *The Oxford Movement in Scotland* (Cambridge, 1933), pp. 78–81.
87 C. Bethell, *A Charge Delivered to the Clergy of the Diocese of Bangor ... 1856* (London, 1856), p. 32.

as applied to the eucharist was open to dispute.[88] Denison was guilty of a 'dangerous opinion' but no more.[89]

Edward Churton took a similar line. Churton regarded the teaching of John Johnson, the Nonjurors and later exponents such as Alexander Knox, as 'more trustworthy and more consonant to antiquity, than Waterland',[90] though like most High Churchmen, he considered Waterland in other respects to be a model of orthodoxy. This attitude distinguished Churton from his Hackney mentors such as Joshua Watson who followed Waterland's line on the eucharist. But Churton insisted that Van Mildert, the Phalanx's leading theologian, though commonly regarded as Waterland's mouthpiece in his generation, had also been critical of his eucharistic doctrine.[91]

Churton, however, pointed out that Denison's teaching contradicted that of the Caroline Divines and Nonjurors, as well as that of Waterland. Yet Churton conceded that Denison had made only 'an unauthorised statement', and had not taught heresy.[92] In later years, Churton pleaded for a 'Catholic toleration' of more advanced eucharistic doctrine than his own. There was also a blurring of doctrinal differences between his own and Tractarian eucharistic views, especially regarding reception of the sacrament by the wicked. In a renewed eucharistic controversy in 1867 after the Tractarian Bishop Hamilton had upheld an objective presence 'without us' and not merely 'in the soul of the faithful receiver',[93] Churton dismissed the difference as a mere dispute over words. Churton's later view was that Christ could be 'really present in the Sacrament, as well to the unworthy as to the faithful receiver' but in a contrary manner. As Churton explained, 'He is present, as the God of Israel was to the Israelites, in the pillar of the cloud, and the pillar of the fire – a sign of wrath to one and protection to the other.'[94] This

---

[88] *Ibid.*, pp. 36–8.   [89] *Ibid.*, p. 9.

[90] E. Churton, ed., *Supplement to Waterland's Works*, p. xi. Churton criticised some Hackney divines for deferring too uncritically to Hanoverian writers on the eucharist. He singled out 'Clagget, Pearce, the semi-Arian, Dr Samuel Clarke, and other Expositors, selected with too little discernment in the Notes to Mant and D'Oyly's Bible'. Churton, *Unity and Truth in Catholic Toleration*, pp. 30–1 n. 3.

[91] Churton, ed., *Supplement to Waterland's Works*, p. vii; A. Knox, 'Treatise on the Use and Import of the Eucharistic Symbols' [1826], *Remains of Alexander Knox*, vol. II, p. 174.

[92] E. Churton, *Ditcher versus Denison* (London, 1856), pp. 17–18.

[93] W. K. Hamilton, *A Charge to the Clergy and Churchwardens of the Diocese of Salisbury at His Triennial Visitation in May 1867*, (2nd edn, Salisbury, 1867), pp. 74–5.

[94] Churton, *Unity and Truth in Catholic Toleration*, pp. 31–2.

was not far from the position of Denison and Bishop Forbes, who had been condemned for maintaining that 'Christ may, in certain cases, be present in the Sacrament, not to bless, but to judge.'[95]

On account of the apparently one-sided Evangelical appeal to the Articles as the ultimate Anglican doctrinal standard,[96] old High Churchmen became anxious to play down their differences with Tractarians. Hook argued that there were 'now two extremes in the Church: the one extreme would receive the Articles without the Prayer Book; the other, the Prayer Book without the Articles. From either extreme all those who love the Church of England as it is must stand apart.'[97] The Tractarians in the 1840s may have posed the greatest threat to the church's equilibrium by explaining away the Articles. During the Gorham and Denison controversies, however, the main challenge to the Orthodox consensus reverted to that from the Evangelical camp. Evangelicals had always been vulnerable to the Orthodox charge that their baptismal teaching was incompatible with the Prayer Book. Evangelicals met the difficulty by offsetting against the latter the private theological views of individual Reformers including continental Calvinists such as Bucer.[98] The Tractarians used this discrepancy to justify their own departure from the formularies in a different direction,[99] increasingly appealing to the 'wise latitude' sanctioned by the Church as a cover for their own eucharistic teaching. Pusey, Denison and Bishop Forbes

---

95 Forbes, *Primary Charge*, p. 26.
96 *The Martyrs' Candle: What Is to Become of It? A Review of the Work of the Rev. W. Goode and the Sermons of Archdeacon Denison on the Doctrine of the Real Presence. Reprinted from the 'Christian Observer' for January 1857* (London, 1857), p. 26.
    The Court at Bath which condemned Denison's teaching, declared that the Thirty-Nine Articles were the only standard of Anglican doctrine. Bishop Bethell indignantly repudiated this position: '*Prima facie* the assertion is sheer nonsense. But if the Court means that these Articles are the only standard of the Church of England doctrine, it is directly contrary and repugnant to truth.' C. Bethell, *Additional Remarks on the Judgment of the Court at Bath, in the Case of Ditcher versus Denison* (London, 1857), p. 4. Nonetheless, High Church defenders of Denison insisted that the Articles and the Prayer Book were not at variance on the Eucharist. See C. S. Grueber, *A Letter to the Rt. Hon Stephen Lushington, Legal Assessor to His Grace the Archbishop of Canterbury, in the Trial of the Venerable the Archdeacon of Taunton* (London, 1856), p. vi.
97 W. F. Hook, 'Our Holy and Beautiful House, Where Our Fathers Praised Thee', Sermon xiii, *The Church and Her Ordinances*, 2 vols. (London, 1876), vol. i, p. 292; F. W. Trenow, *The Thirty-Nine Articles No Test of Heresy. A Brief Examination of a Pamphlet by the Rev. William Goode, Entitled 'A Defence of the Thirty-Nine Articles'* (London, 1848), pp. 13, 15.
98 Goode, *Doctrine of the Church of England as to the Effects of Baptism in the Case of Infants*, pp. vii–viii.
99 Newman, *Apologia*, p. 171.

notably did not claim *ex cathedra* status for their teaching but only a plea for its toleration.

The Evangelical exaltation of the Articles as the church's fixed and final court of doctrinal appeal alarmed the Orthodox because it seemed part of a wider attempt to subvert other traditional Anglican doctrines such as baptismal regeneration. In the eucharistic controversy in Scotland, the attitude of the moderate High Church party among Episcopalians was shaped by sensitivity towards Protestant objections to the status and doctrinal character of the Episcopal Church. Within the Church of England, on the other hand, the Orthodox needed Tractarian support in rebutting what was regarded as Evangelical error on baptism. This made them more inclined to concede that a certain latitude had been allowed by the Church in a 'catholic' direction.[100] Comparing J. B. Sumner's rigid position in supporting his brother's exclusion of Keble's curate from the priesthood for doctrinal unsoundness on the eucharist, with his toleration of Gorham's heterodoxy on baptism, Phillpotts concluded, 'the deacon, if he erred, erred on the side of anxiety for catholic truth; Mr Gorham on the side of Puritanism; and, as the Bishop's sympathies are with the one and against the other, he decided accordingly'. Sumner, Phillpotts complained, 'applauds the latitude conceded to one who denied an article of the Creed, and arrests the fair course of ministerial action of another, who denied nothing which the Church affirms, nor affirmed anything which the Church denied'.[101]

In the earlier stages of the controversy, Denison had felt let down by the attitude of High Churchmen. To Churton, he exclaimed, 'I respect "Evangelicals" who, denying the Doctrine of the Sacraments, do all they can to destroy it from amongst us ... but forgive me when I say it, I do not respect "High Churchmen" who affirm the Doctrine of the Sacraments, but do not defend it, or what is worse, explain it away under Protestant pressure.'[102] To Woodgate, Denison even complained that he 'never expected much support from the High Church, but did not suppose any churchmen would damage the cause ... as Churton and Gresley have done

---

[100] T. H. Britton, *Ditcher versus Denison: an Examination* (London, 1857), pp. iii–iv.

[101] Phillpotts, *A Pastoral Letter to the Clergy of the Diocese of Exeter ... 1851*, pp. 48–9; Grueber, *Letter to the Rt. Hon Stephen Lushington*, pp. 55–6.

[102] L. E. Denison, ed., *Fifty Years at East Brent: the Letters of George Anthony Denison, 1845–1896, Archdeacon of Taunton* (London, 1902), p. 62.

publicly'.[103] The closing of High Church ranks in 1857, however, which followed the Evangelical challenge to any expression of High Church sacramental doctrine, allayed Denison's sense of grievance. As Denison later recalled, '"High Churchmen", with some exceptions, at first looked coldly on ... But as the prosecution went on ... they gathered round me.'[104] The result was a *rapprochement* between old High Churchmen and Tractarians which marked the first check to fifteen years of growing divergence.

SACRAMENTAL ABSOLUTION AND CONFESSION

An ingredient of the High Church doctrine of the authority of the priesthood was the power and efficacy of ministerial absolution. High Churchmen based this doctrine on the delegation of authority implied in Christ's words to his Apostles, 'whosesoever sins ye remit, they are remitted; whosesoever sins ye retain, they are retained'. In the writings of Jones of Nayland, Horsley, Daubeny, Henry Best, Edward Nares, Sikes, Spry, Faussett and the younger Phillpotts, the doctrine of priestly absolution was a recurring theme.

In his 1820 Bampton Lectures, Godfrey Faussett laid emphasis on 'the power which has ever been esteemed the highest assigned to the Christian ministry, that of the remission and retaining of sins'.[105] The doctrine of absolution was important in Orthodox apologetic because the abandonment of such powers by the Dissenting sects undermined the latter's pretensions to spiritual authority. As Jones of Nayland argued, 'without this power there can be no such thing as a Church of Christ'.[106] Moreover the Orthodox were also sensitive to the charges of Roman Catholic controversialists that the Church of England in practice had adopted the Protestant principle of 'every man his own absolver'.[107] Edward Nares sought to discredit this view as a 'fanatical' error of 'sectarists between the reigns

103 PH, Woodgate Papers, 1/7/3, G. A. Denison to H. A. Woodgate, 21 November 1856. Churton's criticism of Denison was largely a protest against the 'kind of spirit' that 'has possessed some who consider themselves the only true High Churchmen in these days'. Churton, *Ditcher versus Denison*, p. 21.
104 Denison, *Notes of My Life*, p. 247.
105 Faussett, *Claims of the Established Church*, p. 215.
106 W. Jones, 'A Short View of the Present State of the Argument between the Church of England and the Dissenters', *Scholar Armed*, vol. II, p. 58.
107 H. Best, *A Sermon on St John XX. 'Whosoever Sins Ye Remit ... ' etc. Preached before the University of Oxford at St Mary's ... 1793* (Oxford, 1793), p. 18.

of Charles I and Charles II'.[108] John Oxlee likewise argued in 1819 that the 'progress of Methodism and the fanatical dogma of percept- ible pardon shall be shown to be unwarranted by the Word of God, and to be as groundless, and as visionary as the revelations of Joanna Southcott'. Oxlee implied that a previous 'culpable indifference to doctrinal points' such as the doctrine of priestly absolution had only played into the hands of Methodists. But he was now confident that 'the full tone of orthodoxy will be openly and uniformly main- tained'.[109] Oxlee concluded 'that the true reason, why the assaults of Methodism make so little impression on the minds of Roman Catho- lics, is that the most ignorant of the latter have at least some notion of the doctrine of remission of sins'.[110]

High Churchmen defended their view of absolution by reference to the relevant offices in the Book of Common Prayer, emphasising the special provision in the Office for the Visitation of the Sick for private confession to a priest in cases of troubled conscience. Low Church divines such as Bishop Burnet were criticised for holding that the absolution prescribed in the Prayer Book was at all times merely declaratory. Such divines were accused 'of deceiving the Church by their insidious and unmanly prevarications'.[111]

Pre-Tractarian High Churchmen drew a distinction between the doctrine of ministerial absolution and the penitential system of sacramental confession as practised by the Church of Rome. For example, in his *Letters to Charles Butler* (1825), Phillpotts asserted that for the Church of England, unlike the Church of Rome, 'confession is not at all required as a necessary service, not as a part of repentance, not even of discipline: that it is merely recommended to those sinners whose troubled conscience admits not of being quieted by self-examination however close and searching, nor any other instruction however diligent'.[112] For the Orthodox, as much as for

---

[108] E. Nares, *A View of the Evidences of Christianity at the Close of the Pretended Age of Reason: in Eight Sermons Preached before the University of Oxford at St Mary's in the Year MDCCCV. At the Lecture Founded by the Rev. John Bampton* (Oxford, 1805), p. 516.

[109] J. Oxlee, *A Sermon Preached . . . at Thirsk, July 10, 1816 . . . in Which It Is Demonstrated . . . that the Full Power of Remitting or Retaining Sins, and of Dispensing Absolution is an Essential Prerogative of the Christian Priesthood* (York, 1819), in '*Three Sermons . . . on the Power, Origin and Succession of the Christian Hierarchy and Especially That of the Church of England*' (York, 1821), p. 91 n. 49.

[110] *Ibid.*   [111] *Ibid.*, p. 79 n. 51.

[112] Phillpotts, *Letters to Charles Butler*, p. 207. Even George Horne in 1778 confided that he exercised private confession and absolution only very occasionally: 'Our church does not seem to require a particular confession to the minister, but in the case of some grievous crime lying heavy on the conscience.' BL, Althorp Papers, Poyntz Letters, E. 18, G. Horne to C. Poyntz, 13 April 1778.

Evangelicals, making forgiveness conditional upon sacramental, auricular confession to a priest was a 'popish' bugbear. In their desire to tie the grace of absolution to auricular confession, the Tractarians abandoned the distinction.

Initially, the Tractarian position was in line with the Orthodox. Tractarians may have urged a more penitential spirit and discipline but at first this was advocated on traditional Anglican lines. The Roman Catholic model was assailed as being synonymous with laxity and worldliness. In 1835 Pusey criticised the Church of Rome for turning 'the hard and tiresome way of repentance into the easy and royal road of Penance'.[113] David Forrester, however, has shown how far Pusey's views on confession, as on other questions, underwent a *volte-face* between 1835 and 1846. By 1846, in a sermon before the University of Oxford, *The Entire Absolution of the Penitent*, Pusey was advocating the regular and systematic use of auricular confession.

Pusey could fall back on the testimony of some of the Reformers, as well as the Caroline Divines, who had recommended auricular confession as useful preparation for Holy Communion and not merely in cases of troubled conscience.[114] Pusey even cited 'lax' late-Georgian divines such as Pretyman-Tomline and Hey as conceding that the church sanctioned the practice. This was more than mere theory. Pusey insisted that 'older clergy told me of remarkable instances of Confession and institution, long before our Tractarian days'.[115]

In citing earlier Anglican authorities on confession, Pusey claimed more than was implied by the bare testimonies themselves. Forrester suggests that Pusey was probably influenced by Hooker's sermon, *Private Confession and Absolution with Us*.[116] But Pusey did not quote Hooker on confession entirely in context. Like other High Church advocates of confession such as Maskell, Pusey claimed the sanction of the Prayer Book and sought to keep within the bounds of Anglican formularies, by conceding that sacramental confession was not 'necessary to salvation'.[117] Yet confession came to be advocated

---

[113] *Tract 67*, 'Scriptural Views of Holy Baptism', p. 59.

[114] Pusey, *Letter to the Lord Bishop of London* (1851), pp. 25–6. For seventeenth- and eighteenth-century examples of the practice, see Wickham Legg, *English Church Life*, pp. 263–9.

[115] E. B. Pusey, *Advice for Those Who Exercise the Ministry of Reconciliation through Confession and Absolution ... Being the Abbé Gaume's Manual for Confessors. Abridged, Condensed and Adapted to the Use of the English Church* (Oxford, 1878), p. vii.

[116] Forrester, *The Young Doctor Pusey*, p. 200.

[117] W. Maskell, *An Enquiry into the Doctrine of the Church of England upon Absolution* (London, 1849), p. 5. Some Tractarians conceded the inexpedience and impropriety of compulsory

on the same grounds as ministerial absolution. The two became inextricably linked. Forgiveness was effectively made conditional upon the sacramental absolution administered by a priest in private confession in a way which the old High Churchmen deplored.[118]

For Pusey, Anglican neglect of confession since the Reformation was a sign of the Church of England's spiritual malaise. It was a growing perception of the Church's defective 'ascetical theology' in the late 1840s that helped carry Manning and Maskell to Rome. Manning complained that, whereas Lutherans and earlier Puritans had retained a tradition of spiritual direction, albeit divorced from priesthood and confession, the Church of England had abandoned it. Manning observed, 'what we [i.e. High Churchmen] call enthusiasm, and fanaticism, and experience, is the disembodied soul of confession'.[119] No compromise on this could be contemplated. Souls were at stake.

Maskell remained a staunchly 'Anglican' exponent of the High Church tradition, but on confession he subjected the Church's most reputable seventeenth-century divines to searching scrutiny in a spirit of free enquiry that he had not conceded on other doctrinal matters. Maskell found most of those authorities to be riddled with 'discordant judgments',[120] so that he ultimately preferred his own private interpretation of the church's formularies to theirs. On this question, Maskell's breach with his friend and mentor Bishop Phillpotts was clear-cut and painful. The result was that, in 1848–50, a new source of division within High Churchmanship, which transcended that between old High Churchmen and Tractarians, opened up on the doctrine of confession, no less than on the issue of church and state.

Phillpotts found himself fighting on two fronts. On the one hand, in the spirit of pre-Tractarian High Churchmanship, he assailed 'ultra-Protestant' impugners of the doctrine of ministerial absolution, with force and sarcasm.[121] On the other hand, he felt the need

---

secret confession as long as clerical celibacy was not the norm. *British Critic*, 34 (April, 1843), 337.

[118] Maskell, *Enquiry into the Doctrine of Absolution*, p. 44.

[119] H. E. Manning to S. Wilberforce, January 1849, cited in Newsome, *Parting of Friends*, pp. 276–7.

[120] Maskell, *Enquiry into the Doctrine of Absolution*, pp. 43–4.

[121] See H. Phillpotts, *Confession and Absolution. A Letter to the Very Rev. the Dean of Exeter, on a Sermon Preached by Him in the Cathedral at Exeter, on Sunday, November 7th, 1852* (London, 1852). See also Davies, *Henry Phillpotts*, pp. 315–19.

to make a stand against the Tractarian reinterpretation of High Church doctrine on confession. Thus, as early as 1839 in a Charge to his clergy, he lamented that the Tract writers had not condemned 'the pretended Sacrament of Penance generally ... though Penance, as taught by the Church of Rome, is the greatest, because the most soul-destroying, of all those "grievances" ... the foulest perversion of God's saving Truth, which the cunning of Satan ever put into the heart of man to conceive'.[122] Moreover, against Maskell, Pusey and Tractarians in his diocese such as George Prynne, Phillpotts restated the old distinction between absolution and private confession which they had blurred.[123] While taking issue with Low Churchmen for denying that absolution was necessary for the forgiveness of sins, he also criticised Maskell's insistence on private confession as necessary for forgiveness precisely because he felt it undermined the efficacy of the general absolution in the communion service. As a High Church critic of Maskell's view put it, 'a real gift is truly bestowed through the office of the priest, and this gift is not in itself less complete or effective, because the more painful path of private confession might render men more apt for its reception. What is before us, at present is the efficacy of absolution in itself.'[124]

In 1848 Phillpotts republished the ninth of his *Letters to Charles Butler* on the subject of absolution. Phillpotts repeated the message he had given Butler in 1825: 'that the Church of England discouraged confession as a general habit'; a view which he restated as late as 1866 in a reprint of the whole of the *Letters*.[125] The notion of private confession as spiritual medicine rather than food was also upheld by Bishop Wilberforce in his complaints over Pusey's practice in his diocese.[126] Hook took this line against Tractarian clergy in

---

[122] Phillpotts, *A Charge to the Clergy of the Diocese of Exeter ... 1839*, pp. 81–2.

[123] See C. Benson, 'The Power of Absolution', *Discourses upon the Powers of the Clergy, Prayers for the Dead and the Lord's Supper Preached at the Temple Church* (London, 1841), especially pp. 50–1, 54, 57; Garbett, *Christ as Prophet, Priest and King*, vol. II, Lecture VII; Goode, *A Vindication of the 'Defence of the Thirty-Nine Articles'*, pp. 31–7.

[124] 'Maskell on Absolution, etc.', *Christian Remembrancer*, 17 (June, 1849), 447. Joshua Watson had taken this view. See J. Watson to H. H. Norris, 5 February 1826, Churton, *Memoir of Joshua Watson*, vol. I, p. 287.

[125] H. Phillpotts, *On the Insuperable Differences Which Separate the Church of England from the Church of Rome. Letters to the Late Charles Butler on the Theological Parts of His Book of the Roman Catholic Church* (new edn, London, 1866), p. 109. See also, H. Newland, *Confession and Absolution. The Statements of the Bishop of Exeter Identical with Those of the Reformers. A Letter to the Rev. J. Hatchard* (London, 1852), pp. 28, 33.

[126] See S. Wilberforce to E. B. Pusey, 30 November 1850, R. G. Wilberforce, ed. *Life of the Rt. Rev. Samuel Wilberforce*, 3 vols. (London, 1880–2), vol. II, p. 89. Volume I (1880) had been edited by A. R. Ashwell.

his Leeds parish.[127] Private confession might be allowed, but it was to be used as a last resort in time of sickness or 'great spiritual emergencies'.[128]

A sense of the seriousness of post-baptismal sin underlay Pusey's advocacy of confession. In contrast to the caution of old High Churchmen, the Tractarian author of the *Little Prayer Book* (1867) advocated confession of sins to a priest 'each time our conscience is burdened by mortal sin'.[129] On the other hand, critics of the Tractarians insisted that the Church of England spoke of repentance as the condition of forgiveness, but nowhere in her official documents mentioned confession or penance in this context. The *Homily on Repentance* seemed conclusive in its maintenance that confession was 'no integral part of penitence, but is superadded for the benefit of scrupulous consciences, and is a spontaneous act, not a formal thing'.[130]

On confession, as on devotional manuals, Pusey found himself in 1850–1 at the receiving end of criticism from converts to Rome such as T. W. Allies and William Dodsworth. Dodsworth, who had been close to Pusey, questioned his freedom of action in the matter of private confession, insisting that sacerdotal orders alone were no qualification to be a confessor, and that episcopal sanction was necessary.[131] Pusey was reminded that English bishops, if appealed to, would never have sanctioned Pusey's practice of going into other parochial cures and receiving auricular confessions. Pusey later maintained that when ministering in Exeter diocese in the 1840s he had been able satisfactorily to explain his policy of habitual confessions when questioned by Phillpotts, on the grounds that these confessions 'had reference to Holy Communion'.[132] Nonetheless, Phillpotts was uneasy, and Dodsworth could point to Phillpotts's opposition to a 'regular regimen' of sacramental confession and cite

---

[127] Stephens, *Life and Letters of Walter Farquhar Hook*, vol. II, pp. 219–20. However, while Edward Churton considered that Hook was right as to the doctrine in his dispute with Tractarian practitioners of confession in Leeds, he doubted 'the expediency of noticing it' because 'the error lies practically at the other extreme'. E. Churton to R. I. Wilberforce, 28 November 1848, PH, Churton Papers, CHUR 2/4/12.

[128] 'Private Confession in the Church of England', *Quarterly Review*, 124 (January, 1848), 84; [C. Wordsworth], *On Confession and Absolution. A Pastoral Letter to the Clergy and Laity of the Diocese of Lincoln* (London, 1874), p. 18.

[129] T. T. Carter, *Repentance: a Manual of Prayer and Instruction* (London, 1867).

[130] 'Private Confession in the Church of England', *Quarterly Review*, 99.

[131] T. W. Allies, *The Royal Supremacy Viewed in Reference to the Two Spiritual Powers of Order and Jurisdiction* (London, 1850), pp. 56–8.

[132] Pusey, *Abbé Gaume's Manual for Confessors*, p. cxxxvii.

evidence to show that Pusey enjoined penitents to use confessors.[133] Pusey never accepted the validity of such arguments. Against Dodsworth and Allies, he maintained that the Church of England left the power of the keys in the hands of her presbyters without restrictions.[134] Against Bishop Wilberforce, he complained that his attempts to limit that power only 'played into the hands of those who were urging to secession'.[135] Furthermore, for all the qualified moral support which Phillpotts had provided Pusey in Exeter diocese after the Oxford Heads had silenced him from preaching for two years in 1843, Pusey was forced to acknowledge the gulf between himself and the Bishop. Pusey's explanation is revealing in its patronising tone:

Bishop Phillpotts, it is known from the legal character of his mind, was one, who would construe any document with strict exactness. Confession to man was in his early days, although used, exceptional. He, probably, never either made or heard a Confession. In speaking then of the supposed disadvantage of frequent Confession, he was speaking of that, of which, however acute, he had no practical experience.[136]

At the root of the differences between Phillpotts and Maskell over confession lay a gulf in their respective understanding of what dogmatic teaching in the Church of England comprised. On the one hand, Phillpotts clung to an old High Church insistence that 'dogmatic teaching, beyond the acceptance and enforcement of the Creeds, is not, of itself, essential to the Catholicity of a Church'.[137] On the other hand, like other seceders to Rome, Maskell sought to extend the range of dogmatic teaching to cover the whole 'sacramental system' of the church, even to points which Phillpotts deemed not 'fundamental'.[138]

The essence of the divergence over confession lay in the fact that advanced High Churchmen expounded a more practical and comprehensive sacramental system than the older school. As Pusey later

[133] W. Dodsworth, *A Few Comments on Dr Pusey's Letter to the Bishop of London* (London, 1851), p. 6; Dodsworth, *Further Comments on Dr Pusey's Renewed Explanation*, p. 5.
[134] Pusey, *Letter to the Lord Bishop of London ... 1851*, p. 3; E. B. Pusey, *The Church of England Leaves Her Children Free to Whom to Open Their Griefs. A Letter to the Rev. W. U. Rickards* (Oxford, 1850); Liddon, *Life of Pusey*, vol. iii, pp. 266–8; W. Gresley, *The Ordinance of Confession* (London, 1851), p. 14.
[135] Liddon, *Life of Pusey*, vol. iii, p. 270.
[136] Pusey, *Abbé Gaume's Manual for Confessors*, p. cxxxvi.
[137] *Correspondence of the Archbishop of Canterbury and the Bishop of Exeter with the Rev. W. Maskell* (London, 1850), Letter vi.
[138] Maskell, *Second Letter on the Present Position of the High Church Party*, pp. 33–42.

admitted, 'the practice [of confession] spread from conscience to conscience, before there was any oral teaching as to the remedy'. The new oral teaching, itself a response to a new spiritual climate, was conveyed in Newman's and Keble's parochial sermons and Charles Wordsworth's influential *Evangelical Repentance* (1842).[139] Such teaching presented a contrast with the model of Orthodox sacramental teaching of a previous generation, expounded, for instance, in Mant's and D'Oyly's annotated edition of the Bible (1820). By the 1840s, this older teaching was no longer deemed spiritually satisfying in High Church circles; it seemed to be too divorced from spiritual practice and reality. As one High Church-man in 1850 argued, the people needed to be won over to the church. This meant that 'sacraments, creeds, ministrations, must not be left as cold theories before their eyes, but must be associated in their ideas with earnestness, affection, and adaptation to their individual wants'. 'Many', the writer concluded, had 'gained the reputation of high churchmen ... while no bell has called their poor to daily prayer, no more frequent communion calls them to gather round their altar, no more energetic teaching in the village schools marks the belief in baptismal regeneration.'[140]

It was later argued that Pusey's teaching on baptism with its emphasis on the seriousness of post-baptismal sin, though opposed for a time by Phillpotts and other High Churchmen, ultimately 'quickened the belief of those who belonged to the old High Church party'.[141] Pusey's teaching on confession, itself a logical response to the implications of post-baptismal sin, challenged the spiritual roots of the older High Churchmanship. The use of confession was the prime example of the way in which Tractarians, and also zealous High Churchmen such as Maskell, Charles Wordsworth and William Gresley, sought to apply the static and abstract older teaching into new practical spiritual directions in order to meet the perceived needs of individual parishioners. The Tractarians hoped to appeal to those for whom the Evangelical tradition was attractive. As a writer in the *Quarterly Review* in 1874 put it, 'the present desire for Confession and absolution is the descendant of the low church and Dissenting movements of the latter portion of the last

---

139 Pusey, *Abbé Gaume's Manual for Confessors*, pp. vi–vii.
140 E. Monroe, *A Few Words on the Spirit in Which Men Are Meeting the Present Crisis in the Church. A Letter to Roundell Palmer Esq. QC MP* (2nd edn, Oxford, 1850), pp. 18–19.
141 'Sacerdotalism, Ancient and Modern', *Quarterly Review*, 136 (April, 1874), 115.

century'.[142] For confession, even more than the eucharist, was the issue in which the Tractarians most perceived High Church deficiencies, and accordingly sought to realise the ideal of 'Catholic Evangelicalism'.[143]

HIGH CHURCHMANSHIP AND THE DOCTRINE OF JUSTIFICATION

The doctrine of Justification represented the main source of theological dispute between Protestants and Roman Catholics at the Reformation. Protestants decisively repudiated what they regarded as the Roman Catholic doctrine of merit and notion of an inherent or infused righteousness in man attainable through obedience and good works. Following Luther, the Reformers held a forensic doctrine of Justification by Faith alone whereby righteousness was imputed to man. Faith, it was insisted, was not a work. The difference between the Tridentine and Reformed theories of Justification was clearly set forth by the Anglican Evangelical controversialist G. S. Faber in 1837: 'the one system grounds our Justification upon our own Intrinsic Righteousness, infused into us by God, through our faith in the Lord Jesus Christ. The other system grounds our Justification upon the Extrinsic Righteousness of Christ, appropriated and forensically made our own by faith as by an appointed instrument.'[144] In the Protestant formulation, Justification was grounded on 'Christ's blood' and not rendered in any way dependent on either individual good works or the efficacy of the sacraments. Justification was regarded as distinct from and anterior to sanctification. According to Faber, the Tridentine system, following that of the Schoolmen, identified 'the Righteousness of Sanctification which is inherent but not perfect, with the Righteousness of Justification which is perfect but not inherent'. On the other hand, the Protestant view carefully distinguished 'both in office and in character and in order of succession, the Perfect Righteousness of Justification which is Christ's, and the imperfect Righteousness of Sanctification which is our own'.[145]

---

[142] *Ibid.*, p. 110.
[143] See D. Voll, *Catholic Evangelicalism* (London, 1963); Newsome, *Parting of Friends*, p. 319n.
[144] G. S. Faber, *The Primitive Doctrine of Justification Investigated Relatively to the Definitions of the Church of Rome and the Church of England* (London, 1837), p. iv.
[145] *Ibid.*, p. v.

Although the doctrine of Justification by Faith was expressed in varying terms, for the century following the Reformation it provided a theological consensus within Anglicanism which encompassed divines who otherwise differed widely in their views on church government and order. Late-Elizabethan, Jacobean and early Caroline Divines such as Whitgift, Bancroft, Hooker, Ussher, Davenant, Hall and Jackson who held moderately High Church views of episcopal authority and even the sacraments, were as Protestant in their theology of Justification and the economy of salvation, as was the Calvinist Presbyterian school of Cartwright and Travers with whom they were otherwise in conflict.[146] In consequence, these Jacobean and early Caroline divines whom the Tractarians cited as exemplars on those points with which they were in agreement, were also not unfairly claimed as spiritual ancestors by moderate Evangelicals such as William Goode and G. S. Faber in the era of the Oxford Movement.

In the post-Restoration era, the earlier Anglican consensus on Justification broke down.[147] The later Caroline Divines such as Jeremy Taylor and George Bull reacted against what they perceived as the excesses of Puritan covenant theology in the Commonwealth era. For the later Carolines, the mid-century Puritan divines had fallen into the error of Solifidianism whereby faith was emphasised to the complete exclusion of works, with the consequent danger of Antinomianism. In reaction, Taylor, Bull, South and others, including the anonymous author of *The Whole Duty of Man* (1657), denied the theory of imputed righteousness as held even by Jewell, Hooker and the early Caroline Divines. The latter had conceded that justifying faith must be fruitful of good works, but Bull in his *Harmonia Apostolica* (1670) extended this argument and reversed the order of priority. It was argued that faith without obedience and observance of the law was dead and useless – in Taylor's words 'like a stomach poweder faith only works if it purges and purifies'.

During the eighteenth century, the Augustinian Protestantism of the English Reformers was modified by an emphasis on the moral and rational dimension of man's nature. The Evangelical Revival, as espoused by George Whitefield, represented a response to a

---

[146] A. McGrath, 'Anglican Tradition on Justification', *Churchman* (1984), 32. See also, L. Weil, 'The Gospel in Anglicanism', in Sykes and Booty, eds., *Study of Anglicanism*, pp. 64–71.

[147] McGrath, 'Anglican Tradition on Justification', 38–9. A. McGrath, *Justitia Dei*, 2 vols. (London, 1986), vol. II, pp. 109–10.

perceived dilution, if not abandonment, of the Reformed tenet of Justification by Faith alone within the Church of England.[148]

The alliance of High Church Hutchinsonians with Anglican Evangelicals in the second half of the eighteenth century, in its repudiation of Tillotsonian moralism, might have predisposed the former to be sympathetic to Evangelical ideas on Justification. As McGrath, however, points out, there was no precise Evangelical consensus on the subject.[149] Prior to the influence on him of the Moravians and his conversion experience in 1738, John Wesley espoused the revisionist High Church Anglican teaching of Hammond, Taylor and Bull with its emphasis on good works as prerequisites to man's justification. Moreover, even following his rejection of this teaching in 1738, Wesley continued to lay much more stress than did Whitefield and Calvinist Evangelicals on repentance and its fruits as something preceding justifying faith.[150]

For all their respect for Methodist spiritual zeal, the Hutchinsonians remained identified with the later Caroline emphasis on 'Justification by works' as well as by faith. The very exceptions proved the rule. In 1767, George Berkeley junior was criticised by another Hutchinsonian, Samuel Glasse, for aping the language of Whitefield's 'Calvinist doctrine of Justification' in a sermon at Oxford. Berkeley's protestations of High Church principles failed to answer the root of Glasse's critique. For in a revealing reply, Glasse contended, 'it matters not whether you are a Lesleian or Wesleian in other respects ... [since] I presume even those who enter the lists with Whitefield etc. are as averse to lay preaching, and have as just notions of the powers conveyed in ordination, as they ought'.[151] George Horne took a similar line. Horne cited his reading of Bull's *Harmonia Apostolica* for 'his own deliverance from all danger of fanatical infection';[152] by which he meant deliverance from the peril of Antinomianism that was deemed a likely consequence of Calvinist

148 Garbett, *Christ as Prophet, Priest and King*, vol. I, pp. 437–8; C. P. McIlvaine, *Oxford Divinity Compared with That of the Romish and Anglican Churches; with a Special View of the Doctrine of Justification by Faith* (London, 1841), pp. iii–iv.
149 A. McGrath, 'Justification in Earlier Evangelicalism', *Churchman*, 98 (1984), 226.
150 Selen, *The Oxford Movement and Wesleyan Methodism in England*, pp. 152–61. Selen (p. 173) points out that Tractarian writers remained unaware of the ambiguity of John Wesley's teaching on Justification, and thus failed to level the charge against nineteenth-century Methodists of diverging from their founder's own views on the subject.
151 BL, Berkeley Papers, Ms Add 39311, fols. 220–1, S. Glasse to G. Berkeley, 22 October 1767.
152 Jones, ed., *Works of George Horne*, vol. I, p. 65.

teaching. In a sermon preached at Oxford in 1761, Horne glowingly referred to Bull's assault on the 'Solifidian or Antinomian heresy ... in all its glory in the last century'. Moreover, in a direct allusion to contemporary Calvinistic Evangelicalism, he warned that 'the time seems to be coming when Antinomianism is to be again rampant among us'.[153]

Differences over the doctrine of Justification between the Orthodox and Evangelicals resurfaced in the controversy between Overton and Daubeny in the late 1790s and 1800s, and between Richard Mant and his Evangelical critics a few years later. For Daubeny, who identified with Bull's standpoint in linking Justification to baptism, the Evangelical schema of salvation presented 'a mutilated sketch of the Gospel'.[154] Similarly, Mant's Bampton Lectures (1812) were particularly directed against what he regarded as the Solifidian interpretation of Justification by Faith advocated by Calvinist Evangelicals such as William Romaine who had appeared to argue that man was not required to obey and perform good works in order to be saved.[155] In private correspondence Alexander Knox also assailed the forensic view of Justification, i.e. the making of God's 'acceptance of our persons' independent of all moral qualification and dependent wholly on an extrinsic ground. Knox argued that 'the Church of England itself, and many of those who deem themselves to be its only true members [i.e. Calvinistic Evangelicals] look absolutely different ways'. Knox accused Evangelical writers of making no distinction 'between our grounds of comfort, when seeking justification, and when actually justified'.[156]

The most strident critique of the Evangelical understanding of Justification came from Arminian divines, such as Richard Warner, who adhered to the Latitudinarian spiritual tradition and were old-fashioned Low Churchmen. In 1818, Warner maintained that the doctrine of Justification by Faith alone was 'a doctrine so repugnant to Scripture, and the principles of our Church; so demoralising in its tendency, and so pernicious in the effects which it is at this moment

---

[153] G. Horne, *Works Wrought through Faith a Condition of Our Justification. A Sermon Preached before the University of Oxford at St Mary's ... 1761* (Oxford, 1761), p. 5.

[154] C. Daubeny, *A Vindication of the Character of the Pious and Learned Bishop Bull from the Unqualified Accusations Brought Against It by the Archdeacon of Ely* (London, 1827), p. 2.

[155] R. Mant, *An Appeal to the Gospel*, p. 93.

[156] Knox, 'A Letter to Mr Parken on Justification' [April 16, 1810], *Remains*, vol. 1, pp. 269–70.

actually working in society; as renders it necessary to drag the monster into light, and to mark it with the strongest disapprobation'.[157] On the other hand, Overton and Sir Richard Hill accused Orthodox and Latitudinarian alike not only of abandoning the Reformed doctrine on the subject but also of espousing Pelagianism or the notion that man could achieve salvation by his own unaided means.[158] Certainly, there was kinship between Orthodox and latitudinarian views on Justification.[159]

Nevertheless behind the differences between the Orthodox and Evangelicals over Justification, there was much Protestant common ground. Donald Greene, A. C. Clifford and others have argued that the eighteenth-century Anglican mainstream, including Tillotson, who himself had a Calvinist background, did not depart so far from the bedrock of Reformed teaching on Justification as Whitefield and various Evangelical writers maintained.[160] The necessity of good works as a condition for salvation may have been given greater emphasis but this was always disassociated from the Church of Rome's doctrine of works as intrinsically meritorious. Even Mant made clear that he excluded 'works from all pretensions to meritorious salvation', and cited approvingly Hooker's dictum: 'the meritorious dignity of doing well we utterly renounce'.[161] The anti-Roman Catholic polemic of Daubeny and Phillpotts revealed the gulf separating the Church of England and Rome on the subject. Mant and Daubeny did not object to the doctrine of Justification by Faith but only to what they regarded as the Evangelical gloss on that doctrine. In his debate with the Evangelical J. W. Middelton in the early 1820s, the Orthodox divine Johnson Grant conceded that Justification by Faith was 'a most wholesome doctrine. But here the author [i.e. Middelton] would edge in his Solifidianism; that is to say, faith without any reference to works.'[162] Yet moderate Evangelicals such as J. B. Sumner equally warned against the perils

---

157 Warner, *Letter to the Rt. Rev. Henry Ryder*, p. 36.
158 Overton, *The True Churchman Ascertained*, p. 179.
159 Overton, *Four Letters to the Editor of the 'Christian Observer'*, pp. 7–9.
160 D. Greene, 'Augustinianism and Empiricism: a Note on Eighteenth-Century English Intellectual History', *Eighteenth-Century Studies*, 1 (1967–8), 33–68; D. Greene, 'How "Degraded" was Eighteenth-Century Anglicanism?', *ECS*, 24 (Fall 1990), 93–108; Clifford, *Atonement and Justification*, 33–5; Abbey and Overton, *English Church in the Eighteenth Century*, vol. 1, ch. 5. See also J. S. Chamberlain, 'Moralism, Justification and the Controversy over Methodism', *JEH* 44 (October, 1993), 652–78.
161 Mant, *Appeal to the Gospel*, pp. 92–3.
162 Johnson Grant, *Summary History*, vol. IV, p. 35.

of Solifidianism. In his influential *Apostolical Preaching* Sumner rejected 'the naked proposition, that works contribute nothing to justification' as constituting the whole truth, and opposed Solifidianism by appealing to Luther's maxim: 'Faith alone justifies, yet Faith alone is not sufficient.'[163] Moreover, Alexander Knox who, as an advocate of the doctrine of a moral as opposed to a forensic view of Justification, is commonly regarded as a precursor of Tractarian teaching,[164] enjoyed amicable relations not only with the Arminian followers of John Wesley but also with Calvinist Evangelicals in the Church of England. Even Overton in his controversy with Daubeny conceded that the Reformed doctrine of Justification also represented 'the doctrine of the most orthodox of his opponents at their most orthodox moments'.[165] Thus, Daubeny's Protestant credentials were not doubted.

The main Evangelical critique of the Tractarians was that the latter had overturned the Protestant doctrine by blending Justification with sanctification, substituting 'another Gospel'. The failure of the Tractarian leaders to give prominence to Justification by Faith alone as the basis of a revived controversy with the Church of Rome in the 1830s did most to check initial Evangelical enthusiasm for the early numbers of the *Tracts for the Times*. When the silence was broken, in Evangelical eyes it was by an actual denial by the Tractarians of Protestant truth.

Evangelical restatements of Protestant teaching on Justification in the late 1830s had been provoked by the views of Alexander Knox revealed in his *Remains* (1834–7). The publication of Knox's controversial essay *On Justification* (1810) in the *Remains* first made the subject one of renewed theological dispute. Knox's views were identified with those of the Schoolmen and Tridentine Fathers and deemed to be anti-Protestant.[166] The partial identification by the Tractarians with Knox's views on Justification ensured that this Evangelical response soon came to be directed at themselves. Newman's debate with Samuel Wilks, the editor of the *Christian Observer* in 1837 focused on their differences over Justification. Some of Newman's followers, sensing that such a debate would prematurely alienate Evangelical support for the Movement, sought to dissuade

163 Sumner, *Apostolical Preaching* (1815 edn), p. 193.
164 Brilioth, *Anglican Revival*, pp. 279–80.
165 Overton, *True Churchman Ascertained*, p. 217.
166 Faber, *Primitive Doctrine of Justification*, p. vi.

Newman from getting drawn into controversy on the subject. In April 1837, Newman was warned by his friend Samuel Wood:

Is not the *peculiar* [i.e. Evangelical] view of justification in some sense their stronghold, inasmuch as it is only false as being partial and distorted, and has there not been a great school on that side ever since the Reformation? It seems to me (and I'm sure it was the case with myself) that men must be induced to drop their notions on this point by being made good Catholics, and not vice versa. The last is like pulling at a horse's tail instead of his bridle. If this be true it follows that the subject should be treated as late as possible.[167]

Newman was not dissuaded. He was convinced that the root of what he regarded as Evangelical spiritual flaws lay in a narrowly forensic understanding of Justification. He felt that Evangelicals overlooked the objects and fruits of saving faith and ignored discussion of a formal cause of Justification.[168] For Newman, the propagation of 'apostolical' principles of sacramental grace entailed a frontal assault on this teaching. Newman used the debate with Wilks as a basis for an exploration of the whole subject in his *Lectures on Justification* (1838) which have been described as 'perhaps the chief theological document of the Oxford Movement'.[169]

In his *Lectures*, Newman seemed to blend two rival systems, the Protestant and the Roman Catholic, when he maintained that whereas Justification was the application of Christ's merits to the individual, it was an inward gift lodged within us by the Spirit.[170] Newman insisted that his own doctrine of the righteousness of Christ, while not 'imputed' to the believer in the external, forensic Lutheran sense, yet differed from the 'inherent righteousness' that constituted the Roman Catholic view. Newman preferred the notion of an 'adhered righteousness' which depended 'wholly and absolutely upon the Divine indwelling'.[171]

Newman's position was presented by Protestant controversialists as much closer to the Roman than to the Reformed position. Certainly as Gilley argues, Newman was nearer the Roman Catholic position in relating Justification not only to the initial act of divine pardon on which Protestants focused but to the whole process

---

[167] S. F. Wood to J. H. Newman, 8 April 1837, *Letters and Diaries*, vol. VI, p. 53.

[168] J. H. Newman to Lord Lifford, 12 September 1837, *Letters and Diaries*, vol. VI, p. 131.

[169] Brilioth, *Anglican Revival*, p. 282.

[170] J. H. Newman, *Lectures on Justification* (Oxford, 1838), pp. 136–8. For discussion of the *Lectures*, see Brilioth, *Anglican Revival*, pp. 282–94; I. Ker, *The Achievement of John Henry Newman* (London, 1991), pp. 106–9; *Newman and the Fullness of Christianity*, pp. 95–7.

[171] Newman, *Lectures on Justification*, especially Lectures V–VIII.

of salvation encompassing renewal as well as pardon.[172] Newman retained a Protestant element in his schema by making God's pardon of the sinner precede his regeneration, whereas Roman Catholics inverted this. Moreover, his emphasis on the indwelling righteousness of Christ in the believer derived not only from the Greek Fathers but also from the writings of the Saxon Reformer Andreas Osiander. Osiander in his day had also been accused of making Justification dependent on sanctification.[173] Furthermore, it was not immediately apparent to moderate Evangelicals such as Faber that Newman's *Lectures* actually contradicted their own teaching. Faber initially gave the *Lectures* a cautious welcome and wrote to Newman in eirenic vein, confident that they agreed on far more than they differed.[174] In response, Newman readily conceded that his own views of Justification partly agreed with those of Faber and partly with those of Knox.[175]

Closer examination of Newman's *Lectures* convinced Faber that Newman's doctrine was as subversive of Reformed teaching as he felt Knox's views had been. In a second edition of his *Primitive Doctrine of Justification* (1839), Faber amended his original text accordingly.[176] Other Evangelicals were stronger in their criticism of the *Lectures*. According to James Bennett, 'there never has been a book published, at least among Protestants, more full of insidious, but determined, opposition to the Lord Jesus Christ as our righteousness'.[177] Moreover, indignation at Newman's views on the subject was not confined to those strictly classifiable as Evangelicals. C. P. Golightly dated his parting of the ways with Newman and subsequent indefatigable opposition to Tractarianism, to the report

---

[172] Gilley, *Newman and His Age*, p. 167; H. Chadwick, 'The Lectures on Justification', in Ker and Hill, eds., *Newman after a Hundred Years*, p. 295.

[173] Toon, *Evangelical Theology*, p. 155. According to Archbishop Laurence of Cashel, Newman affixed 'a peculiar sense to the word Justification which with the exception of Osiander no Protestant ever affixed before him'. R. Laurence, *Visitation of the Saxon Reformed Church* (London, 1839), p. 189.

[174] G. S. Faber to J. H. Newman, 9 April, 12 April 1838, *Letters and Diaries*, vol. VI, pp. 229–33.

[175] J. H. Newman to G. S. Faber, 11 April 1838, *Letters and Diaries*, vol. VI, p. 231. Although Knox can be regarded as a precursor of the Oxford Movement, Newman was dismissive of his influence and regarded him as too eclectic. J. H. Newman to R. I. Wilberforce, 9 June 1838, *Letters and Diaries*, vol. VI, p. 256.

[176] Faber now asserted that the book's 'ingenuity of mystification would seduce incautious admirers into all the grossness of Tridentism'. Faber, *Primitive Doctrine of Justification* (2nd edn, London, 1839), p. 409; G. S. Faber to J. H. Newman, 11 May 1838, *Letters and Diaries*, vol. VI, pp. 241–3.

[177] J. Bennett, *Justification as Revealed in Scripture, in Opposition to the Council of Trent and Mr Newman's Lectures* (London, 1840); McIlvaine, *Oxford Divinity*.

that Newman 'objected to the expression Justification by Faith only in the Article as unscriptural. From this day forward, I have not hesitated to communicate my alarm to others.'[178]

Newman's teaching on Justification fell within one strand of the High Church tradition as represented by Hammond, Taylor and Bull. Newman's debt to Bull's *Harmonia Apostolica*, like that of John Wesley and George Horne before him, was marked. In fact, the *Lectures on Justification* might be interpreted as the first and most ambitious example of his stated attempt to construct a *via media* that would embody a synthesis of various scattered strands of older High Anglican teaching.[179] Yet, as McGrath demonstrates, Newman's case for a *via media* doctrine of Justification rested upon the teaching of only the post-Restoration Caroline Divines over a mere thirty-three year period, from which such notable High Anglican apologists as Hooker and Andrewes were necessarily absent.[180] In appealing to seventeenth-century Anglican tradition to bolster his case, Newman was even more selective than on other doctrinal questions.

The Evangelical Henry Fish complained that there was no 'greater deception than that which is to be found in the "catenae patrum"' of the Tractarians on the subject of Justification and sanctification. Fish was particularly critical of Pusey for citing Hooker and Andrewes 'in confirmation of Mr Newman's views of justification: whereas the views of both those men were the very reverse of Mr Newman's'.[181] The Tractarians conceded that Hooker's sermon on Justification was not in line with their own teaching. But Keble objected to Goode's overlooking Hooker's later abandonment of the Calvinistic system in which he had been reared, and of which his early sermon on Justification still bore traces, for a fuller sacramental position. Thus in 1837 Keble complained to Norris regarding a work by Goode on Hooker and Justification: 'the great difference between the two is that Hooker in his later works dwells so much on the sacraments as essential means in the scripture method of Justification; whereas Mr Goode does not'.[182]

In their own response to Tractarian teaching on Justification, old

---

[178] LPL, Golightly Papers, Ms 1809, fol. 261, C. P. Golightly, 'Narrative of the Oxford Movement'.

[179] R. H. Hutton, *Cardinal Newman* (London, 1891), p. 88; Gilley, *Newman and His Age*, p. 165.

[180] McGrath, 'Anglican Tradition on Justification', *Churchman* (1984), 40; A. McGrath, 'John Henry Newman's Lectures on Justification: the High Church Misrepresentation of Luther', *Churchman*, 97, No. 2 (1983), 112.

[181] Fish, *Jesuitism of the Oxford Tractarians*, pp. 61–2.

[182] Bodl. Lib, Ms Eng Lett c. 469, fol. 92, J. Keble to H. H. Norris, 13 November 1837.

High Churchmen did not speak with one voice. Hugh James Rose gave a glowing review of the *Lectures* in the *British Magazine* which delighted Newman,[183] while in the *British Critic* Newman suffered under private protest a critical review by the Hackney divine Charles Le Bas whose position was closer to that of Faber.[184]

For conservative supporters of the early phase of the Movement such as A. P. Perceval, there was no difference between Tractarian statements on Justification and earlier High Church teaching as expounded by Taylor and Bull. Perceval even went on the offensive on behalf of the Tractarians by assailing J. B. Sumner's critique of Tractarian teaching for itself being full of theological error. If the Tractarians blurred Justification and sanctification then they were in the good company of Bull and Taylor who had asserted, 'no one is justified without being in some measure sanctified'.[185] But other High Churchmen, notably Samuel Wilberforce and Hook as well as Le Bas, interpreted Justification by Faith in a more Protestant sense and were as critical of the Tractarians for combining Justification and sanctification as were Evangelicals.

David Newsome has traced the source of Samuel Wilberforce's theological differences with Newman to their very different understanding of the relationship between Justification and sanctification as revealed in private correspondence in 1835. Newsome has shown that what helped make Robert and Henry Wilberforce 'Apostolicals' and devoted followers of Newman in contrast to their brother Samuel, was their thorough identification with Newman's teaching on Justification.[186]

Hook's break with the Tractarians came rather later than that of Samuel Wilberforce's but also focused on the doctrinal issue of Justification. As late as 1840 Hook appeared to be at one with Tractarian writers in his insistence that 'Justification by Works is as much a doctrine of Scripture as Justification by Faith. The fact is

183 J. H. Newman to H. J. Rose, 8 July 1838, *Letters and Diaries*, vol. VI, p. 262.
184 J. H. Newman to Mrs J. Mozley, 5 June 1838, *Letters and Diaries*, vol. VI, p. 253. See [C. W. Le Bas], 'Newman and Faber on Justification', *British Critic*, 24 (July, 1838), 82–119. For Charles Le Bas (1779–1861), one-time tutor to Bishop Pretyman-Tomline's sons, Principal of Haileybury College 1837–43, see *DNB*.
185 A. P. Perceval, *A Letter to the Rt. Rev. John Bird, Lord Bishop of Chester, with Remarks on His Late Charge, More Especially as Relates to the Doctrine of Justification* (London, 1841), especially pp. 16, 27. Henry Handley Norris commended Perceval's 'scriptural condemnation of his [Sumner's] opinions so dogmatically propounded'. PH, Pusey Papers, LBV [Transcripts], H. H. Norris to A. P. Perceval, 29 December 1841.
186 D. Newsome, 'Justification and Sanctification: Newman and the Evangelicals', *Journal of Theological Studies*, new series, 15 (1964), 51.

that too many Protestants make Justification by Faith only which is an important doctrine of Scripture, to be the very foundation of Scripture; whereas the one thing necessary is mystical union with Christ.'[187] Hook, however, repudiated the Tractarians when he became convinced that they had forsaken the cardinal principle of Protestantism by failing to assert 'the grand doctrine of justification by faith only, independent of works' and 'the distinction between justification and sanctification, infused and imputed righteousness'.[188]

Like Samuel Wilberforce, Hook implicitly rejected the teaching of Bishop Bull and Alexander Knox and identified his views on Justification with those of Hooker and even modern High Church Evangelical writers such as Faber. In a sermon on Justification in 1849 Hook approvingly quoted Hooker's dictum: 'concerning the righteousness of sanctification, we deny it not to be inherent; we grant, that unless we work, we have it not; only we disregard it as a thing different in nature from the righteousness of justification'.[189] Citing G. S. Faber's treatise on Justification as in full accord with his own views, Hook argued that the rise of what he regarded as Romanising opinions within the Church had been promoted by a conscious explaining away of the doctrine of Justification by Faith independently of works. He conceded that for many years in the early part of the century the Orthodox had focused their attention on the opposite error to that presented by the Church of Rome. The renewed challenge from Rome, he argued, had necessitated a reorientation on the part of Protestant High Churchmen:

that Antinomianism prevailed among us to a great extent not many years ago, is a fact not to be denied. And they, therefore, who attacked that as the Protestant doctrine obtained a patient hearing. But the result being a tendency to Romanize, we must go back to our first principles, and maintain with discretion, but with firmness, the doctrine of justification by grace.[190]

Bishop Phillpotts challenged the Tractarians for apparent dereliction of the Reformed doctrine of Justification. In his Charge of 1842, he accused them of countenancing 'the fatal error ... that the

---

187 Stephens, Life and Letters of Walter Farquhar Hook, vol. ii, p. 49.
188 For Hook's critique of Newman on Justification, see his letter of 24 April 1848, Stephens, Life and Letters of Walter Farquhar Hook, vol. ii, pp. 231–2.
189 W. F. Hook, The Necessity of Romish Saints and the Inanity of Romish Ordinances. Two Sermons (London, 1849), p. 36.
190 Ibid., p. 24.

regenerate man can fulfil the Law of God by perfect obedience –
that their good works can satisfy for sins – that they can stand before
the Judgment seat of God and claim everlasting life as due to their
own deservings'.[191] Phillpotts's continued Protestant emphasis was
in accord with earlier broadsides on the Roman Catholic doctrine of
merit in his *Letters to Charles Butler* (1825). Nonetheless the ambivalence within High Churchmanship on the subject was revealed by
Phillpotts's later assault on the Evangelical position during his
controversy with Archbishop Sumner in 1850–1. Phillpotts now
echoed the earlier critique of Sumner's position by A. P. Perceval
and implied that the Archbishop was guilty of Solifidianism. For
Phillpotts, all other ingredients of the Christian life appeared to be
reduced to nothing in Sumner's schema of salvation by an over-
emphasis on Justification by Faith alone.[192] Phillpotts argued that
Sumner's apparent unsoundness on Justification was directly related
to his unsoundness on baptism, in that he denied the Orthodox view
propounded by Waterland that baptism 'concurred towards our
Justification'. Thus Phillpotts now rebutted the Evangelical critique
of Tractarianism by asserting against Sumner, 'the shaft aimed at
the Tractarians does in truth strike no less a name than Waterland'.
Phillpotts also complained that Sumner's strictures on 'Tractarian'
notions of Justification applied no less to the views expounded in
Bull's *Harmonia Apostolica*, in which Bull had argued that forgiveness
of sins or works of mercy could avail in obtaining a remission of sins.
Phillpotts's concluding thrust against Sumner was pointed: 'I think
it was his duty to tell his clergy, that it was Bishop Bull, rather than
the Tractarians, whose false teaching he thus denounced.'[193]

Bishop Kaye also displayed the same tension between a high
Catholic view of the efficacy of sacramental grace and Protestant
doctrine of Justification. Like Hook, Kaye interpreted Article 11 on
Justification in a judicial or forensic sense and inclined to the earlier
Caroline view of imputed righteousness rather than to the later
Caroline view of infused righteousness preferred by Perceval and
Phillpotts.[194] Whereas Phillpotts and Bishop Bethell, following
Waterland, were happy to employ the expression 'Sacramental

---

[191] Phillpotts, *A Charge to the Clergy of the Diocese of Exeter ... 1842*, p. 94.
[192] Phillpotts, *A Pastoral Letter to the Clergy of the Diocese of Exeter on the Present State of the Church*, pp. 21–2.
[193] *Ibid.*, p. 26.
[194] J. Kaye, *A Charge to the Clergy of the Diocese of Lincoln ... at the Triennial Visitation, in MDCCCXLIII* (3rd edn, London, 1843), p. 27.

Justification', Kaye cited Burnet in altogether rejecting the notion as 'among the most mischievous of all the practical errors that were in the Church of Rome'.[195] By implication, Kaye accused the Tractarians of falling into the same error. Yet at the same time Kaye qualified these sentiments by urging his clergy not to run 'into the opposite extreme'. Citing Bishop Bethell, Kaye cautioned against the denial of any connection between baptism and Justification.[196]

The Tractarians claimed continuity on Justification with the High Church tradition as represented by Bishop Bull, Newman's favourite Anglican divine.[197] As there had never really been an Anglican consensus on the doctrine, it was easy for opponents of the Movement also to claim impeccable Anglican testimony for their decisive repudiation of Tractarian teaching on the subject. The issue remained much more a point of divergence between Evangelicals and the older school of High Churchmanship than between the latter and the Tractarians. But some High Churchmen allied themselves with Evangelicals in repudiating the Tractarian expression of the doctrine, while others such as Bishop Blomfield appeared to look both ways. In assailing the Orthodox bugbear of Antinomianism and the Roman Catholic doctrine of merit in his controversial Charge of 1842, Bishop Blomfield alienated both sides.[198]

The difference between old High Churchmen and Tractarians on the question was one of emphasis and tone rather than of substance. But the difference was enough to ensure that the Orthodox generally clung to a more Protestant outlook that inhibited them from adopting the fuller sacramental system which the Tractarians advocated. Newman's concept of 'imparted righteousness', deriving more from patristic than from Anglican sources, enabled the Tractarians to embrace what Brilioth called 'sacramental mysticism'[199] to an extent which distinguished them from old High Churchmen such as Le Bas, who criticised Newman's writing on the subject for 'shadowy and mystical fancies'.[200] In W. G. Ward's *Ideal of a Christian Church*, the anti-Protestant implications of the Tractarian critique of Justification by Faith were taken to their logical conclusion. Newman's notion of an 'indwelling righteousness' was developed and the full

195 *Ibid.*, p. 37.   196 *Ibid.*, p. 39.   197 Newman, *Apologia*, p. 195.
198 C. J. Blomfield, *A Charge Delivered to the Clergy of the Diocese of London at the Visitation in October MDCCCXLII* (2nd edn, London, 1842), pp. 23–5.
199 Brilioth, *Anglican Revival*, p. 286.
200 [Le Bas], 'Newman and Faber on Justification', *British Critic*, 24 (1838), 87.

Roman doctrinal position appropriated.[201] When viewed alongside such teaching, some Evangelicals later recognised that older High Churchmen, for all their anti-Calvinist rhetoric, had upheld a soundly Protestant view of Justification in the tradition of the earlier Carolines, which enabled them to keep their sacramental 'doctrine within the Gospel limits'.[202] The implication was that the Tractarians had overstepped those limits. Yet, as on baptism, the Tractarians revealed a greater sensitivity than the Orthodox to Evangelical concerns in insisting that teaching on Justification be grounded on the reality and consequences of original sin. One Tractarian writer in 1843 concurred with J. B. Sumner's view that, in their dislike of Calvinism, the Marsh–Tomline school had neglected this emphasis and inclined towards Pelagianism. His complaint was that Sumner had made this charge also against the Tractarians. Sumner, according to this author, had been misled 'in his judgment of the Oxford writers by the recollections of his youth'. But it was 'not of Tomline or Marsh that he now speaks, but of Mr Newman and Dr Pusey; yet we find no disposition in his recent controversial writings to give them, or those who have been guided by them, the benefit of this distinction'.[203]

---

[201] Ward, *Ideal of a Christian Church*, ch. 5.

[202] Garbett, *Christ as Prophet, Priest and King*, vol. 1, p. 248.

[203] 'Bishop J. B. Sumner on Justification', *British Critic*, 34 (July, 1843), 70. Some Evangelicals conceded that the Tractarians were less inclined to Pelagianism than some of their High Church predecessors. See the comment of one Evangelical: 'There was a time when the pulpits of High Churchmen rang with eulogies of good works as opposed to faith; but the tone has been greatly changed of late, and faith has been more spoken of, if not better understood than formerly.' King, *Letter Addressed to the Churchmen of Hull* (1846), p. 18.

CHAPTER 6

The old High Churchmen and Tractarians in historical relation

TRACTARIANISM IN CONTEXT: HISTORICAL BACKGROUND, 1760–1833

From the 1710s until 1760, High Churchmen were marginalised from the inner counsels of church and state. There were, however, High Church Whigs such as Bishop Gibson, Archbishop Wake and Archbishop Potter. As Mather shows, the preferment of High Churchmen to the bench such as Thomas Sherlock, Thomas Gooch and Henry Stebbing helped ensure the survival of High Church values within the establishment into the second half of the century.[1] If Latitudinarians were dominant among the mid-century episcopate, they had no absolute monopoly. The fact that there were many other sources of patronage apart from that of the crown, such as Oxford colleges, meant that avenues to higher preferment were not closed to High Churchmen. High Church resistance to Hoadlyism remained alive even during the nadir of High Church fortunes in the 1740s and 1750s. The accession of George III in 1760 opened a new era. The tide of ministerial preferment turned in favour of High Churchmen. Although Jones of Nayland obtained no high recognition, various Hutchinsonian divines such as Nathaniel Wetherell, George Berkeley junior, George Horne and Samuel Glasse, all obtained deaneries or royal chaplaincies from the late 1760s onwards. By the late 1790s, the prevailing character of the episcopate was Orthodox, with John Warren, Charles Moss, Samuel Horsley and the Hutchinsonian, John Douglas, Bishop of Salisbury, being particularly High Church.[2] A similar trend was discerned among the lower clergy. In 1790, the Unitarian minister, Joseph Priestley, observed: 'the body of the clergy seem to be more ortho-

[1] Mather, *Horsley*, p. 7.
[2] *Ibid.*, pp. 9, 15, 210–13. Jones of Nayland and Horne owed their preferment to the former's old school friend, Charles Jenkinson, political counsellor to George III in the 1770s and 1780s. Sack, *From Jacobite to Conservative*, pp. 76–7.

dox than they were in the last reign, and more bigotted. We see what a court and an establishment can do.'[3]

Until the 1790s, the organisational coherence and identity of High Churchmen remained limited. High Church influence was felt throughout the century in the SPCK. But it was only with Jones of Nayland's foundation of the *Society for the Reformation of Principles* in 1792, that High Churchmen had their own organisation and ideological agenda. Thereafter, with the foundation of the *National Society* in 1811 and the *Church Building Society* in 1818, a greater sense of High Church unity and purpose was fostered. The emergence of the Hackney Phalanx in the 1800s was indicative of this trend. A coherent body of defenders of Orthodoxy emerged where, previously a less co-ordinated basis of action had been the norm. Moreover, with the foundation of the *Orthodox Churchman's Magazine* in 1801, High Churchmen entered the expanding field of popular journalism. In this publication, High Church theological themes, no longer subservient to Tory political concerns as in the *Anti-Jacobin Review*[4] and the early *British Critic*, were propagated in a way which prefigured Tractarian literary methods. The transference of publication in 1804 to Rivingtons heralded the beginning of an involvement of that publishing house with High Churchmanship which would span several generations: Rivingtons would achieve fame as the publisher of Tractarian literary works.[5] Consequently, the failure of the *Orthodox Churchman's Magazine* in 1816 was more of a blow to High Church self-esteem than the closure of the *Anti-Jacobin* in 1821, though the former was partly offset by the foundation of the *Christian Remembrancer* in 1819.

Between 1805 and 1828, the Hackney Phalanx dominated the episcopal bench, archdeaconries, royal chaplaincies and Oxbridge collegiate headships. The Archbishop of Canterbury from 1808–28, Charles Manners-Sutton, was linked with the Phalanx; around him was grouped the 'Canterbury party' of High Church dignitaries – the archetypal 'Zs' of Tractarian parlance.[6] Hackney dominance

---

[3] J. Priestley to T. Lindsey, 22 January 1790, in J. T. Rutt, ed., *Theological and Miscellaneous Works of Joseph Priestley* (London, 1832), pp. 50–1.

[4] Mather, *Horsley*, pp. 215–16. For a list of early contributors to the *Anti-Jacobin Review*, see E. L. de Monthuzon, *The Anti-Jacobins, 1798–1800: the Early Contributors to the 'Anti-Jacobin Review'* (London, 1988). Sack, *From Jacobite to Conservative*, ch. 1.

[5] S. Rivington, *The Publishing House of Rivington* (London, 1919). See also, J. L. Althoz, *The Religious Press in Britain, 1760–1900* (New York, 1989), ch. 4. L. N. Crumb, 'Publishing the Oxford Movement: Francis Rivington's letters to Newman', *Publishing History*, 28 (1990), 5–53.

[6] W. N. Molesworth, *History of the Church of England from 1660* (London, 1882), p. 317.

reached an apogee under the administration of Lord Liverpool in 1815–27, when ecclesiastical appointments appeared to be largely in the hands of one of the Hackney Phalanx leaders, Henry Handley Norris, popularly known as the 'Bishop maker'. Some Evangelicals were also given preferment to the bench at this time, though some recently so designated such as John Kaye and George Murray were in fact Phalanx High Churchmen.[7]

As Corsi's evidence of Hackney *rapprochement* with the *Noetics* and Waterman's of an Orthodox–latitudinarian axis at Cambridge suggests, the theological party character of pre-Tractarian High Churchmanship remained indistinct.[8] Hackney identity was always as much cultural and social as strictly ideological. R. D. Hampden, the Oxford liberal bogey figure of the Tractarians in the 1830s, not only edited the Orthodox journal the *Christian Remembrancer* in the early 1820s, but was also a curate to Norris at Hackney. Corsi's identification of the later liberal, Baden Powell, as the author of several articles in the Hackney-run *British Critic* as well as *Christian Remembrancer* between 1823 and 1826, is also significant.[9]

Theological consensus in pre-Tractarian Anglicanism owed something to the diversity and eclecticism of Orthodox Churchmanship in the period. The primacy of the challenge from Dissent ensured that alliances could be forged without regard to theological unanimity. From a later Tractarian perspective, this appeared a sign of weakness rather than strength. Newman's perception of such apparent weakness set him on his own confrontational course with those whom he regarded as exponents of theological liberalism. But it also set him on the path of collision with those representatives of older High Churchmanship whom he felt were wedded to what he called 'cold Arminian doctrine' and had become either too compromising or too worldly to be regarded as heirs of his own image of seventeenth-century Anglicanism; an image which we have shown to have been not entirely in accord with reality.[10]

The overlap between church parties renders precise numerical quantification of grass-roots support for pre-Tractarian High Churchmanship very difficult. Some estimates for the 1790s as 'no

[7] W. Gibson, 'The Tories and Church Patronage, 1812–30', *JEH*, 41 (April, 1990), 269.
[8] Corsi, *Baden Powell*, chs. 1 and 2; Waterman, 'A Cambridge Via Media', 429–36.
[9] Corsi, *Baden Powell*, p. 22.
[10] Weatherby, 'The Encircling Gloom: Newman's Departure from the Caroline tradition', 58.

more than one hundred in all',[11] can be regarded as suspect. Yet
clerical rhetoric did not always match parochial reality. A silent
majority may have belonged to no particular sub-group in the
Church. Particular pressure-groups were not necessarily representative of the mainstream. Even Edward Churton, who was always
urging his Tractarian friends to emphasise the 'standing witness' of
the Hutchinsonian divines in the late-Georgian era, could admit: 'I
do not at all mean to say that or suppose that Bishop Horne and
Jones of Nayland and their friends were in the majority in the latter
half of the eighteenth century.'[12] But for a moderate High Churchmanship, stiff against Dissent and Calvinism and 'High' in the sense
of 'High for the Church of England' rather than as denoting adherence to full-blown sacramental teaching, support was considerable.
One indication is provided by the circulation figures for the mildly
High Church *British Critic* at the end of the 1790s, which amounted
to three thousand.[13]

If there was a blurring of theological differences between High
Church and liberal churchmen in the 1820s, this can partly be
explained by recognising that such *Noetics* as Baden Powell and
Hampden were not then the obvious theological liberals that Tractarian rhetoric depicted them as in the 1830s. Polarisation may have
taken place in the 1830s, destroying an earlier theological consensus,
but this was not a one-sided process. For if the future Tractarians
moved in one direction after the cathartic experience of the Peel
election in 1829, some *Noetics* moved no less far in the liberal direction.[14] By the end of the 1820s, the Orthodox had shed earlier
illusions about the character of *Noeticism*.[15] It was a growing perception of the threat from this quarter as well as from Dissent,
combined with a consciousness of their own weakness and intellectual vulnerability, that made the Orthodox welcome new and
younger allies. Disorganised in the wake of the loss of former political influence in 1828–30, the Hackney Phalanx found in the
Oxford zealots the prospect of much-needed energy to revitalise the

11 Murray, 'The Influence of the French Revolution on the Church of England', p. 4; Braine,
'Life and Writings of Herbert Marsh', p. 4n. Murray (p. 51) restricts numbers of High
Churchmen in *c.* 1800 almost exclusively to her own estimate of the fifty to one hundred
laymen and clergymen connected with the Hackney Phalanx.
12 PH, Churton Papers, CHUR 2/4/98, E. Churton to R. I. Wilberforce, 19 July 1854.
13 Mather, *Horsley*, p. 213.
14 Nockles, 'An Academic Counter-Revolution', 149.
15 Bodl. Lib, Norris Papers, Ms Eng Lett c. 789, fols. 200–1, J. H. Spry to H. H. Norris, 10
December 1829.

High Church cause. Thus, it was the Oriel *Noetics* and not future Tractarians to whom the Hackney divine Archdeacon Pott was referring when he complained in 1830 of the threat posed by 'a set of conceited dogmatising Oxonians who are reaching very singular notions ... when they should give us ... support'.[16] In contrast, Tractarian Oxford represented 'new wine' for 'old bottles'. In short, the rise of Tractarianism was in the context of the decline of Hackney.

SUPPORT, CO-OPERATION AND THE SEEDS OF DISUNION, 1833–7

Hugh James Rose was the 'Z' most supportive of the early Tractarians. Under his editorship, the *British Magazine* in 1832–6 carried several influential articles from the pens of Froude and Newman. Other High Church organs such as the *Christian Remembrancer* were more cautious, but even the latter in 1836 could hail the *Tracts for the Times* and allied publications 'as almost forming a new era in the Church – an era of the revival and renovation of the principles of her earlier and better days'.[17] As long as the external challenge from Dissent remained potent, not only Protestant High Churchmen but conservative Evangelicals welcomed the articulate advocacy of the Church's interests from the young Oxford divines. Manifestations of the danger from Dissent and Whig Latitudinarianism within Oxford itself in the mid-1830s strengthened this trend. The attempt to subvert the confessional nature of the university by the proposed admission of Dissenters in 1834–5, and the affront presented by the Whig government's appointment of Hampden as Regius Professor of Divinity in 1836, helped solidify a 'triple alliance' of Protestant High Churchmen, Tractarians and Evangelicals in defence of Church and University.[18]

The early Tracts struck a chord with the country clergy, to whom they were primarily directed. All who in the context of the challenge of Dissent and Whig ecclesiastical reform in the early 1830s felt conservatively disposed in religion and politics, rallied to the Tractarian standard. As a writer in the *Christian Remembrancer* in 1841 recalled,

16 Bodl. Lib, Norris Papers, Ms Eng Lett c. 790,. fol. 2, J. H. Pott to H. H. Norris, 6 January 1830.
17 *Christian Remembrancer*, 18 (November, 1836), 645.
18 For further discussion of this theme, see Nockles, 'The Great Disruption: The University and the Oxford Movement, 1829–54' (forthcoming).

we apprehend that with the earlier numbers of that series [*Tracts for the Times*] the great mass of the clergy fully agreed. They were glad to find men bold enough to advance opinions which they themselves had always implicitly received, and able to vindicate them against their common adversaries. They witnessed the total and invincible overthrow of the dissenting party in the church ... In the very moment when they were calling upon the church to abandon her established principles, at this very moment arose a company of men, strong in knowledge, faith and self-denial, who proved, in a manner which could not be questioned, that those truths instead of being abandoned, needed only to be acted upon; that what we needed was not a new reformation, but a return to the old one'.[19]

Tractarian *élan* harnessed to the restatement of old truths enshrined in the Church's formularies seemed an irresistible combination. The expectation was that the Tractarians would harmonise, if not merge their identity, with the 'established orthodoxy of the land, and not only harmonise with it, but materially strengthen its cause, and enlarge the sphere of its knowledge and usefulness'.[20]

Disillusionment only slowly set in. The year of Newman's classic statement of the *via media*, 1837, probably represented the high-water mark of the alliance between old High Churchmen and Tractarians. Misgivings and suspicions had eased over the preceding four years. For all Rose's strongly expressed private unease, outward relations had never been better. High Church reception of Newman's *Prophetical Office* was surprisingly favourable, given Rose's private doubts and the later identification of seeds of theological error. The work was deemed to have allayed earlier fears.[21] Moreover, the long-standing grounds of antipathy between Orthodox and Evangelicals on some issues ensured that, when the *Record* and *Christian Observer* began to assail the Tractarians, this was taken as a very healthy omen by old High Churchmen.[22]

Old High Church hopes would not be fulfilled, because the Tractarians had their own theological agenda. The latent differences of *ethos* between the two sides were well represented by the contrasting personalities of the provocative Froude and the

[19] *Christian Remembrancer*, New Series, 1 (April, 1841), 425–6. See Bishop Bethell's admission: 'In the early stages ... there were, I believe, few members of our church, of moderate views, and attached to no party interest, who did not look with some degree of favour on these writings [i.e. the *Tracts for the Times*].' Bethell, *Charge to the Clergy of the Diocese of Bangor ... 1843*, pp. 15–16.
[20] *British Critic*, 21 (April, 1837), 496.   [21] *Christian Remembrancer*, 19 (June, 1837), 330.
[22] *Church of England Quarterly Review*, 2 (July, 1837), 169. As late as the summer of 1835, sales of the *Tracts for the Times* were limited. By 1836, however, sales were great and Francis Rivington could scarcely keep up with demand. Crumb, 'Publishing the Oxford Movement'.

cautious Palmer of Worcester. As William Copeland observed, 'it is extremely important to keep the movement, which was from within, as clear as possible from the external circumstances, with which it came into contact'.[23] In short, the 'Apostolicals' were not prepared merely to react to events in a defensive posture. Froude relished the soubriquet of 'conspirator'. The defence of the church in 1833–5 was but the start of a counter-revolution. Whereas for Froude and Newman, a 'living idea had got hold of their minds' and they 'did not quite know whither it would ultimately lead them', 'Zs' like Palmer were not concerned with 'the speculative questions "whence" and "whither"'.[24] The objectives of the 'Zs' were as definite as they were limited.

Newman's early alliance with Palmer, from which Froude weaned him, was tactical. Palmer's proposals for a committee of revision clashed with Newman's 'principle of personality' and contempt for boards 'of safe, sound, sensible men',[25] and were successfully resisted. The Tractarians were never prepared to act merely as the mouthpiece of Hackney among the rising Oxford generation, in the way that even Edward Churton hoped. Behind the outward unanimity which episodes such as the Hampden controversy confirmed, an underlying tension emerged. As Copeland recalled, 'London thought Oxford too eager and hasty: Oxford fancied London too shy and timid, and most interesting it was to see how both felt about matters.'[26] Hackney still hoped to be able to control the Oxford men. Therefore, during the massed rally at Oxford of Orthodox clergy from London and the country to vote against Hampden in May 1836, an opportunity for a closer scrutiny of the Movement's followers was taken. The impressions formed were not entirely favourable. Such clergy, according to Thomas Mozley, 'found Newman in companionship with free spoken men who might wreck a cause in a day'. J. H. Spry of Oriel was deputed by Hackney 'to arrange matters with the university' so that 'the larger body [the metropolis] was not to be hastily compromised by the impulses or caprices of the smaller [Oxford]'. Such efforts were in vain. It was clear that for Spry, Newman was not 'a safe person'; but Hackney had lost the initiative and was no longer in a position to dictate terms.[27]

23 KCA, Keble Papers, W. J. Copeland to the Warden of Keble [E. Talbot], 22 September 1879.
24 Ward, *William George Ward and the Oxford Movement*, p. 53.
25 Newman, *Apologia*, p. 109.
26 PH, Ollard Papers, W. J. Copeland to T. Bowdler, 6 December 1841 (copy).
27 Mozley, *Reminiscences Chiefly of Oriel College and the Oxford Movement*, vol. I, pp. 387–8.

The disavowal of party spirit by the Orthodox[28] may often have been a self-serving rhetorical device. Yet the Orthodox complaint that the Tractarians were disturbers of the peace and divisive, was not without substance. For Archdeacon Sinclair, Tractarian partisanship was 'the natural effect ... of exclusive intercourse' and 'sodalities'.[29] A party line in the manner against which Whately had warned in 1822 was engendered.[30]

RETREAT OF THE HACKNEY PHALANX; THE *BRITISH CRITIC* AND A TRACTARIAN COUP D'ÉTAT, 1837–8

It was a measure of Hackney weakness, as it had been of the *British Critic*'s founder Jones of Nayland in the 1790s, that its leaders often were unable to impose their theological stamp on the review.[31] It was dislike of the tone of several articles under the editorship of Archibald Campbell and James Shergold Boone between 1829 and 1836, that prompted Norris and Edward Churton to invite Newman and his Oxford friends to contribute.[32] Such an arrangement seemed suited to raising the overall tone of the review above the mild liberalism espoused by Boone, while at the same time keeping the Tract writers under some control.

By 1837, Tractarian dissatisfaction with Boone was such that, to

[28] The following avowal of non-partisanship is characteristic: 'As true churchmen ... we thoroughly dislike parties as parties, and schools as schools ... Our chief quarrel, indeed, with the Evangelical party is its disposition to erect itself into a school or sect ... For ourselves, we fairly avow, our object is to consolidate and cement the old orthodox party – but no, a party we will not call it – the old orthodox body of the Church of England.' *British Critic*, 19 (April, 1836), 429.

[29] J. Sinclair, *Church Difficulties of 1851. A Charge Delivered to the Clergy of the Archdeaconry of Middlesex* (London, 1851), p. 11. See also Edward Churton's angry private objection to Pusey's reference to his [Churton's] 'school': 'God forbid ... that we should have any school or wish to form one. If we can but serve God as faithful sons of the English branch of the Church Catholic, let our names perish rather than be remembered as the founders of any school.' PH, Gresley Papers, GRES 3/7/44, E. Churton to W. Gresley, 22 February 1843. Churton later maintained: 'All went wrong at Oxford from the time that the leaders began to form a party.' PH, Gresley Papers, GRES 3/7/81, E. Churton to W. Gresley, 20 July 1847.

[30] R. Whately, *The Use and Abuse of Party-Feeling in Matters of Religion Considered in Eight Sermons Preached before the University of Oxford in the Year MDCCCXXII, at the Lecture Founded by the Late Rev. John Bampton, M.A.* (Oxford, 1822), especially Lecture II.

[31] *Review of the Review of a New Preface to the Second Edition of Mr Jones's Life of Bishop Horne, in the 'British Critic' for February 1800* (London, 1800), pp. 17–23; Carter, *Undercurrents of Church Life in the Eighteenth Century*, p. 216.

[32] PH, 'British Critic Papers' [1836–43], E. Churton to J. H. Newman, 17 November 1837. For an account of Campbell's editorship, see E. R. Houghton, 'A *New* Editor of the *British Critic*', *Victorian Periodicals Review*, 12, No. 3 (Fall, 1979), 102–4. James Shergold Boone (1799–1859). Incumbent of St John's, Paddington. *DNB*.

the dismay of the Hackney leaders, they threatened to pull out altogether unless they could be allowed completely to take over the journal. In alarm, the 'Zs' pressed the merits of Archbishop Howley's librarian, S. R. Maitland, a High Churchman but not identified with the Tract writers, as Hackney's preference for a new editor. As Rose explained to Newman,

You know his [views] go very far with yours. It appears to me too that as matter of policy, it is better for your friends to state their opinions in a journal not ostensibly their mere party organ, as they will thus reach quarters which otherwise could not see them. As soon as a work is a declared organ of certain opinions, its influence becomes exactly proportionate to the influence of those opinions, but it is not carried forth by ... aid ... from any other quarter.[33]

Newman consulted Pusey. Pusey's advice accorded with what Newman wanted to hear. Disappointed with Rose's line, Pusey told Newman that he wanted him 'to have an organ of your own'. He pressed the claims of Manning as editor, since he liked 'Manning's ethos much better than Maitland's'. The message was that the exclusivity and independence of the Movement was paramount. The conclusive point was that 'Maitland does not altogether go along with us, although he would do nothing against us.'[34]

The Hackney elders were exasperated. Norris complained that Newman and his friends were 'making distinctions amongst those who though not up to Oxford proof are still sound upon church principles'.[35] Yet Hackney did not wish entirely to forfeit Oxford support. Edward Churton began his long-term role as mediator between the two sides. As Churton later recalled to Copeland, 'I was often writing one thing to you at Oxford, and by the same post perhaps, defended you to good Mr Norris and Joshua Watson.'[36] Thus, on the one hand, Churton insisted to Norris, 'I feel more and more every day that the cause of truth and of the Church is most deeply indebted to these good men at Oxford, who have with most generous imprudence, thrown themselves into the breach, and are bearing the brunt of all the obloquy which is hurled against us.'[37]

[33] *Ibid.*, H. J. Rose to J. H. Newman, 18 December 1837; H. J. Rose to W. F. Hook, 18 December 1837, Stephens, *Life and Letters of Walter Farquhar Hook*, vol. I, p. 414.
[34] PH, '*British Critic* Papers', E. B. Pusey to J. H. Newman, December 1837.
[35] Bodl. Lib, Norris Papers, Ms Eng Lett c. 790, fol. 75, H. H. Norris to J. Watson, 12 January 1838.
[36] SC, Churton Papers, E. Churton to W. J. Copeland, 28 February 1860.
[37] *Ibid.*, E. Churton to H. H. Norris, 7 December 1837.

On the other hand, Churton struck a different note when pleading with Newman that he use his influence with his friends,

that they will not combine against the good old men who really have done something for right principles in their day, and who I know, will engage no editor who will not be ready to avail himself of your assistance and be proud of your support. Let us not have anything that looks like a spirit of separation, especially from those who are in heart and mind one with you.[38]

Newman proved resistant to such blandishments. In a subsequent letter, Churton expressed dismay that 'your friends ... should have so little confidence in Mr Watson's fidelity and zeal (the world will never know half the good he has done, or half the evil he has prevented) and in his feelings towards the defenders of Catholicity at Oxford ... if he is not up to your high water mark, I fear I shall never be'.[39]

Churton's pressure ensured that Maitland took over the *British Critic*, but he resigned after a few months. The Tract writers now staged a *coup* and won exclusive control of the journal in early 1838. They immediately infused the *British Critic* with their own distinctive party line and *ethos*. Moderation was jettisoned. Newman explained the Tractarian agenda in a revealing letter:

We want a Review conducted, i.e. morally conducted, on the Catholic temper – we want all subjects treated on one and the same principle or basis – not the contributors of a board of men, who do not know each other, pared down into harmony by an external editor, but our editor must be the principle, the internal idea of Catholicism itself, pouring itself outwardly, not trimming and shaping from without.

He concluded with a hit at the Hackney ideal, insisting that 'all great things are done by concentration and individuality. We have been ruined by coalitions – if we are saved, it must be by God's single instruments.'[40]

Newman's application of this principle as editor of the *British Critic* proved divisive. Samuel Wilberforce, who had been as unhappy as Newman with Boone's editorship, had his offer of a contribution coldly rejected on the grounds of his having publicly criticised Pusey's views on post-baptismal sin. Newman informed

[38] PH, '*British Critic* papers', E. Churton to J. H. Newman, 17 November 1837.
[39] *Ibid.*, E. Churton to J. H. Newman, 28 November 1837.
[40] *Ibid.*, J. H. Newman to E. Churton, 21 November 1837.

Wilberforce, 'I am not confident enough in your general approval of the body of opinions which Pusey and myself hold, to consider it advisable that we should cooperate very closely.'[41] Newman's note in his own hand attached to his copy of Wilberforce's offer of support confirms the ground of rejection: – 'July 8, 1838. answered that he differed from Pusey and me too much to co-operate. If his opposition in the University pulpit was unintentional, still more hopeless was cooperation in the Review'.[42] Wilberforce had cause to complain of this as 'another mark of party spirit'.[43]

Newman allowed one Phalanx High Churchman, Charles Le Bas, to continue to contribute, but his was the exception which proved the new rule. Certainly, the retention of Le Bas scarcely warranted Newman's later claim in a note, dated 1875, attached to a letter of 1839, in which he stated that this proved, 'that, in spite of my want of sympathy with Le Bas's view of things, I still urged him, as being one of the old high and dry staff of the "British Critic" (whom I wished to retain) to write in it'.[44] However, other old High Church contributors could not accept Newman's rigid editorial conditions, and Churton refused to contribute after the spring of 1839.

While on most occasions the Tractarians distanced themselves from the Hackney cause, sometimes Tractarian rhetoric flattered the Phalanx. For example, in 1839 Pusey defended the Movement by sheltering behind Watson's good name. He gloried in being recognized by Watson 'as carrying on the same torch which we had received from yourself, and those of your generation.'[45] In his *Letter to the Archbishop of Canterbury* in 1842, Pusey was still more abject in his flattery of Hackney, but he had a purpose in doing so. Pusey had been informed of Thomas Sikes's prophecy, in Hackney rectory in about 1833, that once the cardinal doctrine of the one Holy Catholic Church had been revived, there would 'be one great outcry of

---

[41] J. H. Newman to S. Wilberforce, 18 July 1838, *Letters and Diaries*, vol. VI, pp. 267–8.

[42] PH, '*British Critic* Papers', J. H. Newman, 18 July 1838; J. H. Newman to S. Wilberforce, 18 July 1838, in A. R. Ashwell, ed., *Life of the Rt. Rev. Samuel Wilberforce* (London, 1880), vol. I, p. 125. See Newman's later comment: 'I think Samuel Wilberforce redeemed his early career by his later; but he had a great deal to redeem.' PH, Pusey Papers, LBV [Transcripts], J. H. Newman to W. J. Copeland, 30 December 1879.

[43] S. Wilberforce to C. Anderson, 31 August 1838, Ashwell, ed., *Life of Samuel Wilberforce*, vol. I, p. 128; PH, '*British Critic* Papers', S. Wilberforce to J. H. Newman, 19 July 1838.

[44] PH, '*British Critic* Papers', note in Newman's hand on copy of letter to C. Le Bas to J. H. Newman, 25 February 1839.

[45] PH, Pusey papers, LBV [Originals], E. B. Pusey to J. Watson, 30 October 1839; PH, Pusey Papers, LBV [Transcripts], E. B. Pusey to J. H. Newman, 11 September 1839.

Popery from one end of the country to the other'. In his *Letter* Pusey turned this prophecy to Tractarian advantage by identifying all opposition to the Movement as an illegitimate outcry against 'catholicity'.[46] This use of Sikes's prophecy became part of later Tractarian historiography.[47] The indignant repudiation, however, by contemporary old High Churchmen of 'the memory of the late excellent Mr Sikes' being 'very improperly used by Dr Pusey'[48] has been overlooked. Both Norris and Watson felt that Sikes's words as quoted did not support the sense which Pusey made of them, while Sikes's widow found no record of such a prediction having been made.[49]

A PARTING OF THE WAYS AND WATERSHED OF FROUDE'S *REMAINS* 1838–9

Newman's and Keble's ill-fated publication in 1838 of the private writings and diaries of their revered late friend, Hurrell Froude, marked the opening of a new era of public opposition to the Tractarians from within Old High Churchmanship.

The sternest response to the publication of the *Remains* came from Godfrey Faussett's 1838 *Revival of Popery* sermon. Other old High Churchmen confined their strong expressions of displeasure to private remonstrance. Samuel Wilberforce condemned the 'mischievous delirium of publishing Froude's unguarded thoughts to a morbidly sensitive and unsympathetic age as this. I feel assured that that work has put back church principles for fifty years.'[50] Edward Churton agreed. 'This publication', he wrote, 'has involved us in difficulties, which we ought not to have met with.'[51]

Why did Newman and Keble publish what was almost designed to offend? Keble appears to have been guileless. Edward Churton explained Keble's part by the fact 'that poets must live in a world of their own, and so are incapable of calculating those consequences

---

[46] Pusey, *Letter to His Grace the Archbishop of Canterbury*, pp. 33–5.
[47] See Liddon, *Life of Pusey*, vol. 1, pp. 257–8; Cornish, *English Church in the Nineteenth Century*, vol. 1, p. 66.
[48] Bodl. Lib, Ms Eng Misc. e. 117, fol. 135, E. Churton to J. C. Crosthwaite, 13 April 1842.
[49] PH, Pusey Papers, LBV [Transcripts], H. H. Norris to A. P. Perceval, 28 October 1842. In his biography of Watson, Churton only hinted that Pusey had altered the context of Sikes's prophecy. Churton, *Memoir of Joshua Watson*, vol. 11, p. 30.
[50] Bodl. Lib, Ms Wilberforce d. 38, fol. 130.
[51] PH, Pusey Papers, LBV [Transcripts], E. Churton to A. P. Perceval, 23 February 1839; H. J. Rose to J. Watson, January 1838, Burgon, *Lives of Twelve Good Men*, vol. 1, p. 136.

which are foreseen by prosy people'.[52] Such an excuse did not suffice in Newman's case. Newman knew what he was doing, and calculated the likely consequences. He was quite prepared to alienate the large 'orthodox body' of the Church of England whose early support had proved the Movement's lifeblood, if the Movement's hold over the rising generation at Oxford could thereby be assured. Far from seeking to conciliate or disarm Faussett, he hit back hard. In private, his expression of contempt for the Lady Margaret Professor was unrestrained. Faussett was unflatteringly likened to 'an old piece of ordnance, which can do nothing but fire – or like an old macaw with one speech ... He can do nothing but fire, fire.'[53]

The tone of Faussett's attack did earn Newman some Hackney sympathy, with Churton indulging in his own paraody of 'Il Dottore Falsetto'.[54] Moreover, Newman rightly sensed that, however Froude's self-revelations were received in Hackney rectories, the mixture of romantic historicism, youthful zest and ascetic holiness which those revelations contained, would exert an almost hypnotic appeal on his own younger followers. By publishing the *Remains*, argues Sheridan Gilley, Newman 'was giving orthodoxy the notoriety and excitement of revolution and heresy, and thereby multiplying his followers'.[55] In short, Newman realised that he was in 'hot water', but hoped to 'turn it into steam, and direct it aright'.[56] It was a hope that was not to be fulfilled. Newman might have increased the Movement's appeal among a new constituency, but he had strained the loyalty of the Hackney school to breaking-point.

THE BREACH CONFIRMED: THE HACKNEY PHALANX AND *TRACT 90*

One observer in the early 1840s contended that the Tractarians had 'brought *old High Churchism* to a "complete stand still"'. The original relation between the two was likened to that of patron and client, with the latter, on reaching maturity, casting off its early protector the old High Churchmen, and following its own indepen-

---

[52] SC, Churton Papers, E. Churton to W. J. Copeland, 28 February 1860.
[53] J. H. Newman to Mrs J. Mozley, 5 June 1838, *Letters and Diaries*, vol. VI, p. 254.
[54] E. Churton to J. H. Newman, 18 September 1838, *Ibid.*, p. 324.
[55] Gilley, *Newman and His Age*, p. 165.
[56] Bodl. Lib, Manning Papers, Ms Eng Lett c. 654, fol. 25, J. H. Newman to H. E. Manning, 4 April 1838.

dent career.[57] If Froude's *Remains* had begun the breach, Newman's *Tract 90* made it irrevocable.

Tract 90 seemed designed to appeal to one constituency, Newman's younger followers, at the expense of another, his older, original supporters and would-be guardians. Hackney dismay at *Tract 90* was deep. According to Churton, Joshua Watson 'felt very strongly the wrongfulness of the words in the Introduction to No. 90'.[58] Watson informed Norris that he had told Keble that he was 'a terrible alarmist on the subject of No. 90' and had had to decline Keble's offer of the dedication to him of a pamphlet in defence of that Tract.[59] According to his niece, Mary, Watson 'dared not reason out his fears'. Too many hostages to fortune were being given to the Movement's enemies. As Watson warned, 'the enemy's cry "see what these things will lead to" is harmless until it gains a colour of truth, and it can be said, "see what they do lead to"'.[60]

For Watson, *Tract 90* was the natural product 'of party leaderships, which will ordinarily be little different in a Newman or a Simeon'.[61] Yet if only caution and quiet were observed, Hackney insisted all was still not lost. But it was in vain that Watson urged Keble to refrain from 'heaping fuel on the fire'.[62]

Newman's surrender of effective control of the *British Critic* in 1841 to Thomas Mozley dashed Hackney hopes that the Movement might revert to a more moderate course. Hackney mourned the premature death of Hugh James Rose in 1838 the more deeply because of a well-founded conviction that, had he lived, the subsequent history of the Movement might have been very different. Watson confided to Rose's widow in 1841 that the first number of the new *British Critic* showed how far his 'restraining hand ... is

57 *Letters from Oxford in 1843. By 'Ignotus'* (Dublin, 1843), pp. 24–5.
58 SC, Churton Papers, E. Churton to W. J. Copeland, 28 February 1860.
59 Bodl. Lib, Norris Papers, Ms Eng Lett c. 790, fol. 82, J. Watson to H. H. Norris, 5 April 1841.
60 M. Watson, Ms. 'Reminiscences', fol. 118, 20 August 1843.
61 M. Watson, Ms. 'Reminiscences', fol. 105, 25 February 1843. Churton later made clear that Newman's dedication of a volume of sermons to Watson in 1840 had been an 'unsanctified offering'. Churton, *Memoir of Joshua Watson*, vol. II, p. 142. But Newman's regard for Watson remained high. See Copeland's later comment to Pusey: 'I do not know whether you knew him [i.e. Watson], a man of singularly fine mind and large heart. N[ewman], I remember, was greatly struck with him.' PH, LBV [Originals], W. J. Copeland to E. B. Pusey, 16 March 1855.
62 Bodl. Lib, Norris Papers, Ms Eng Lett c. 790, fol. 82, J. Watson to H. H. Norris, 5 April 1841.

missed, and how likely to be more and more missed every day we lived'. Newman was no longer editor, and technically not answerable for its contents. Yet as Watson remarked, 'the world will not know this, and if it did, would not probably be charitable enough to acquit the master of much responsibility for the excesses of the latter'.[63] Hackney suspicions that the leaders were not inclined to repudiate such excesses had some basis, the elder Christopher Wordsworth informing Watson that though 'Pusey and Keble etc. see many things in their children and pupils which they do not like ... yet they will not lift up a little finger to warn or keep them in check'.[64]

A NEW ERA OF HIGH CHURCH OPPOSITION TO TRACTARIANISM, 1840–3

High Church opposition to Tractarianism assumed a variety of forms. Faussett's outburst in 1838 was not typical of old High Churchmen as a whole. On the contrary, many engaged with Tractarianism in a spirit of constructive criticism that distinguished them from less discriminating assailants.[65] Two organs that represented constructive opposition to the Movement were the *Church of England Quarterly Review*, re-established under a new editor, Henry Christmas, in January 1840, and the *Churchman*, similarly reconstituted in January 1841. Henry Christmas coined the term 'Evangelical High Churchman' or 'True Churchman' to delineate the churchmanship of his journal.[66] Christmas does not appear thereby to have signified a 'High Church Evangelical' though that genus did exist, possible examples being G. S. Faber, William Goode, and C. S. Baird.[67] On the contrary, Christmas consciously wished to reappropriate for High Churchmen a term that the 'Evangelical party' had unfairly monopolised for itself; hence, his use of such phrases as 'the so-called evangelicals' and 'self-styled evangelicals'.

---

63 LPL, Watson Papers, Ms 1562, fol. 67, J. Watson to Mrs Rose, 10 July 1841.
64 M. Watson, Ms. 'Reminiscences', fols. 73–4. C. Wordsworth (Sen.) to J. Watson, 26 September 1842.
65 *Letters from Oxford*, p. 25.
66 For Henry Christmas (1811–68), Librarian of Sion College, London, see *DNB*.
67 G. S. Faber also appropriated the term 'Evangelical High Churchman'. See Faber's avowal to Golightly: 'If I wished to designate our principles, perhaps I could not do it better than by the name of Evangelical High Churchmanship.' LPL, Golightly Papers, Ms 1805, fol. 230, G. S. Faber to C. P. Golightly, 4 March 1841. On Golightly's churchmanship, see Introduction, n. 142.

Christmas defined 'Evangelical High Churchmanship' in terms of the tradition of seventeenth-century Anglican divines, which he insisted was distinct from both Tractarianism and Evangelicalism.[68] Likewise, the *Churchman* described its editorial views as those

of the Church of England – not as expounded by the "Tracts for the Times" – still less, as understood by the Calvinistic divines who still remain in the communion of our Church; but as taught in her own liturgy – as elucidated by Hooker, and Bramhall, and Hammond, and Hall, and Sanderson, and Blackhall, and Comber, and Waterland, and Wheatley, and Mant ... in a word, our views are those of *Evangelical High Churchmen* ... That our views are those of a large majority in the Church we have been long convinced.[69]

The gulf between this theological system and Evangelicalism was confirmed with the claim that even such Tractarian heroes as Andrewes, Robert Nelson and Bishop Wilson were exponents of 'Evangelical High Churchmanship'.[70]

The Tractarians were not unreservedly condemned in this quarter. Commendation and credit were given where they were felt due. As an editorial in the *Church of England Quarterly Review* in 1840 explained,

it must not be imagined that, on the whole, they have done harm ... they have caused sound men to reflect upon matters which they had hitherto forgotten; they have in cases, made those who would have been latitudinarians, *Evangelical High-Churchmen*; and these have spread their own sound views of doctrine and discipline.[71]

It was conceded that for some years, 'the Tracts and their authors were assailed, not by argument, but by declamation and assertions, which evinced only the ignorance and passion of the writers'. It had become necessary to 'remedy the mischief of these injudicious opponents'.[72] The opposition to Tractarianism needed to be conducted on High Church principles. Although as Peter Toon has shown, the list of contributors to the *Churchman* included avowed Evangelicals such as Edward Bickersteth,[73] the editorial line generally made clear that Evangelicalism, even as represented by Goode, was not a natural nor appropriate ally in the opposition to Tractarianism. Even Goode's *Divine Rule of Faith and Practice* (1842), for all its appeal

[68] *Church of England Quarterly Review*, 7 (January, 1840), 7–21.
[69] *Churchman*, 5 (July, 1841), iv.
[70] *Church of England Quarterly Review*, 16 (July, 1844), 47–8.   [71] *Ibid.*, 7 (July, 1840), 124.
[72] *Ibid.*, 12 (July 1842), 223.   [73] Toon, *Evangelical Theology*, pp. 42–3.

to patristic and seventeenth-century sources, was criticised as defective by the self-styled Evangelical High Churchmen. For as one contributor explained.

a Low Churchman is not a fair match for the writers of the Tracts; he does not come up to their mark – he has not weapons of the same power – he scarcely comes within arm's length of them. And a Low Churchman does really often misapprehend their point, and so is generally greatly undervalued, if not despised by them, and fails to do them good.[74]

Evangelical High Churchmen welcomed the Evangelical-inspired publications of the Parker Society, expecting that, by reprinting the English Reformers' works, it would serve as much as an antidote to modern Evangelicalism as to Tractarianism. Evangelicals were denounced by High Churchmen for 'perjury' in their failure to teach the doctrines of absolution and baptismal regeneration enshrined in the Book of Common Prayer to which they had given, 'hearty and unfeigned assent'. It was hoped that the *Parker Society* publications, by illuminating the true opinions of the Reformers on these questions, would reveal the extent of such 'perjury'.[75] In short, it cannot be said that such High Churchmen opposed Tractarianism in a pan-Protestant eirenical spirit of accommodation with their traditional opponents, the Evangelicals.

THE YOUNGER 'ZS' OR 'CHURCH PRINCIPLES' PARTY AND THE TRACTARIANS, 1841–4

Younger traditional High Churchmen such as Hook, Palmer of Worcester, Churton, Sewell and Jelf, remained more reluctant than their Hackney elders to break with the Tractarians. Their aim was to preserve 'church principles' from the fury of the rising anti-Tractarian reaction in the Church. They wished 'to use the drag-chain, not to attempt to stop the movement' or to act in 'downright opposition'. They resorted to similar propaganda and organisational techniques to those used by the Tractarian leaders, setting up literary ventures such as the *Englishman's Library* as a medium for the dissemination of 'Reformed Catholic' views.[76]

This group attracted as much popular opprobrium from

---

[74] *Church of England Quarterly Review*, 11 (April, 1842), 363.
[75] *Ibid.*, 12–13. See also strictures on those 'whose Christianity consists in Pusey-phobia, and whose churchmanship may be defined as a sabbath attendance upon some favourite divine'. *Church of England Quarterly Review*, 7 (July, 1840), 23.
[76] Bodl. Lib, Ms Eng Misc. e. 117, fol. 137. E. Churton to J. C. Crosthwaite, 21 April 1842.

Evangelical and other anti-Tractarian quarters as the Oxford leaders themselves. One contemporary described them as 'endeavouring the most difficult of all positions, that on the side of a steep hill, half way between the inert torpidity of the old high churchmen at the top, and the startling activity with which their more forward friends are "developing Romish tendencies" below them'.[77] Edward Goulburn was no kinder, complaining that their 'object seems to be to put Newmanism in a popular view, to soften its excrescences ... really holding Newmanistic principles, only not liking to act them out to their extreme results ... they deck themselves out in a sheeps-clothing of moderation, Conservatism etc. etc. and in this garb, plead the cause of the Tracts'.[78] Such critics implied a closer ideological affinity between the two than was merited; but the 'church principles' party did adopt a tactical position which rendered it vulnerable in the theological climate of the early 1840s.

The tendency of this party to give the Tractarian leaders the benefit of the doubt was exemplified in the *Tract 90* controversy. Palmer of Worcester's personal ties with Newman led him, in contrast with the Hackney elders, to defend *Tract 90* as 'the most valuable of the series of Tracts that has come under my observation'.[79] There is strong evidence, overlooked by Adams, to suggest that this expression of agreement was designed to placate Newman and confirm his Anglican allegiance.[80] As shown above, Palmer's letter did not accurately represent his real theological estimate of *Tract 90*. For Edward Churton made clear to Perceval that privately, Palmer 'condemns No. 90, as Mr Joshua Watson and all good men of my acquaintance do'.[81] Likewise, Hook admitted that he 'had intended to answer *Tract 90* and had begun to do so, but I would not attack my friends when they had fallen'.[82]

---

77 *Letters from Oxford*, p. 27.
78 LPL, Golightly Papers, Ms 1806, fols. 175–6, E. M. Gouburn to C. P. Golightly, April 1842.
79 PH, Pusey Papers, LBV [Transcripts], W. Palmer [of Worcester] to J. H. Newman, 9 August 1841.
80 According to James Mozley, 'Palmer sent this letter quite spontaneously, and it does him great credit, especially as he and Newman were rather on cool terms some time ago.' J. B. Mozley to A. Mozley, 13 March 1841, *Letters of J. B. Mozley*, p. 113. Cf. W. S. Adams, 'William Palmer's *Narrative of Events*', pp. 87–9. Owen Chadwick takes Palmer of Worcester's cordial reception of the Tract too much at face value. See O. Chadwick, 'The Mind of the Oxford Movement', *The Spirit of the Oxford Movement*, pp. 43–5.
81 PH, Pusey Papers, LBV [Transcripts], E. Churton to A. P. Perceval, 20 December 1841.
82 Birmingham Oratory, Newman Papers, 'Tract 90 Correspondence', W. F. Hook to W. G. Ward, 20 March 1841. See also Hook's comment to Newman: 'if these were fitting times of peace I should have a little quarrel with you for some things in Tract 90'. *Ibid.*, W. F. Hook

In order to prevent the opposition to *Tract 90* from discrediting 'church principles', a declaration in favour of 'Reformed Catholic principles', was drawn up, while renunciation was made of 'those ulterior views of which suspicions have been raised'.[83] The Hackney elders criticised this action as an unfortunate 'demonstration of warm feeling', a 'running ahead of judgment'. For J. H. Spry, the episode showed 'how desirable it is that cooler and older heads, worn on the shoulders of persons a little removed from the heat and turmoil of the conflict, should interpose, and prevent hasty though well-intentioned measures'.[84]

As late as 1843, Palmer's concern to shield and defend the Tractarian leaders remained evident. While the Hackney elders condemned Pusey's Oxford sermon on the eucharist, Palmer took a different line, insisting that the Heads of Houses had exceeded their powers. With characteristic generosity, rarely reciprocated by his Tractarian friends, Palmer identified himself with Pusey, assuring him, 'I should think you can have little doubt that I like your sermon and that I feel surprise at the sentence. If you deserve such a sentence, I deserve one much more severe.'[85]

The realisation of the logic of Tractarian theological developments proved a bitter blow for Palmer. He confided to Hook,

the world mixes us and our principles entirely with the ultra men ... And what must be the result? I do not speak of individual sufferings, for that is nothing – but of the result to the church at large. Does it not tend to the revival of Puritanism, to the destruction of Church Principles, to the expulsion of them from the church and from our formularies?[86]

Palmer admitted that he had been blinded to the reality and extent of the Romeward drift in the Movement. 'It was with horror', he told Perceval, 'that I found the danger impending over us. I had no

to J. H. Newman, 17 March 1841. Hook later remarked to Gladstone: 'I do not wish to act unkindly by the good men at Oxford. I sacrificed my own character rather than give them up on the publication of Tract 90.' W. F. Hook to W. E. Gladstone, 15 December 1841, Stephens, *Life and Letters of Walter Farquhar Hook*, vol. II, p. 136.

83   DCL, Thorp Papers, No. 363, E. Churton to C. Thorp, 19 March 1841; *ibid.*, No. 364, C. Thorp to E. Churton, 20 March 1841; PH, Gresley Papers, GRES 3/7/29, E. Churton to W. Gresley, 19 March 1841.

84   PH, Bagot Papers [Transcripts] ['A Collection of Letters bearing on the Oxford Movement, and especially on Bishop Bagot's Connexion with it'], J. H. Spry to Bp R. Bagot, 7 April 1841.

85   PH, Pusey Papers, LBV [Transcripts], W. Palmer [of Worcester] to E. B. Pusey, n. d.

86   W. Palmer to W. F. Hook, August 1843, Stephens, *Life and Letters of Walter Farquhar Hook*, vol. II, pp. 106–7; BL, Gladstone Papers, Ms Add 44360, fols. 299–301, W. Palmer to W. E. Gladstone, 9 November 1843.

conception that men who had been disciples of Newman and Pusey etc. were really unsettled in their views.'[87] Palmer could keep silent no longer. Thus, his *Narrative of Events Connected with the Publication of the "Tracts for the Times"* (1843), sought to draw a clear 'line between sound church principles and Ultra & Romanising views'.[88]

To the dismay of other old High Churchmen, Palmer still refused to pass censure on the Tracts themselves or to include Newman and Pusey in his censure of 'Ultra' views. This same ambivalent attitude even coloured his editorial policy for the *English Review*, a new periodical which he founded after the demise of the *British Critic*. With continued loyalty to his old friends, Palmer insisted that 'unless the Review can take something of a party line – unless it can distinctly take its side and defend Newman – it will not give satisfaction to the large body of men who are under his influence, and amongst whom are many whom I should delight to see contributing to the Review'.[89] Palmer opposed Hackney attempts by Bishop Kaye and J. H. Spry to give the review a too harshly anti-Tractarian tone. As he told Gladstone, 'nothing could be more injurious in every respect than to let' it 'fall into the hands of the High Church party of 20 years ago'.[90]

Palmer's generosity was respected even by some Evangelicals who disagreed with his policy of conciliation. Thus, the Evangelical Francis Close later conceded that noble intentions had prompted Palmer's early connection with the Tract writers. Close merely concluded that 'it would have been happy for the world and for the Church of England if Mr Palmer had taken somewhat less than seven years to satisfy himself of the dangerous tenets of his fellow-workers, and to expose them'.[91] As Bishop Kaye pointed out, however, since the publication of Palmer's *Narrative*, Newman had 'done all he can to show' that the 'line of separation' between himself 'and his more ardent followers' drawn by Palmer, no longer existed.[92] It was widely felt, as William Bricknell put it, that Palmer

87 PH, Pusey Papers, LBV [Transcripts], W. Palmer to A. P. Perceval, 3 August 1843.
88 PH, Gresley Papers, GRES 3/40/6, W. Palmer to W. Gresley, 15 September 1843.
89 BL, Gladstone Papers, Ms Add 44361, fol. 127, W. Palmer to W. E. Gladstone, 21 May 1844.
90 BL, Gladstone Papers, Ms Add 44360, fol. 318, W. Palmer to W. E. Gladstone, 21 November 1843. Churton took a similar view – PH, Gresley Papers, GRES 3/7/84, E. Churton to W. Gresley, 16 September 1847; see [Conybeare], 'Church Parties', 338.
91 F. Close, *The Footsteps of Error Traced through a Period of Twenty-Five Years; or Superstition the Parent of Modern Doubt* (London, 1863), p. 6.
92 LPL, Golightly Papers, Ms 1808, fol. 17, Bp J. Kaye to C. P. Golightly, 20 February 1844.

had 'been more successful in reprobating the "British Critic" and excusing himself, than in vindicating the leaders of the Tract school'.[93] For G. S. Faber, Palmer's failure was 'a somewhat chivalrous patronage of Newman, who will be as great a burden to any determined excuser as the old man of the sea was to Sinbad the Sailor.'[94]

THE DIVIDED MANTLE OF HUGH JAMES ROSE, 1839–43

Palmer's *Narrative* can be regarded as the first documentary record of the Oxford Movement.[95] Yet the controversial background to the work ensured that, like Newman's *Apologia*, it was as much personal self-justification as objective history.

Palmer's *Narrative* brought to the surface a latent divergence in interpretation of the Movement between 'Zs' and 'Apostolicals'. The work did not receive, as has been suggested, 'a chorus of approval by all save the party against which it was directed'.[96] On the contrary, many 'Zs' distanced themselves from Palmer's version of events. Edward Churton later referred disparagingly to 'William Palmer's hasty and egotistical *Narrative*',[97] and in his own account emphasised that he had not done as William Palmer, i.e. written 'on the first spur of the moment, as if I was over-anxious about any consequence to myself'.[98]

The Hackney elders disputed Palmer's portrayal of unanimity between old High Churchmen and the Tract writers in the 1830s. Joshua Watson privately faulted the *Narrative* because he 'thought it claimed to an unjustifiable degree to represent the opinions of others, and he [Watson] was especially jealous for the name of Hugh James Rose'. Watson felt that Palmer overlooked the gulf between Rose and Newman as revealed in their private correspondence in 1836–8, about which Palmer must have been aware.[99] Watson's concern was fuelled by his knowledge that Palmer's friend, John Miller of Worcester College, was preparing a biography of Rose. During the last four years of his life, Rose had corresponded regularly with Miller. Miller hoped to make use of these letters in which

[93] *Ibid.*, Ms 1805, fols. 87–8, W. S. Bricknell to C. P. Golightly, 9 November 1843.
[94] *Ibid.*, Ms 1805, fol. 255, G. S. Faber to C. P. Golightly, 14 November 1843.
[95] Adams, 'William Palmer's *Narrative of Events*', p. 99.   [96] *Ibid.*, p. 98.
[97] SC, Churton Papers, E. Churton to W. J. Copeland, 28 May 1860.
[98] *Ibid.*   [99] M. Watson, Ms 'Reminiscences', fol. 126, 16 November 1843.

Rose was reputed to have been unsparing in his criticisms of the Tractarian leaders. According to Burgon the letters contradicted the picture of old High Church and Tractarian harmony painted by Palmer.[100]

The Tractarians put a different historical gloss on the first ten years of the Movement from that of either Watson or Palmer. While ascribing the Catholic Revival to their own exertions, the Tractarians could enhance their respectability by claiming Rose as their patron. In the early days of the Movement, there was truth in this. The fact that the Tractarians themselves had concluded that Rose 'has not the firmness for these times' and had distanced themselves from him,[101] was now explained away. Tractarian rehabilitation of Rose commenced in the wake of his death, with Charles Marriott confiding to Newman: 'there was a time when I thought him much more allied to the establishment than was really the case, and it was only latterly that I had begun to see that he was so much more than I had thought'.[102]

Tractarian apprehension arose when Newman and Pusey learned of Miller's collection of Rose's correspondence and projected biography. Pusey paid a diplomatic visit to Rose's widow, whose sympathies with the Movement were known to be pronounced. Pusey obtained her permission to modify or qualify any potentially damaging admissions or revelations that Miller's proposed biography might throw up. 'She said', Pusey assured Newman,

that her own impression was, that the difference of opinion between you (or us) and her husband were quite on subordinate matters ... She seemed to be very anxious, as on the part of her husband, that nothing should be said, which should in any way create any misgiving, as to you, whom she feels to be an instrument in God's Hand for some great good to the Church, and also on her own, that his views as to us should not be misunderstood. I think then everything is quite safe.[103]

It was conceded that Newman and Rose had had differences, but Pusey feared that 'one like Miller would very likely misunderstand, what was written between you'. Pusey told Newman, 'Rose had something akin to Miller, something to you'. He feared 'Miller

---

[100] Burgon, *Lives of Twelve Good Men*, vol. i, pp. 116–17.
[101] Rowlands regards Froude's letter of 20 November 1833 urging him to break with Rose as crucial in determining Newman's later course. Rowlands, *Church, State and Society*, p. 102.
[102] PH, Ollard Papers, C. Marriott to J. H. Newman, 31 January 1839.
[103] PH, Pusey Papers, LBV [Transcripts], E. B. Pusey to J. H. Newman, 23 January 1840.

might just miss that part of him which was akin to you'. Consequently, Pusey explained that he had suggested to Rose's widow, that 'as I was a third person, and felt that I understood you certainly, and Rose probably better than Miller, it might be well that I might possibly correct impressions, or suggest points to Mr Miller. This she assented to readily, or any thing else we could think of.'[104] Ultimately, Tractarian anxiety was not tested, because Miller only produced a brief memoir which had limited circulation, and which did not fully use the materials at his disposal. Many years later, Edward Churton offered a revealing explanation, 'it looks as if he [Miller] felt too sad to speak reproachfully'.[105] If the biography had appeared earlier and been more revealing, later Oxford Movement historiography might have been less slanted in favour of the Tractarians than was to be the case. For Burgon's candid biographical study in 1888, which made use of some of Miller's materials and emphasised Rose's points of difference with Newman, soon came to be overshadowed by Dean Church's classic account.

FURTHER CONFLICTS IN HISTORIOGRAPHY OF THE MOVEMENT, 1843–5

If Palmer's *Narrative* annoyed the Hackney elders for its representation of Rose's role, the Tractarians disputed its interpretation of events as a whole. It was conceded by Keble and other Tractarians that Palmer had been as fair as could have been expected. If 'one believes', Keble told Copeland, 'there are any old fashioned Anglicans at all (and God forbid there should be not many) I do not see how they can well take any other view than he does of what has been going on lately'.[106] Keble even wrote to thank Palmer for his restrained line. Newman was less charitable. Offended by Palmer's treatment of Froude, he sent an indignant note to Copeland who passed it on to Keble. Keble's response reveals his emotional and intellectual dependence on Newman even in the late stages of the latter's Anglican career, a trait for which he was criticised by the more anti-Newmanite 'Bisley school'.[107] For Keble at once confessed to Copeland,

---

104 *Ibid.*   105 SC, Churton Papers, E. Churton to W. J. Copeland, 24 December 1862.
106 LPL, Keble Dep 2/6, J. Keble to W. J. Copeland, 24 September 1843.
107 Isaac Williams told Keble: 'we are quick enough at spying out each other's weak points, and I should have thought yours was that of losing your own judgment in that of those

I wish I had had your note when he [Newman] wrote it to you: it would have made me write to Palmer in a different tone from what I did. As it is I fear I have seemed to separate myself in feeling from you and Newman. The truth is I am so used to hear people coolly give the account he does of R. H. F. [Froude] and had so entirely made up my mind to that being Palmer's view, that it did not strike me as anything new or worth protesting against.

Keble assured Copeland that as a result of Newman's note, he had written to Palmer 'again to say that I could not be easy without protesting, and that I was sure a time would come when he would be sorry for having treated them [editors of the *Remains*] either as dealers in paradox or insincere churchmen'.[108]

Palmer's interpretation of events was most effectively challenged from a more detached quarter. Newman always emphasised the inner dynamic inherent in the Movement from the start. This had been Froude's conviction, and it was this perception that was missing in Palmer's account precisely because he had never shared or understood it. William Scott of Hoxton, in an influential article in the *Christian Remembrancer* which he edited, upheld the claims of the 'dynamic' Tractarian theory of the Movement against Palmer's 'static' understanding. Like his friend, William Maskell, Scott was not formally identifiable as a 'Tractarian' in a party sense, but he was convinced that the Tractarian leaders in 1833 had 'anticipated a change much more extensive' and 'likely to be more general' than early allies such as Palmer or Perceval 'then contemplated, or are even now disposed to acknowledge'.[109] Palmer's 'kind and courteous language ... respecting Mr Newman' was recognised,[110] but Scott felt that he had suffered under a delusion in his assumption of the Movement's conservative credentials. Scott concluded 'that the division which Mr Palmer would seem to ascribe to subsequent steps really existed at the time ... [of the Movement's] formation too strongly and seriously to make their continued concealment compatible with honesty on either side'. The only surprise was 'how Mr

whom you much regard from thinking more highly of them than they deserve. My great comfort is that I can fall back on your former self when you were free from these troubles and perplexities.' LPL, Williams Dep 2/58, I. Williams to J. Keble, 20 September 1843. In 1854, Keble told Isaac Williams: 'I look upon my time with Newman and Pusey as a sort of parenthesis in my life; and I have now returned again to my old views such as I had before.' G. Prevost, ed., *Autobiography of Isaac Williams* (London, 1892), p. 118.

108 LPL, Keble Dep 2/5, J. Keble to W. J. Copeland, 7 September 1843.
109 *Christian Remembrancer*, 6 (November 1843), 538.
110 *Ibid.*, 549–50.

Palmer's strictly technical and formal view of the Anglican Church could, for any practical purpose, long remain combined with those larger aspirations of his colleagues'.[111] Certainly, both Palmer and Perceval ascribed more significance to the conservative proceedings of the Hadleigh conference than its subsequent significance warranted.

Palmer himself came to accept Scott's contention that there was an underlying division of outlook at the commencement of the Movement.[112] Yet for too long, old High Churchmen lamented, 'the movement was kept up, without a general recognition of this distinction'. Thus, 'it was credited alike with the good of the one and the evil of the other, as if it were all one and the same movement'.[113]

HIGH CHURCH REACTION: NEWMAN, *TRACT 90* AND THE BISHOPS, 1841-5

Newman used the outcry against *Tract 90* as a reason for withdrawal from the public role in the Church of England. 'I considered', he recalled bitterly, 'that after the Bishops' Charges and the general disavowal of the Tract on the part of the clergy, it was not for me to represent or to attempt to champion, the Church to which I belonged.'[114] Newman complained that the 'Charges were unsettling men's minds, and I fear laying the seeds of something deplorable to come'.[115] By 1842 he was complaining to Pusey about 'the growing consensus of the episcopal bench against Catholic truth'.[116] He blamed the first secessions to Rome directly on episcopal toleration of 'protestant error'.[117] In short, Newman's Anglican world now crashed around him. Even John Keble, who set less store on the import of 'a Bishop's lightest word', expressed a lack of 'any confidence in the Bishops as a body' and 'few signs of good information among them'.[118] Was this fair?

Newman's perception of the episcopal response to the Movement

111 *Ibid.*, 551.
112 W. Palmer, *Narrative of Events Connected with the Publication of the Tracts for the Times with an Introduction and Supplement Extending to the Present Time* (London, 1883), pp. 233-43.
113 *Anglo-Catholic Principles Vindicated*, p. 3.
114 Birmingham Oratory, Newman Papers, Ms note, 7 April 1863.
115 Bodl. Lib, Ms Eng Lett d. 102, fol. 103, J. H. Newman to H. A. Woodgate, 8 November 1841.
116 PH, Pusey Papers, LBV [Transcripts], J. H. Newman to E. B. Pusey, 24 August 1842.
117 J. H. Newman, *Sermons on Subjects of the Day* (London, 1843), pp. 384-6.
118 Bodl. Lib, Ms Eng Lett d. 134, fol. 37, J. Keble to Sir J. T. Coleridge, 24 November 1841.

was misleading and unjust. His attitude partly stemmed from an apparent inability to come to terms with the fact that his theory of the Articles in *Tract 90*, which he admitted was an 'experimentum crucis',[119] did not find acceptance from the ecclesiastical authorities. Why was he so surprised?

Never slow to sense a personal affront, in human terms, Newman found the episcopal disowning of *Tract 90* a humiliation. Newman appears to have deluded himself into believing that, in condemning *Tract 90*, the bishops had committed some kind of betrayal of himself, by breaching an 'understanding' which Newman felt he had reached with his sympathetic diocesan, the benign Bishop Bagot. For Newman, this 'understanding' was that, in response to his ending the series of *Tracts for the Times*, the bishop would not only refrain from criticising *Tract 90*, but would also influence other bishops to act accordingly.[120] Newman's contemporary evidence for such an 'understanding' was as slender as it was confused and contradictory. It was only in 1868 that Newman confided to Copeland the source of this apparent bargain; that R. W. Jelf 'came to me, on the beginning of the row about it [*Tract 90*], from Archbishop Howley to say that, if my friends would consent not to move, nothing should be done on the other side'.[121] Yet even Newman's Roman Catholic friend, J. D. Coleridge, expressed doubts that a formal understanding could have restrained a bishop such as Phillpotts from speaking out.[122]

Newman did not appear to keep to his part of the supposed bargain for, contrary to expectations, *Tract 90* continued to be reprinted.[123] Newman was disingenuous in assuming that Bishop Bagot could tie the hands of his fellow bishops. Therefore, Newman should hardly

[119] Newman, *Apologia*, p. 232.
[120] J. H. Newman to Mrs J. Mozley, 30 March 1841, Mozley, ed., *Letters and Correspondence of Newman*, vol. II, p. 341; Newman, *Apologia*, pp. 241, 243.
[121] J. H. Newman to W. J. Copeland, 1 July 1868, C. S. Dessain, ed., *Letters and Diaries* (London, 1973), vol. XXIV, p. 96.
[122] J. D. Coleridge to J. H. Newman, 17 October 1864, *Letters and Diaries*, vol. XXI, p. 262. For further discussion of Newman's 'understanding' with the bishops, see P. B. Nockles, 'Oxford, *Tract 90* and the Bishops', in D. Nicholls and F. Ker, eds., *John Henry Newman: Reason, Rhetoric and Romanticism* (Bristol, 1991), pp. 28–97.
[123] [C. P. Golightly], *Correspondence Illustrative of the Actual State of Oxford with Reference to Tractarianism, and of the Attempts of Mr Newman and His Party to Unprotestantize the National Church* (Oxford, 1842), pp. 33–4. Nonetheless, Bishop Bagot later assured Pusey that, while he 'regretted the original publication of Tract 90, it formed no part of my injunction or request (from well-considered reasons at the time) that there should be no republication of that Tract'. PH, LBV [Transcripts], Bp. R. Bagot to E. B. Pusey, 11 October 1843.

have been surprised that a majority of the bishops ultimately exercised their right to censure *Tract 90* in their Charges. It was partly because Newman considered the bishop to be a 'Pope' in his diocese, that he was so troubled when the Charges came down against him. In theory, this mentality might have been expected to induce an extreme submissiveness to episcopal authority. Yet, for all Newman's protestations otherwise, it was to be submission on his terms, and accompanied by somewhat undutiful invective against apparent episcopal 'denial' of 'Catholic truth'. Newman's own explanation of the apparent contradiction is revealing: 'the more implicit the reverence one pays to a Bishop, the more keen will be one's perception of heresy in him'.[124]

Newman's conditional view of episcopal authority predated the crisis over *Tract 90*. Ever since his early patristic researches, he had made rhetorical use of episcopal capitulation to Arian heresy in the early church.[125] The Arian example had served as a defence when individual bishops first questioned his own theological soundness on particular points as early as 1833. Certainly, Newman's sensitivity to criticism from this quarter was evinced in his rather petulant response to Bishop Kaye's criticism of his account of the *disciplina arcani* in the *Arians*. Newman was reduced to protesting privately that his own learning was though 'truly little enough ... [yet] far more than he [Kaye] thinks'.[126] Newman got his own back in his somewhat patronising review of Burton's *History of the Christian Church* in the *British Critic* in 1836. Newman commended the writings of 'the present very learned Bishop of Lincoln'[127] but most of the compliments he bestowed were decidedly back-handed and double-edged.

The episcopal reaction to *Tract 90* encouraged Newman to draw a more explicit analogy between the contemporary episcopate and that of the epoch of Arianism. In their opposition to 'catholic truth' in the 1840s, the bishops were behaving like those who compromised with Arianism in the fourth century. But Newman's sense of personal defeat was as important a motivation as any theological rationale. Thus, after Bishop Kaye's condemnation of *Tract 90* and defence of the Jerusalem bishopric, Copeland, in a private note written over a letter in his possession, recorded Newman's having

[124] Newman, *Apologia*, p. 275.   [125] Thomas, *Newman and Heresy*, pp. 20–49.
[126] J. H. Newman to R. H. Froude, 15 June 1834, A. Mozley, ed., *Letters and Correspondence of Newman*, vol. II, p. 49.
[127] [Newman], 'Burton's History of the Christian Church', *British Critic*, 19 (July, 1836), 214.

said, 'it was all very well for Kaye to write upon Tertullian but he had no learning'[128] – a verdict which contradicted his earlier statements.

Thomas Gornall's psychological explanation of Newman's double-edged relationship to the Anglican episcopate is persuasive. As Gornall puts it, in 1841 'Newman was cornered by the Bishops in the sense that he had failed to win any of them ... the objective situation was that he had been given a very fair run for his money and had failed'.[129] Faced with this failure, Newman rationalised after the event, and came up with a subjective and confused explanation – a supposed 'understanding', the terms and basis of which Newman altered as circumstances dictated.

Newman's hostile opinion of the Charges was not shared by all Tractarians. In contrast to Newman's view, Frederick Oakeley, in the 'Romanising' vanguard, could defend the episcopate, maintaining, 'we are ... under especial obligation to our Bishops, to aid them in the course of moderation and forebearance which they have hitherto maintained, amid many temptations to deviate from it, under the excitement of this anxious controversy'.[130] Reviewing the Charges of the previous year in the *British Critic* in January 1843, Oakeley was no less generous. He maintained that even the 'very complaints of those persons who are most opposed to us' indicated that 'the general tenor of the Charges delivered during the past year have been in an unprecedented degree in favour of Catholic views'.[131] Likewise, Pusey in his *Letter to the Archbishop of Canterbury* (1842), which Newman sought to dissuade him from writing, conceded that many of the bishops had been very guarded and circumspect in their criticisms.[132]

Newman's complaints also need to be put into the context of intense Evangelical and Low Church dissatisfaction with the

128 Note appended to a copy of a letter in PH, Bagot Papers, W. Palmer [of Worcester] to Bp R. Bagot, 4 September 1843.
129 T. Gornall, 'Newman's Lapses into Subjectivity', *Heythrop Journal*, 23 (1982), 46–7.
130 Oakeley, *Subject of Tract 90 Examined*, p. 26.
131 [F. Oakeley], 'Episcopal Charges', *British Critic*, 33 (January, 1843), 274.
132 Pusey, *Letter to His Grace the Archbishop of Canterbury*, pp. 96–7. Pusey wished to demonstrate 'that we [i.e. the Tract writers] were not really so condemned as we seemed to be'. NLS, Hope-Scott Papers, Ms 3692, fol. 210, E. B. Pusey to J. R. Hope, 31 January 1842. This portion of the letter was cited in Ornsby, *Memoirs of James Robert Hope-Scott*, vol. II, pp. 8–9. But in part of the same letter, marked 'private', Pusey stated: 'Newman was against it [i.e. the *Letter to the Archbishop*] from the first; he thought Harrison wanted to commit me to say things which Newman thought I would not say; in a word to Harrison's own views.'

bishops for not speaking out against the Tractarians much more strongly. Daniel Wilson lamented that 'many even of those bishops who in their Charges expressed their disapproval of those doctrines mingled their admonitions with so many expressions of respect for the motives of the movement party, as greatly to weaken the effect of their reproof'.[133] Similarly, for William Goode, Bishop Bagot was 'a weak' man, 'evidently completely taken in by the representations of the Tractarians'.[134]

For old High Churchmen, the episcopal response to the Movement broadly reflected their own line of critique. Of course, not all bishops adopted the gentle, considerate tone of Richard Bagot.[135] Samuel Wilberforce could criticise the Charge of Henry Pepys, Bishop of Worcester, as 'essentially unchurch', while he felt the Charge of J. B. Sumner, Bishop of Chester, betrayed 'the thorough ingraining of Puritanism'.[136] Samuel Wilberforce thought that even Charles Sumner, Bishop of Winchester, for whom he had retained an enduring regard, in his Charge in 1841 was 'too little church in his conscientious opposition to Tract errors'. Wilberforce feared that opposition to Tractarianism would 'form all into sects; one "Anti-church", the other "Tract", instead of Church-anti-Tract versus Newman'.[137] In fact, the episcopal consensus remained more akin to

133 D. Wilson, *Our Protestant Faith in Danger* (London, 1850), p. 9; *Christian Observer*, No. 145 (October, 1850), 716.
134 LPL, Golightly Papers, Ms 1804, fol. 102–3, W. Goode to C. P. Golightly, 9 June 1842. Another Evangelical later castigated Bishop Bagot for having 'fondled and petted the movement when it first arose in his Diocese'. *The Martyrs' Candle*, p. 6.
   Goode also privately condemned the 'culpable apathy or worse of the heads of the church in this matter and I might almost say derision to the whole of Protestant Europe and America'. LPL, Golightly Papers, Ms 1804, fol. 108, W. Goode to C. P. Golightly, 29 May 1843. Goode later explained the rise of Tractarianism as but the natural termination of 'the prevailing tone of theology in the high places of our Church' which 'had long been tending in the same direction'. W. Goode, *The Case of Archdeacon Wilberforce Compared with That of Mr Gorham* (London, 1854), p. 15.
135 Roundell Palmer commented on Bishop Bagot's Charge: 'he censures in the most uncompromising manner the character of the opposition which they [the Tractarians] have encountered. In truth, therefore, he puts himself at their head, and takes the responsibility of publicly approving their acts and avowing their doctrines up to a certain point – and what is more – nothing less than the furthest limits of Anglo-Catholicism.' LPL, Selborne Papers, Ms 2498, fol. 28, R. Palmer to J. R. Godley, 27 January 1842. Palmer held that the Charges of Bagot, Phillpotts, Denison, Blomfield and Thirlwall showed that 'a very large portion of Catholic ground both in practice and in principle, having been fought for and won by our light armed friends at Oxford' had been 'permanently recovered to the Church of England'. *Ibid.*, fol. 24, R. Palmer to J. R. Godley, 24 January 1842.
136 Bodl. Lib, Ms Eng Lett. d. 367, fols. 69–70, S. Wilberforce to J. W. Croker, 19 April 1843.
137 Ashwell, ed., *Life of Samuel Wilberforce*, vol. I, p. 202.

'Church-anti-Tract' than 'Anti-Church'; old High Church rather than 'ultra-Protestant'.

Newman's followers who remained in the Church of England, did much to perpetuate a myth of their hero's ill-treatment of blundering bishops. They assumed that the episcopal Charges were the cause, not the consequence, of the Romeward drift in the Movement. Palmer's earlier modest historical self-justification was overshadowed by the later pro-Newman historiography propagated by Church and Liddon, though Copeland's incomplete manuscript narrative of the Movement remained unpublished. Yet the older, alternative interpretation, though finding only muted public expression in his *Memoir of Joshua Watson* because of a charitable desire not to give offence,[138] was sustained by Churton in private correspondence over several decades.

In the early 1840s, Churton repudiated Copeland's suggestion that Newman was being treated like 'a criminal under sentence pronounced by the rulers of our own church'.[139] A quarter of a century later, Churton still disputed Copeland's view that the bishops and Oxford Heads had driven Newman out of the Church of England. 'How any of their acts', he informed Copeland, 'could be considered to enforce the secession of J. H. Newman, or to justify it, I do not see, nor shall I ever see. You love the man too much to see the question in its true light.'[140] Churton explained to Copeland what he regarded as the true relation of the bishops to the Movement:

The bishops seem then [in the 1840s] to have thought it their duty to act the part of the Isthmus of Corinth, and were only afraid lest the encroaching tide on one side or the other would burst over them. We are all inclined to prefer a course which may leave us to take our ease. They little thought of the tragical consequences to a mind of such fine fibres as John Henry Newman's. They only wished to be left alone, safe on shore, 'high and dry' as before.[141]

Joshua Watson complained about the 'almost frantic desire for persecution'[142] which he perceived in the Tractarian leaders. Of course, zeal for what one regarded as the truth regardless of

138 SC, Churton Papers, E. Churton to W. J. Copeland, 1 August 1860.
139 *Ibid.*, E. Churton to W. J. Copeland, 18 September 1843.
140 *Ibid.*, E. Churton to W. J. Copeland, 23 November 1860. Churton even regarded Newman's impending secession in 1845 as 'a proof of something like insanity'. PH, Gresley Papers, GRES 3/7/52, E. Churton to W. Gresley, 29 May 1845.
141 SC, Churton Papers, E. Churton to W. J. Copeland, 7 February 1865.
142 M. Watson, Ms 'Reminiscences', fol. 116, 7 August 1843.

consequences was a virtue. But a distinction had to be made, Churton warned Pusey, 'between those who patiently abide under persecution, and those who do all they can to bring it upon themselves'.[143] The comment was aimed at Newman. It was not without basis. Even Newman's friend, John Bowden, felt the need to caution him in 1841: 'check your zeal for martyrdom'.[144] But Isaac Williams, who accepted that Newman had much to put up with from the ecclesiastical authorities, detected also an opposite fault. For the disillusioned Williams, one of Newman's weaknesses was that 'he had not more learned to look on persecution as a matter of course, what a good man must expect to meet with'.[145] These two faults were not mutually exclusive.

A PARTING OF FRIENDS: PALMER'S FINAL BREACH WITH NEWMAN

Palmer's defence of Newman continued until 1844. The extent of Palmer's confidence in Newman's allegiance to the Church of England was evident even in 1843 when, after Newman's resignation as Vicar of St Mary's, he told Pusey that he 'never had, any the least doubt of his [Newman's] steadfastness in the church, and his wish to prevent Romish tendencies – and I am sure that this step, however it may be interpreted, is not to be understood as any symptom of defection'.[146]

Palmer still hoped that Newman might emerge from his Littlemore retirement to repudiate Ward, Oakeley and the 'Romanisers'. It was only when he came to analyse Newman's last volume of Anglican sermons in the *English Review*, that illusions were laid to rest. Palmer was provoked by a footnote in Newman's *Sermons on Subjects of the Day*, in which the episcopal censures of *Tract 90* were criticised. Given Newman's own recent admission that his principles would lead to Rome 'without a strong safeguard' and Newman's

---

143 PH, Pusey Papers, LBV [Transcripts], E. Churton to E. B. Pusey, 9 December 1841.
144 Birmingham Oratory, Newman Papers, 'Tract 90 Correspondence', No. 21, J. W. Bowden to J. H. Newman, 18 March 1841.
145 Prevost, ed., *Autobiography of Isaac Williams*, p. 110.
146 PH, Pusey Papers, LBV [Transcripts], W. Palmer [of Worcester] to E. B. Pusey, 12 September 1843. As late as 1841 Palmer asserted: 'The writings of these men render it, in my opinion, totally impossible for them to become papists; and that if they should become so, I should not be surprised if Mr Bickersteth [a staunch Evangelical] or the Archbishop of Canterbury follow their example.' PH, Gresley Papers, GRES 3/40/2, W. Palmer [of Worcester] to W. Gresley, 20 November 1841.

failure to provide such a safeguard, Palmer regarded this criticism as unfair. In a new note of personal criticism, Palmer concluded, 'it seems as if there were in this, some want of humility – some reluctance to take blame, unless it were shared with others. We are of the opinion that, considering all this, Mr Newman ought to have abstained from such very severe condemnation of the church, and of her prelates.'[147]

Gladstone reached a similar conclusion. Convinced of the enormous advance in the progress of Catholic principles over the preceding decade, Gladstone was puzzled that Newman seemed unable to acknowledge that the Church was in a healthier state and with better prospects than when the Movement was launched. As Gladstone remarked,

that he [Newman] does not see the English Church in her members to be growing more Catholic from year to year, I am astonished. Yet can he be not aware how much more plain and undeniable the sway of Catholic principles has become in the Church of England, since the time when he entertained no doubt about it? Can he have measured the drifting movement of his own mind, seen what the most vulgar observer, the most cursory reader, cannot fail to see? Is he under the delusion that he is fixed, and that others are moving away from truth, when in fact all have been running in the same direction but he faster than others, and I fear somewhat past his peak.[148]

In the supplement to the 1883 edition of his *Narrative*, Palmer modified his own earlier restraint from criticism of Newman, maintaining that anti-Roman statements in the original draft of the first edition had been removed or softened at Bishop Bagot's recommendation. Palmer now wrote of Newman,

If this great man had been really faithful to the Church of England, his own condemnation (however unjust in his own opinion) should not have prevented him from interfering to check the excesses of young writers, which were doing such harm to the church. But he was detached from the church. He was like the shepherd 'that seeth the wolf coming, and leaveth the sheep, and fleeth', whose 'own the sheep are not'.[149]

Something of the personal bond between the two, at least on Palmer's part, survived the breach of 1843–5. Palmer harboured no personal ill-will to his old friend, and there is no evidence for the

---

[147] *English Review*, 1 (July, 1844), 309.
[148] BL, Gladstone Papers, Ms Add 44247, fols. 173–4, W. E. Gladstone to H. E. Manning, 24 October 1843.
[149] Palmer, *Narrative of Events* (new edn, London, 1883), p. 237.

view that he felt 'bitterness and jealousy and even rage' at having the leadership of the Movement 'snatched' from him in 1833.[150] On the contrary, Palmer had never sought such leadership and remained ever anxious to submerge the whole idea of 'personality' in all campaigns in defence of the Church. Of course he was grateful for recognition even though he did not seek it. In a typically generous gesture, Palmer wrote effusively to Newman to thank him for the notice – in truth, not altogether flattering – of him taken in the *Apologia*. Palmer appreciated being described as 'the only really learned man among us'. Yet Newman's power of insinuation of other limitations found expression even in this notice of his former comrade.[151] This Palmer no less characteristically chose to overlook.

ROUT AND REALIGNMENT: PALMER, THE OLD HIGH
CHURCHMEN AND PUSEY, 1845–52

The condemnation of W. G. Ward at Oxford on 13 February 1845 and Newman's secession to Rome in October of that year represented 'catastrophe' for Dean Church, and marked the end of a chapter. Nevertheless, these events did not signal the demise of the Oxford Movement. At the parochial level the Movement was only just beginning to make itself felt. Pusey, aided by Keble and Marriott, took over the mantle of leadership from Newman, and the residue of the Movement's followers regrouped.

As shown, the Gorham and the Denison controversy in the 1850s helped blur lines of division between old High Churchmen and Tractarians and made possible periodic realignments of the two. Yet the growth of religious pluralism within the Church, and the rise of ever more extreme sacerdotalism among the embryonic Ritualists meant that the earlier rift between 'Zs' and Tractarians never quite healed. The hopes of Palmer and other 'Zs' that under Pusey's leadership the Movement would swing back to a more moderate course were not realised, and new sources of dispute arose. Between 1845 and 1851, Pusey found himself locked in conflict with his own moderate High Church diocesan, Samuel Wilberforce, as well as his old friend W. F. Hook. Both Palmer and Churton lamented that

---

150 M. O'Connell, *The Oxford Conspirators: a History of the Oxford Movement* (London, 1969), p. 398.
151 Newman, *Apologia*, p. 108. J. R. Griffin, however, has denied that Newman caricatured Palmer in the *Apologia*. See J. R. Griffin, 'Newman and William Palmer: a Note on the *Apologia*', *English Language Notes*, 28 (December, 1986), 33–6.

Pusey neglected the opportunity to bury differences with themselves, in the wake of Newman's secession. Palmer made clear this disappointment in the 1883 edition of the *Narrative*. He confessed,

that Pusey's proceedings as the self-constituted leader of the Tractarian party often caused me very great unhappiness. I shared in the opinions of Dr Wilberforce and Dr Hook on this point. I should have gladly seen Pusey attempt to reform mistakes introduced by Newman, and endeavouring to correct, instead of seeming to go along with the ultra-Tractarian mistakes.[152]

The Hackney elders were still more disapproving of Pusey's course. In 1846, Christopher Wordsworth senior lamented to his son, Christopher, that 'those Oxford notions' were 'not yet abandoned', and that 'these men will go blundering on, in their narrow-minded and bigoted follies, rejoicing too in the mischief that they do'.[153] More moderate supporters of the Tractarians such as Charles Marriott, J. T. Coleridge and William Gresley were urged not to veer too close towards 'Oxfordism'.[154]

The Gorham Judgment elicited a variety of responses, not always in accord with the division between High Churchmen and Tractarians. But such a division remained apparent in the different tactics and methods of combating an evil on which all were agreed. Pusey may actually have been more personally sensitive to Evangelical spiritual concerns in the Gorham affair than were old High Churchmen, but the tone of some of the numerous memorials and remonstrances which he and his followers drew up, alarmed the Hackney elders. As Norris complained to Watson in October 1850, 'where are we, on our head or our heels? or like so many shuttlecocks tossed to and fro by the cunning craftiness of Dr Pusey and his junto?'[155] Old High Churchmen did not deny the necessity of public protest. On the contrary, even Palmer was willing to adopt extreme measures in 1850–1. Yet, as in 1833–4, most old High Churchmen preferred the caution and control of a 'board of sound, safe men', to the irregular exertions of individuals bent on confrontation.

Palmer's outspokenness in the wake of the Gorham Judgment was qualified by his extreme unwillingness that the anti-Gorham

---

152 Palmer, *Narrative of Events* (new edn), p. 241.
153 LPL, Wordsworth Papers, Ms 2149, fols. 364–5, C. Wordsworth (Sen.) to C. Wordsworth (Jun.), 14 May 1846.
154 *Ibid.*, fol. 329, C. Wordsworth (Sen.) to C. Wordsworth (Jun.), 17 May 1845.
155 Bodl. Lib, Norris Papers, Ms Eng Lett. c. 790, fol. 163, H. H. Norris to J. Watson, 22 October 1850.

campaign be identified in any way 'with views commonly called "Tractarian"'. He remonstrated with Pusey 'against the appearance of names in positions calculated to create such an impression'.[156] Given Phillpotts's primary part in bringing the whole controversy to a head and the non-Tractarian basis of much of the objection to the Judgment, Palmer's concerns might seem unfounded. Having previously overlooked the possibility of moderate High Churchmen being confounded with Tractarians, Palmer now exhibited great sensitivity to the possibility.

There were reasons for Palmer's misgivings. His repeated warnings to Pusey and his friends were brusquely brushed aside. He was not well treated by the Anglo-Catholic followers of Pusey in the early-1850s. To the Tractarians, Palmer remained stuck in the mental groove of 1833, unwilling to acknowledge that the world had changed. Pusey got some of his allies to answer Palmer in as telling a way as possible. One of Palmer's letters of protest to Pusey was passed on to James Beresford-Hope. In Beresford-Hope's view, Palmer's new-found anti-Tractarian obsession was needlessly crippling the 'services of good men to the cause of true religion'. Palmer's charge of 'what is called "Tractarianism"' was thrown back at him. 'You must allow me', observed Beresford-Hope, 'who never wrote a line in the Oxford Tracts, to say that it puzzles me coming from one, who was confessedly one of the authors of that series.'[157] This was something which Palmer now preferred to forget. He was, however, not deterred from insisting on that gulf between the two schools which he had chosen to ignore in the *Narrative*. Thus, in December 1852, he was again lamenting 'that the new High Church party to so great an extent identifies with Tractarianism, and through this, with Romanisers'.[158]

Palmer's rearguard battle was unsuccessful. His 'extreme sedateness, shyness and seeming coldness of manner', according to

[156] LPL, Mill Papers, Ms 1491, fol. 134, W. Palmer [of Worcester] to E. B. Pusey, 25 September 1850 (copy); W. Palmer, *A Statement of Circumstances Connected with the Proposal of Resolutions at a Meeting of the Bristol Church Union, October 1850* (London, 1850), pp. 11, 23.

[157] LPL, Mill Papers, Ms 1491, fol. 81, A. J. Beresford-Hope to W. Palmer [of Worcester], 27 September 1850. See also Pusey's comment on Palmer at this time: 'I feel sorry for Palmer. I fear he has got among friends who do him no good ... He went along with us, in earlier days, but his was what I should call, the political line. And yet in his book on the church, he said things, utterly at variance with the line he is now taking.' PH, LBV [Transcripts], E. B. Pusey to A. J. Beresford-Hope, 28 September 1850.

[158] LPL, Wordsworth Papers, Ms 2144, fol. 315, W. Palmer [of Worcester] to C. Wordsworth (Jun.), 23 December 1852.

Thomas Mozley, always had 'stood much in the way of his general acceptance'[159] at Oxford. His manner of attempting to check Romanising zealotry in the wake of Newman's secession alienated even some of those closest to him in terms of churchmanship. Former allies such as Edward Churton privately criticised Palmer's tone in this period, especially his articles as editor of the *English Review*. Palmer now was described by Churton as being 'suspected of some little personal vanity; and he also is without influence'.[160] Churton deplored Palmer's public letter to Archdeacon Thorp in 1850 as 'the letter of a mad Irishman. Who would think for a moment of taking him for a leader, who has so little command over himself?'[161] After 1853, documentary evidence for Palmer's involvement on the public stage of church politics dwindles. Disillusioned at being disowned by former associates, he retreated into the unobtrusive world of his remote Dorset living. On grounds of ill-health Palmer removed to London in the mid-1860s but continued to take little part in public controversy. His near silence in the Denison affair of 1853–7, the *Essays and Reviews* controversy of 1860–1, and in the legal cases involving ritual matters in the 1860s and 1870s, was striking in one who had hitherto played such a conspicuous part in the literary and theological as well as political aspects of church life. In 1875, Palmer entered the controversy between Newman and Gladstone over 'Vaticanism' but his contribution was made under cover of an anonymous pseudonym.[162] It was only the premature valedictory of Thomas Mozley in the first edition of his *Reminiscences* in 1882[163] that metaphorically brought Palmer back to life. For Mozley's unfortunate action not only called forth the reply that he was still alive, but ushered in a final burst of literary activity in 1883, retracing the ground which had so preoccupied him half a century earlier and restating, with slight modifications, the principles which he expressed at that time. The *Narrative* was republished verbatim with the addition of an eighty-page historical introduction and a sixty-page supplement, while an article in the *Contemporary Review*

---

[159] Mozley, *Reminiscences Chiefly of Oriel College and the Oxford Movement*, vol. i, p. 320.

[160] PH, Gresley Papers, GRES 3/7/53, E. Churton to W. Gresley, 18 June 1845.

[161] PH, Gresley Papers, GRES 3/7/92, E. Churton to W. Gresley, 7 October 1850.

[162] [W. Palmer], *Results of the 'Expostulation' of the Rt. Hon W. E. Gladstone in Their Relation to the Unity of Roman Catholicism. By Umbra Oxoniensis* (London, 1875). Palmer had not been entirely silent in his Dorset retreat. In 1854–5, he had engaged in Protestant polemic with the Catholic Mr Weld of Lulworth. See J. Wolffe, *Protestant Crusade in Great Britain*, pp. 148–9.

[163] Mozley, *Reminiscences Chiefly of Oriel College and the Oxford Movement*, vol. i, p. 322.

represented a condensation of that which appeared in the *Narrative*. But this final literary flowering was too late to forestall the ultimate near eclipse, in Newman's literary shadow, of Palmer's memory in later years, and to prevent him from becoming the 'forgotten man' in the history of the Oxford Movement.

Conclusion

'We have advanced ... but it has been in spite of the Movement of 1833, and not through it or by it.'[1] Charles Drury's comment to G. A. Denison might seem to undervalue the Tractarian achievement, but it represented a common mid-century view among old High Churchmen which only the later ascendancy of Tractarian historiography eclipsed. In the 1850s Edward Churton advocated a quiet 'rebuking of the upstart self-satisfied spirit' of the Tractarians whom, he complained, had been 'preaching up their noble selves, as if ... knowledge would die with them'.[2] In truth, the significance of 1833 in the annals of the nineteenth-century Church of England has been misunderstood. The Tractarians sharpened a sense of High Church party identity in the Church, but they did not and could not create it. In their church principles, sacramental teaching, spirituality and even political theology, they owed more than they usually acknowledged, not only to the Caroline phase of the High Church tradition but to the eighteenth- and early-nineteenth-century witnesses to that tradition. But 1833 was in another sense a genuine watershed. For Tractarianism diverged both spiritually and theologically from old High Churchmanship. Thus Tractarian historiography was mistaken in suggesting that the Oxford Movement first rediscovered 'Anglicanism' and that what became known as 'Anglo-Catholicism' was a natural or lineal evolution.

The damaging consequences fostered by the later course of the Movement should not be underestimated. The Movement's negative impact on the fortunes of native High Church traditions in the Church of Ireland and Scottish Episcopal Church has been explored elsewhere.[3] Certainly, it is ironic that a Movement whose origins

---

[1] PH, Denison Papers, 2/24/12 C. Drury to G. A. Denison, 26 May 1852.
[2] SC, Churton Papers, E. Churton to W. J. Copeland, 29 October 1855.
[3] See Nockles, 'Continuity and Change', vol. 1, chs. 5, 7.

were linked to a protest on behalf of the embattled Irish Church should after 1833 so studiously turn its back on the cause of a sister church. The High Church revival within the Church of Ireland in the 1840s was encouraged by old High Churchmen such as William Sewell and not by the Tractarians as such. The remnant of the Hackney Phalanx gave moral support to Sewell's foundation of St Columba's College, encouraged by the patronage of the Archbishop of Armagh, J. C. Beresford, himself a friend of Watson and Norris.[4] The efforts of Irish High Churchmen such as Pusey's friend J. H. Todd, however, were hampered by what they viewed as the excesses of English Tractarians. As a result, Archbishop Beresford distanced himself from the St Columba's project.[5] Similarly, Scottish episcopalians suffered the negative consequences of an outcry against 'Puseyism' in the 1840s largely provoked by events south of the Tweed. It was in vain that representatives of the Nonjuring and Hutchinsonian traditions within Scottish episcopalianism protested their independence from the Tractarians.

For old High Churchmen, the view propagated by Newman's loyal Anglican friends Copeland and Dean Church that he was persecuted and driven from the Church of England by intolerant authorities was one of many Tractarian myths. Isaac Williams insisted that Newman's attraction towards Rome predated *Tract 90* and was no product of Hebdomadal censure.[6] The Hackney elders also defended the actions of the Oxford Heads. For Joshua Watson, 'the cards were dealt to them [i.e. the Heads], and if they had refused to play, they had surely failed in their duty to the university'.[7] Edward Churton remained less inclined to side with the Heads, but his patience wore increasingly thin with Copeland's assiduous repetition of charges of episcopal persecution. Owen Chadwick has suggested a psychological reason for Church's restatement of this discredited theory. Church's obsession against the Heads, Chadwick argues, stemmed from his unwillingness to accept 'that Newman went because he chose'. For Church, Chad-

---

[4] *Ibid.*, vol. II, p. 420 n. 2.   [5] *Ibid.*, pp. 422–3.
[6] Prevost, ed., *Autobiography of Isaac Williams*, p. 108.
[7] Churton, *Memoir of Joshua Watson*, vol. II, p. 152. Even Isaac Williams commented: 'Copeland has never ceased to inveigh against the Heads of Houses as the causes of so much mischief ... but I doubt whether harm was done by it ... There were also in some cases grounds for their distrust.' Prevost, ed. *Autobiography of Isaac Williams*, p. 100. By 1861, however, Churton (*Memoir of Joshua Watson*, vol. II, p. 153) conceded that Pusey had 'lived to refute the calumnies and suspicions which were then [1843] rife in many quarters'.

wick says, 'the heads of colleges became a scapegoat, which bore away the blame, and so rescued the integrity and honour of his former leader, and enabled him to retain his own former convictions'.[8]

The Tractarian suggestion of an unholy alliance of 'Puritan' and latitudinarian official opposition to themselves was wide of the mark. The two Vice-Chancellors of Oxford University most involved in anti-Tractarian measures, A. T. Gilbert and Philip Wynter, were commonly regarded as High Churchmen and Tories, with a pronounced bias against Low Churchmen.[9] Tractarian designations of the Board of Heads as a 'board of Puritan divines'[10] represented a misrepresentation of a body which had a moderate High Church majority. Moreover, it can be argued that the episcopal bench of the 1830s and early 1840s was more High Church than at any time since the Revolution of 1688. The leaven of Latitudinarian theology allied to Erastianism in high places, had largely been eradicated by Evangelical as well as Orthodox campaigning long prior to the rise of the Movement. Ever since about 1760, most old-style Latitudinarians had found their path to episcopal preferment effectively blocked, with Richard Watson (who died in 1816) being the last of that line prior to the rise in the 1830s of a new breed of liberal bishops such as Maltby and Thirlwall (the latter not unfriendly to the Movement).[11] Thus the Charges of the bishops in 1841–3 largely reflected the judgment of the old High Churchmanship upon the new.

There was an uncomfortable contrast between Tractarian theoretical exaltation of the episcopal office and defiance of that office in practice. The Hackney elders disliked even Pusey's supposedly conciliatory *Letter to the Archbishop of Canterbury* in 1842 as 'threatening'

[8] Chadwick, 'The Oxford Movement and Its Reminiscencers', pp. 151–2.

[9] Churton maintained: 'He [Gilbert] has so little love for the Low Church, that a few years ago he was deliberating, when my poor brother, took to those [Evangelical] views, whether he should desire him to give up his tutorship.' SC, Churton Papers, E. Churton to W. J. Copeland, 1 February 1842.

[10] Bucklebury, Hook Papers, J. Williams to W. F. Hook, 24 December 1844.

[11] Gascoigne, 'Anglican Latitudinarianism and Political Radicalism in the Late Eighteenth Century', 22–38. On the decline of Anglican latitudinarianism in the late eighteenth century, see M. Fitzpatrick, 'Latitudinarianism at the Passing of the Ways: a Suggestion', in Walsh, Taylor and Haydon, eds., *Church of England, c. 1689–c. 1833*, pp. 209–27. Even in 1853, W. J. Conybeare calculated that thirteen out of twenty-eight bishops and archbishops of England 'belonged to various shades of High Church'. [Conybeare], 'Church Parties', 338.

in tone.[12] Edward Churton described that *Letter* 'as written in the style of a leader of mutineers'.[13] For Hackney, the Oxford men were aping the insubordinate tactics of Evangelicals of earlier years. Churton complained, 'it must tend to loosen the bonds of church government if Bishops's Charges are to be replied, however inoffensive the manner of reply'.[14] A few years earlier, it was argued, 'no person (who did not choose to be thought a dissenter or a semi-dissenter) would have dreamed of attacking a bishop in the newspapers', but now it was the so-called 'friends of catholicity' who were 'labouring, day after day, to make the episcopal office odious and contemptible'.[15] Bishop Blomfield remarked in 1842 to Archbishop Howley, 'we [i.e. the Bishops] have been worse treated by the Oxford writers than we have ever been by the Evangelical party in the whole course of our government in the Church'.[16]

The Tractarians did not set out to defy the bishops, but submission had to be on their terms. This discrepancy between high episcopal theory and an almost Congregationalist or Presbyterian practice became an unhappy legacy of the Movement, and so much a feature of later Anglo-Catholicism that in 1868 John Lonsdale, Bishop of Lichfield, an old High Churchman of the Hackney school, complained 'that he had only one high-churchman in his diocese who ever submitted to him'.[17] William Sewell even branded Ritualists as 'Revolutionists' bent on overturning the whole ecclesiastical order.[18] Likewise, Burgon argued in 1888 that to 'the partial miscarriage of the Tractarian movement' was 'to be attributed, in no slight degree, that miserable lawlessness on the part of a section of the Clergy, which is among the heaviest calamities of these last days'.[19]

When compared to the apparent theological polarisation of the post-1833 Church of England, the pre-Tractarian era seemed to exemplify a church characterised by relative internal harmony and party fluidity based on a certain consensus; a consensus forged by the primacy of allegiance to establishment and the somewhat undoctrinal focus of pre-Tractarian High Churchmanship. The pre-

[12] SC, Churton Papers, E. Churton to W. J. Copeland, 16 February 1856.
[13] PH, Gresley Papers, GRES 3/7/68, E. Churton to W. Gresley, 21 May 1846.
[14] PH, Pusey Papers, LBV [Transcripts], E. Churton to E. B. Pusey, 9 December 1841.
[15] *British Magazine*, 26 (October, 1844), 452.
[16] In T. Henderson to E. B. Pusey, Ash Wednesday, 1842, Liddon, *Life of Pusey*, vol. II, p. 275.
[17] E. B. Denison, ed., *Life of the Rt. Rev. John Lonsdale, Bishop of Lichfield* (London, 1868), p. 120.
[18] *Anglo-Catholic Principles Vindicated*, pp. 438–9.
[19] Burgon, *Lives of Twelve Good Men*, vol. I, p. 225.

Tractarian Church of England, while comprising different church parties, was not riddled with that 'mutual suspicion, and an apartheid of personalities, theological colleges, journals and publishing imprints' which characterised the post-Tractarian Church.[20] Warm theological disputes, as over baptismal regeneration and the interpretation of Article 17, might divide the Orthodox and some Evangelicals. Yet even these exceptions proved the rule. For example, in the 1820s in the wake of Bishop Marsh's campaign to 'catch Calvinists' in his Peterborough diocese, centrifugal pressures averted the damaging split that characterised the later Gorham controversy in 1850.[21] Many noted the striking contrast between the way in which the dispute provoked by Marsh in 1821 and that provoked by Phillpotts in 1847–50 were respectively resolved.[22] It was not that pre-Tractarian High Churchmen were undogmatic, but that, once other political props of establishment had been removed in 1828–33, dogma assumed a greater importance as a test of churchmanship than it generally had thirty years previously.

Hanoverian Orthodox churchmen had tended to stress what the Church of England was not, rather than what she was. The real change introduced by the Tractarians was a raising of the doctrinal temperature of the Church of England; highlighting in an often provocative way theological issues that had lain dormant. Newman's theory of the *via media* was not the Hanoverian ideal of 'moderation' as an end in itself nor even quite the Laudian 'middle way' between Puritanism or Geneva on the one hand and Rome on the other, but rather, a 'middle way' between Protestantism *per se* and Romanism. This subtle shift in the place assigned to Anglicanism in the theological spectrum in effect forced High Churchmen to decide whether they were Protestant or Catholic. Even the many High Churchmen who clung to a combination of the two, were forced to take sides more unreservedly.

The Tractarians helped to absolutise pre-existing party positions. As a consequence, the traditional High Churchmanship of non-Tractarians such as Phillpotts and Maskell took on more of a dogmatic character. This in itself provoked division. As the debate between Phillpotts and Maskell in 1850 revealed, a wide gulf

---

[20] Avis, *Anglicanism*, p. 86; Avis, 'Tractarian Challenge to Consensus and the Identity of Anglicanism'.
[21] *Thirty Years' Conflict in the Church of England and Its Remedy* (London, 1855), p. iii.
[22] *Quarterly Review*, 101 (April, 1857), 552; *Edinburgh Review*, 92 (January, 1850), 26.

emerged between old High Churchmen and those who seceded to Rome as to what precisely were the parameters of dogmatic teaching.

In the wake of the rise of the Oxford Movement, cross-fertilisation for a time became less common – the battle-lines were more sharply drawn. It was a process well portrayed by a perceptive writer in the *Quarterly Review* in 1858, who made clear that, while the divisions between High Church and Low Church were not products of the Oxford Movement, yet prior to 1833, such divisions had tended to be 'a matter of feeling much more than of reasoning'. While the Tractarians only solidified pre-existing party divisions, they also encouraged many who had been hitherto High Church 'in sentiment' or on primarily constitutional grounds to embrace a more theologically systematic and sacramental form of High Churchmanship.[23] Bishop Phillpotts himself, while remaining independent of the Tractarians,[24] was perhaps more influenced by the Tracts than he was aware[25] and can be regarded as an example of this trend. As late as 1842, Phillpotts's anti-Romanist credentials were such that the Evangelical Francis Close hailed him 'as one of the ablest champions of Protestant truth'.[26] Phillpotts's *rapprochement* with Pusey and Manning in the 1840s as well as his role as protagonist in the rubrical and Gorham controversies drastically modified his reputation in Low Church circles. The example of Phillpotts can be cited to show that what has been called the Anglican Renaissance was something broader than the Oxford Movement and that its influence was not confined to the Tractarians proper but, like the earlier Evangelical Revival, overflowed into the church at large, encouraging an evolution even in the character of old High Churchmanship itself. With Phillpotts, the evolution was from a primarily political to a more sacerdotalist emphasis. A similar trend is discernible in the churchmanship of G. A. Denison. Denison had been a rather political High Churchman while at Oriel in the 1830s, keeping his distance from and even giving offence to the Tractarian

---

23 *Quarterly Review*, 104 (July, 1858), 155.

24 Thurmer, 'Henry of Exeter and the Later Tractarians', 210–20; Nias, *Gorham and the Bishop of Exeter*, p. 10.

25 Davies, *Henry Phillpotts*, pp. 289–90.

26 ECA, Spencer Gift, Phillpotts Papers, 11/4, F. Close to Bp H. Phillpotts, 16 November 1842. On the shift in perceptions of Phillpotts, see J. R. Wolffe, 'Bishop Henry Phillpotts and the Administration of the Diocese of Exeter, 1830–1869', *Transactions of the Devonshire Association*, 114 (1982), 108–10.

leaders. According to Tom Mozley, however, Denison deserved to be listed 'among the number of those upon whom Newman was long making a continual and silent impression, undetected or suppressed at the time, but destined to show itself all the stronger afterwards'.[27] The result was the combative, sacerdotalist High Church protagonist of the eucharistic controversies of the mid-1850s. In truth, even 'the moderate party' among High Churchmen in the 1840s, while following the line of the older tradition more strictly than the Tractarians, underwent something of the same spiritual rejuvenation and drew on the same *secunda aura*[28] which infused the Movement. Thus when the Tractarian W. J. Butler, Vicar of Wantage, in 1859 distinguished two schools of High Churchmen as 'the spiritual' and 'the ecclesiastical', the implication that only the Tractarians conformed to the former type was rejected by Samuel Wilberforce. For Wilberforce insisted that 'I, Leighton, Burgon and others belong really to the spiritual and not to the ecclesiastical division of the school.'[29]

The old High Church party lived on into the second half of the century, with remnants of the Hackney constellation surviving among numerous clerical dynasties, that of the Lyall family being only one of the more notable.[30] As Arthur Burns has demonstrated, the continued vitality of the Orthodox at the organisational level was such that they, rather than the Tractarians, were at the forefront of the diocesan revival from the late 1820s onwards.[31] While more local studies are needed, there is evidence of Orthodox dominance in certain dioceses. According to the, albeit partisan, view of Bishop Phillpotts in 1842, in Exeter diocese there were not more than thirty of what he called 'modern Puritans', 'out of a body of clergy of 800. The great mass of the clergy are very staunch.'[32] From her study of the Lincoln diocese, Frances Knight has concluded that in the period 1827–53, 'among archdeacons and rural deans a form

---

[27] Mozley, *Reminiscences Chiefly of Oriel College and the Oxford Movement*, vol. II, p. 98.
[28] PH, Bagot Papers, E. Cooper to Bp R. Bagot, 11 January 1842. According to W. J. Conybeare in 1853, compared to 'the good old days of Eldonian Toryism', a better spirit had been breathed into hundreds of the old High Church party 'who but for this new movement would have remained, as their fathers were before them, mere Nimrods, Ramrods, or Fishing rods'. [Conybeare], 'Church Parties', 306.
[29] S. Wilberforce to W. J. Butler, 26 January 1859, in R. G. Wilberforce, ed., *Life of Samuel Wilberforce*, vol. II (London, 1881), p. 372.
[30] Dewey, *Passing of Barchester*, ch. 8.
[31] Burns, 'Diocesan Revival in the Church of England', p. 315.
[32] ECA, Spencer Gift, Phillpotts Papers, 11/3, Bp H. Phillpotts to T. Baker, 2 September 1842.

of high churchmanship' akin to that of its diocesan, John Kaye, 'was virtually a prerequisite of office holding'.[33] Even in the 1880s the episcopal bench could boast exponents of the older High Church tradition such as Harold Browne and Christopher Wordsworth junior. Furthermore, old High Church ideological influence continued to be felt. In 1877 a compendium of divinity claiming to represent an 'old historic High Church' school was published.[34]

Yet whereas in the 1820s the Orthodox seemed to be centre-stage and dominant in the Church of England, by the 1850s their loss of ideological dominance in the face of rival extremes seemed complete. For those reared in the Hackney tradition, this loss was felt in family and hereditary terms. As Edward Churton sadly observed in 1839,

> my friends from childhood, and all my friends and counsellors for many years, are now breaking up ... and when one thinks of the wise and benevolent influence they have long exercised in the church's counsels, and the many dangers against which they have helped it to stand firm, one cannot but look with sad forebodings to the changes which may abide it when their influence is withdrawn.[35]

For mid-century old High Churchmen, it was the loss of an earlier relative internal harmony that was cause for lament. In 1858, Henry John Rose suggested that the High Church revival spearheaded from Cambridge in the 1820s by his more famous brother, Hugh James Rose, had aimed to promote unity. He contrasted what Dean Burgon later presented as Hugh James Rose's inclusive vision with the divisive and sectarian vision of catholicity which Burgon ascribed to Newman and the Tractarians.[36] Had the *Tracts for the Times* followed the pattern and line of such earlier Orthodox publications as the *Scholar Armed* and *Churchman's Remembrancer*, and had the Tractarians merely banded together for the same defensive purposes as the *Society for the Reformation of Principles* in the 1790s, there could have been no such grounds for complaint. Had Rose

---

[33] Knight, 'John Kaye and the Diocese of Lincoln', p. 303. Nonetheless, in his clergy sample for South Lindsey in 1851, Obelkevitch found that as many as forty-six per cent could be identified as 'Evangelical' or 'moderate Evangelical', compared to thirty-seven per cent as 'moderate High Church'. Obelkevitch, *Religion and Rural Society*, p. 122.

[34] *Anglo-Catholic Principles Vindicated*, p. xxix.

[35] SC, E. Churton to T. T. Churton, 18 June 1839; E. Churton to T. T. Churton, 17 April 1841.

[36] *Encyclopaedia Metropolitana*, ch. 11, [H. J. Rose], 'Ecclesiastical History from A.D. 1700 to A.D. 1858. The Church of England' (1858), pp. 375, 379.

lived longer, it was later maintained, the Catholic Revival 'would have been wholly primitive and Nicene'.[37] An interesting parallel was drawn between the Oxford Movement and Methodism. As one old High Churchman later noted, the former, like the latter, 'has passed into the life of the church, in one form, and is going out of it in another'.[38]

The betrayal felt by the 'Zs' was understandable. They did not fail to note the significance of the fact that Newman and others who seceded had never been hereditary High Churchmen. A writer in the *Christian Remembrancer* in 1841 observed,

The leading minds among these [Tractarian] writers had not the advantage of being trained themselves in the Anglo-Catholic School; they had to grope for their principles, as men suddenly beset by nightly robbers catch at such weapons as the moment allows ... Their sentiments, therefore had not been worked out by a previous development of the English system, but were taken up by persons who came rather as allies than as subjects to the defence of the Church.[39]

Likewise, when Joshua Watson surveyed what for him was the 'wreckage' of 1845, his verdict was that the fatal mistake had been that the Oxford divines had begun 'to fight before they scarcely knew the weapons wherewith they should arm themselves'.[40] Churton and Palmer put up with great provocations from the Tractarian leaders. Newman could be exasperating in his 'fierce' phase as exponent of the *via media*. Newman himself admitted to the offensive mixture of 'fierceness and of sport' in his behaviour at this time. 'I was not unwilling to draw an opponent on step by step to the brink of some intellectual absurdity, and to leave him to get back as he could ... Also I used irony in conversation, when matter-of-fact men would not see what I meant',[41] Newman later confessed. Rose, Palmer and Churton were sometimes victims of this verbal sparring, and felt that they were too often left to allay alarms raised by Tractarian excesses. Churton would never forgive the affront that he saw in Froude's *Remains*. In 1860, he was even prepared to assert, 'God in His righteousness chastised such a leading mind as J. H. N's, because he cared so little for the responsibility he incurred

---

[37] Rt. Rev. Cleveland Coxe [Bishop of Ohio], in *Anglo-Catholic Principles Vindicated*, p. 22.
[38] *Ibid.*, p. 22.   [39] *Christian Remembrancer*, 3 (April, 1841), 426.
[40] M. Watson, Ms 'Reminiscences', fol. 166, 18 May 1845.
[41] Newman, *Apologia*, pp. 114–15.

in publishing those unhappy things in the "Remains".[42] *Tract 90*
tarnished Newman's reputation still more in old High Church eyes.
As one old High Churchman later recalled, the Tract was viewed in
this quarter as 'a tissue of cruel hints and cunning reservations, like
Iago's in the play'.[43]

Yet while Newman's personal demeanour can be faulted, it would
be wrong to blame the Tractarians entirely for the misunderstanding that arose with the 'Zs'. The Oxford Movement could never,
under Newman's leadership, have rested content with the limited
role which Hackney evidently assigned for it. The Oxford Movement was something greater than one more manifestation of a long
tradition of High Church resistance to the 'Church in danger'.
William Scott of Hoxton in his profound article in 1843, appreciated
this essential point, but Henry John Rose, like Palmer and the
Hackney elders, never grasped it.

Any focus on the negative impact of the Oxford Movement must
be offset by an appreciation of what its leaders really set out to
achieve. By that yardstick, the achievement of Tractarianism on the
life and thought of the Church of England was enormous. Hackney
and Oxford may have fallen out with each other, but this division
can in the last resort be ascribed as much to the limitations and
weaknesses of the former as to the apparent excesses and undoubted
provocations of the latter.

While the divisive impact of the Oxford Movement cannot be
denied, it can be overstated. Some old High Churchmen, bereft of
their former influence, by the middle of the century, had an interest
in recalling the past more fondly than it deserved, and in exaggerat-
ing the Movement's negative legacy. The image of pre-Tractarian
theological harmony later portrayed by Rose and the Hackney
elders never quite accorded with the reality of the trend towards
party strife evident after the demise of the Hutchinsonians and death
of Horsley in 1806. In truth, polarisation predated the rise of
Tractarianism.

Horsley's truly inclusive vision of High Church episcopal and
sacramental principles allied to a tolerance towards doctrinal
Evangelicalism, even of the moderate Calvinist variety, represented
an essentially pre-Laudian churchmanship characteristic of early-
seventeenth-century divines of the school of Ussher, Davenant,

[42] SC, Churton Papers, E. Churton to W. J. Copeland, 28 February 1860.
[43] Bishop Coxe in *Anglo-Catholic Principles Vindicated*, p. 8.

Carleton, Jackson and Hall. As late as the 1690s there were a few Calvinist churchmen such as Dr Jane who took the High Church side in controversy with the Whig interest, but in general the 1662 settlement had dealt a near fatal blow to the pre-Laudian consensus.

The early Hutchinsonians first recaptured the older High-Church–Calvinist entente. Thus Horne defended the six Calvinistic Methodists expelled from St Edmund Hall, Oxford, in 1768, while Hutchinsonians collaborated with Calvinist Evangelicals in resisting Latitudinarian attempts to alter the Articles and liturgy in 1772–3. A common determination to reassert the paramountcy of revealed theology ensured that this High-Church–Evangelical alliance prospered in the era, *c.*1760–*c.*1800. But the entente did not survive the two decades of controversy sparked by Daubeny's attack on Evangelicalism at the end of the 1790s. Disputes arose as disagreement over the precise content of revealed theology surfaced. Horsley's demise made the divide less bridgeable. William Van Mildert, on whom the mantle of High Church leadership increasingly would fall, was never able to match his mentor Horsley's breadth of intellectual sympathy.[44] Bishop Jebb and Alexander Knox remained committed to the earlier eirenicism but they increasingly stood out as exceptions to a growing mood of High Church intolerance towards Roman Catholicism as well as Anglican Evangelicalism.

It was not the confrontationalism of Newman and the Tractarians alone that destroyed an earlier *rapprochement* between High Churchmanship and Evangelicalism. Archdeacon Daubeny and Phalanx High Churchmen such as Sikes and Norris, as well as the Arminian churchmen Bishop Randolph, Archdeacon Thomas and Bishop Marsh, adopted as divisive a course as the Tractarians did at a later date. Daubeny attracted Evangelical opprobrium in a way which sharply contrasted with their view of Horsley, who for all his no less Laudian credentials remained an Evangelical favourite for generations to come,[45] while being strangely neglected by the Tractarian fathers.[46]

Daubeny not only provoked Evangelicals but also acted as a

[44] Varley, *Van Mildert*, p. 63.
[45] For example, H. McNeile, *The Church and the Churches; or, the Church of Christ, and the Churches of Christ Militant Here on Earth* (London, 1846), p. 24; *The Charge of John Bird [Sumner], Lord Archbishop of Canterbury, to the Clergy of His Diocese, at His Visitation, 1857* (London, 1857), pp. 21–2; [G. Townsend], *A Few Remarks on the Idolatrous Tendency of Some Parts of the Oxford Tracts* (London, 1839), pp. 23–5.
[46] Mather, *Horsley*, p. 301.

brake on the more broad-minded High Churchmen such as William Stevens in the 1800s.[47] Although during the 1810s collaboration between Hackney and Clapham extended to education, missions to India and church building,[48] growing High Church fears over Evangelical attempts to purchase advowsons increasingly soured relations. As Sikes's ill-tempered quarrel with Bishop Porteus in 1806[49] and Orthodox attempts in 1817–18 to outlaw the Bath Church Missionary Society[50] suggest, eirenicism towards Evangelicals, still upheld by Knox and Jebb, ceased to be the norm among pre-Tractarian High Churchmen. Thomas Mozley considered that it was only Norris's readiness 'to close with anybody who was not an "Evangelical"', that led him into taking on even apparent liberals such as Hampden, Baden Powell and Samuel Hinds as curates at Hackney.[51]

In the 1810s and 1820s, many of the Orthodox became consumed by the bogey of a 'Puritan' conspiracy to overthrow the Church from within. Tractarian rhetoric against Evangelicals could be similarly unfair, but there was a difference. Tractarians, partly because many had been reared in the Evangelical tradition, appreciated the spiritual dimension of Evangelical religion better than most pre-Tractarian High Churchmen of the era 1805–30. In fact, Tractarian complaints against contemporary Evangelicals were mainly grounded on the latter's new-found apparent alliance with the worldly and irreligious. Certainly, Tractarians exhibited less political jealousy of Evangelical spiritual influence than did their

47 ESCRO, Locker-Lampson Papers, B/5/3, C. Daubeny to J. Boucher, 28 December 1798; *ibid.*, C. Daubeny to J. Boucher, 29 May 1801. Daubeny even impugned the honesty of the eirenic Bishop of London, Beilby Porteus. *Ibid.*, C. Daubeny to J. Boucher, 27 February 1800.
48 Varley, *Van Mildert*, pp. 75–85. As late as 1826, Bishop Jebb could assert: 'a moderate spirit is growing up both in high churchmen and in the better kind of Evangelicals'. Bp J. Jebb to A. Knox, 30 May 1826, *Thirty Years' Correspondence between John Jebb and Alexander Knox*, pp. 539–40.
49 Ms 'Minutes of a Conversation with Bishop Porteus on His Own Invitation, Occasioned by the Foregoing Pamphlet, March 1806' [in Thomas Sikes's hand], appended to T. Sikes, *An Humble Remonstrance to the Lord Bishop of London, Vice-President of a New Association Called the British and Foreign Bible Society* (1806).
50 Bodl. Lib, Ms Eng Lett. c. 789, fol. 89, 85, Archdeacon J. Thomas to H. H. Norris, 22 December 1817; J. H. Spry to H. H. Norris, 12 December 1817; J. Thomas, *A Protest against the Church Missionary Society* (Bath, 1818); *A Defence of the Protest of the Rev. Archdeacon Thomas in Reply to the Rev. Daniel Wilson* (Bristol [1818]).
51 Mozley, *Reminiscences Chiefly of Oriel College and the Oxford Movement*, vol. 1, p. 339. Even Hugh James Rose privately maintained that 'malice and falsehood' were the chief characteristics of Evangelicals 'as a party and, I believe, always have been'. Bucklebury, Hook Papers, H. J. Rose to W. F. Hook, 21 March 1838.

Orthodox forebears or old High Church contemporaries. Evangelicalism might have been assailed by Tractarians as doctrinal heresy as in the Gorham affair but never as a political conspiracy with the good faith of its adherents malignantly traduced as it was by Sikes and Marsh. The contrast shows that the greater doctrinal fluidity and indistinctness of the pre-Tractarian Church of England was not always accompanied by a greater genuine charity or sense of fair dealing in controversial debate. It was a contrast generously conceded in favour of the Tractarians even by some of their sternest Evangelical critics.[52]

It is easy to exaggerate the depth and extent of party strife in the Tractarian era. Arthur Burns has shown how an Orthodox-inspired diocesan revival acted as a powerful brake upon centrifugal forces in the church. Again, as shown, in the wake of the Gorham and Denison cases, there was some *rapprochement* between old High Churchmen and Tractarians, with even a diminution of doctrinal differences as on the Eucharist. Moreover, for all the detestation of moderate High Churchmen for Ritualists, the doctrinal implications of verdicts in ritual cases such as the Purchas Judgment in 1871 furthered this trend.[53] Furthermore, the controversies in Oxford of 1841–5 centring on subscription culminated in a tactical alliance between younger liberals and Tractarians. This alliance would later bear fruit in the fragile new plant of 'liberal catholicism' within High Churchmanship.[54]

Ironically, it was the liberal Protestant comprehensiveness of the Church of England against which the Oxford Movement reacted, which ultimately ensured for Anglo-Catholics the freedom to protest and advance their views. As early as 1837, Newman observed that some liberals might give support to the Movement, 'from really feeling ... in our views ... some indulgence of latitudinarianism'.[55] It suited Newman to play down or ignore support from this quarter when it came. Yet while most Tractarians may not have approved of the way that A. P. Stanley equated the defence of *Tract 90* along with the Gorham Judgment as landmarks in a latitudinarian cam-

[52] *Christian Observer* (February, 1837), 166; Sidney, *Life of Sir Richard Hill*, pp. 129–30.
[53] O. Shipley, *Secular Judgments in Spiritual Matters; Considered in Relation to Some Recent Events* (London, 1871), p. 15.
[54] W. R. Ward, 'Oxford and the Origins of Liberal Catholicism in the Church of England', *SCH*, 1 (1964), 236–7.
[55] PH, Ollard Papers, J. H. Newman to F. Rogers, 19 June 1837 (copy).

paign for the Church's freedom from tests,[56] it was precisely in the context of the Church's post-1845 move towards greater internal religious pluralism, that the future strength of the Anglo-Catholic cause lay. While Catholic principles were tolerated in the 1860s to an extent that might have seemed unthinkable in the 1840s, this did not signify the triumph of Tractarianism. Catholic latitude was itself only a product of the breach of doctrinal and confessional barriers associated with the old Protestant High Church orthodoxy. In short, the Tractarians of the 1860s owed their position in the Church in part to the latitudinarian advocacy of Stanley whose principles they otherwise abhorred. For example, while the republication of *Tract 90* by Pusey in 1866 was received in relative silence, contrary to Tractarian polemic Bishop Jackson pointed out that this reflected 'not so much approval of the principles therein assumed, as acquiescence in a licence which can be no longer questioned'.[57]

Later High Churchmen came to insist that the 'Catholic interpretation' of the Articles which Newman first expounded was in their eye the only true and exclusive sense[58] and not a merely permissible option as Newman had implied.[59] But the many and varied legal judgments inflicted on the Church from the 1840s onwards, some favouring one party and others another, in effect created a new practical theory of subscription which matched, albeit unintentionally, the catholic inclusiveness which Maurice and Stanley in different ways had long advocated. The comprehensiveness of the Church of England thereafter was strained to a new degree of doctrinal elasticity. As one writer observed, in effect 'any interpretation is allowed which does not openly impugn the Articles, instead of the opposite, which excluded every sense but one. The three parties in the Church have successively been shielded in this way from prescription by their rivals.'[60] In short, the Oxford Movement caused the Church of England to become theologically more tolerant when, in fact, its aim had been to make it more dogmatic.

[56] A. P. Stanley, *A Letter to the Bishop of London on the State of Subscription* (London, 1863), p. 23; A. P. Stanley, *Essays Chiefly on Questions of Church and State from 1850 to 1870* (London, 1870), p. 15; A. P. Stanley, 'Subscription', *Macmillan's Magazine*, 43 (January, 1881), 209–11.

[57] J. Jackson, *A Charge Delivered to the Clergy and Churchwardens of the Diocese of Lincoln at His Triennial Visitation in October 1867* (London, 1867), p. 33.

[58] 'The Bishop of Brechin and the Articles', *Christian Remembrancer*, 56 (July, 1868), 69–70.

[59] For Newman's explanation of his differences with Pusey on this point, see J. H. Newman to H. J. Coleridge, 20 October 1865, in C. S. Dessain, ed., *Letters and Diaries*, vol. XXII (London 1972), p. 79.

[60] Heard, *National Christianity, or Caesarism or Clericalism*, pp. 138–9.

The Tractarians retained common ground with Evangelicals. Robert Wilberforce was not alone in regarding the Oxford Movement as the legitimate continuation of the Evangelical Revival.[61] Many Evangelicals such as Charles Sumner approved of the early numbers of the Tracts.[62] Although disputes over Tradition and Justification would produce a breach in the later 1830s, Evangelicals and Tractarians remained united by a common quest for holiness.[63] Both held the view that religion must involve a personal response to divine favour, the only difference being that the one stressed individual conversion and the other corporate holiness. This common emphasis sometimes overcame the doctrinal divide. It ensured that Robert Wilberforce would always feel closer to Charles Sumner, than Richard Mant had to Thomas Scott. The debate between the former was not the 'dialogue of the deaf' of the latter. It was precisely because, as Wilberforce put it, 'persons who had been most influenced by the one, often most readily entered into the other',[64] that Tractarianism became such an object of suspicion for old High Churchmen such as John Crosthwaite, for whom it was merely 'puritanical mar-prelacy' revived.[65]

As David Newsome observes, for a long time, it was not even 'at all clear that sacramentalism, and all that followed from high sacramental teaching, might become a dividing factor' between Evangelical and Tractarian.[66] Moreover, on the subject of antiquity, we have shown the influence of the Evangelical Milner on Newman. Even Liddon conceded that Milner's *Church History* 'gave evidence of a sense of the spiritual beauty of the ancient Church'.[67] Furthermore, as the example of Edward Bickersteth's enthusiasm for the *Library of the Fathers* project showed, even later moderate Evangelicals were not averse to Tractarian patristic priorities *per se*.[68] Until the later 1830s, 'Oxford and Clapham should be regarded as complementary rather than antagonistic spheres of influence.'[69]

The eirenical potential of shared spiritual concerns was translated into common political action. The episode of the Hampden con-

---

61 R. I. Wilberforce, *The Evangelical and Tractarian Movements: a Charge ... 1851*, pp. 10–11.
62 Y. Brilioth, *Evangelicalism and the Oxford Movement* (London, 1934), p. 28.
63 Newsome, *Parting of Friends*, p. 14. For evidence of shared spiritual concerns of the two parties, see PH, Tyndale Papers, CUP 5/104, A. Tyndale to E. B. Pusey, 29 January 1834.
64 R. I. Wilberforce, *The Evangelical and Tractarian Movements: a Charge ... 1851*, p. 10.
65 Bodl. Lib, Ms Eng Misc. e. 117, fol. 310, J. C. Crosthwaite to E. B. Pusey, April 1842.
66 Newsome, *Parting of Friends*, p. 14.   67 Liddon, *Life of Pusey*, vol. I, p. 414.
68 *Ibid.*, vol. II, p. 435.
69 Hilton, *Age of Atonement*, hardback edn, p. 28.

troversy in 1836 showed that an alliance between High Churchmen and Evangelicals could be reactivated to meet a particular danger from another quarter. While Newman's efforts to woo the Evangelicals at the beginning of the Movement were soon abandoned, Pusey quite matched Bishop Horsley in eirenic and sympathetic understanding of the distinctive emphases of Evangelical and Methodist spirituality. It has also been suggested that their 'victory' in the Gorham Judgment made many Evangelicals thereafter somewhat more accommodating towards at least moderate High Churchmen and to concede that there had been good as well as error in the Movement.[70] Even the Evangelical Francis Close approved of what he took to be the initial aim of the Oxford Tracts, 'to level the hydra-headed monster of latitudinarianism, and to bring back indifferentists to the church of their fathers'.[71] Moreover by the 1870s, according to the old High Churchman Bishop E. H. Browne, there had been a mutual watering or fusion of the High Church and Evangelical traditions at several levels; a fusion promoted rather than retarded by the Oxford Movement.[72] This view was also taken by some Evangelicals.[73]

The testimony of Arthur West Haddan provides evidence of renewed cross-party fertilisation. Haddan, who was a detached supporter of the Tractarians, argued in 1861 that the bitterness of party division over the preceding thirty years had been exaggerated. Haddan maintained that the most striking development in that era was the almost unconscious way in which opponents of the Tractarians came to adopt some of the latter's 'clothes' and weapons. The result was that the Oxford Movement had lifted 'the bulk of the Church ... into a more substantial orthodoxy' so that even the Church's opponents in 1860 were occasionally more

---

[70] Carter, 'Evangelical Seceders', vol. II, pp. 497–8. Anglican Evangelicals also softened their anti-Tractarian rhetoric when they perceived that the motives of Dissenters in attacking the Tractarians were more Voluntaryist than Protestant. Wolfe, *Protestant Crusade in Great Britain*, p. 304.

[71] Close, *Footsteps of Error*, p. 6.

[72] E. H. Browne, *The Position and Parties of the English Church: a Pastoral Letter to the Clergy of the Diocese of Winchester* (London, 1875), pp. 58–9.

[73] J. Guinness Rogers, *Church Systems of England in the Nineteenth Century* (London, 1881), p. 172; *J. Guinness Rogers: an Autobiography* (London, 1903), p. 291; A. M. Fairbairn, *Studies in Religion and Theology: the Church in Idea and History* (London, 1910), p. 124. In 1853, W. J. Conybeare made the point that the journals representing the High Church and Evangelical parties respectively, tended to be more extreme than the bulk of their readership. [Conybeare], 'Church Parties', 318–19.

Orthodox upon disputed points than some of its supporters of thirty years since.[74]

In opposing Tractarianism, even Evangelicals could lay claim to High Church principles. As one Evangelical churchman in 1849 insisted, 'the Church system ... does not, of right, belong to the class who have so long occupied it, and who have it still in possession. It belongs to the justified, not to the unrenewed man.'[75] Another example of this trend towards 'Catholic Evangelicalism' was that of James Garbett. In the early 1840s it was Garbett's anti-Tractarian theological credentials which had ensured his election to the Professorship of Poetry at Oxford against the Tractarian candidate Isaac Williams. As Archdeacon of Chichester at a later date, however, Garbett assumed a more eirenical posture. Thus, in a Charge in 1867, Garbett maintained that the early Tractarian emphases on apostolical succession and on the evils of schism had been 'supplementary of the Truths of the everlasting Gospel' which the Evangelical revivalists had proclaimed. Referring specifically to the High Church doctrines of the succession and apostolic commission, Garbett concluded, 'I shall never, so God help me, cease to value that part of the great Church Movement which has brought into fuller light, and pressed home to men's consciences those great and precious truths.'[76]

The difference in substance as well as style of Tractarianism from older High Churchmanship partly explains why no equivalent movement had occurred in the 1790s or 1810s. Several ingredients were lacking, both in the external circumstances of the earlier period, and also in the *ethos* and moral and philosophical character of the High Churchmanship of that time. The reaction against the French Revolution and the patriotism engendered by the war against Napoleon inspired a High Church religious as well as merely political revival. Nevertheless, that reaction was still too dependent upon a negative recoil from 'French principles', and too subservient

---

[74] A. W. Haddan, 'On Party Spirit in the English Church' [1861], in A. P. Forbes, ed., *Remains of the Late Arthur West Haddan* (Oxford, 1876), pp. 478–9. On the positive impact of Tractarianism on Nonconformity, see D. A. Johnson, 'The Oxford Movement and English Nonconformity', *Anglican and Episcopal History*, 59 (1) (1990), 76–98.
    Party spirit could also be regarded as evidence of renewed life within Anglicanism. See J. H. Blunt, *Parties and Principles in the Church of England* (Oxford, 1870), p. 6.
[75] *A Letter to His Grace the Archbishop of Canterbury, on the Restoration of the Church's Unity. By an English Presbyter* (London, 1849), p. 10.
[76] J. Garbett, *Rome and the Church of England. A Charge Delivered ... at Chichester ... 1867* (London, 1867), p. 21.

to the antagonism of political parties in the state to acquire an independent and scientific character.[77] What most dismayed Victorian High Churchmen about their Georgian forebears, the Hutchinsonians excepted, was not merely a perception of spiritual torpor and 'miserable tone' but a want of philosophical depth or ethical insight. It was precisely these qualities in Tractarianism which earned the respect even of liberal opponents such as Baden Powell.[78]

For all its apparent insularity and reputation for obscurantism, the intellectual and pan-European credentials of the Movement have been recently vindicated.[79] As even Bishop Knox appreciated, the Oxford Movement formed a chapter in the intellectual history of nineteenth-century Europe, and was in tune with such deep cultural currents as Romanticism.[80] The same could not be said of Georgian High Churchmanship, even in its most spiritual forms. For neither Non-jurism nor Hutchinsonianism attained the intellectual or spiritual sway that Tractarianism would achieve.

Some of the Hackney forebodings about the Movement would prove unfounded, even if others were realised. It had been Joshua Watson's half-expectation that there would be the 'same result from the Oxford Movement as from the Nonjuring, when carried to extremes – that it would die away in the bulk of the nation and leave a greater coldness throughout'.[81] Events proved this prophecy to be seriously mistaken. Of course, some of the claims on behalf of the Movement by its more zealous protagonists might be regarded as far-fetched. One Pembroke undergraduate claimed in 1841, that 'the "Tracts for the Times" have completely altered the tone of thought not only in England but they have produced as great and powerful a change in France, Austria, Italy, Greece, Russia etc.' 'People would stare', he maintained, 'if they were told of the correspondence kept up between Oxford and all parts of the world, and I dare say they would not believe some one who told them that

---

[77] 'Personal Influences on Our Present Theology: Newman – Coleridge – Carlyle', *National Review*, 3 (1856), 450.
[78] Baden Powell, *Tradition Unveiled*, pp. 8–9.
[79] Nockles, 'An Academic Counter-Revolution'; D. Newsome, 'Newman and the Oxford Movement', in A. Symondson, ed., *The Victorian Crisis of Faith* (London, 1970), pp. 74–5.
[80] E. A. Knox, *The Tractarian Movement, 1833–1845: a Study of the Oxford Movement as a Phase of the Religious Revival in Western Europe in the Second Half of the Nineteenth Century* (London, 1934) ch. 3; A. M. Fairbairn, *Catholicism: Roman and Anglican* (London, 1899), p. 294.
[81] M. Watson, Ms 'Reminiscences', fol. 36.

the Oxford publications had been attentively read by the Maronites of Syria and the Christians of St Thomas in India.'[82] The Archbishop of Moscow apparently enquired about Oxford views and sought a copy of Pusey's work on baptism. There was even a report that the fame of the Oxford Tracts had spread to Transylvania.[83]

A unique combination of moral strength and religious dynamism, imbued with the spirit of Romanticism, proved to be the winning, almost secret power which enabled the Movement to capture the hearts as well as minds of the rising generation in the Oxford of the 1830s. The Tractarian leaders were superb propagandists among the young and impressionable.[84] They understood the vital importance of an external bond of union between individuals which their natural counterparts in Cambridge never did. Newman relished the comparison with the sister university: 'Are they not like Greeks, and we like Romans?'[85] Moreover, as its later enemies such as Mark Pattison recognised, the spread and momentum of the Oxford Movement rendered it a social phenomenon, 'its significance concealed under the guise of a theological squabble'.[86]

By the early 1830s, the old High Churchmen had 'run out of steam' and lacked the power to move or inspire the new generation, unaided. One observer likened 'the old High Church party, which [has] long ruled in high places at Oxford' to 'a dynasty outliving the principles and energy which called it into existence and power'[87] – a view which Alexander Knox had himself expressed as early as 1816 when he declared, 'the old High Church race is worn out'.[88] Much of the evidence from our study contradicts such assumptions, but there was certainly some truth in the Newmanite perception that 'love had grown cold' and that fresh weapons and armour were needed to fight new battles. There was always a limit to Hackney's intellectual influence. Although Hackney acted as a sort of High Church rival and counterpoise to Clapham, it was never quite able

---

[82] PCA, Renouf Papers, 63/9/1, P. Le Page Renouf to Mrs Le Page Renouf, n.d.
[83] Liddon, *Life of Pusey*, vol. II, p. 160.
[84] G. S. Faber commented: 'In buying up the public prints of all descriptions, they [the Tractarians] have precisely adopted the tactics of Voltaire and the Encyclopaedists.' LPL, Golightly Papers, Ms 1805, fol. 235, G. S. Faber to C. P. Golightly, 14 December 1841.
[85] J. H. Newman to F. Rogers, In Festo SS. Innocent, 1838, *Letters and Diaries*, vol. VI, p. 365. Newman developed the comparison at the expense of Cambridge: 'These [Cambridge] fellows take up everything as a matter of literature – and their opinions come and go like Spring fashions.' J. H. Newman to G. Cornish, 28 December 1838, *ibid.*, p. 363.
[86] Ellis, *Seven against Christ*, p. 248.   [87] *Letters from Oxford*, pp. 24–5.
[88] *Remains of Alexander Knox*, vol. I, pp. 49–50.

to match it in terms of men, measures or literature. By the early 1830s there was something of a vacuum waiting to be filled. Even Rose admitted that, for many of the country clergy at that time, the 'first real ground of hope' had been 'the existence of a body of men at Oxford' prepared to bolster the efforts of individuals who 'had from time to time "in much fear and trembling" ventured to proclaim the same truths after their strength, or their feebleness'.[89]

In the short term, the Oxford Movement might be deemed a failure. The Church of England was weakened by the theological fragmentation of Anglicanism into constituent parts which the Tractarian 'rediscovery' of the seventeenth-century tradition spawned. Disunion, extremism and party spirit were all apparent consequences of a relentless quest for true catholicity and apostolic purity. While originally only aiming to restore to the Anglican tradition its understated continuity the Tractarians eventually tested that tradition to destruction. Another weakness was the Movement's opting for a 'separate tradition' in place of its earlier ideal – most apparent within the university context – of spreading a 'catholicising' leaven throughout the church.[90] Dean Burgon was not alone in blaming the later recoil from established religion in the ancient universities directly to 'the miscarriage of the Tractarian movement'.[91] Furthermore, for seceders like William Maskell, in appearing to settle for a mere 'permission to hold' catholic doctrines in the Church, the later Tractarians betrayed the original principles of the Movement.[92] As the convert Newman complained, the result was a sect-like posture and a practical eclecticism quite at variance with the original spirit of 1833.[93]

Yet on Newman's own reckoning, a sect was all that Anglo-Catholicism could ever hope to become. Even when formulating his *via media* Newman doubted whether doctrinal historical Anglicanism had ever had a popular hold. As a Roman Catholic, he concluded that the 'movement of 1833' had been alien to the popular and national consciousness. Of course, this mirrored the contention of 'Ultra-Protestants' and High Churchmen always rebutted such a claim. But Newman had a point. As the church of the English nation

---

[89] H. J. Rose to E. B. Pusey, 30 April 1836, Burgon, *Lives of Twelve Good Men*, vol. 1, p. 208.
[90] Nockles, 'An Academic Counter-Revolution', 173–4, 180–1.
[91] Burgon, *Lives of Twelve Good Men*, vol. 1, p. 225.
[92] Maskell, *Protestant Ritualists*, p. 12.
[93] See J. R. Griffin, 'Newman's *Difficulties Felt by Anglicans*: History or Propaganda?', *Catholic Historical Review*, 59 (July, 1983), 371–83.

and as an establishment, Anglicanism had always been able to draw on vast reservoirs of support. Yet popular Anglicanism, as manifest in the tradition of 'Church and King' riots from Sacheverell to Priestley, which Hurrell Froude and other Tractarians wanted to reestablish, had never been primarily theological. The often hostile popular lay response to the Oxford Movement suggested that John Bull was not on the side of the Tractarians.

In the last resort, however, the Movement's breadth of spiritual influence overrode its increasing tendency towards a churchy sectarianism. The impact of Newman's preaching and example transcended party boundaries. It left an indelible mark on many, such as the future Broad Churchman, Frederick Temple, who opposed the ecclesiastical principles of the Movement[94] and earned respect from some of its bitterest opponents. The commendation of the Evangelical, James Garbett, in his otherwise hostile Bampton Lectures of 1842 and long prior to his later eirenicism, deserves to stand as representative of a whole genre of anti-Tractarian polemic thus softened by such admissions:

Whatever judgment may be formed of their [i.e. the *Tracts for the Times*] ultimate tendency ... so wide an influence could never have been exerted, or the approbation, however qualified, of wise and good men have been obtained, unless they had successfully struck some deep chord – had hit on some real wants of the period – and brought out distinctly into light certain substantive principles which, before their appearance, had required an adequate exponent, and had formed none ... they possessed ... occasionally a moving and almost tragic eloquence; and a rich scattering over them of really profound thoughts, which probed unsparingly the religious and political deficiencies of the times.[95]

It is a moving tribute. If it were an epitaph, it would be one of which the leaders of the Oxford Movement could have been proud.

[94] E. G. Sandford, ed., *Memoirs of Archbishop Temple by Seven Friends*, 2 vols. (London, 1906), vol. II, pp. 401–87.
[95] Garbett, *Christ as Prophet, Priest and King*, vol. II, pp. 462–3.

Select bibliography

A comprehensive bibliography of printed works relating to this subject, even if it were confined to primary sources, would very considerably swell the length of the present book. Therefore, reasons of space have led me to confine my bibliography to the original manuscript sources consulted, some of which will be unknown to many readers. For the extensive primary printed as well as secondary sources consulted, the reader is referred to the full references cited in the footnotes. The excellent bibliography of Oxford Movement sources compiled by Laurence N. Crumb of Oregon University Library is also strongly recommended. See Laurence N. Crumb, *The Oxford Movement and Its Leaders: a Bibliography of Secondary and Lesser Primary Sources* (Metuchen, 1988). A Supplement (1993) is also available.

MANUSCRIPT SOURCES

The most useful collections consulted are listed below under the repositories in which they are located.

Balliol College, Oxford
 Jenkyns Correspondence
 Scott Correspondence

Birmingham Oratory Library
 Newman Papers
 Miscellaneous Papers
 Tract 90 Papers

Bodleian Library
 Add. MSS. d. 30, Nonjuror Papers
 Add. MSS c. 290
 MSS Eng Lett. b. 27
 MSS Eng Lett. d. 123–4, Ogilvie Correspondence
 MSS Eng Lett. c. 199
 MSS Eng Lett. c. 297
 MSS Eng Lett. c. 653–8, d. 526–7, Manning Papers
 MSS Eng Lett. c. 789–90, H. H. Norris Papers
 MSS Eng Lett. d. 38
 MSS Eng Lett. d. 102, Newman–Woodgate Correspondence

MSS Eng Lett. d. 367–8, Croker Correspondence
MSS Eng Misc. d. 134, Keble–J. T. Coleridge Correspondence
MSS Eng Misc. d. 137, J. T. Coleridge–J. T. Randall Correspondence
MSS Eng Misc. e. 117, Crosthwaite–Pusey Correspondence
MSS Top. Oxon d. 353–6, Randolph–Lambard Correspondence
MSS Oxf. Dioc. c. 656, Skinner–Randolph Correspondence
MSS Wilberforce c. 5, c. 7–8, d. 17, d. 38–9, S. Wilberforce Papers

British Library
   Add. MSS 39,311–12, Berkeley Correspondence
   Add. MSS 44,152; 44,154; 44,204; 44,213–14; 44,247–8; 44,283; 44,300;
      44,343; 44,356–65; 44,369–70; 44,728; 44,735; 44,769; 44,777;
      44,790–1, Gladstone Papers
   Add MSS 46,136, Wordsworth Papers
   Althorp Papers, E 16–19

Cambridge University Library
   Add. MSS 8134, Horne

Library of Christ Church, Oxford
   Burton Correspondence (microfilm)

Durham University Library
   Thorp Papers

East Sussex County Record Office, Lewes
   Locker-Lampson: Sec. I, Park, Locker, Watson Correspondence A.I,
      B.1, 2, 3, and 5, Boucher Letters

Exeter Cathedral Library
   Spencer Gift: Phillpotts Papers

Gloucestershire County Record Office
   Prevost Papers

Keble College, Oxford
   Heathcote Correspondence
   Keble Papers
   Miscellaneous Correspondence

Lambeth Palace Library
   MSS 1491, Mill Papers
   MSS 1562, Watson Papers
   MSS 1604
   MSS 1767, Horsley Papers
   MSS 1804–11, Golightly Papers
   MSS 2497–8, 2836, Selbourne Papers
   MSS 1822, 2140, 2143–4, 2147–50, Wordsworth Papers
   MSS Keble Dep. 2, 4–5, 9, Keble Papers
   MSS Williams Dep. 1–4, I. Williams Papers
   Tait Papers

Lincoln Record Office
  Kaye Papers
  Massingberd Papers

Magdalen College, Oxford
  Horne Correspondence
  Routh Papers

National Library of Scotland
  MSS 3670, 3672–3, 3675, 3678–9, Hope-Scott Papers

Oriel College, Oxford
  Hawkins Papers (11 Letterbooks)

Pembroke College, Oxford
  Le Page Renouf Correspondence

Pusey House, Oxford
  Pusey Papers (originals, and Liddon Bound Volumes, mainly transcripts)
  Ollard Papers
  Bagot Papers
  British Critic Papers
  Copeland Papers
  Churton Papers
  Gresley Papers
  Hamilton Papers
  Marriott Papers
  Bricknell Papers
  Morris Papers
  Denison Papers
  Henderson Papers
  Woodgate Papers

St Edmund Hall, Oxford
  MS 'Diary of John Hill'

Sion College, London
  Maskell–Scott Correspondence

Trinity College, Cambridge
  Whewell Papers
  Wordsworth Correspondence

Trinity College, Dublin
  Crosthwaite–Pusey Correspondence
  J. H. Todd–Pusey Correspondence
  Jebb Papers

Wadham College, Oxford
  Martyrs Memorial Correspondence
  Symons/Griffiths Correspondence

West Sussex Record Office, Chichester
S. Wilberforce Correspondence

The collections consulted and listed below remain in the following private hands:

Mr Victor Churton, Sutton Coldfield, Warwicks.
  Churton Family Papers

Mrs Coatelen, Lamberhurst, Kent (formerly, Bucklebury, Oxon., when originally consulted).
  Hook Family Papers

Canon E. Reade, Marychurch, Torquay
  Watson Family Papers

HIGH CHURCH PERIODICAL LITERATURE

The different High Church periodicals cited in this work often have more than one series. To alleviate potential confusion, the following bibliographical information may serve as a useful guide to the reader.

Anti-Jacobin Review and Magazine: or monthly political literary censor. 1798–1821. [Edited by John Gifford, pseud. i.e. John Richards Green] 61 vols. (London, 1799–1821). This work was united in 1816 with the *Protestant Advocate*, and became a vehicle of strident anti-Catholicism.

British Critic; A New Review. May 1793–Dec 1813. [Edited by W. Beloe and R. Nares], 42 vols. (London, 1793–1813).
New Series. Jan 1814–June 1825 [Edited by T. F. Middleton, W. R. Lyall and others], 23 vols. (London, 1814–25).
Third Series. Oct 1825–Oct 1826. 3 vols. The work was united at the end of 1826 with the *Quarterly Theological Review*.

British Critic, Quarterly Theological Review and Ecclesiastical Record. Jan 1827–Oct 1843. [Edited successively by E. Smedley, J. S. Boone, J. H. Newman and others], 34 vols. (London, 1827–43). After years of identification with the old High Church party, the journal became a vehicle of Tractarian thought in 1838. On the role of the *British Critic* in the High Church revival, see E. R. Houghton and J. L. Althoz, 'The *British Critic*, 1824–1843', in *Victorian Periodicals Review*, 24, 3, (Fall, 1991), 111–18; E. R. Houghton, 'The *British Critic* and The Oxford Movement', *Studies in Bibliography*, 16, (1963), 119–37.

British Magazine and Monthly Register of Religion and Ecclesiastical Information, Parochial History, etc. [Edited successively by H. J. Rose, S. R. Maitland, J. C. Crosthwaite], 36 vols. (London, 1832–49).

Christian Remembrancer; or the Churchman's Biblical Ecclesiastical and Literary Miscellany, 22 vols. (London, 1819–40). Initially a product of the Hackney circle and edited by the Rev Frederick Iremonger, the magazine was reconstituted in 1840, and became identified with the Tractarians.

Christian Remembrancer: a Monthly Magazine and Review. vols. 1–8. (a quarterly review, vols. 9–56). [Edited by W. Scott]. (London, 1840–68).

The Churchman. 3 vols. (London, 1835–7). Continued as: *The Churchman: a Monthly Magazine in Defence of the Church and Constitution*. [Edited by H. Christmas] [New Series] 8 vols. (London, 1838–43).

Church of England Quarterly Review [Edited successively by E. Thompson and others], 44 vols. (London, 1837–58).

English Review; or Quarterly Journal of Ecclesiastical and General Literature. [Edited by W. Palmer of Worcester], 19 vols. (London, 1844–53). Described by Bishop Kaye in 1845 as 'The only Quarterly publication which appeared to me likely to represent Church of England opinions as distinguished from Romish exclusiveness on the one hand and Low Church laxity on the other'.

Orthodox Churchman's Magazine: or, Treasury of Divine and Useful Knowledge. (By a Society of Churchmen). March 1801–December 1808. 15 vols. (London, 1801–1808).

Index

Abbey, C. J. 161, 182
Abbott, Edwin 2, 112, 132
absolution 248–9, 251, 252, 286
Adams, William S. 23, 140, 220
adiaphora 124
Alliance between Church and State (Warburton) 54n, 56 and n, 64
Allies, Thomas William 97, 180, 253, 254
American Episcopal Church 88–9, 153
Andrewes, Lancelot, 239, 240, 264
'Anglican' as epithet 39–41
'Anglo-Catholic' as epithet 41–2
Ango-Catholicism *see* Oxford Movement
anti-establishmentism 79, 81, 82, 85, 87, 89, 103
Anti-Jacobin Review 44, 271
Antinomianism 257, 259, 266, 268
antiquity, appeal to 104–45
anti-Rationalism and High Churchmanship 200–6
anti-Romanism 164–70
Apologia pro vita sua (Newman) 2, 3, 69, 79, 112, 171n, 290, 302, 315n
'Apostolicals' 20, 35, 79
Apostolical Succession 119, 157, 169 and Tractarians 146–52, 323
Arians of the Fourth Century (Newman) 110, 112, 113, 144, 145, 198, 296
Arminian/Calvinist divide 31, 141, 194, 236
Arminian divines 202 and n, 236, 259
Arnold, Thomas 74, 87, 109–10
asceticism (High Church) 184–90
auricular confession 250, 253
Avis, Paul 7–8

Bagot, Richard, Bishop of Oxford/Bath and Wells 135, 295, 298 and n, 301
Bampton Lectures 64, 79, 106, 110, 149, 186, 195, 212, 248, 259, 327
baptismal regeneration 94, 119, 229–35, 247, 286, 311

Barrington, Shute, Bishop of Durham 26, 167
Barrow, Isaac, Master of Trinity, Cambridge 153, 192
Barter, William Brundell 180, 182
Bath 210
Bath Judgment (1856) 242, 243, 246n
Baxter, Richard 27
Bayley, Henry V., Archdeacon of Stowe 19 and n
Becket, Thomas, Archbishop of Canterbury 81 and n, 83, 84, 86 and n
Bellenger, D.A. 168
Bennett, James, 263
Bennett, W.J.E. Vicar of St. Barnabas Pimlico 6, 216, 241 and n
Benson, Christopher, Master of the Temple 36 and n, 157
Beresford, J.G., Archibishop of Armagh 308
Beresford-Hope, James 304 and n
Berkeley, George junior 14, 211, 258 and n, 270
Bethell, Christopher, Bishop of Gloucester/Bangor, 82n, 148, 173, 229, 231, 244, 246n, 267, 268, 275n
Biber, George Edward, Vicar of Roehampton 88n, 95, 180
Bible Society controversy 107–8, 155, 200
Bickersteth, Edward 110–11, 285, 300n, 321
Bingham, Joseph 157
Bird, Charles Smith, Rector of Gainsborough 32 and n, 34 and n, 134 and n, 135
'Bisley school' 39 and n, 178n, 226, 292
Blackburne, Francis, Archdeacon of Cleveland 28n, 56n, 141, 142, 147, 149, 194
Blomfield, Charles James, Bishop of London 12n, 146–7, 152, 163, 214, 215, 220, 235, 268, 310

333

Remains 187, 189, 315: publication of
281–2

Garbett, James, Archdeacon of Chichester
134 and n, 135, 323, 327
Gaskin, George, Rector of Stoke Newington
14 and n
George III, King of England 58, 60, 75
Gilbert, A.T., Principal of Brasenose 17,
309 and n
Gilley, Sheridan 24, 78, 177, 196, 204, 262,
282
Gisborne, Thomas 49
Gladstone, William Ewart, M.P. 23, 26, 83,
86–8, 90–1, 92, 96, 99n, 103, 146,
147n, 226n, 228–9, 230, 240n, 301, 305
Glasse, Samuel 13 and n, 15, 211, 258
Gleig, George, Bishop of Brechin 204
'Glorious Revolution' *see* Revolution of
1688/9
Glover, George 108 and n, 169
Golightly, Charles P. 34 and n, 263
Goode, William 121 and n, 135 and n,
136, 139, 141, 152n, 158–9, 230–1, 232,
233, 257, 264, 284, 285, 286, 298
and n
Gorham, George Cornelius 94, 101, 230,
231, 247
Gorham case 93–103, 142, 180, 230, 232–3,
246, 302, 303, 322
Gornall, Thomas 297
Goulburn, Edward 34, 287
Grant, Johnson, 11, 30, 49, 195, 212–13,
260
Greek Orthodox Church 161–3
Green, William, fellow of Magdalen 57
Greene, Donald, 9, 260
Gresley, William 21 and n, 22, 33, 40, 41,
255, 303
Grotius, Hugo 202, 236
Grove, H.C. 236

'Hackney Phalanx' 13, 14 and n, 29, 47, 51,
58, 64–5, 88, 89, 90, 106, 120–1, 148,
149, 185, 197, 200, 201, 204, 205, 212,
218, 237, 244, 271, 272, 273, 280, 288,
303, 308, 309, 313, 325
Haddan, Arthur West 322
Hadleigh (Essex) conference 124
Hamilton, William Keir, Bishop of
Salisbury 245
Hammond, Henry 132, 239
Hampden, R.D. Regius professor of
Divinity at Oxford, later Bishop of
Hereford 93 and n, 242, 272, 273, 276,
321

Hare, Julius, 160 and n
Harrison, Benjamin, Archdeacon of
Maidstone 12, 21 and n, 33, 37, 95,
115
Hawkins, Edward, Provost of Oriel 106,
108, 109, 110, 152, 187
Heligoland, proposed Anglican bishopric
164 and n
Henriques, Ursula 56 and n
Herring, G.W. 217n
Heylin, Peter, 31n, 135
Hickes, George 46, 64, 121–2
Hicks-Smith, James 17n
'High and Dry' party 40, 41, 43, 197
'High Church'
as opprobrious label 26–7
Hook/Maurice controversy concerning
35; *see also* 'Orthodox'
'High Churchman', pre-Tractarian
definition 25–6
Hill, Sir Richard 155–6, 260
Hoadly, Benjamin, Bishop of Winchester 7,
53, 63, 105, 147, 236, 237, 238
Hobart, John Henry, American bishop
89
Hole, Robert 45, 49n, 61
Hook, Walter Farquhar, Vicar of Leeds 20
and n, 35, 89, 93, 100, 126, 166, 185,
187, 215 and n, 234, 240, 252–3, 253n,
265, 287 and n, 288n, 302
Hooker, Richard 4n, 54, 83, 207, 237 and
n, 242, 250, 257, 264
church–state theory 53–4, 55, 56, 60, 63,
64, 79, 83, 87 and n, 96
Hope, James, later Hope-Scott 94n, 97,
164
Horne, George, Bishop of Norwich 4, 13
and n, 26, 46 and n, 58, 66, 74, 148,
193, 203–4, 207, 208, 209, 211, 249n,
258–9, 264, 270, 317
Horsley, Samuel, Bishop of St David's/St
Asaph/Rochester 12n, 22, 27, 49, 50n,
59n, 63, 66, 70, 74, 102, 106, 147, 168
and n, 194–5, 204, 218, 229, 237, 238,
316, 317
Howley, William, Archbishop of
Canterbury 135–6, 243, 295
Hutchinson, John 13, 45–6, 209n
Hutchinsonians 13, 13n, 45–6, 47, 51, 71,
149, 184, 196, 197, 205, 208, 209 and
n, 270, 316, 324
anti-rationalism of 203
and ceremonial 211
and Evangelicals 193, 258

Imberg, Rune 24 and n, 37, 124

Index